THE CIVIL WAR

ADVISORY EDITOR: BETTY RADICE

GAIUS JULIUS CAESAR was born in 100 B.C. into an ancient patrician family. He was an adolescent during the period of the proscription of Marius (his father's brother-in-law), the dictatorship of Sulla and the early career of Pompey. His family were traditionally against the patrician senatorial oligarchy and Caesar followed suit. He was imprisoned for a short time by Sulla, but managed to maintain good relations with the nobles for ten years after his release: he was even co-opted into the college of priests (73 B.C.). During the sixties, he advanced through the senatorial *cursus* to the rank of praetor, while supporting the 'popular' side in politics. In 60 B.C. he formed with Pompey and Crassus the combination known to us as the 'first triumvirate', to overcome conservative senatorial opposition, and he was elected consul for 59 B.C. He was then created governor to Transalpine Gaul, a task which was to occupy him for nine years. He had left the two triumvirs to safeguard his interest in Rome but they had many differences and met him in 56 B.C. in an attempt to solve them. Pompey was appointed sole consul in 52 B.C. after the death of Crassus, which resulted in civil war and the defeat of the Pompeian faction in Spain (45 B.C.). Caesar came back to Rome as dictator. He tried to improve conditions for the Roman citizen and increase the honesty and efficiency of the government. His dictatorship was declared perpetual in February 44 B.C., but his many bitter enemies hatched a conspiracy and assassinated him in March 44 B.C.

JANE GARDNER was born in 1934, and has degrees in Classics from Glasgow and Oxford Universities. She is a Senior Lecturer in Classics and Curator of the Ure Museum at Reading University. Her publications include the revised edition of S. A. Handford's *Caesar: The Conquest of Gaul* (Penguin Classics 1982), *Women in Roman Law and Society* (1986) and (with T. Wiedemann) *The Roman Household: A Sourcebook* (1991).

CAESAR

THE CIVIL WAR

together with
The Alexandrian War,
The African War,
and The Spanish War
by other Hands

*

TRANSLATED
WITH AN INTRODUCTION
BY
JANE F. GARDNER

PENGUIN BOOKS

PENGUIN BOOKS

Published by the Penguin Group

Penguin Books Ltd, 80 Strand, London WC2R 0RL, England

Penguin Putnam Inc., 375 Hudson Street, New York, New York 10014, USA

Penguin Books Australia Ltd, 250 Camberwell Road, Camberwell, Victoria 3124, Australia

Penguin Books Canada Ltd, 10 Alcorn Avenue, Toronto, Ontario, Canada M4V 3B2

Penguin Books India (P) Ltd, 11 Community Centre, Panchsheel Park, New Delhi – 110 017, India

Penguin Books (NZ) Ltd, Cnr Rosedale and Airborne Roads, Albany, Auckland, New Zealand

Penguin Books (South Africa) (Pty) Ltd, 24 Sturdee Avenue, Rosebank 2196, South Africa

Penguin Books Ltd, Registered Offices: 80 Strand, London WC2R 0RL, England

www.penguin.com

This translation first published 1967

26

Translation, Introduction and Notes copyright © Jane F. Mitchell, 1967

All rights reserved

Printed in England by Clays Ltd, St Ives plc

Set in Linotype Juliana

GEORGE MORRISON
OPTIMO MAGISTRUM
D.D.
DISCIPULA QUONDAM

CONTENTS

CONTENTS

CONTENTS

NOTES

INTRODUCTION

Historical background

CAESAR'S *Civil War* starts when the point of no return has been reached. The narrative of the *Civil War* itself, however, is only the penultimate chapter of a story which ends with the defeat of Mark Antony by Octavian in 31 B.C., but which started at least a century before. One must therefore go back and trace the developments which led to the great upheavals which finally put an end to the Republic in all but name.

The careers of the brothers Tiberius and Gaius Gracchus and the military innovations of Marius fundamentally changed the character of Roman politics. The Gracchi set the pattern for their successors by showing that the sovereign power of the people could be used to break the Senate's *de facto* control of government. Their fates showed that civil power was not enough; the senators were prepared to resort to physical force, if necessary, in defence of their monopoly. This made it certain that, if a successful assault on their entrenched power was ever made, it would not come from a mere tribune. It came in fact from men who, while using Gracchan methods, took care also to secure military command, and with it, wealth, patronage and – not least important – armed power.

The effects were already visible by the time of Gaius Julius Caesar's entry into politics. He was born in 100 B.C. (according to tradition), the year of the second tribunate of Saturninus. His father was the brother-in-law of Marius. He was a child at the time of the murder of Livius Drusus and the ensuing war with the Italian allies. He was growing through adolescence in the period of the proscriptions of Marius and the dictatorship and proscriptions of Sulla. He had before him an object lesson in extra-constitutional advancement in the early career of Gnaeus Pompeius Magnus (to whom I shall hereafter refer by the more familiar name, in English, of 'Pompey').

By the time of Caesar's first magistracy as quaestor in 68 B.C.,

Pompey had held a series of important military commands. In his early twenties, he commanded troops under Sulla and extorted a triumph from him. Then, without ever having held a magistracy, he was from 77 to 71 B.C. in almost continuous tenure of military command – against Lepidus, against Sertorius, against Spartacus – and on his return to Rome proceeded immediately to the consulship. At this period, he was using the support of the 'popular' element in the Senate and, as consul, honoured his election promises by legislation restoring the powers of which the tribunes had been deprived by Sulla. The sixties saw two more commands, carrying with them enormous civil and military powers in the provinces of the Roman empire – the special command against the pirates, conferred on Pompey in 67 B.C., and that against Mithridates, conferred on him in the following year and retained for some four years for the reorganization of the East. In both cases, the activity of tribunes secured him these appointments. At Rome, there was widespread apprehension as to how the victor would behave when he brought his armies back – apprehension that found expression as early as 65 B.C. in the abortive plot which Cicero successfully deluded subsequent generations into calling the 'first Catilinarian conspiracy'; in fact, it appears to have been an attempt by a group of the conservative aristocracy to ensure by violence, since electoral corruption had failed, that the key magistracies at Rome should be in the hands of Pompey's opponents on the latter's return.

To everyone's surprise, Pompey returned in 62 B.C. and promptly disbanded his armies and relapsed into private life. The action was, however, not untypical of him. Pompey was ambitious; he had a constant appetite for prestige and acclaim. He had considerable military and administrative talents; but although the immense authority he had won, thanks to these gifts, more than once put supreme power within his grasp, had he ventured to take it, he would let the opportunity go. The explanation has sometimes been offered that he was by temperament a constitutionalist; but it may be rather that Pompey was aware that it needed more than talent to make a success of the supreme direction of the Roman empire – and perhaps also he was conscious that he lacked that touch of genius. Caesar had it, and Octavian had it, and in both it was accompanied by sufficient self-confidence to make them independent of the senatorial *auctoritas* and allow them to use the Senate as their instrument. Pompey, on the other hand, could never quite bring himself to do without the Senate. In the constitutional theory of the Republic the Senate was the *consilium* – the advisory council – of the magistrates; when it came to the point Pompey could not cut loose and trust to his own judgement. 'Constitutionalism' is a partial explanation, no doubt – years of *de facto* governing had left the Senate in the enjoyment of almost unquestioned veneration and authority; but there were some individuals who were prepared to question its right to rule, and in the last resort Pompey was not one of these. This uncertainty, and the consequent vacillations in his policy in the fifties, largely contributed to creating the situation which led to the outbreak of the Civil War.

Pompey soon found that when he gave up his troops he also lost his influence with the Senate. Delays and excuses were interposed to the ratification of his settlement of the Eastern provinces and the granting of land to pension off his veterans. Cicero at this time had hopes of putting a final end to political strife at Rome by inducing all classes to cooperate in defence of the constitution; in particular, he wanted to secure cooperation between the ruling élite, the Senate, and the class with vested interests in finance and commerce, the so-called 'equestrian order' (or 'knights'). He hoped that this 'harmony of the orders' would be stabilized round Pompey as its leader and rallying-point.

In itself, this was essentially a barren ideal; it presented merely an attempt to shore up the *status quo* and not to deal with any of the real problems of the day. In any case, Cicero's hopes were dashed by the behaviour of the Senate. The latter made the mistake of alienating three ambitious men – Caesar, Pompey and Crassus. As said above, they deliberately delayed their consent to Pompey's routine requests. Crassus was rebuffed when he supported the request of a company of tax-farmers for the remission of part of their contracted price for the taxes of Asia – this also alienated the equestrians. Caesar returned in 60 B.C. from his service as governor in Further Spain. He wanted a triumph for his victories over recalcitrant Spanish tribes; but he also wanted to be consul in 59 B.C. Legally, he would have to appear in person as a candidate at the elections; but if he entered the city he would forfeit his military command and have to disband his army; that would mean losing his triumph. He asked permission to be a candidate in absence. The debate on his request was 'talked out' by Marcus Porcius Cato, who had also been instrumental in the rebuffs to Pompey and Crassus. Caesar gave up his triumph, came and stood as consular candidate and was elected.

Things then began to move. Caesar persuaded Pompey and Crassus to patch up their long-standing grievances and the three men formed an unofficial coalition, known to modern historians as the 'first triumvirate'. Unlike the later coalition, of Octavian, Mark Antony and Lepidus, it had no official standing; it was merely a private combination for mutual self-help in the teeth of conservative senatorial opposition.

Caesar used his position as consul to satisfy the immediate requests of Pompey and Crassus. He also looked after his own interests, in defiance of the Senate. By a law of Gaius Gracchus, the provinces to be held by the consuls of a given year after their term of office had to be assigned before they were elected. The Senate, realizing that Caesar was bound to be elected, had tried to curtail his influence as far as possible by assigning as provinces for the consuls of 59 B.C. various trivial departments in Italy – the supervision of the forests and cattle-pastures. Caesar retorted by using a tribune, Vatinius, to put a law through the popular assembly giving him Cisalpine Gaul and Illyricum – for a period of five years and with the right of appointing his own lieutenants. When the governor of Transalpine Gaul died suddenly the Senate assigned that province to Caesar as well – partly perhaps in order to save themselves the humiliation of seeing it awarded to him in any case by a popular assembly.

Caesar's consulship at Rome in itself gave his opponents cause to be apprehensive of what might happen when he should return from his Gallic command. He had used the methods of the Gracchi to by-pass senatorial opposition; and he had also shown himself ready to intimidate his opponents, if necessary, by force (Pompey had supplied bands of his veterans for this purpose). As his colleague Bibulus had declared a formal block on all business (on the grounds that he was 'watching for omens'), all the legislation carried through by Caesar in defiance of this announcement was technically null and void; but no one ventured to set himself up against the triumvirate on these grounds.

Caesar withdrew to Gaul to take over what was to prove a nine-years' task, leaving the other two triumvirs to safeguard his interests at Rome. By 56 B.C., however, the triumvirate appeared to be in danger of collapse. Publius Clodius Pulcher, who had been elected tribune for 58 B.C. as a tool of the triumvirs, subsequently began to terrorize Rome with a gang of thugs. He also tried to whip up public hostility specifically against Pompey, and it was inevitably suspected that in this he was instigated by either Caesar or Crassus. Pompey's own influence was enhanced by his appointment in 57 B.C. to a five-year commission, with proconsular power, to control the corn supply; but relations between him and Crassus were damaged by their rivalry to secure a military command for the restoration of the king of Egypt. Pompey finally went so far as to allege that he was in danger of his life at the hands of agents of Crassus. Meanwhile, there was a threat to Caesar's position in the declaration by Lucius Domitius Ahenobarbus, a member of the conservative senatorial opposition, that if elected consul for 55 B.C. he would propose Caesar's immediate recall from Gaul.

Caesar had to act to save the triumvirate. He met Pompey and Crassus at Luca in the spring of 56 B.C. and there they settled their plans for the futures of themselves and the state. About 120 of the senators made the journey to Luca to ingratiate themselves with the masters.

On their return to Rome Pompey and Crassus proceeded to put the decisions of the conference into operation. They were elected consuls for 55 B.C. A tribune, Gaius Trebonius, put forward a bill assigning provinces to them for a five-year term. Crassus was to have Syria; Pompey was to have the two Spains, with permission to govern in *absentia* through lieutenants, so that he himself could remain near Rome. The consuls jointly sponsored a law (the *Lex Licinia Pompeia*) extending Caesar's command in Gaul for five years.

However, neither Rome nor the triumvirate were to enjoy stability. One of the links binding Pompey to Caesar had been his marriage to the latter's daughter, Julia. She died in 54 B.C. Another unforeseen blow was the death of Crassus in 53 B.C. while campaigning against the Parthians. Meanwhile rioting and violence continued in the streets of Rome. Clodius and his gang were opposed by a rival gang under Milo, with the secret approval of Pompey. Constant rioting prevented the holding of the consular elections throughout the year 53, and finally Clodius was murdered in a scuffle. This set off further rioting; the mob took his body to the Senate house for cremation, and in the confusion the building itself was destroyed by fire.

Pompey, who as proconsul had to remain outside the city but was within easy reach of Rome, did nothing. The inevitable moment came when the Senate offered him power. A state of public emergency was proclaimed and Pompey was given authority to levy troops and restore public order. This was a temporary measure; some longer-lasting authority was needed, and there were even rumours of a dictatorship for Pompey. Finally, he was appointed sole consul* for the year 52 B.C. and took immediate steps to restore public order, as well as passing a more general measure designed to make judicial bribery virtually impossible.

Now that the emergency had been dealt with, the question of relations between Pompey and Caesar would have to come up. On the one hand there might be some reassurance for Caesar in the fact that, although Pompey was in possession simultaneously of proconsular *and* consular power, he had been careful not to set himself up as a dictator; on the other hand it was disturbing that one of his first acts as consul was to secure the renewal of his proconsulship for a further five years, without a corresponding provision for Caesar.

It was now that Pompey's personality, as noticed above, played a decisive part in the course of events. He was being torn two ways – between loyalty to his partner, Caesar, on the one hand, and the forces of constitutionality, as represented by the conservative senators, on the other. The main link holding him to Caesar had been the usefulness of the latter in assisting his self-advancement. Now that the formerly hostile Senate was actually offering

* He added his new father-in-law, Scipio, as colleague in July/August.

him power the temptation to break his promises to Caesar must have been very great. These promises, however, ought to be kept – if not from a sense of honour, at least from the consideration that Caesar, with his veteran army in Gaul, was in a position to fight for his claims.

Pompey therefore found himself in a dilemma; and the outcome of three years' vacillating was the Civil War. Caesar's requirements were that when he gave up his Gallic command, he should immediately be able to enter Rome under the shield of official power as consul. Two things were therefore necessary : that he should be allowed to stand as candidate *in absentia*, and that since he was not legally eligible for the consulship until 48 B.C., the Senate must be prevented from appointing a successor who could take over his province before he became consul-elect. Pompey, before being appointed sole consul, had secured the passage of a law granting Caesar the privilege of standing *in absentia*. As consul, he carried a law insisting that candidates appear in person, then subsequently added a clause exempting Caesar. His law on the interval between magistracies and provincial governorships (see note on *Civil War*, I. 9) threw Caesar's province open for re-allocation immediately; but Pompey himself in 51 B.C., and again in 50, helped to block discussion of a successor.

By 50 B.C., however, the situation had seriously worsened. On news of a Parthian threat to Syria the Senate voted that Pompey and Caesar should each contribute a legion for the Eastern campaigns; Pompey announced that his legion would be the one which in 53 B.C. he had lent to Caesar, whose forces were thus weakened by the loss of two legions. In fact, the rumours came to nothing, and the legions remained in Italy. The consuls elected for 49 B.C. were Gaius Claudius Marcellus and Lucius Cornelius Lentulus, both enemies of Caesar; Pompey had evidently not exerted himself on Caesar's behalf.

Matters finally came to a head in a senatorial debate at the beginning of December. The consul Gaius Claudius Marcellus (cousin of the consul-elect for 49) put two questions to the vote in the Senate: Should a successor be sent to replace Caesar? Should Pompey be required to resign his command? The first received an affirmative answer; the second was rejected by a large majority. The Caesarian tribune Curio promptly put another motion: that *both* Caesar and Pompey should resign their commands and disband their armies. Many of the senators seem to have clutched eagerly at this suggestion as affording a chance of avoiding the war that now seemed imminent. Three hundred and seventy voted for the motion and only twenty-two against. Curio's efforts, and theirs, were, however, futile – a tribune was found to veto the proposal. On the following day another attempt by Marcellus was vetoed by Curio; the consul thereupon declared a state of emergency on his own initiative. Going to Pompey, he called on him to save the State, authorizing him to command the two legions in Italy and to raise additional levies.

When it was put to him as bluntly as this Pompey could no longer evade the issue, and accepted the commission. The decision had in effect been made for him, and probably this solution was the most satisfactory to his conscience.

Caesar's friends sent the news to him, and Curio on the expiry of his office went to join him in winter quarters at Ravenna. Caesar still attempted to maintain the *status quo*; he proposed a compromise solution – that he should retain the provinces of Cisalpine Gaul and Illyricum, with two legions, until the start of his consulship. Pompey appears to have been willing to accept this and to avoid war; but the consuls rejected it. Caesar therefore tried again; he sent Curio with the letter referred to in the opening paragraph of the *Civil War*. In this, he offered to resign his command if Pompey would do the same; but if the offer were rejected, he would be obliged to act in defence of his own rights and those of the State.

At this point Caesar's narrative takes over and, with the continuations by other hands (the *Alexandrian War*, the *African War* and the *Spanish War*), the story is taken down to the defeat of the remnants of Pompeian opposition in Spain in 45 B.C. Caesar returned to Rome as dictator with less than a year to live, and continued the programme of financial and social legislation which he had begun in his brief visit to Rome in 46 B.C. between the African and Spanish campaigns. There were no blood-baths and confiscations of property, such as had characterized the reign of the dictator Sulla; instead, a series of measures designed to improve conditions for Roman citizens and provincials alike, to increase the efficiency and honesty of government and to accelerate the Romanization of the provinces. His haste led him on occasion to deal rather summarily with the machinery of senatorial government and this further embittered his enemies who were smarting under what they considered his autocratic rule. They muttered that Rome was reverting to the days of the kings, and when, in February 44 B.C., his dictatorship, which had originally been bestowed for only ten years, was declared perpetual, they realized that only his death could now remove him from power. A conspiracy was hatched, and on 15 March 44 B.C. Caesar was assassinated at a meeting of the Senate.

The murderers found to their chagrin that the removal of the dictator had solved no problems. The constitution had fallen into such disrepute and disrepair that public order and efficient government would not come of themselves. There was a need for some overriding authority which could compel obedience. Thirteen years and another civil war later, that authority emerged in the person of Octavian, later known as Augustus.

Caesar – the man and his aims

Caesar came from a patrician family of great antiquity. It was said that the Julii Caesares had come to Rome from Alba Longa when the latter town was destroyed by the Roman king Tullus Hostilius. The family claimed an even longer and more glorious line of descent – through Iulus (otherwise Ascanius) the son of Aeneas the Trojan. Aeneas was the son of Venus herself. Caesar referred to this legend of his family's descent in his funeral speech for his aunt Julia, the wife of Marius.

The Julii Caesares seem to have had little else to boast about. They do not figure largely in Roman Republican history and when Caesar was born it was some considerable time since any of the family had risen beyond the praetorship. However, the marriage of Caesar's aunt to Gaius Marius gave them a connexion with a potentially important political group; both his father and his uncle supported Marius. This connexion meant that the family was regarded as belonging to the *populares* (the 'radicals', or – to their opponents – 'demagogues') and were therefore regarded with suspicion by the *optimates* (the 'good men'), i.e. the conservative supporters of the entrenched power and privilege of the senatorial oligarchy.

This Marian connexion and his own marriage to a daughter of Cinna exposed Caesar to the suspicions of the dictator Sulla. He refused to obey the latter's order to divorce his wife, and had his property and his wife's dowry confiscated. He was captured by Sullan agents and in danger of his life, but the dictator was persuaded by influential friends to let him go. He gave the 'good men' no trouble for the next ten years or so and was sufficiently highly regarded by the patrician nobles to be co-opted in 73 B.C. to the college of priests.

Within two years the patricians realized that they had been mistaken in him. He came out into the open as a supporter of popular measures, backing Pompey in his programme rescinding the Sullan constitution.

The reason for Caesar's apparent change of side is inevitably a matter for speculation. His denigrators would no doubt ascribe it to mere opportunism. Lily Ross Taylor (*Greece and Rome*, March 1957, p. 14) suspects that the reason was 'policy, that, with his sure sense of timing in politics, he waited to join the fight for the destruction of the Sullan constitution until Pompey's championship made victory sure'. This does not necessarily mean that his sole, or even main, motive was self-advancement; after all, it would have been possible to build up respectable connexions among the *optimates*. Caesar, however, right down to the Civil War, is found consistently supporting popular legislation and reforms, and his legislation as dictator, in marked contrast to that of Sulla, was directed towards bettering the conditions of Roman citizens and inhabitants of the empire in general, rather than to strengthening the power and prosperity of the noble few.

This is not to say that Caesar was not ambitious; on the contrary, ambition seems to have been one of his predominant characteristics, and in pursuit of self-advancement he was prepared to brush aside constitutional obstacles. I believe, however, that his ambition was limited to the achievement of that degree of prestige and power within the state which he felt he merited; I do not believe that his aim, at the outset of the Civil War, was to enforce himself as dictator upon the Roman people or, after the Civil War, to establish himself as any sort of king, as the hostile tradition alleges.

His requirements from the Senate at the earlier period have been described in the previous section of the Introduction; and it was necessary as much (if not more) for his self-preservation, as for the satisfaction of his ambition, that a consulship should follow uninterruptedly upon his military command. As things stood he dared not become a private citizen again. Nor, I think, can it be convincingly demonstrated that he did not sincerely try to reach a negotiated settlement and avert war.

As for the period of his dictatorship at Rome, the myth that he wanted to make himself a king, or even a Hellenistic-type king worshipped with divine honours, was first put about by his enemies of the time; it has been taken up by historians and others in later generations who have shown themselves ready to accept the gossip put about by his detractors and their representation of his actions and remarks.

Honours were heaped on him, by senatorial decree – quasi-regal dress (in fact, the traditional garb of the Roman *triumphator*), a golden throne in the Senate house, his image on coins, a statue in the temple of Quirinus, etc. How these decrees were inspired is again a matter for speculation. The most obvious interpretation would be that they were the product of adulation based on fear; some may perhaps have been the work of the misguided enthusiasm of Caesar's supporters. But it is extremely unlikely that they were instigated by Caesar himself – for, as many recent commentators have pertinently asked, when Caesar as dictator held the reality of power what need was there to insist on the invidious outward trappings?

His enemies were always ready to look for signs of arrogance and contempt for the Senate. They construed in this way his appointment of Caninius to fill the vacancy caused by the sudden death of a consul on the last day of his term of office; whereas all that Caesar need necessarily have been blamed for was excessive punctiliousness in carrying out his duties as dictator and in observing the requirements of the constitution. Again, the story was put about of his failure on a certain occasion to rise to receive the Senate when they came to inform him of their latest honorific decrees; but there is some reason to believe that a sudden attack of faintness (often the forewarning of one of his epileptic fits) kept him in his seat. Certainly, he did on occasion betray his impatience with opposition, and may even have been ashamed of it afterwards. He does not tell us in his narrative of the Civil War that in fact he gained access to the State treasury in 49 B.C. only by using physical force against the tribune who attempted to bar his way. In 44 B.C. he had two tribunes deposed by the popular assembly. This reversion to Gracchan techniques was bound to inflame general indignation, especially in view of the occasion. The tribunes had summarily arrested and committed for trial, first a person who had placed a diadem on the head of Caesar's statue in the forum and secondly one who had saluted Caesar as king when he was riding in procession from the celebration of the Alban festival. Caesar initially did not interfere; but, when the tribunes then published an edict complaining that they had no liberty of action, he had them deposed. The incident lent itself to misrepresentation as evidence of Caesar's autocracy and desire for monarchy. In the writer's view, however, the tribunes were, at best, officious, at the worst, *agents provocateurs*, and it was understandable, if not prudent, that Caesar should lose patience.

Suetonius in his biography of Caesar (Ch. 77) cites (from a Pompeian source) several remarks of Caesar's which were preserved by a hostile tradition as demonstrating his arrogance, presumption and scorn for the constitution and, even, his desire to overthrow the Republic. The most notorious of these remarks perhaps is the pronouncement that Sulla was a dunce to resign the dictatorship. This is ambiguous; Caesar's enemies would interpret it to mean that Caesar wanted autocratic power for its own sake; but – supposing that Caesar ever said anything of the sort – his meaning might simply have been that Sulla had not retained power long enough for the restoration of public order and had, moreover, been too short-sighted to see that his attempts to botch up the constitution could not possibly have any lasting effectiveness.

Such remarks may have escaped Caesar in moments of impatience (and then probably in private). His attitude appears to have been, 'I know that I can save this country and that no one else can', and lack of cooperation with his efforts or opposition to them made him lose patience. His behaviour as dictator in many respects recalls his consulship.

The care he took to associate the Senate with himself, consulting it on the minutest details of public business, does not suggest that he seriously contemplated scrapping the machinery of the Republic. There are many hostile references in the ancient tradition to the alleged ignoble origins of the new senators he enrolled in the house – centurions, scribes, sons of freedmen, newly-enfranchised aliens, etc. In fact, centurions might often be men of notable Italian families who had risen to equestrian financial status. Scribes and the sons of freedmen (on whom there was no legal bar) could also be men of quite high social standing. As for foreigners, the enfranchisement of deserving provincials was no new thing; some of the inhabitants of Narbonensis were by now second- or third-generation Roman citizens. The evidence, admittedly, is sparse, but only a very small number of Roman citizens from the provinces is attested in the Senate at this time, and those are from the more Romanized provinces; Gallia Comata ('Long-haired Gaul' – Caesar's newly-won territory) is not represented. His enrolments were, of course, interpreted as displaying his contempt for the Senate, in turning it into a body of compliant placemen. This overlooks the fact that the necessities of the government of Rome and the provinces required an increase in the number of magistrates. In 44 B.C. the number of quaestors elected annually was raised to forty and, since the quaestorship gave automatic entry to the Senate, this in itself meant an increase in the numbers of the latter. Besides, the depletion in the ranks of the Senate due to the Civil War had to be made good. Lastly, what the carping critics ignored was the simple fact that if Caesar had felt secure enough in his position to display (on this view) such blatant contempt for the Senate, then it is unlikely that he would have hesitated to abolish this mockery of a government.

Had Caesar seriously intended to convert Rome into a monarchy it would be expected that we should find evidence that he had taken or was contemplating steps both to remove his own position from popular control and to provide for a successor. Neither can be shown to be the case.

His acceptance of the title *dictator perpetuus* shows that he did intend to retain power indefinitely. His status, however, had been bestowed on him by the vote of the sovereign Roman people and was still in theory revocable by them. There is no positive evidence that he had considered doing what was necessary to convert the dictatorship into a monarchy. The incident at the Lupercalia (known to all readers of Shakespeare, if not of the classical sources) is mysterious; if sponsored by Caesar, it may have been intended as a demonstration to the people that he did not want the title of king. The rumour that spread about Rome, that the keeper of the Sibylline books was going to find an oracle saying that the Romans would need a king to defeat the Parthians, appears to have been part of a smear campaign by Caesar's enemies.

The clearest possible evidence that Caesar intended to set up a monarchy would be provided if it could be shown that he had taken steps to bind the Roman people to accept a hereditary successor. Such evidence is not available. According to Dio, one honour awarded to Caesar in 44 was the decree that his son, if he should beget one, or adopted son should inherit his position as head of the college of priests. Although honorific, this would not carry any political power. Octavian, some months after the dictator's death, secured recognition as the latter's adopted son, allegedly by the provisions of his will. It is in fact doubtful whether testamentary adoption in this way was legal; in any case, it certainly could not be used to transfer constitutional powers. It would have been open to Caesar, in his lifetime, to make his wishes so plain and so to build up the *auctoritas* of Octavian that on his death the Senate would have to confer the same constitutional powers on Octavian to prevent a civil war. In fact, Caesar did not do so. In any case, Caesar, now married to a young wife, apparently still had hopes of begetting sons of his own, and had taken account of that possibility in his will. On balance, it does not seem that Caesar contemplated the foundation of a personal dynasty.

Very different views have been taken of Caesar's actions and ambitions in the closing period of his life. The ancient tradition is mainly hostile and has influenced many modern scholars. Others believe that what is known of Caesar's actual government and legislation cannot easily be reconciled with the hostile view. It is impossible, in an essay on the scale of this Introduction, to deal adequately with even a fraction of the evidence; the foregoing is merely a brief treatment of some of the salient points. It will no doubt have emerged that the writer has a strong predilection in Caesar's favour; nevertheless, an attempt has been made to deal fairly with the evidence, bearing in mind the great difference in circumstances, and therefore in general attitudes towards politics and government, between Rome in the first century B.C. and the States of the twentieth century A.D.

As well as Caesar the administrator, politician and man of ambition, something should be said of Caesar the orator and the author. Little need be said here of Caesar the soldier. The accounts of his campaigns by himself and others are testimony to his qualities as a general. He was not infallible; on more than one occasion, as he himself acknowledges, it was not so much tactics that won a battle for him as the effect of his personal intervention on the morale of his troops or some small incident that turned the tide of battle; but these instances do not detract from the total impression produced by the narrative of his campaigns. These reveal not only a sound grasp of the principles of all branches of military organization – strategy, tactics, commissariat, engineering – but imagination and energy in their application. Last, but by no means least, he succeeded in binding his men to him by strong ties of loyalty; he did this by making a point of close personal contact with small sections, if not with every individual, in the army. Particular instances of good service were noted and recalled when appropriate; and he took pains to be acquainted with the centurions – the company-sergeant-majors – of his legions, treating them not merely as subordinates but as experienced soldiers whose advice was to be heeded and respected. This policy reaped its rewards.

As author, Caesar earned the praise of Cicero in 46 B.C. for his work on the Gallic War (and possibly also the 'Commentaries' on the Civil War, at least in part). Cicero says in the *Brutus*:

They [sc. the *Commentaries*] are like nude figures, upright and beautiful, stripped of all ornament of style as if they had removed a garment. His aim was to provide source material for others who might wish to write history, and perhaps he has gratified the insensitive, who may wish to use their curling-tongs on his work; but men of good sense he has deterred from writing.

This is praise of an unusual kind. Cicero held the general view that style, as much as veracity and lucidity, was essential to the writer of history; but Caesar's work has an important difference from ordinary history. He gave his narratives the title 'Commentaries' (on the Gallic War, on the Civil War). The word *commentarius* originally meant something like 'memoir' or 'report'. Cicero himself had written such a 'commentary' on his own consulship, in Greek, which was not intended as a literary work, but as source material for working up into a historical narrative. Caesar, in calling his works 'Commentaries' was therefore disclaiming the status of literary work for them, but representing them merely as bald, unvarnished reports of his campaigns. The point of Cicero's praise, as he goes on to make clear, is that these terse 'reports' are nevertheless so elegantly and lucidly written that they compel admiration without the addition of further ornament. Cicero's praise is echoed by Caesar's former officer, Hirtius, who wrote the final book of the *Gallic War* after the dictator's death.

Caesar's oratory also won the praise of Cicero, as well as that of Quintilian and Fronto. Quintilian went so far as to assert that, had Caesar had the leisure to devote himself to forensic oratory, he would have been the one orator who could have been considered a rival to Cicero. The particular qualities he ascribes to him are penetration, energy and elegance of language.

Caesar had, in fact, definite views on elegance of language. He wrote a work in two volumes, dedicated to Cicero, entitled *de Analogia* ('On Selection of Words'). From such references to the work as survive, it appears that Caesar advocated careful selection of vocabulary, rather than the uncritical acceptance of everyday colloquial usage. On the one hand, the orator should purge his speech of foreign coinages and colloquial corruptions; on the other, he should avoid bizarre and unfamiliar words. The aim should be a clear, pure Latinity. His *Commentaries* are some indication of how far he himself succeeded in this aim. The pitfall into which a practitioner of his theories might readily fall is that of dullness and repetitiveness of vocabulary; Caesar himself is very rarely guilty of this, in contrast to the lesser writers who continued his narrative in the *Alexandrian War* and the *African War*.

Caesar's youthful literary efforts were suppressed by Augustus as unworthy. Other lost works of which we hear are *Anticato* (an answer to Cicero's pamphlet in praise of M. Porcius Cato), a work on astronomy, perhaps connected with his reform of the calendar, and a poem called *The Journey*, allegedly written on a journey from Rome to western Spain, which took twenty-four days. Of his poetry, six lines survive – a literary judgement in hexameters on Terence; he laments his lack of 'comic force' but praises him specifically as a 'lover of pure speech'.

The Civil War *and the continuations*

The three parts of Caesar's *Civil War* take the narrative down to the beginning of the Alexandrian War in the autumn of 48 B.C. The narrative is continued down to the battle of Munda in 45 B.C. in three works by other hands called respectively, after the campaigns featuring most prominently in them, the *Alexandrian War*, the *African War* and the *Spanish War*.

Part III of the *Civil War* does not end at a natural break, such as the death of Pompey, or Caesar's return to Rome in 47 B.C. The presumption is that, as far as Caesar was concerned, the work was unfinished. It is difficult, however, to draw any conclusions from this fact alone as to the period or periods at which it was composed. It has, for instance, been suggested that it was the Ides of March which put a stop to the writing. On the other hand, the work bears many signs of being intended as propaganda to win over some of the less violent opponents of the new regime (just as, possibly, the *Gallic War* was rushed out in order to catch votes for his intended candidature for the consulship of 49 B.C.). Such propaganda was more urgently necessary during the successive campaigns of the Civil War than once his power was assured in 44 B.C. It seems therefore a reasonable inference that the *Civil War* was written during the course of the Civil War; but that is as far as we can go. The state of our knowledge does not really admit of precise allocations of dates and times of writing. Nor is it known for certain that the *Civil War* was published in his lifetime. Cicero's comment in the *Brutus* (see above) may refer only to the *Gallic War*, and we have no other contemporary reference.

Caesar is concerned to present himself and his cause in the best possible light. To this end he does in some cases omit mention of setbacks and of actions not altogether creditable (some of which are mentioned in the Notes at the end of this book). He does also take pains to point out examples of behaviour discreditable to his opponents, e.g. the implacable hostility of his senatorial enemies in the debate which opens the work and the self-seeking of the Pompeians before Pharsalus, and he perhaps rather exaggerates the degree to which his virtually bloodless conquest of Italy was due to his own popularity. On the other hand I feel that some modern writers, such as Rambaud (see Bibliographical Note), rather exaggerate the amount of distortion and deliberate mis-representation to be found in these books. Rambaud's Caesar, in particular, is a much meaner figure than the man whose character appears in the reading of the text itself. Especially one should not be ready to disbelieve in Caesar's *clementia* – after all, he persisted in it, even though those he had spared time and again repaid him with further attacks. His statement of his case, e.g. in various speeches in Part I, is remarkably temperate in tone and free from emotionalism. For the famous crossing of the Rubi-con with its attendant heart-searchings, of which Appian, Lucan and Plutarch make so much, the reader will search in vain in Caesar's narrative.

According to Suetonius, Asinius Pollio, himself a historian and an officer in Caesar's army during the war, criticized the memoirs as showing signs of carelessness and inaccuracy. Caesar, he said, did not always check the truth of the reports received and was either disingenuous or forgetful in describing his own actions. The apparent harshness of the latter criticism is, however, softened by the following remark that he believed Caesar must have intended to revise the work. The former point is important. Substantial portions of Caesar's narrative (e.g. much of the account of the siege of Massilia and the African campaign in Part II) concern actions at which he himself was not present; for these he had to rely on the reports made by his lieutenants.

Caesar's *Civil War*, as indicated above, is no mean literary achievement; his style is clear, terse and restrained without being monotonous or drab. The authors of the sequels were rather less successful.

As early as the beginning of the second century A.D. the authorship of the three books was unknown. Hirtius, who was known to have written the continuation to the *Gallic War*, and Oppius, another adherent of Caesar, were suggested as likely authors. Modern scholars have laboured on analysis of vocabulary and style and searched for internal evidence in an attempt to identify the authors. Nothing certain has emerged. Many are inclined to accept the view that the *Alexandrian War* was the work of Hirtius. It is the nearest of the three in style to Caesar's own work, though lacking in the latter's liveliness.

A wide variety of ascriptions has been made for the *African War*. Sallust and Asinius Pollio, both of whom participated in the Civil War, are the most famous among the candidates; but, as a French editor, M. Bouvet (Budé edition, 1949), observes, this ascription is flattering to neither writer. The narrative shows clear signs of being based on eye-witness experience; the author appears to have been in Caesar's army, perhaps as a junior officer. His junior status is suggested by his lack of knowledge of the reasons for many strategic or tactical decisions taken by the commander. His partisanship is warm and enthusiastic. This enthusiasm, itself suggestive of youth, is reflected in his style. He is at some pains to produce 'fine writing': little rhetorical flourishes such as balanced clauses, alliteration, assonance, chiasmus and rhythmical sentence-endings abound. On the other hand, there is a certain monotony of expression, particularly in the choice of phrase for transition from one topic or period of time to another, and many of the more complex sentences are clumsy and ill-controlled, if not downright ungrammatical. These, together with the uncertainty of taste indicated in his use of Greek words and slangy expressions normally avoided by good prose writers, may be indications of youthful inexperience.

The *Spanish War* is clearly not the product of someone accustomed to literary effort; and the wretched condition of the text which has come down to us, full of gaps and corruptions as it is, accentuates rather than cloaks the literary deformities of the work. The author was apparently an eye-witness of the events described; his status is totally unknown. It was Lord Macaulay who first suggested that the work may have been the fruits of the enthusiasm of 'some sturdy old centurion, who fought better than he wrote'. The author shows little sense of perspective; trivial details are recounted while important information on troop numbers and movements, strategy, etc., is omitted. He has little ability to organize a historical narrative; repeatedly, some detail or incident is inserted with a prefatory phrase explaining that the author omitted to mention it at the proper place. His vocabulary is limited, his grammar poor and his expression often muddled and ambiguous. Nevertheless, he is evidently trying hard to make his work reflect something of his own enthusiasm, and uses his acquaintance with Ennius (the 'schoolboy classic' of the Romans) and Homeric legend to elevate the tone of the narrative. Whatever its defects, the *Spanish War* does preserve for us some form of contemporary account of the campaigns.

BIBLIOGRAPHICAL NOTE

FOR those mainly interested in the history of the period, T. Rice Holmes, *The Roman Republic* (3 vols., O.U.P., 1923), remains important. I have also found it useful in suggesting occasional turns of phrase and in helping me decide between variant readings in the text. The period is also covered by Volume IX of the *Cambridge Ancient History*. More recent is the two-volume biography, with useful bibliography and notes, *Caesar*, by Gérard Walter (translated into English by Emma Crauford, Cassell, 1953). Ronald (now Sir Ronald) Syme, *The Roman Revolution* (O.U.P., 1939; corrected edition now available in Oxford Paperbacks, 1960), writes on the political background of the revolution.

The book by M. Rambaud, mentioned in the Introduction, is entitled *L'art de la déformation historique dans les commentaires de César* (Paris, 1953). A further list of works on the veracity of Caesar is given at the end of the article, 'The Veracity of Caesar', by J. P. V. D. Balsdon in *Greece and Rome* (second series, vol. IV, no. 1; March 1957). This issue of *Greece and Rome* is devoted mainly to articles on Julius Caesar; it commemorates the bimillenium of his assassination in 44 B.C.

An English translation is now available of Matthias Gelzer, *Caesar: Politician and Statesman* (P. Needham, Blackwell, 1968), a work justly famous in the world of scholarship and now happily accessible to a wider readership.

TRANSLATOR'S NOTE

THE Roman mile (subdivided into one thousand 'paces') was rather less in length than an English mile; I have, however, translated X Roman miles simply as X (or 'about X') English miles, to avoid confusion for the reader. There are a few instances, mainly in *Civil War* Part I, where a fragment of a Roman mile (X hundred paces) is mentioned; in these instances, I have converted to the roughly equivalent length in English yards, and have rendered the expression either in yards or in the nearest fraction of an English mile.

In reckoning time, the Romans divided the day (from sunrise to sunset) into twelve equal divisions and the night (from sunset to sunrise) into four 'watches'. There would obviously be seasonal differences in the beginning, end and duration of these periods. To render time in terms familiar to a modern reader, I have taken a standard 6.00 a.m. sunrise, 6.00 p.m. sunset and converted accordingly. Obviously times of night can be expressed only approximately. Dates have been converted into modern terms.

I have not attempted to find modern substitutes for monetary and military terms. It may be helpful to the reader to bear in mind the equations six centuries = one cohort, ten cohorts = one legion.

The text followed is in the main the Oxford Classical Text of Renatus du Pontet. Variations are listed in an appendix.

Footnotes in the translation, unless in square brackets, are part of the original text.

In the Notes, Appendices and Glossary, the books are referred to by the abbreviations C.W. (*Civil War*), Al. (*Alexandrian War*), Af. (*African War*), Sp. (*Spanish War*).

I am indebted for much helpful advice and criticism to my colleague A. E. Wardman. The flaws that remain are due to my own stubbornness.

University of Reading
June, 1965

CAESAR : THE CIVIL WAR

PART I: THE STRUGGLE BEGINS

1. Intransigence at Rome

1. The dispatch from Gaius Caesar[1] was delivered to the consuls; but it was only after strong representations from the tribunes that they gave their grudging permission for it to be read in the Senate. Even then, they would not consent to a debate on its contents, but initiated instead a general debate on 'matters of State'. This was opened by the consul Lucius Lentulus, who promised that, if the Senate was prepared to state its views courageously and firmly, he would not fail in his duty to the State; but if they had regard for Caesar's possible reactions, and tried to ingratiate themselves with him, as on previous occasions, then he would choose his own line of action and would not obey the voice of the Senate. He reminded them that he too could take refuge in the good-will and friendship of Caesar. Scipio spoke in the same vein. Pompey, he said, intended to stand by his duty to the State, if the Senate would support him; but if they hesitated and showed weakness, then, should they want his help later, they would ask for it in vain. 2. The Senate was meeting in Rome, and Pompey was near by[2]; and so Scipio's speech seemed to come from the mouth of Pompey himself.

Some few expressed themselves in milder terms. First, Marcus Marcellus launched into a speech to the effect that the topic should not be introduced in the Senate until a levy had been held throughout Italy and troops enrolled under whose protection the Senate might dare, freely and with impunity, to pass whatever decrees it wished. Marcus Calidius urged that Pompey should set out for his provinces, so that there should be no grounds for hostilities. He alleged that Caesar was apprehensive that Pompey was holding on to the two legions he had taken from him, and keeping them near Rome, in order to do him some harm. Marcus Rufus took substantially the same line.

Lucius Lentulus took up all the speakers and routed them with a withering reply. He refused point blank to put Calidius's motion, and his strictures cowed Marcellus, so that he too gave up his motion. And so the majority, under pressure from the consul's tirades together with fear at the proximity of the army and the menaces of Pompey's friends, were driven reluctantly to support Scipio's motion. The terms of this were that Caesar should disband his army before a date to be fixed; if he failed to comply, he would be deemed to be meditating treason against the State. Mark Antony and Quintus Cassius, tribunes of the people, then interposed their veto. There was a hurried debate on this veto and harsh measures were advocated; and the more savage and vindictive the speaker, the more he was applauded by Caesar's enemies.

3. When the Senate was dismissed towards evening, all its members were summoned out of the city by Pompey. Those who were prompt to obey he praised and encouraged to continue so; the less quick he reproved and urged to do better. Many veterans from Pompey's old armies were called out from their homes by the prospect of rewards and advancement, and many troops were summoned from the two legions handed over by Caesar. The city, the approach to the Capitol and the *comitium* [3] were full of tribunes, centurions and recalled veterans. All the friends of the consuls, all the adherents of Pompey and of those with old grudges against Caesar were mustered in the Senate. Their numbers and the uproar they made intimidated the timorous, made up the minds of the waverers and robbed the majority of the power to decide freely.

The censor Lucius Piso and a praetor Lucius Roscius undertook to go and inform Caesar of these events, and asked for a period of six days to fulfil their mission. Some speakers further suggested that a deputation should be sent to Caesar to acquaint him with the feelings of the Senate. 4. All these suggestions were opposed in speeches by the consul, by Scipio and by Cato, each for his own reasons. Cato was an old enemy of Caesar's and, besides, he was stung by his defeat at the elections. Lentulus was actuated by the size of his debts, and by the prospect of a military command and a province and bribes from native rulers for the recognition of their titles. He boasted among his friends that he would be a second Sulla and hold supreme command in the State. Scipio had the same hopes of a province, and of military command, for he expected to share the armies with Pompey as a relative of his by marriage[4]. Besides, he had a dread of the law courts and was susceptible to the flattery of certain persons of great influence in politics and in the courts at the time, as well as being swayed by his own and their love of display.

Pompey, for his part, was reluctant to let anyone stand on the same pinnacle of prestige as himself. For this reason, and also because he had been listening to Caesar's enemies, he had completely severed his friendly connexions with Caesar. He had become reconciled with their common enemies – most of whom he had himself inflicted on Caesar at the time when he contracted a marriage alliance with him. Moreover, he was perturbed by the discredit attaching to his behaviour over the two legions, which he had diverted from the expedition to Asia and Syria, in order to advance his own power and supremacy. Pompey, therefore, was anxious to force a decision by war.

5. Accordingly, haste and confusion characterized every transaction. Caesar's friends were not given time to acquaint him with these events, while the tribunes were given no chance of protesting at the threat to themselves, or even of retaining, in the exercise of the veto, their most fundamental right, which Lucius Sulla had not taken away from them; and whereas in the old days those notoriously unruly tribunes had been wont to look ahead anxiously to the end of several *months* of exercise of authority, in the present instance the tribunes were given only six days in which to secure their own safety. The Senate had recourse to that ultimate decree of emergency, which was never employed before except when the city was on the verge of destruction and when everyone expected inevitable ruin at the hands of unscrupulous law-makers. The decree ran : 'The consuls, praetors, tribunes of the people and proconsuls in the vicinity of the city shall take steps to see that the State suffer no harm', and was recorded on the seventh of January. And so, not counting the two election days, during the first five days after Lentulus's entry into office on which meetings of the Senate could be held, resolutions of the harshest and most severe nature were passed concerning Caesar's command, and concerning those distinguished officials, the tribunes of the people. The latter at once fled from Rome and went to join Caesar, who was then at

Ravenna, awaiting a reply to his very moderate demands and hoping that some human sense of justice might make a peaceful settlement possible.

6. During the following days, the Senate met outside the city, and Pompey pressed the same policy that he had indicated through Scipio. He praised the courage and steadfastness of the Senate; he revealed the strength of his own resources, announcing that he had ten legions ready[5]; he claimed, moreover, to have reliable information that Caesar's troops were disaffected and could not be induced either to defend him or to follow him. Remaining business was put at once to the Senate, and it was decided to levy troops throughout Italy and to make Pompey a grant from the treasury. It was also proposed that King Juba should be given the title 'ally and friend', but Marcellus refused to tolerate this at present; another proposal, that Faustus Sulla be sent speedily to Mauretania, was blocked by the tribune Philippus. On the rest of the business, there are senatorial decrees in the records.

The provinces – two consular, the rest praetorian – were assigned to private individuals. Syria was allotted to Scipio and Gaul to Lucius Domitius, while Philippus and Cotta were passed over, by private agreement, and no lots were cast for them; praetors were sent to the rest. Then, without waiting for their commands to be referred to the people for ratification, the governors donned the military cloak, made the usual vows, and departed. The consuls, before they left the city, had their attendants going about in the city and on the Capitol in military cloaks, something which had never happened before and was contrary to all ancient practice. Troops were being levied all over Italy, weapons were being requisitioned, and money was exacted from the Italian towns and carried off out of temples with complete disregard for the distinction between divine and human.

2. Caesar reacts

7. When news of these events reached Caesar, he assembled his men and addressed them, retailing to them all the wrongs done to him at various times by his enemies. 'They have seduced Pompey,'

he protested, 'and led him astray, through jealous belittling of my merits; and yet I have always supported Pompey, and helped him to secure advancement and reputation. A precedent has been created in government; in the recent past, armed force restored the tribunes' veto; now armed force is repressing and overriding it. When Sulla stripped the tribunes of the rest of their prerogatives, he none the less left them the free exercise of the veto; Pompey has the credit of having restored their lost powers, but he has taken away even what they previously had. The decree calling upon the magistrates to act to save the State from harm, a decree by which the Senate called the Roman people to arms, was never passed before now except in the case of pernicious legislation, or violence by tribunes, or a mutiny of the people, when the temples and heights commanding the city were seized; and these earlier precedents were atoned for by the fates of Saturninus and the Gracchi. But in the present instance, none of these things has taken place, or even been contemplated; there has been no law proposed, no attempt to appeal to the people, no mutiny.

'I have been your commander for nine years; under my leadership, your efforts on Rome's behalf have been crowned with good fortune; you have won countless battles and have pacified the whole of Gaul and Germany. Now, I ask you to defend my reputation and standing against the assaults of my enemies.'

The men of the Thirteenth legion* clamoured that they were ready to avenge the wrongs done to their general and to the tribunes; and being thus assured of their support, Caesar took them to Ariminum, ordering the remaining legions to leave their winter quarters and follow him [6]. 8. At Ariminum, he met the tribunes who had fled to join him, and young Lucius Caesar, the son of one of his lieutenants. After Lucius had discharged the business for which he had come [7], he revealed that he had a message from Pompey concerning personal relations between himself and Caesar. Pompey wanted to clear himself in Caesar's eyes, and begged him not to take as a personal affront what he had done for the sake of the State; for he had always put the good of the country before the claims of personal friendship, and Caesar too, as befitted his

* He had summoned this legion at the beginning of the troubles; the others had not yet arrived.

position, should subordinate his personal ambitions and grievances to the good of Rome, and should not allow his anger against his personal enemies to lead him into damaging Rome, in his efforts to do them harm. Lucius added a few more remarks in the same vein, with excuses for Pompey's behaviour. The praetor Roscius appealed to Caesar more or less with the same arguments and in the same words, and expressly said that he was quoting Pompey directly.

9. In all this, there was no apparent move to repair the wrongs done. None the less, having thus obtained suitable agents to convey his wishes to Pompey, Caesar said to them both that, since they had brought Pompey's message to him, he hoped they would not object to taking his terms back to Pompey. 'Only consider,' he said, 'that by a small expenditure of effort you can put an end to grave dissensions and release all Italy from fear. Prestige has always been of prime importance to me, even outweighing life itself; it pained me to see the privilege conferred on me by the Roman people being insultingly wrested from me by my enemies, and to find that I was being robbed of six months of my command[8] and dragged back to Rome, although the will of the people had been that I should be admitted as a candidate *in absentia* at the next elections. However, for the sake of Rome, I bore this loss of privilege with a good grace. When I wrote to the Senate suggesting a general demobilization, I was not allowed even that. Troops are being raised all over Italy, my two legions, which were taken from me on the pretext of a Parthian campaign, are being retained, and the whole State is in arms. What is the aim of all these preparations but my destruction? However, I am ready to submit to anything and put up with anything for the sake of Rome. My terms are these: Pompey shall go to his provinces; we shall both disband our armies; there shall be complete demobilization in Italy; the regime of terror shall cease; there shall be free elections and the Senate and the Roman people shall be in full control of the government. To facilitate this and fix the terms and ratify them with an oath, I suggest that Pompey either comes to meet me or allows me to meet him. By submitting our differences to mutual discussion, we shall settle them all.'

10. Roscius accepted the commission and went with young

Lucius to Capua, where he found Pompey and the consuls and reported Caesar's demands. They discussed them and sent back in reply, by the same messengers, written orders the gist of which was that Caesar should leave Ariminum, return to Gaul, and disband his army, and that if he did so Pompey would go to the Spanish provinces. Meanwhile, until they received a pledge that Caesar would do as he promised, the consuls and Pompey would not suspend the levy of troops.

11. It was unfair that Pompey should require Caesar to leave Ariminum and return to his province, while he himself kept his own provinces, and another man's legions as well; that Pompey should expect Caesar's army to be disbanded while he levied troops; that Pompey should promise to go to his province without fixing a date by which he must do so, so that even if he still had not gone when Caesar's consulship expired, he could not be held to have broken his oath. Further, the fact that he offered no opportunity for a conference and made no promise to come to meet Caesar made it likely that hopes of peace must be abandoned. Caesar therefore sent Mark Antony from Ariminum to Arretium with five cohorts, while he himself stayed with two cohorts and began levying troops on the spot, and also put one cohort each into Pisaurum, Fanum and Ancona.

12. Meanwhile, word came that the praetor Thermus was holding Iguvium with five cohorts and fortifying the town, but that the townspeople were all strong partisans of Caesar; he therefore sent Curio with the three cohorts which he had at Pisaurum and Ariminum. When Thermus heard of Curio's approach, not trusting the mood of the townsfolk, he withdrew his cohorts from the town and fled; on the journey, the troops deserted him and went home. Curio took over Iguvium amid general good-will. On learning of this, Caesar decided he could rely on the support of the Italian towns, and taking the cohorts of the Thirteenth legion out of their garrisons he set off for Auximum. Attius Varus was holding this town with cohorts which he had installed there and was sending the local councillors around to levy troops throughout Picenum.

13. When the town council heard of Caesar's approach, they came in a body to Attius, saying that, while they were not

competent to judge the issue, neither they nor their fellow-townsmen could allow Gaius Caesar, a holder of military command, a man who had served the State well and had many brilliant achievements to his credit, to be shut out of the town. They warned Attius therefore to think of the future and of his own danger. This speech alarmed Attius, who removed the garrison he had installed in the town and fled. He was pursued by a small detachment from Caesar's advance guard and compelled to stop; and after a token resistance his troops deserted him and a number of them went off home, while the rest made their way to Caesar, taking with them in custody Lucius Pupius, a chief centurion, who had previously held the same rank in the army of Pompey. Caesar commended Attius's troops, let Pupius go, and thanked the people of Auximum, promising to remember what they had done.

14. The news of these events raised a panic at Rome; so much so, that when the consul Lentulus came to open the treasury, in accordance with the decree of the Senate, to withdraw funds for Pompey, he opened the treasury reserve[9] and immediately fled from Rome – for there were reports that Caesar was on his way, and his cavalry with him, and would arrive at any minute. These were false alarms; nevertheless Marcellus followed his colleague, accompanied by most of the magistrates. Pompey had left the neighbourhood of Rome the day before and was on his way to join the legions taken from Caesar, which he had stationed in Apulia for the winter. The troop-levies around Rome were suspended, as it was felt that nowhere between there and Capua could be relied on. It was at Capua that they first rallied and recovered their spirits; there they began to hold a levy among the old soldiers who had been settled there by the Julian law[10]. Lentulus brought into the market-place the gladiators whom Caesar kept in a school there and, promising them their freedom, he issued them with horses and ordered them to follow him; later, however, on the advice of his supporters, since his action had met with universal disapproval he dispersed them for safe-keeping among the slave-gangs in Campania.

15. Leaving Auximum, Caesar hurried through the district of Picenum. All the prefectures[11] in the area gave him a hearty wel-

come and assisted his army with supplies of all kinds. A deputation even came from Cingulum – a town founded by Labienus and constructed at his own expense – promising to show the utmost zeal in carrying out any commands he might give. He asked them for soldiers, and these were supplied. Meanwhile, the Twelfth legion overtook Caesar, and with this and the legion he already had he made for Asculum, which Lentulus Spinther was holding with ten cohorts. On word of Caesar's approach, Lentulus abandoned the town, and tried to take the cohorts with him, but most of them deserted, and he was left abandoned on the road with only a small force of men. He then met Vibullius Rufus, who had been sent by Pompey to Picenum to ensure the loyalty of the local inhabitants. He received a report from Lentulus of what was going on in Picenum, took over his soldiers, and dismissed him. He then proceeded to muster what cohorts he could from the levies ordered by Pompey, as well as the six he caught fleeing from Camerinum with Lucilius Hirrus, who had commanded them in garrison there, and altogether he made up thirteen cohorts. With these he made his way by forced marches to Domitius Ahenobarbus at Corfinium and reported that Caesar was on his way with two legions. Domitius, for his part, had raised about twenty cohorts from Alba, the Marsi, the Paeligni and the surrounding districts.

3. The siege of Corfinium

16. Caesar accepted the surrender of Firmum; he also gave orders that a search be made for the men who had deserted Lentulus after the latter's expulsion, and that fresh troops be levied. He himself stayed where he was for one day to collect supplies of corn, and then hurried to Corfinium. On arrival there, he found that five cohorts sent out by Domitius from the town were breaking down the bridge over the river*, about three miles from the town. Domitius's men engaged Caesar's advance-guard, but were soon beaten back from the bridge and retreated into the town. Caesar then led his forces over the river and, halting near the town walls,

[*The Aternus.]

set up camp. 17. On learning this, Domitius by dint of offering a large reward succeeded in finding men with a knowledge of Apulia, and sent them to Pompey with dispatches begging him to come and help; he reported that two armies, aided by the confined nature of the country, could easily hem in Caesar and prevent his getting supplies. He warned Pompey that, if he failed to help, he himself and more than thirty cohorts, as well as a good many Roman knights and senators, would be put in danger. While awaiting a reply, he delivered encouraging speeches to his men, set up ballistic machines at various points on the walls, and assigned each of his men to specific duties for the defence of the town. In an address to the troops, he promised grants of land from his own possessions, at the rate of twenty-five acres per man, and proportionately larger grants to centurions and re-enlisted veterans.

18. Caesar in the meantime heard that the people of Sulmo, a town seven miles from Corfinium, were eager to support him, but were being restrained by the senator Quintus Lucretius and by Attius, a Paelignian, who were holding the town with a garrison of seven cohorts. Caesar sent Mark Antony there with five cohorts of the Thirteenth legion, and as soon as the people of Sulmo saw our standards they opened the gates and, one and all, troops and citizens, came out joyfully to meet Antony. Lucretius and Attius threw themselves from the walls, but Attius was brought to Antony and asked to be sent to Caesar. Antony returned on the same day as he had set out, with the cohorts and Attius, and Caesar incorporated the cohorts into his own army and released Attius unharmed. During the next few days, Caesar began to construct large defence-works about his camp and to gather in provisions from the neighbouring towns, while waiting for the rest of his forces. Within three days the Eighth legion arrived, together with twenty-two cohorts from the latest levies in Gaul and about three hundred cavalry from the king of Noricum. On their arrival, he set up a second camp on the other side of the town, and put Curio in charge of it. During the following days he began surrounding the town with earth-works and redoubts.

When the major part of this work was finished, the messengers sent to Pompey arrived back. 19. Domitius read the dispatch they brought; and then, in his council of officers, he concealed its contents, and announced that Pompey would shortly arrive with help; he urged them to keep up their spirits and make all necessary arrangements for the defence of the town. He himself then held a secret conclave with a few friends and decided to attempt an escape. Domitius's looks, however, belied his words; indeed, his whole demeanour was much more anxious and fearful than usual. When to this was added the fact that, contrary to his usual custom, he spent a lot of time talking to his friends in private, making plans, while avoiding a meeting of the officers or an assembly of the troops, then the truth could not be concealed or misrepresented for long. In fact, Pompey's reply had been that he was certainly not going to put his cause in jeopardy; that Domitius had not asked his advice or consent in going to Corfinium; and that if he could get the chance Domitius should come at once with all his forces and join him. This, however, was being rendered impossible by the building of siege-works around the town.

20. When word of Domitius's plans got about, the soldiers in Corfinium gathered in groups in the early evening and, led by tribunes, centurions and the more reputable men of their own class, began discussing the situation. They were being besieged by Caesar, and his siege-works were almost completed; they had stood steadfastly by their commander Domitius because of their confidence in and reliance on him, and now he was proposing to abandon them all and run away. The best course, it seemed, was for them to look after themselves. At first, the Marsi, not knowing about Domitius's intended flight, disagreed with this view and took possession of that part of the town which seemed best fortified; indeed, the disagreement grew so heated that they almost resorted to weapons. Presently, however, by an exchange of messengers between the two groups, the Marsi too were informed of the truth. Thereupon, the whole army unanimously had Domitius brought out and, surrounding him and putting him under guard, they sent a deputation from their own ranks to Caesar, saying they were ready to open the gates and take orders from him, and that they would surrender Domitius alive into his hands.

21. Caesar was fully aware of the importance of taking possession of the town and bringing the cohorts into his own camp as
soon as possible, before bribes, or a renewal of courage, or some
false rumours, should make the men change their minds; for he
knew that in warfare slight events can often turn the scales and
produce serious reversals. However, he was afraid that the entry
of his troops into the town, in the mood of licence engendered
by night, might lead to looting; on receipt of the message, therefore, he commended those who had brought it and sent them back
to the town, with orders that careful guard was to be kept on the
walls and gates. For his own part, he stationed his men around the
partly-built earth-works, not at fixed intervals as during the preceding days, but in a continuous line of sentries and guard-posts,
within touching distance of each other and covering the whole
length of the works. He sent the prefects and military tribunes[12]
around the guard-posts with injunctions to keep a look-out not
only for sallies from the town but also for stealthy exits by individuals. Indeed, not a single one of his troops was indifferent or
lazy enough to take any rest that night. So keen was their anticipation of the final settlement that each found his thoughts and
feelings caught up with some question or other. What was going
to happen to the people of Corfinium, to Domitius, to Lentulus?
What would happen to the rest? How would each man fare?

22. Towards the end of the night, Lentulus Spinther called
down from the walls to our men on guard, saying that he would
like to be allowed to have an interview with Caesar. He was given
permission and escorted from the city, although Domitius's men
did not leave him until they had brought him right into Caesar's
presence. He pleaded for his life, begging to be spared, and re-
minding Caesar of their old friendship and of all the benefits he
had received at Caesar's hands*. Caesar interrupted his speech : 'I
did not leave my province with intent to harm anybody. I merely
want to protect myself against the slanders of my enemies, to
restore to their rightful position the tribunes of the people, who

* These were indeed very great. Through Caesar he had been
admitted to the college of pontiffs[13], he had held Spain as his
province after his praetorship and he had received help in his candidature for the consulship.

have been expelled because of their involvement in my cause, and to reclaim for myself and for the Roman people independence from the domination of a small clique.'

Lentulus was so reassured by this speech that he asked permission to return to the town. 'The fact that I have been granted my life will bring great comfort and hope to the others; some have been so terrified that they have been driven to think of violence against themselves.' He was given permission; and went.

23. At dawn, Caesar ordered all the Roman senators and their families, the military tribunes and the knights to be brought out to him. There were five senators, Lucius Domitius, Publius Lentulus Spinther, Lucius Caecilius Rufus, Sextus Quintilius Varus, a quaestor, and Lucius Rubrius, as well as the son of Domitius and several other youths, and a large number of Roman knights and councillors summoned by Domitius from the local towns. When these were produced, Caesar protected them from the insults and jeers of the soldiers and, merely commenting briefly that he had received no thanks from them for the great benefits he had bestowed on them, he set them all free. The magistrates of Corfinium brought him six million sesterces, a sum which Domitius had brought and deposited in their treasury; these he restored to Domitius, to show that he had as little eagerness to take money as to take human life, even though it was clearly public money and had been given by Pompey for paying the troops. He ordered Domitius's soldiers to take the oath of allegiance to himself and, on the same day, after spending seven days at Corfinium, he did a full day's march, going to Apulia via the territories of the Marrucini, the Frentani and the Larinates.

4. Pompey leaves Italy

24. On learning of the events at Corfinium, Pompey left Luceria and went first to Canusium and from there to Brundisium. He ordered all the forces raised in the recent levies to be assembled there; he issued weapons and horses to slaves and shepherds, from whom he made up about three hundred cavalry. A praetor, Lucius Manlius, fled from Alba with six cohorts, and another

praetor, Rutilius Lupus, from Tarracina with three. These last, however, seeing in the distance Caesar's cavalry under the command of Vibius Curius, deserted their praetor and transferred themselves and their standards to Curius. Similarly, during the rest of his journey, several cohorts joined Caesar's infantry column on the march, and some also his cavalry.

Numerius Magius of Cremona, one of Pompey's officers in charge of engineers, was captured *en route* and brought to Caesar, who sent him back with a message for Pompey. Since up till now there had been no opportunity for a conference, Caesar said, and since he himself would be coming to Brundisium, he thought it would be in the interests of the State and of the general welfare if he and Pompey had a talk; they could not accomplish so much while they were a long distance apart and sending their proposals by intermediaries, as they could by an exhaustive discussion face to face. 25. After sending this message, he himself came to Brundisium with six legions, of whom three were seasoned troops and the other three had been raised in his recent levies and made up to strength on the march*. He found that the consuls had left for Dyrrachium with a large part of the army, while Pompey had remained in Brundisium with twenty cohorts; although he could not find out for certain whether he had stayed there in order to hold on to Brundisium and so control more easily the whole Adriatic from the end of Italy as well as from the Greek side, and carry on operations on both sides of the sea, or whether he had been held up by lack of shipping. However, since he feared that Pompey might be determined not to leave Italy, he decided to blockade the harbour of Brundisium and stop its operation as a port. He set about this as follows: at the narrowest part of the entrance to the harbour, he built out a great earth breakwater on either side, where the sea was shallow, but as the work advanced and it proved impossible to keep the earth-works together in the deeper water, he placed two rafts, thirty feet square, at the ends of the breakwater and moored these with an anchor at all four corners to keep them still in the waves. Once these were in position, he joined on other rafts of similar size and built a causeway of earth out over them, to remove any hindrance to approach-

* He had sent Domitius's cohorts straight from Corfinium to Sicily.

ing and boarding them for defence. In front and on either side he
put up screens and mantlets for protection and on every fourth
raft he built a tower two storeys high, to help in defence against
attacks by sea and against firebrands. 26. Against these Pompey
was fitting out large merchant ships which he had commandeered
in the harbour of Brundisium. He was raising towers on them,
three storeys high, and stocking these with ballistic engines and
missiles of all sorts, then bringing the boats up to Caesar's works,
in order to break up the rafts and disrupt the siege-works. They
went on fighting at a distance like this with arrows and missiles
every day.

Caesar, however, was taking care to keep open the possibility
of a peaceful settlement. He was surprised that Magius, whom
he had sent with proposals to Pompey[14], was not yet sent back to
him, and indeed such persistent attempts to negotiate were a check
to the speedy execution of his plans; nevertheless, he felt that he
ought to persevere and try everything he could. Accordingly he
sent his lieutenant Caninius Rebilus, a close friend of Scribonius
Libo, to talk with the latter; his instructions were to urge Libo
to try to effect a peace, and in particular to ask him to speak personally to Pompey. The arguments put before Libo were that
Caesar was certain that if Libo managed to see Pompey then hostilities could be terminated by an equitable peace, and a great
deal of the credit would go to Libo if it was at his instance and
by his efforts that the settlement was reached. Libo, breaking off
his talk with Caninius, went to see Pompey, and presently came
back with the reply that, in the absence of the consuls, no negotiations about a settlement could be conducted. And so Caesar
finally determined to abandon these repeated vain efforts and to
wage war in earnest.

27. He had completed about half of his siege-works, which took
him nine days, when the ships which had been sent back by the
consuls after transporting the first part of the army over to Dyrrachium arrived back at Brundisium. Pompey at once prepared to
leave Italy, either because he was alarmed by Caesar's preparations
or because he had intended to do so all along. In order to check
an assault by Caesar and prevent his troops from breaking into
the town while the withdrawal was in progress, he blocked up the

gates, built barricades in all the streets, and dug trenches across the roads, in which sharpened stakes were fixed and wicker and earth laid on top to make a flat surface. He put fences of large pointed beams round the two roads outside the city walls which gave access to the harbour. After all these preparations, he picked a small force of archers and slingers from his veterans and stationed these, in light marching order, at intervals along the walls and on the towers, while the rest of the army, under orders, embarked in silence. He arranged to recall this covering guard at a fixed signal once all the rest had embarked, and left some swift vessels in an accessible spot to pick them up.

28. The people of Brundisium resented their ill-treatment by Pompey's troops and the insulting behaviour of Pompey himself, and favoured Caesar's cause. When, therefore, they learned of Pompey's intended departure, while his men were still milling about, preoccupied with preparations for embarking, they signalled the news from the roof-tops. Caesar ordered the scaling-ladders to be got ready and the troops to arm, so as not to lose the opportunity for action. Pompey cast off towards nightfall. The guards on the wall were recalled by the agreed signal and hurried down to the ships by marked paths. Caesar's men got their scaling-ladders up and climbed the walls, but were warned by the citizens to beware of the trenches and the concealed stakes. They therefore halted, and under the guidance of the townsfolk were conducted round by a long detour to the harbour. They put out in skiffs and dinghies and managed to catch and take possession of two of Pompey's ships, with their passengers, which had run foul of Caesar's breakwater.

29. Caesar felt that the best course, to settle the issue, would be to gather a fleet and cross in pursuit of Pompey before the latter could strengthen his forces with overseas contingents. However, he was afraid of the long delay that this would involve, since Pompey by collecting all the available ships had robbed him of the means of pursuit for the time being. The remaining alternative was to wait for ships to come from remoter places, i.e. Gaul and Picenum, and from the Sicilian strait, but this, owing to the time of year, was likely to be a protracted and hazardous operation. Meanwhile, he was unwilling to allow an established army

and the two Spanish provinces, one of them under a heavy debt of
gratitude to Pompey [15], to be confirmed in their allegiance; he did
not want to let auxiliaries and cavalry be raised there and harry
Italy and Gaul in his absence.

5. Caesar's Senate

30. Accordingly, he gave up for the time being his plan of following Pompey and decided to proceed to Spain instead. He ordered
the chief magistrates of all the Italian townships to collect ships
and have them conveyed to Brundisium. He sent his lieutenant
Valerius to Sardinia with one legion and sent Curio to govern
Sicily with two, with further orders to take his forces to Africa
once he had secured Sicily. Sardinia was in fact the province of
Marcus Cotta, and Sicily of Marcus Cato, while Tubero was due
to take over Africa as his allotted province. As soon as the people
of Caralis in Sardinia heard that Valerius was being sent to them,
even though he had not left Italy yet, they spontaneously expelled Cotta from their town. Cotta panicked, realizing that the
whole province shared their feelings, and fled from Sardinia to
Africa. In Sicily, Cato was displaying great energy in getting old
ships repaired and ordering the towns to supply new ones. He had
his lieutenants out in Lucania and Bruttium, enlisting Roman
citizens, and was trying to raise a certain number of cavalry and
infantry from the Sicilian towns. When these preparations were
nearly complete he heard of the approach of Curio and complained
in a public speech that he had been abandoned and betrayed by
Pompey. Pompey had undertaken an unnecessary war when everything was in a state of total unreadiness and, when questioned by
himself and others in the Senate, he had declared that he was
fully prepared and ready for war. Having made his protest, Cato
fled from the province.

31. Valerius and Curio thus obtained provinces without
governors and made their way to them with their armies. When
Tubero arrived in Africa, he found Attius Varus in command
there. Attius, as we related above, on losing his cohorts at
Auximum, continued his flight and went straight to Africa.

Finding the province without a governor, he had of his own initiative taken command, and had made up two legions by holding a levy, an undertaking on which he was able to embark thanks to his familiarity with the people and the locality, and the experience of the province which he had gained a few years previously, when he had been governor there after his praetorship. As Tubero approached Utica with his ships, Attius denied him access to the town and its harbour, refusing even to allow him to land his son, who was ill, but forced him to lift anchor and depart.

32. After making these dispositions, Caesar distributed his troops among the neighbouring towns to spend the remaining time resting while he himself went to Rome. He summoned the Senate and detailed the wrongs done him by his enemies. He declared that he had sought no exceptional privilege; he had been content to wait for the statutory interval[16] between consulships, and to have the rights accorded to all citizens. A proposal had been put forward by the ten tribunes that he should be allowed to be a candidate in absence, and this had been carried, even though his enemies spoke against it, and Cato in particular opposed it bitterly, following his old tactics and dragging the dispute out for days. 'Pompey,' he said, 'was consul then[17]; if he disapproved, why did he let the bill go through? If he approved, why has he prevented me from availing myself of the people's generosity? I think I showed extreme forbearance, in actually suggesting myself that the armies be disbanded, although this would have meant a loss of position and power for me. The vindictiveness of my enemies can be seen in their refusal to submit themselves to the demands they made of someone else, and in their readiness to cause a universal upheaval rather than give up control of their armies. I was wronged, by the confiscation of two of my legions; I was insulted and outraged by the interference with the rights of the tribunes; yet I offered terms, I asked for a meeting – and I was refused. Therefore I earnestly ask you to join with me now in taking over the government of Rome; if timidity makes you shrink from the task, I shall not trouble you – I shall govern by myself. Envoys must be sent to Pompey to discuss terms. I am not frightened by his recent statement in this assembly, that the sending of deputations merely enhances the prestige of those to

whom they are sent and reveals the fears of the senders. These are the reflections of a weak and petty spirit. My aim is to outdo others in justice and equity, as I have previously striven to outdo them in achievement.'

33. The Senate agreed to the sending of a deputation, but they could find no one to send. Everyone was afraid for himself and shirked the task; for they all remembered how, when Pompey was leaving Rome, he had said in the Senate that he would draw no distinction between those who remained in Rome and those in Caesar's camp. Three days were spent in discussion and excuses. What was more, Lucius Metellus, a tribune of the people, had been suborned by enemies of Caesar to postpone a decision on this matter and to hold up any other business that he might try to transact. Caesar found out this plot, after several days had been wasted, and to save spending any more time he gave up the rest of his projected business and left Rome for Further Gaul.

6. Resistance at Massilia

34. On arrival, he learned that Vibullius Rufus, whom he himself had captured and released again at Corfinium a few days before, had been sent by Pompey to Spain. He learned also that Domitius had gone to take over Massilia, with seven fast ships which he had requisitioned from private persons in Igilium and around Cosa, and had manned with his own slaves, freedmen and tenants. Moreover, some young Massiliote noblemen had been sent ahead to their homeland as messengers, and as they were leaving Rome Pompey had exhorted them not to let Caesar's recent generosity blot out the memory of his own past kindness to them. The Massiliotes had obeyed this injunction and had closed their gates against Caesar; they had sent for the Albici, a barbarian tribe, who lived in the mountains above Massilia and had rendered allegiance to them ever since the remote past; they had gathered corn from the neighbouring districts and from all the forts into the city, set up forges for making weapons, and begun repairing the walls, the gates and the fleet.

35. Caesar sent for the Massiliote Grand Committee of Fifteen

and urged them not to let the Massiliotes be guilty of starting hostilities; they ought rather to follow the lead of the whole of Italy than to bow to the will of one man. He added such further considerations as he thought might serve to bring them to their senses. The deputation reported what he said to their senate, and on its instructions came back with the following message. 'We understand that the Roman people is split in two. It is not within our powers of judgement to determine which side has the juster cause; however, the protagonists on either side, Gnaeus Pompeius and Gaius Caesar, are both benefactors of our state; the one offici-ally granted to us the territories of the Volcae Arecomici and the Helvii, and the other, after defeating the Sallyes, made them tributary[18] to us and increased our revenues. Since, therefore, we are equally indebted to both, we think that we ought to show equal good-will to both, and ought not to help one against the other, nor admit either to our city and harbours.'

36. While these negotiations were going on, Domitius arrived with his ships at Massilia, where he was admitted and put in charge of the city, and entrusted with the entire conduct of mili-tary operations. On his instructions they sent ships out in all directions; wherever they found transport vessels they seized them and brought them back to harbour. They used the nails, timber and tackle from those that were inadequately fitted out for equip-ping and repairing the rest. Any corn that they found in them they distributed publicly and other goods and foodstuffs were stored up, in case the city should be laid under siege. Caesar was stung by these misdemeanours and brought three legions up to Massilia; he also began to bring up siege-towers and screens, in preparation for a siege. He ordered twelve ships to be built at Arelate; these were finished and fitted out within thirty days from the cutting of the timber and were brought to Massilia. He put Decimus Brutus in charge of them, and left Gaius Trebonius as the officer in charge of the siege of Massilia.

7. The first Spanish campaign – Ilerda

37. While he was occupied with these preparations, he sent his lieutenant, Gaius Fabius, ahead to Spain with three legions which he had stationed in and around Narbo for the winter. Fabius's orders were to make haste to seize the passes over the Pyrenees, which at that time were being held by the troops of Pompey's lieutenant, Lucius Afranius. He ordered the remaining legions, which were wintering farther away, to follow on. Fabius, obeying orders, lost no time in dislodging the guards from the pass and proceeded by forced marches to encounter Afranius's army.

38. Afranius held Hither Spain with three legions; of Pompey's other lieutenants, Petreius and Varro, the latter held Further Spain from the pass of Castulo to the river Anas with two legions, and Petreius held the territory of the Vettones, from the river Anas, and Lusitania, also with two legions. On the arrival of Lucius Vibullius Rufus* they re-allocated their spheres of duty. Petreius was to proceed from Lusitania through the territory of the Vettones, with all his forces, to join Afranius, while Varro was to hold the whole of Further Spain with those legions which he commanded. These arrangements were duly made, and Petreius summoned cavalry and auxiliary troops from all over Lusitania, while Afranius summoned soldiers from Celtiberia, from the Cantabrians and from all the barbarian tribes on the western seaboard. Petreius mustered his forces and passed quickly through the Vettones to join Afranius. The two of them then conferred together and decided to conduct their campaign in the region of Ilerda, because of the favourable opportunities offered by the terrain there.

39. Afranius, as shown above, had three legions, and Petreius two, and there were also about eighty cohorts of auxiliaries – those from Hither Spain armed with long shields, and those from Further Spain with targets – as well as about five thousand cavalry drawn from both provinces. Caesar had sent six legions ahead to Spain; he had no auxiliary infantry; he had about three thousand

[* Sent by Pompey; see Ch. 34.]

cavalry, whom he had had with him in all his previous campaigns, and a similar number from Gaul, whom he himself had collected by summoning individually all the noblest and bravest members of the Gallic tribes. To these he had added some first-class men from the Aquitani and the mountain tribes bordering on the province of Gaul. He had heard that Pompey was on his way through Mauretania with his legions, making for Spain, and would shortly arrive. At once, he borrowed money from the tribunes and centurions and distributed it among his troops, thus killing two birds with one stone – he took a security for the loyalty of the centurions, and won the good-will of the troops by his bounty.

40. Fabius was attempting, by letters and emissaries, to suborn the neighbouring tribes. He had built two bridges over the river Sicoris, four miles apart, and sent men across them to forage, since he had used up all the supplies of fodder on the near side of the river during the preceding days. The commanders of the Pompeian army were doing much the same thing and for the same reason, and there were frequent skirmishes between their cavalry forces. On one occasion, two of Fabius's legions had gone out, as was the daily custom, to guard the foragers. They had crossed the river by the nearer bridge and the wagons and all the cavalry were following, when there was a sudden squall of wind and a rush of water that broke down the bridge and cut off a good part of the cavalry. Petreius and Afranius realized what had happened when they saw earth and wood-work being carried down the river, and Afranius quickly led four legions and all the cavalry across the bridge connecting the town with his camp, and went to encounter Fabius's two legions. On word of his approach, Lucius Plancus, who was in command of the legions, bowed to necessity and took up his position on high ground, with his two legions facing in opposite directions to avoid being surrounded by the cavalry. In this way, although fighting against superior numbers, he held out against strong attacks by the legions and the cavalry. When the cavalry had engaged, both sides saw some distance away the standards of two legions, which Fabius had sent across by the farther bridge, suspecting that just this would happen, i.e. that the enemy commanders would take advantage of their good luck

to try to overpower our men. The arrival of these legions put an end to the fighting, and both sides led their forces back to camp.

41. Two days later Caesar arrived with nine hundred cavalry, whom he had kept as a personal bodyguard. The bridge which had been broken down by the storm was almost rebuilt; he ordered it to be completed that night. He himself ascertained the nature of the surrounding country and leaving behind all the baggage train, together with six cohorts to protect the bridge and the camp, he set off on the following day towards Ilerda, advancing with his forces in a triple column. He halted close to Afranius's camp and kept his men there under arms for a short time, offering battle in the plain. Afranius thereupon led out his forces and halted them half-way down the hill below the camp. Caesar, realizing that Afranius did not intend to have a battle, decided to make camp, rather less than half a mile from the base of the hill. He ordered his men not to build a rampart, which could not fail to be prominent and visible at a distance, in case while they were engaged on this the enemy should make a sudden attack, terrorize them and force them to give up the work. Instead, they were to dig a trench fifteen feet wide on the side facing the enemy; the actual digging was carried on secretly by the men of the third line, while the first and second lines were drawn up in front of them still under arms. As a result, the work was finished before Afranius realized that defences for a camp were being constructed. Towards evening, Caesar led his legions behind the trench and they waited there under arms during the following night.

42. The next day, he kept the whole army behind the trench, and since materials for a stockade would have to be fetched from a considerable distance, he kept the men for the time being on the same kind of work, setting one legion to fortify each side of the camp, with instructions to dig trenches of the same dimensions as the first; the remaining legions he stationed under arms, but without their marching kit, to ward off the enemy. Afranius and Petreius, hoping to frighten our men and make them break off their work, brought their forces right down to the foot of the hill and tried to provoke a battle; but in spite of this Caesar carried

on with the defence-works, relying on the protection afforded by
the trench at the front and the three legions. The enemy did not
linger long; without advancing farther from the foot of the hill,
they withdrew into their camp again. On the third day, Caesar
had a rampart built round the camp and ordered the cohorts and
baggage which had been left in the previous camp to be brought
up.

43. Between the town of Ilerda and the neighbouring hill where
Petreius and Afranius had their camp there was a level space
about five hundred yards wide and almost in the middle of this
there was a small hillock. Caesar was certain that if he seized and
fortified this eminence he would cut off the enemy from the town
and the bridge and all the supplies which they had collected together in the town. With this intention, he led three legions out
of camp and drew them up for battle in a suitable position; then
he ordered the front line of one of the legions to advance at the
double and seize the hillock. Observing this, Afranius hastily
sent the cohorts guarding the front of his camp round by a shorter
route to capture the position. There was fighting, but since
Afranius's men had reached the hillock first our men were beaten
off and, as enemy reinforcements came up, they were forced to
turn and go back to the legionary standards.

44. The method of fighting employed by the Pompeian troops
was simply to charge violently at the outset and seize a position;
they had no particular concern about keeping their ranks but
fought dispersedly; if they were being worsted, they did not think
shame to retreat and give ground. They had grown accustomed
to this sort of fighting with the Lusitanians and other barbarian
tribes – naturally, since it usually happens that troops are influenced by the habits of the natives of any region in which they
have spent a long period of service. This upset our troops, who
were not at all accustomed to this sort of fighting; when they saw
individuals running forward, they thought that they were going
to be surrounded on the flanks, where they were exposed; and
they believed that they ought to keep in their lines and should
never leave the standards nor allow themselves to be dislodged
from a position they had taken up, except for some very serious
reason. The result was that the advance-guard were thrown into

confusion and the legion posted on that wing did not stand its
ground but retreated to higher ground near-by.

45. Panic spread through almost the whole force. Seeing this
unexpected and unusual occurrence, Caesar began urging his men
on, and led up the Ninth legion to support the others; he beat
back the enemy, who were boldly rushing in hot pursuit of our
men, and forced them in their turn to retreat and withdraw to
Ilerda, under whose walls they halted. However, the men of the
Ninth were carried away by their eagerness to repair the setback
and, rashly pursuing the enemy's flight too far, they found themselves in a dangerous position at the foot of the hill on which
Ilerda stands. When they tried to withdraw from this position,
the enemy once again began pressing on them from above. They
were on a slope, falling away steeply on both sides; the ground
was just broad enough to admit three cohorts drawn up abreast;
and no reinforcements could be sent up on the flanks, nor could
the cavalry bring any help if they got into difficulties. Towards
the town, the ground descended in a slight slope for about seven
hundred yards. In this place our men attempted to rally since,
carried on by their zeal, they had thoughtlessly advanced thus
far; they had to fight in a position that was disadvantageous both
because of its narrow confines and because it was right up against
the base of the hill, so that no missile could fail to find a mark.
None the less, they fought with courage and endurance, sustaining innumerable wounds. The enemy's numbers were increasing,
and fresh cohorts were constantly being sent up from the camp
through the town, so that their men could be replaced as they
grew tired. Caesar was forced to do the same and send up fresh
cohorts so that he could draw the weary men out.

46. After five hours of continuous fighting, our men had used
up all their missiles, and their inferiority in numbers was beginning to tell on them. They drew their swords and, charging up-
hill against the enemy cohorts, they cut down a few and forced
the rest to give ground. The enemy retreated right up to the walls,
and some in their panic were driven right into the town, so that
the way was left open for our men to withdraw. In addition, our
cavalry, although they had been posted low down on the slopes,
struggled up valiantly at either side to the top, and rode up and

down between the two armies giving cover for our men to retire. And so the day's fighting was a blend of successes and reverses. About seventy of our men fell in the first encounter, and among them was Quintus Fulginius, leading centurion[19] of the Fourteenth legion, who had risen to this position from the ranks because of his outstanding valour; more than six hundred were wounded. Among Afranius's troops, over two hundred ordinary soldiers were killed and five centurions, including Titus Caecilius, a senior centurion.

47. However, each side was of the general opinion that it had come off better in that day's fighting. Afranius's men claimed the victory because, although they were generally acknowledged to be inferior, they had none the less kept fighting at close quarters for so long and withstood the onslaught of our men, and they had initially captured the hillock which had been the object of contention and had forced our men to give way at the first encounter. Our men thought they themselves had won because, although they were on unfavourable ground and at a disadvantage in numbers, they had sustained the battle for five hours; because they had charged up-hill with drawn swords; and because they had forced their adversaries, who were actually on higher ground, to withdraw and had compelled them to take refuge in the town. Afranius's men built substantial defence-works on the hill which had been the object of the fighting and put a guard on it.

48. Two days later, moreover, we suffered an unexpected misfortune. A great storm arose, with what was agreed to be the heaviest rainfall the district had ever had, and this washed down the snow from the mountains and made the river flood over its banks, bursting in one day both the bridges built by Fabius. This put Caesar's army in great difficulties; since their camp, as shown above [20], was between two rivers, the Sicoris and the Cinga, about thirty miles apart, and neither of these rivers could be crossed, the soldiers were imprisoned in this confined space. The tribes which had established friendly relations with Caesar could not reach them with supplies of corn, while foraging parties which had gone too far afield were cut off by the rivers and unable to return, and the large stocks of provisions which were on their way from Italy and Gaul could not get through to the camp. Besides, it was

the most awkward time of the year, when there was none of last
year's grain in the winter stores and this year's was not quite
ripe; the tribes had no supplies of their own, as Afranius had
carried off practically all the grain to Ilerda before Caesar had
arrived; and Caesar himself had used up in the previous days what
little there was left. The local cattle might have served as an
alternative source of food in need; but they had been taken to a
distance by the neighbouring tribes because of the fighting. The
parties which had gone out to gather food and fodder for the
beasts were being harried by Lusitanian light-armed infantry and
targeteers from Hither Spain, who knew the district and who
found no difficulty in swimming across a river, since it is their
universal custom to take bladders with them when they go campaigning. 49. Afranius's army, on the other hand, had ample
supplies of everything. There was a large stock of corn that had
been gathered earlier and a lot more was being brought in from
all over the province. There was plenty of fodder as well. The
bridge at Ilerda gave them access to all these, and the countryside
across the river, from which Caesar was completely cut off, offered
untouched resources.

50. The floods lasted for several days. Caesar attempted to repair
the bridge, but the height of the river and the presence of enemy
cohorts stationed on the river bank prevented the work from
proceeding. The nature of the river itself and the force of the flood-
water were effective deterrents; and besides, our men were working in a confined space, into which, from all along the bank, the
enemy could pour showers of missiles; and the soldiers found it
difficult to finish their work while simultaneously struggling
against the strong current and dodging the missiles. 51. Word was
brought to Afranius that large convoys of supplies on their way
to Caesar had halted at the river. Archers from the Ruteni had
arrived as well, and cavalry from Gaul, with large trains of
wagons and baggage, as is the Gallic custom. There were besides
about six thousand men of various sorts, as well as domestics and
children; but there was no organization, no defined authority, as
everyone followed his own judgement and they all travelled on
confidently, in the same informal way as they had always done.
There were also several young men of good family, sons of

senators or of equestrian rank; there were official deputations from tribes; there were some of Caesar's lieutenants. All these were held back by the rivers. Hoping to overpower them, Afranius made a sortie at night with all his cavalry and three legions. He sent the cavalry ahead and took them by surprise; however, the Gallic horsemen lost no time in forming up and engaging battle, and although they were greatly outnumbered, held their own as long as it was possible to fight on equal terms. When, however, the standards of the legions began to approach, the Gauls withdrew to the near-by hills with the loss of a few men. The period of this battle was decisive for the safety of the rest of our people; for it gave them time to withdraw to higher ground. On that day about two hundred archers were lost, as well as a few cavalry and some – not many – camp followers and pack animals.

52. All these circumstances, however, had sent up the price of corn[21], as tends to happen not merely because of present shortage but also because of fears for the future. The price had already risen to fifty denarii a peck, and shortage of corn was sapping the soldiers' strength, while their difficulties grew from day to day. In a mere handful of days, circumstances had totally changed and there had been a reversal of fortunes; our men were now labouring under shortages of all the necessities of life, while their opponents had plenty of everything and were considered the stronger force. As the supply of corn dwindled, Caesar asked the tribes that had come out on his side to supply cattle, and sent the camp followers off to the more distant tribes, while for his own part he tried to remedy the present want with such aids as he could.

53. Afranius and Petreius and their friends wrote to their adherents in Rome about this, with plenty of exaggerations and amplified detail. Rumours added further embroideries and it was thought that the war was almost over. When the messengers with the dispatches reached Rome, great crowds gathered at Afranius's house and congratulations were lavished on him; many people left Italy to join Pompey, some in order to have the credit of being the first to bring such news, others to avoid turning up last of all and appearing to have waited for the outcome of the wars.

54. In these straits, with all the routes blocked by Afranius and his men and no possibility of repairing the bridges, Caesar ordered

his men to build boats of the type that his experience in Britain a few years before had taught him to make. The keels and ribs were made of light wood; the rest of the hulk was made of woven withies and covered with hides. When the boats were finished, he had them conveyed by night, on wagons joined together, some twenty-two miles from the camp. He conveyed his men across the river in these boats, and so captured unexpectedly a hill adjoining the bank and fortified it before his opponents realized what he was doing. He then transferred a legion here, and started the building of a bridge from both sides, finishing the work in two days. He was thus enabled to recover safely the supply convoys and the foraging parties, and ease the difficulties of the corn supply.

55. On the same day he sent across the river a large part of his cavalry and these, falling unexpectedly upon a foraging party who were scattered about with no fear of attack, captured a large number of beasts and of men. When cohorts of targeteers were sent to the rescue, the cavalry cunningly divided themselves into two groups, one to guard the spoils, the other to meet and repel the oncoming forces, and they succeeded in isolating and annihilating one cohort, which had incautiously come on ahead of the main body. Then they themselves returned unharmed to camp, by the same bridge, with a large quantity of booty.

8. A naval fight at Massilia

56. Meanwhile, the people of Massilia, following Lucius Domitius's instructions, prepared seventeen warships, eleven of them decked over, and added to these many smaller boats, hoping to intimidate our fleet by their sheer numbers. On board the ships they put large numbers of archers, and also of the Albici whom we mentioned previously, bribing them with promises of rewards. Domitius asked for a special detachment of ships for himself, and manned them with farmers and herdsmen whom he had brought with him. When the fleet was thus fully prepared, they proceeded confidently against our ships, which were stationed under the command of Decimus Brutus by an island off Massilia.

57. Brutus's fleet was greatly inferior in numbers, but Caesar had manned it with a special corps of men selected from all the legions for their courage, as well as front-line men and centurions who had demanded the privilege. These troops had prepared hooks and grappling-irons and had supplied themselves with large quantities of javelins, throwing-darts and other missiles. So, learning of the enemy's approach, they sailed from their moorings and engaged the Massiliotes. Both sides fought with courage and spirit; and indeed the Albici almost matched the valour of our own men. They are a mountain people, used to warfare; and besides, on this occasion, the promises of the Massiliotes, from whom they had just come, were fresh in their minds. Domitius's herdsmen, too, were spurred on by the promise of freedom and were anxious to demonstrate their keenness before their master's eyes.

58. The Massiliotes themselves, relying on the speed of their ships and the skill of their steersmen, repeatedly evaded our men and baffled their onslaughts while they themselves stretched out their line as far as space permitted and kept attempting to surround our fleet, or pick off single ships with groups of several of their own, or sail close alongside our ships and snap off the oars. If any ships were forced into combat at close quarters, the practical skill of the steersmen would give way to reliance on the courage of the mountain people. We had less practised rowers and less experienced steersmen, who had been recruited hastily from transport ships and did not yet know even the names of the gear. The weight and slowness of the ships were also serious handicaps; they had been made in a hurry out of unseasoned timber and were less capable of quick manoeuvre. Therefore, when an opportunity offered of combat at close quarters, our men willingly set one ship against two of the enemy; they used grappling-irons to catch both and then fought on both sides, boarding the enemy vessels and killing many Albici and herdsmen. Some of the ships they sank, a considerable number they captured along with their crews, and the rest they drove back to harbour. On that day the Massiliotes lost nine ships including the captured vessels.

9. Spain – a war of attrition

59. The result of this battle was reported to Caesar at Ilerda; at the same time, the completion of the bridge brought a swift change of fortune. The enemy had been shaken by the bravery of our cavalry, and now made their forays with less freedom and confidence. Sometimes they would venture only a short distance from camp, in order to be able to retreat to safety quickly, and would forage over a small area; sometimes they would make a long detour and try to avoid our guardposts and cavalry squadrons, and if they had the least setback or saw our cavalry in the distance they would drop their loads in their tracks and flee. Finally, contrary to all usual practice, they began to go out foraging only at night and at intervals of several days.

60. Meanwhile, the people of Osca and of Calagurris, a tributary of Osca, sent envoys to Caesar, undertaking to obey his commands, and their example was followed by the people of Tarraco and the tribes of the Iacetani and Ausetani and, a few days later, the Illurgavonenses, who live by the Ebro. He asked them all to help by supplying corn. This they promised to do, and collecting pack animals from all parts of their territory they conveyed the corn to his camp. A cohort of Illurgavonenses also went over to him, on learning the policy of their tribe, and transferred their standard from their former post. The whole situation had changed rapidly; the bridge was complete, five important peoples had opened friendly relations, the problem of the corn supply had been settled and, further, as the rumours about the auxiliaries of the legions said to be coming with Pompey through Mauretania were exploded, many of the more distant tribes defected from Afranius and made friendly overtures to Caesar. All of this thoroughly frightened Caesar's opponents.

61. Now, in order to avoid always sending the cavalry a long way round by the bridge, he found a suitable spot and gave orders for the digging of several trenches thirty feet wide, with which to divert part of the flow of the Sicoris and make a ford over the river. When the work was almost completed, Afranius and

Petreius became afraid that they might be cut off from their source of corn and fodder, because of Caesar's great cavalry strength. They decided accordingly to leave the district and transfer the war to Celtiberia. Their decision was also influenced by the fact that Caesar's name was less well known among the barbarians there, while, of the two different classes of tribes, i.e. those who had supported Sertorius in the earlier uprising and those who had remained loyal, the former, once conquered, had remained in awe of the name and authority of Pompey, even in his absence, while the latter, on whom great rewards had been bestowed, were devoted to him. In this district, they were expecting to obtain large numbers of cavalry and of auxiliary troops, and they were hoping, since the locale would be of their own choosing, to be able to prolong the war right into the winter. Once they had decided on this course, they began requisitioning boats all along the course of the Ebro, and ordered them to be mustered at Octogesa, a town on the Ebro about twenty miles from their camp. They ordered a bridge to be built there by joining these boats together, and taking two legions across the Sicoris they built a camp, fortifying it with a twelve-foot rampart.

62. Scouts brought word of these operations to Caesar. By setting his troops working night and day at the diversion of the river, he had by now reached the stage at which the cavalry, albeit with some difficulty, found it practicable to cross the river, and did in fact venture to do so, although the infantry found the water was still breast-high, and were prevented from crossing by the depth and also by the force of the current. However, the Sicoris was becoming fordable about the same time as the reports were coming in that the bridge over the Ebro was nearing completion.

63. Afranius and Petreius now thought it all the more urgent that they should hasten their departure; and so they left two cohorts of auxiliaries to guard Ilerda and, crossing the Sicoris with the rest of their troops, they set up camp with the two legions that they had sent across a few days before. The only course left to Caesar was to use his cavalry to harass and impede the enemy's column on the march, for his own bridge required a long detour, and so the enemy could reach the Ebro by a much shorter route. Accordingly, he sent cavalry across the river, and when the Pom-

peian commanders broke up camp in the small hours of the morning, these cavalry suddenly showed themselves at the rear of the column and, milling around in great numbers, began to hinder and obstruct the march. 64. When dawn came, it was observed from the high ground adjoining Caesar's camp that our cavalry were pressing hard on the rear of the enemy column, which was sometimes being held up and even cut off from the rest; at other times, the rear cohorts would form up behind their standards and charge, and our men would be driven back, but would then rally and go after them again.

All over the camp, our troops began getting into little groups and lamenting that the enemy were being allowed to slip through our fingers, and that the war was being protracted unnecessarily; they approached the centurions and military tribunes and begged them to be their spokesmen and tell Caesar not to hesitate to expose them to toil or danger; they said they were ready, able and bold enough to cross the river in the same place as the cavalry had crossed. Caesar yielded to this clamorous display of their zeal; and, although he was anxious about exposing the army to so powerful a river, he felt that he must make the experiment and attempt a crossing. Accordingly, he ordered the weaker soldiers, those whose courage or whose physique did not seem adequate to the enterprise, to be picked out from all the centuries. These he left with one legion to guard the camp; he stationed large numbers of pack animals in the water above and below the crossing-place, then led out the rest of the legions in light marching order and took them across. A few of these men were swept away by the river, but were caught and rescued by the cavalry, so that no one was killed. Once the army was safely over he formed them up and began to lead them on in a triple line. Such was the eagerness of the troops that, although the detour to the ford had added six miles to their journey, and although the crossing of the river had caused considerable delay, nevertheless before three in the afternoon they caught up with those who had left in the small hours of the morning.

65. When Afranius, with Petreius, saw them some distance away, he was appalled at this unexpected development and, halting his men on high ground, he drew them up ready for battle.

Caesar allowed his men to rest on the plain so as not to make them fight when they were tired, and when they attempted to move on again he went after them and stopped them. The enemy were forced to make camp sooner than they had intended, for they were close up to the mountains and only five miles farther on they would find themselves in country where the tracks were narrow and difficult. They were anxious to get in among these mountains, in order to shake off Caesar's cavalry, and to block the army's route by placing guards on the passes while they themselves, without danger or alarm, led their forces across the Ebro. This they must attempt to do, and must at all costs accomplish; but they were worn out by a whole day's fighting and a toilsome journey, and put off the attempt until the following day. Caesar, likewise, set up camp on a neighbouring hill.

66. About the middle of the night, a party that had ventured too far from the Pompeian camp to fetch water were captured by the cavalry, and they informed Caesar that their commanders were leading their forces out of the camp in silence. At once Caesar ordered the signal to be sounded and the usual command for striking camp to be called. Hearing the noise, Afranius and Petreius were afraid that their army might be forced to engage by night while encumbered with their packs or that they might be penned up in a narrow pass by Caesar's cavalry; they therefore checked their departure and kept the troops in camp. On the following day, Petreius went out secretly with a small force of cavalry to explore the region, and a similar expedition went out from Caesar's camp, consisting of a few horsemen under the command of Lucius Decidius Saxa. Both parties made the same report back to their respective armies, that for the next five miles the route was over level ground but after that there was rocky, mountainous country, and that the first to seize the narrow passes there could hold an enemy off with no trouble.

67. Petreius and Afranius held a council of war. They discussed the report and sought a decision about the time to start off. The majority favoured a journey by night, since they could then reach the passes before they were observed. Others took the fact that the order to strike camp had been given by Caesar the previous night as a proof that it was impossible to get away

secretly. They said that Caesar's cavalry spread all around at night
and beset every position and every route. Besides, a night battle
was to be avoided, since the soldiers in the panicky atmosphere
of a civil war were more likely to be swayed by their fears than
by their sense of duty; daylight, on the other hand, was apt of
itself to impose a sense of shame, under the gaze of everyone,
while the presence of the military tribunes and centurions was
also a restraining influence. It was by such circumstances that
soldiers were usually kept in hand and maintained in their loyalty.
Therefore, at all costs, they should make their break by day; and
even if they should suffer some losses, nevertheless the bulk of
the army would be safe, and they would be able to take the place
they were making for. This view prevailed in the council, and
they decided to set off at dawn the following day.

68. Caesar had reconnoitred the district, and as soon as the sky
grew light he led the whole army out of the camp and round by a
detour, not following any marked track; this he did because the
direct routes to Octogesa and the Ebro were commanded by the
enemy camp. His men had to cross deep and difficult gullies and
in many places the way was blocked by precipitous rocks, so that
they had to pass their weapons along from hand to hand; they
covered a good part of the way without their weapons, helping
one another over. However, no one jibbed at this exertion, since
they thought that they would have an end to all their toils, if they
could bar the enemy's way to the Ebro and cut him off from corn
supplies.

69. At first, Afranius's men joyfully ran out of camp to watch,
and pursued our men with taunts, saying that they had been
forced to leave from lack of necessary provisions and were going
back to Ilerda – for our movement was in a direction away from
our destination, and it looked as if we were going off in the
opposite direction. Meanwhile, their generals were congratulating
themselves on having decided to stay in camp; and their opinion
was strongly backed by the fact that they saw our men going off
without packs or pack animals, so that they believed that we were
unable to endure the lack of supplies any longer. When, however,
they saw the column gradually turning round to the right and
observed the head of the column working round above the camp,

everyone was for leaving the camp at once and intercepting us. There was no hanging back and no shirking; the call to arms was given and, leaving only a few cohorts on guard, the entire army marched out along the direct route to the Ebro.

70. It was a race to reach the mountain passes and everything depended on speed; and while Caesar's army was delayed by the difficulties of its route, his cavalry was following closely behind Afranius's forces and delaying them. However, Afranius's men had brought themselves into a situation in which, if they did manage to reach the mountains for which they were aiming first, they would get themselves out of danger but would be unable to recover the cohorts they had left behind and the baggage of the entire army, since the way to these was barred by Caesar's army and there was no means of conveying help to them. Caesar finished the journey first, and finding some level ground among the crags he drew up there to meet the enemy. Afranius, seeing the enemy ahead of him, and having the rear of his column harassed by cavalry, halted on a hill and from there sent four cohorts of targeteers to the highest mountain in sight, with orders to storm it and take possession of it. His intention was to make for that position with the rest of his forces and then to alter his route and turn off towards Octogesa over the mountain ridges. While the cohorts were on their way to the mountain by a side route, they were seen and attacked by Caesar's cavalry; they held out against them for a considerable length of time, but then they were all surrounded and killed in view of both armies.

71. An opportunity now presented itself for achieving success. Caesar was fully aware that the enemy army, shaken at witnessing so dreadful a loss, would not be able to hold out, especially as the engagement would take place on flat, open ground, which meant that they would be entirely surrounded by cavalry. Indeed, all sections of his own army urgently demanded an engagement; the lieutenants, centurions and military tribunes crowded round him, urging him to engage at once, as the troops were all keyed up in readiness. They pointed out that Afranius's men, on the other hand, had given many indications of fear, in that they had not come to the rescue of their own men, they were not moving down from the hill, they were scarcely holding ground against

the attacks of the cavalry, and they had huddled together with their standards massed in one place, without any attempt to keep their ranks or stay by their own standards. 'Perhaps,' they said, 'you are uneasy because their present position puts you at a disadvantage. But you will have a chance of battle in some place or other. Afranius is bound to come down; he cannot stay up there without water.'

72. Caesar had come to hope that, since he had cut off his opponents' food supply, he might be able to settle the conflict without involving his men in fighting or bloodshed. 'Why,' he wanted to know, 'should I sacrifice some of my men, even for a victory? Why should I allow the troops who have done me such excellent service to be wounded? Why, in fine, should I tempt providence? – especially as I know that a good commander should be able to gain as much by policy as by the sword. Besides, I am stirred by pity for the citizens whom I see must be killed; I would rather gain my ends without any harm befalling them.' This view of Caesar's did not meet with general approbation; indeed, the soldiers openly avowed to each other that, since such a chance of victory was being thrown away, they would not fight even when he wanted them to. Caesar stuck to his decision, and withdrew a little from his position, to lessen the enemy's fears. This gave Petreius and Afranius a chance, which they took, to return to their camp. Caesar set guards on the hills, completely blocking the way to the Ebro, and pitched camp as near as possible to the Pompeian camp.

73. On the following day, the enemy commanders, dismayed at the total loss of their hopes of reaching the Ebro and securing a corn supply, discussed what still lay open to them. There was one route they could take, if they should decide to return to Ilerda, and another, if they made for Tarraco. While they were deliberating, reports came that the men sent out to fetch water were being harried by our cavalry. Thereupon they posted detachments of cavalry and auxiliary cohorts close together on guard, putting legionary cohorts in between, and began to construct a rampart from the camp to the water, to allow their men to fetch water within their own defence-works, without apprehension and without guards. Petreius and Afranius shared this work between their

forces, and themselves went out a considerable distance to see to its completion.

74. Their departure left the soldiers free to fraternize. There was a general exodus from the Pompeian camp; the men began asking after personal friends and fellow-townsmen in Caesar's camp, and called them out. Firstly, they all expressed their thanks to all of our men for having spared them the day before, when they were utterly terror-stricken. 'We owe our lives to you,' they said. They then asked whether Caesar could be trusted, and whether they would be right to put themselves in his hands; they expressed regret for not having done so in the first place and for having joined battle with their own friends and kinsmen. This discussion emboldened them to ask assurances from Caesar that the lives of Petreius and Afranius would be spared, since they did not wish to incur the guilt of a crime and bear the stigma of having betrayed their own people. When assurances were given, they promised to bring their standards over at once, and sent a deputation of leading centurions to discuss a settlement with Caesar. Meanwhile, some took their friends to visit them in their own camp, so that the two camps seemed to have become one; and a number of tribunes and centurions came to Caesar and offered their services. This example was followed by the Spanish chieftains whom they had commandeered and were holding in the camp as hostages. They too sought acquaintances and traditional family friends, through whom they might each have access to Caesar, to demonstrate their good-will. Even Afranius's young son tried to negotiate with Caesar, through the latter's lieutenant Sulpicius, for his father's life and his own. The whole scene was one of joy and self-congratulation, one side thankful at their escape from such great peril, the other rejoicing at having, as it seemed, brought so great a conflict to a conclusion without bloodshed. Everyone recognized that Caesar was reaping the benefits of his original clemency and his decision met with universal approval.

75. When Afranius received word of these events, he left the work in progress and came back to the camp, ready, as it appeared, to accept whatever had happened calmly and without perturbation. Petreius, however, retained his presence of mind. He armed

the slaves of his own personal staff and with these, the cohort of targeteers who formed his bodyguard, and a few barbarian cavalry, he swooped unexpectedly on the camp, interrupting the soldiers' conversations, and drove our men out of the camp, killing those whom he captured. The remainder rallied and, gripping their shields on their left arms and drawing their swords, they defended themselves against the targeteers and cavalry, relying on the nearness of their own camp; then, withdrawing there, they had the protection of the cohorts on guard at the gates. 76. After this, Petreius made a tour of his companies, weeping, and begged them not to betray himself and not to betray Pompey, their commander, in his absence and yield him up to his enemies for punishment. His men flocked to the parade-ground. He exacted an oath from them that they would not desert the army and its leader and that they would not act individually in their own interests, abandoning the others. He himself was the first to take the oath; he compelled Afranius to follow suit; then the tribunes and centurions swore, and the soldiers were brought up by centuries and took the same oath. Everyone who had one of Caesar's men in his quarters was ordered to produce him, and all who were given up were publicly put to death on the parade-ground. However, most of those who had received visitors kept them concealed and got them out over the rampart during the night. In this way, by intimidating their men, by exacting ruthless punishment and by imposing the bond of a fresh oath, Afranius and Petreius quashed hopes of a surrender for the time being; they swayed the feelings of their soldiers and restored the war to its old footing.

77. Caesar ordered that those of the opposing army who had come into his camp during the period of fraternization should be sought out with the utmost care and sent back; however, an appreciable number of the tribunes and centurions stayed behind with him of their own volition. To these he afterwards showed signal honour, restoring the centurions to their former ranks and those of equestrian status to the position of tribunes.

78. Afranius's men were finding it difficult to secure supplies of fodder and water. The legionaries did have some supplies of corn, since they had been ordered to bring twenty-two days' supply from Ilerda; but the auxiliaries and targeteers had none,

and not only had they scant facilities for obtaining any, but they were physically unaccustomed to carrying loads. As a result, large numbers of them were deserting to Caesar every day. The situation, then, was very grave; of the two alternatives proposed by the commanders, the easier seemed to be a return to Ilerda, since they had left a little corn there, and they trusted that once there they could deliberate about further action. Tarraco was farther away, and they realized that the greater the distance, the greater the number of misfortunes that might befall them. They decided, therefore, on the former alternative, and set off. Caesar sent on his cavalry to harry and hinder the rear of their column and himself followed on with the legions. The rearguard were engaged in fighting with the cavalry almost at once.

79. The nature of the fighting was as follows. The rear of the column was covered by cohorts in light marching order, and on level ground several of these would halt and cover the retreat of the others. If they had to go up a slope, the nature of the terrain itself helped to ward off danger, for those who had gone ahead could protect, from their higher position, their companions who were still climbing up; but when they had a valley or a slope down before them, then the situation was very perilous, since those who had gone ahead could not bring help to those falling behind, while the enemy cavalry were able to throw down missiles on their backs from higher ground. The alternative was, when they approached a position of the latter kind, to order the legionary standards to halt and to charge at the enemy and rout them, then all rush at full speed down into the valleys, cross them, and then halt again on higher ground. They did have a large number of cavalry; but so far were these from being any help to them that they actually had to be taken into the middle of the column for protection, since they had completely lost their nerve as a result of the earlier skirmishes; and none of them could leave the line of march without being picked off by Caesar's cavalry. 80. As usually happens with this sort of skirmishing, their advance was slow and gradual, with frequent stops to help their own men.

When they had advanced about four miles, hard-pressed by the cavalry, they took a high hill and camped there, without unload-

ing the baggage animals. When they saw that Caesar's camp was
pitched and his tents up and he had sent his cavalry out to forage,
they suddenly sallied out (this was at about noon on the same day)
and having succeeded, as they hoped, in delaying us because of
the absence of our cavalry, they resumed their journey. Realizing
this, Caesar followed with his legions, now rested, leaving a few
cohorts to guard the baggage. He ordered them to follow at four
o'clock and the cavalry and the foragers to be recalled. The cavalry
soon resumed the daily routine of the march, fighting energetically at the rear of the Pompeian column, so much so that they
almost put them to rout, and a number of troops, including
several centurions, were killed. Caesar's main column was following closely behind and menacing the enemy *en masse*.

10. The Pompeians capitulate

81. Then, since the enemy were given no opportunity either of
going forward or of looking for a place suitable for a camp, they
were obliged to stop and pitch camp far from a water supply and
in an unfavourable position. But for the same reasons as set forth
above, Caesar did not provoke a battle. From that day on, he did
not allow tents to be pitched, so that everyone might be ready
more quickly to go in pursuit, whether the enemy tried to break
away at night or during the day. The Pompeians, realizing the
defects of their camp, spent all night extending their lines of fortification, and exchanged one camp for another. However, the more
they extended the camp and moved it forward, the farther away
they were from water, and they cured their existing troubles only
by creating fresh ones. During the first night, no one left the
camp to fetch water; on the following day, they left a guard in
the camp and led out the entire army to fetch water, but sent no
one out for fodder. Caesar preferred that they should be subjected
to these hardships and forced to surrender, rather than that they
should fight it out; none the less, he tried to hem them in with an
earth-work and ditch, to put as much of an obstacle as possible in
the way of sudden attempts to break out, to which he thought
they would be forced to resort. They, for their part, ordered all the

baggage animals to be killed, both because they had no fodder for them, and also in order to disencumber their progress.

82. Two days were spent in planning and constructing Caesar's earth-works; by the third day, the work was far advanced. The Pompeians, to stop the construction going any further, gave the signal at about three in the afternoon, led out the legions, and formed them up for battle just below the camp. Caesar recalled his legionaries from the earth-works, ordered all the cavalry to muster, and formed up his battle line; for his reputation would suffer a severe setback if he gave the appearance of shunning a battle, contrary to the general feeling among his troops and to his reputation in the world at large. However, he had the same motives as have already been described for not wanting a battle, the more so because the small space available could be of little help in securing a decisive victory, even if the enemy were routed; for the two camps were not more than two miles apart. The two armies occupied two thirds of this space; the remaining third was left for charging and attacking. If they joined battle, the proximity of the camp would allow the beaten side to retreat and find refuge quickly. He determined, therefore, to offer resistance if the enemy came against him, but not to take the initiative in starting a battle.

83. Afranius's first two lines were made up of five legions, while in the third he had auxiliary cohorts as reserves. Caesar had a threefold line; in the first line he had four cohorts from each of his five legions, while the second and third had three cohorts each in reserve from each of the legions. The archers and slingsmen were posted in the centre, and the cavalry covered the flanks. The armies being thus drawn up, each commander seemed to have gained his object – Caesar, not to join battle unless he was forced to, the enemy, to hinder Caesar's constructions. However, the stalemate was prolonged and the battle formations maintained until sunset; then both sides went back to camp. On the following day, Caesar made ready to complete the earth-works; the Pompeians set themselves to try to ford the Sicoris, if it was possible. Observing this, Caesar sent his German light troops and part of the cavalry across and posted a heavy guard on the banks.

84. The Pompeians were now completely cut off. They were on the fourth day without any fodder for the animals they had kept, and they needed water, wood and corn. Afranius and Petreius finally sought a conference, to be held, if possible, in some place away from the troops. Caesar refused the latter request, but agreed to confer with them in public, if they were willing; they then gave him Afranius's son as a hostage, and a meeting took place in a spot chosen by Caesar. Afranius spoke in the hearing of both armies. 'You should bear no ill-will,' he said, 'against Petreius and myself and our armies, for having wanted to keep faith with our own commander, Pompey. However, by this time we have adequately fulfilled our duty, and we have been adequately punished by having to endure privation. We are now penned in like beasts; we cannot reach water, we cannot move on, and we can no longer endure our physical sufferings and our sense of disgrace. We admit we are beaten; we earnestly beg, if there is any room for pity left, that you will not feel obliged to exact the supreme penalty.' Afranius made this plea in the most humble and abject manner possible.

85. Caesar's reply was: 'No one in the whole army has less right to complaints and self-pity than you. All the rest acted as they should; I did, in that I refused to fight, even when conditions, time and place were suitable, in order to avoid, as far as possible, prejudicing the chances of peace. My army did, since, even when they were subjected to outrage and some of their members were killed, they preserved and protected the men they had in their power. Your army did, since of their own initiative they sought a reconciliation, thinking that thereby they ought to have regard for the lives of all their comrades. Thus, the part played by all sections was a compassionate one; you alone shrank from peace. It was you who did not observe the conventions of a truce and a conference; you who brutally put to death guileless men, who had been deceived by the offer of a chance to talk. And so you have suffered the fate that commonly befalls those who are too stubborn and arrogant; you are now forced to have recourse to the very thing you spurned only a little while ago, and indeed to beg for it. I do not now intend to take advantage of your humiliation and of the present circumstances so as to increase my own

resources; I require only the disbanding of those armies which you have maintained against me these many years.

'I say "against me", for it was for no other reason that six legions were sent to Spain and a seventh enrolled here, and so many large fleets [22] prepared and experienced commanders [23] sent in to lead them. None of these preparations was intended for the pacification of Spain or the administration of the province; it has been at peace for a long time, and had no need of them. All these preparations have been going on, for a long time, to attack me. To attack me, a new kind of military command has been created, in which the same person can stay at the gates of Rome and supervise politics in the city, and at the same time hold command for so many years, in absence, of two provinces fully equipped for war. To attack me, the rights of magistrates have been tampered with [24], so that, instead of governors being sent out immediately after being praetors and consuls, as has always happened, they are now approved and elected by a small clique. To attack me, the plea of age has been disregarded, and men who have already done good service in earlier wars have been called out again to command troops. I alone have been denied the right always accorded to all commanders – that is, the right of coming home, after successful campaigns, with some honour, or at least without disgrace, and disbanding one's army. None the less, I have borne all this patiently, and I shall go on doing so; nor do I intend in the present instance to take your army and keep it myself – although I could do that perfectly easily – but merely to see to it that you will not have an army to use against me. This is my one and final condition for peace.'

86. The troops, of course, were delighted that, instead of the punishment they expected and deserved, they should actually be granted, without asking, the reward of a free discharge. They showed their delight quite plainly; for when the time and place of the discharge came under discussion, they began to shout and gesture from the ramparts, where they were standing, to indicate that they wanted immediate demobilization; they did not believe that they could rely on getting it, no matter what pledges might be given in the meantime, if it were postponed to a later date. There was a brief argument, and it was finally settled that those

who had homes and possessions in Spain should receive discharge at once, and the rest when they reached the river Var. Caesar promised that there would be no victimization, and that no one would be compelled to take the military oath against his will.

87. He further promised to provide them with corn from then on until they reached the Var, and added that any property lost by any of them in the course of the war and now in the hands of his own men should be restored. He had the soldiers make a fair evaluation of this property and paid them cash in lieu. Afterwards, whatever disputes arose among the soldiers were spontaneously referred to Caesar for judgement. When the Pompeian legions began clamouring for their pay and almost mutinied, and Afranius and Petreius made the excuse that it was not yet payday, the men demanded that Caesar should investigate the dispute, and both sides accepted his decision.

He disbanded about a third of the army within the next two days, then sent two of his own legions on ahead, ordering the Pompeians to follow close behind, so that they should camp close together. He put Quintus Fufius Calenus in charge of the escort. Obeying instructions, they marched out of Spain to the river Var, and there the rest of the army received discharge.

PART II: SECURING THE WEST

1. The siege of Massilia

1. During these events in Spain, Caesar's lieutenant Gaius Trebonius, who had been left behind to conduct the siege of Massilia, began building siege-walls on two sides[25] of the town and bringing up screens and siege-towers. One of these walls was near the harbour and dockyards, the other near the gate affording access to the town from the direction of Gaul and Spain, close to the coast beside the mouth of the Rhône*. To carry out this work, Trebonius conscripted large numbers of men from all over the province, commandeered beasts of burden and ordered supplies of withies and timber to be collected. With these resources he built his wall up to a height of eighty feet.

2. However, the Massiliotes had long since collected in the town such a stock of armaments and so large a collection of missile engines that no screens of woven osiers could possibly stand up against their salvoes. Beams twelve feet long, with spikes fixed at the end, and fired, moreover, from enormous ballistas, went crashing through four thicknesses of wickerwork and planted themselves in the ground. Our men therefore covered the protective galleries with timbers a foot thick and under the shelter of these they passed up materials for the siege-wall from hand to hand. A 'tortoise'[26] sixty feet long went in front to level the ground; this also was made of strong timbers and covered with every sort of material that could give protection against stones and firebrands. In spite of all this, such was the size of the works, the height of the walls and towers and the number of missile engines, that the work as a whole proceeded very slowly. A further cause of delay was frequent sallies by the Albici, who threw firebrands on to our siege-wall and towers; our men easily fended

* Massilia is washed by the sea on three sides; the fourth alone affords approach by land, and since part of this side is occupied by the citadel, a natural fortification rising steeply out of a valley, a siege is a long and difficult process.

off these missiles, besides inflicting serious damage on the attackers and driving them back into the town.

3. Meantime, Lucius Nasidius had been sent by Pompey with a fleet of sixteen ships, a few of them fitted with bronze rams, to help Lucius Domitius and the people of Massilia. Curio was not expecting him and had taken no precautions, with the result that Nasidius was able to sail through the Sicilian straits and put in at Messana. There, the local council and its leaders panicked and fled; he took a ship from the dockyards, added it to his own fleet and continued his journey to Massilia. He sent some small boats ahead to notify Domitius and the Massiliotes of his approach, and urged them strongly to combine their fleet with the reinforcements he was bringing and engage Brutus again.

4. After their previous setback[27], the Massiliotes had brought old ships out of the dockyard to replenish their fleet and had worked hard at repairing them and fitting them out; they had plenty of steersmen and rowers for them. They had added fishing boats, which they had decked over to protect the rowers against missiles, and these they filled with archers and ballistic engines. When the fleet was ready they embarked, amid the tears and prayers of all the old men, mothers and young girls, who begged them to rescue their city in its dire need. Their courage and confidence were as great as when they had fought before; for it is a common fault in human nature that the unseen and unknown provoke excessive confidence or excessive fear, and so it happened on this occasion. The arrival of Lucius Nasidius had filled the people with optimism and enthusiasm. When they got a suitable wind they left harbour and joined Nasidius at Taurois, which is one of their forts. There they prepared the ships for action, screwed up their resolution to fight again, and discussed their plans. The Massiliotes held the right of the line, Nasidius the left.

5. Brutus hurried there also. He had a larger fleet than before, for to those made at Arelate on Caesar's orders had been added six captured from the Massiliotes. These Brutus had repaired and completely fitted out during the preceding days. And so, exhorting his men to scorn the men they had already conquered, since they had defeated them already when their force was undamaged, he advanced, full of confidence and courage, against the enemy. From

the camp of Gaius Trebonius and from all the high ground it was
easy to look into the city and to see how all the men of military
age who had remained in the town, all the older men, and the
wives and children, were stretching up their hands to heaven in
the public squares or at look-out points or on the wall, or were
going to the temples of the immortal gods and prostrating themselves in front of the statues of the gods and begging for victory.
There was no one who was not convinced that all his future fortunes depended on the result of that day; for all the best warriors
and the men most highly esteemed from every age-group had been
called out by name and had responded to entreaties and gone on
board ship. As a result, if the Massiliotes should suffer a reverse,
they could not see that there would be any possibility left even of
attempting a resistance; whereas, if they were victorious, they
could rely for the protection of the State on their own resources
and on help from outside.

6. When the battle started, the courage of the Massiliotes left
nothing to be desired. They remembered the injunctions their
people had given them a little while before. They fought in the
belief that they would have no second chance, and that those who
jeopardized their lives in the battle would not, they thought,
anticipate by very long the fate of the rest of the citizens, who
would have to submit to the same fortune of war, should the city
be captured. Our ships gradually became separated, and this gave
the enemy an opportunity to make use of the skill of their steersmen and the manoeuvrability of their ships; and whenever our
men took an opportunity of fastening on a ship with grappling
irons, they would come in from all directions to rescue their
comrades from difficulties. They also acquitted themselves well in
hand-to-hand fighting, along with the Albici, and did not fall far
short of our men in courage. At the same time, volleys of missiles
were being hurled from the smaller boats standing off at a distance, and these inflicted many wounds unexpectedly on our men,
who had not foreseen this and were embroiled in the battle. Two
triremes had sighted the ship of Decimus Brutus, which could
easily be recognized from its ensign, and bore down on it from
different directions. Brutus, however, had just enough forewarning to make an effort and propel his ship a little way ahead of

them. The two triremes collided at speed so hard that both were severely damaged by the impact, and in fact one had its beak broken off and began to founder. Observing this, the ships of Brutus's fleet which were nearest the spot attacked the crippled ships and soon sank them both.

7. Nasidius's ships, on the other hand, were of no help and quickly withdrew from the battle; for their crews had not the sight of their homeland nor the injunctions of their kinsfolk to urge them on into mortal danger. And so none of that contingent of ships was lost. Of the Massiliote fleet, five were sunk, four captured and one fled with those of Nasidius, all of which made for Hither Spain. One of the remaining ships had been sent ahead to Massilia to convey the news. On its approach, the whole population poured out to hear the result; and when they heard it, there was such consternation that it seemed as if at the same time the city itself had been taken by the enemy. None the less, the people set themselves to do all that remained to be done for the defence of the city.

8. The legionaries who were engaged on the right-hand part of the siege-works observed that they would obtain substantial protection against the frequent sallies of the enemy if they built a tower of brickwork there close up against the wall as a sort of fort and place of refuge. At first they made only a small, low structure, against sudden onslaughts. Into this they would retire; from this, whenever there was an exceptionally vigorous attack, they would defend themselves; from this they would sally out to repel and pursue the enemy. The tower was thirty feet square, but the walls were five feet thick. Later, however, their natural intelligence told them (experience, as usual, being instructive) that it could be extremely useful if this tower was built up high. This was done in the following manner.

9. When the tower was built up as high as the first floor, they built this flooring into the walls in such a way that the ends of the beams were covered by the brickwork of the walls, so that there should be no parts projecting on which enemy firebrands could take hold. Above this timber-work, they built up the sides with bricks as high as the protection afforded by siege-hut and screens allowed; then above that they put two beams across, not

far from the ends of the walls, on which to support the wooden
framework that was going to act as a roof for the tower. On top
of these beams they put joists across at right angles and fastened
these with tie-beams. They made the joists rather longer so that
they stuck out beyond the ends of the walls, to provide something
on which to hang the coverings to ward off and repel blows, while
the walls were being built up inside this wooden frame. The top
of this woodwork they covered with bricks and clay, to prevent
the enemy damaging it with fire, and they laid pads of rag on top
of that again, so that javelins from ballistas should not break
through the timber or blows from catapults dislodge the brickwork.

They also made three fenders four feet broad out of anchor-
cables to fit along the length of the walls of the tower, and
fastened these so that they hung from the projecting ends of the
joists on the three sides of the tower that were exposed to the
enemy; for their experience elsewhere [28] had taught them that this
was the one type of covering that no missile or ballistic engine
could penetrate. Now, once that part of the tower which was
completed had been roofed over and protected against all enemy
missiles, they removed the siege-huts to other parts of the works.
Then they began to poise and lift up the roof of the tower, all in
a piece, by leverage from the flooring of the first storey. When
they had raised it as far as the cover provided by the fenders
permitted, they went on, concealed and protected by these shields,
building up the walls with bricks, and levering the roof up farther
to allow room for working. When it seemed to be time to make a
second storey, they built in beams, as before, protected by the
outside brickwork, and above this flooring they again raised up
the roof and the fenders. In this way, safely and without casualties or danger, they built six storeys, and left apertures where it
seemed suitable in the course of building for discharging missiles
from ballistic engines.

10. When they were certain that from this tower they could
protect all the surrounding works, they began making a covered
gallery [29] sixty feet long, of boards two feet square, to be taken
from the brick tower up to a bastion of the enemy's wall. The
structure of the gallery was as follows. First, two beams of equal

length were laid on the ground four feet apart, and on these were fixed posts five feet high. They joined these together with wooden stays forming a slight gable, on which to lay the timbers for roofing the gallery, and laid on top boards two feet square which they fastened with plates and bolts. At the edge of the roof of the gallery and at the ends of the timbers they fixed poles with a square section, about three inches square. These were to hold the bricks which were to be laid on top of the gallery.

When the gallery had been gabled and methodically built up in this way, and the timbers had been laid on the stays, it was covered with bricks and clay, as a protection against fire thrown from the wall. Hides were laid over the bricks, so that water could not be discharged on the bricks from pipes and split them up. The hides themselves were covered with pads of rags as a protection against fire and stones. They completed the whole of this work, under the protection of screens, as far as the bastion, and suddenly, when the enemy were off their guard, they used a naval trick and put rollers under the gallery, bringing it right up to the bastion so that it lay alongside the building.

11. Dismayed at this sudden calamity, the inhabitants pushed up with levers the largest rocks they could manage and sent them toppling down from the edge of the bastion on to the gallery. The strength of the construction stood up to the impact and anything that fell on the gable of the gallery rolled off. Seeing this, they changed their tactics; they filled barrels with firewood and pitch, lit them and rolled them down from the wall on to the gallery. The barrels rolled and fell off, and as they fell at the sides they were pushed away from the construction with poles and forks. Meanwhile, under the gallery, the soldiers were using crowbars to pull apart the stones which held together the foundations of the bastion. Some of our troops kept up a protective fire from the brick tower with javelins and missile engines; the enemy were driven back from the wall and the bastion and were not given free scope to defend the wall. When several of the stones in the wall under the bastion had been withdrawn, part of the bastion suddenly collapsed, and the rest began keeling over on top of it. The enemy were thrown into consternation at this breach in their city and all rushed out of the gates unarmed, wearing white

bands[30] and stretching out their hands in supplication to the officers and the army.

12. This new development put a complete stop to military operations. The troops left their action stations and came eagerly to see and hear. When the enemy reached the officers and the army, they all flung themselves down at their feet, and begged them to await the arrival of Caesar. They said, 'We see our city taken, the siege-works complete, the bastion undermined; and so we are abandoning the defence. When Caesar does arrive, if we do not carry out orders at his behest, there can be no hindrance to the immediate sack of the city. If the bastion collapses completely, there is no possibility of restraining your troops from bursting into the town in search of plunder and destroying it.' These and other pleas of the same sort, as one might expect from skilled orators[31], were delivered with much weeping and so as to excite much compassion.

13. The officers were touched by this appeal and withdrawing their men from the siege-works they suspended the siege, leaving only a guard on the works. Yielding to compassion, they thus established an informal truce and waited for Caesar's arrival. No missiles were launched from the wall, and none from our side; everyone relaxed their conscientiousness in attending to duty, as if the job was done. For Caesar, in a dispatch, had strongly impressed on Trebonius that he was not to allow the city to be stormed by force, in case the combined effects of resentment against the rebels, the contempt displayed towards themselves and their prolonged labours should inflame the soldiers' feelings to such a degree that they should kill all the men of military age. This indeed they were threatening to do, and it was only with difficulty that they were being restrained at this time from breaking into the town. They bitterly resented the fact that through Trebonius's fault, as it seemed, they were not taking over the town.

14. The enemy, however, were not acting in good faith. They were merely seeking the time and opportunity for trickery. A few days later, when our men were relaxed and off guard, some of them away, others resting after their long labours on the siege-works, with their weapons all put away and covered up, the enemy

suddenly burst out of the gates at midday and set fire to the siege-works.

There was a strong following wind, which spread the fire, so that the siege-wall, the screens, the 'tortoise', the tower, the missile engines all went up in flames at once and were all consumed before it could be seen how it had happened. This sudden blow stung our men to action; they snatched up such weapons as they could, and more men rushed out of the camp to join them. They charged at the enemy as they fled, but were prevented from pursuing them by showers of arrows and missiles from the town wall; meanwhile the enemy rallied close to the wall and there without hindrance set fire to the gallery and brickwork tower. And so the work of many months perished in a moment, thanks to the faithlessness of the enemy and the strength of the wind. The Massiliotes tried to repeat their exploit on the following day. They had the same wind, and with even greater boldness they sallied out fighting and brought large quantities of firebrands against the other tower and siege-wall. But whereas our men had previously relaxed all their earlier watchfulness, they had now made preparations for defence, warned by the events of the day before. The result was that they killed many of the enemy and drove the rest back into the town before they could achieve their object.

15. Trebonius began to reorganize and rebuild those siege-works which had been destroyed. His men worked with increased zeal, for they had seen the utter collapse of the contrivances that had cost them so much work and they were stung by the thought that their courage would be held up to ridicule as a result of this criminal breach of truce. There were no materials left at all that could be collected to make a siege-wall, since all the timber for a long way around in the territory of Massilia had been felled and carried off. They therefore began to build a wall using a novel and unexampled method of construction. They built two walls of brick, six feet thick and with a timber roof between them; this made a siege-wall of about the same width as the old wall of piled timbers had been. Where the space between the walls or the weakness of the structure seemed to demand it, they drove piles into the ground between the walls and laid cross-beams on these

to strengthen the wall. The timber roofing was covered with wickerwork, which was plastered with clay. The soldiers, with a roof over them, walls to the right and left and a screen in front, were able to bring up whatever was needed for the construction without danger. The work proceeded quickly; the good sense and hardiness of the troops soon repaired the loss of their prolonged labours. Gateways were left in the wall at suitable places to allow them to sally out.

16. The enemy saw that the siege-works, which they had hoped were incapable of repair except at the expense of a great deal of time and effort, had been so far restored after a few days' work that there was no scope for treachery or for breaking out, and no way left at all of injuring the men with missiles or damaging the works by fire. They realized also that that whole part of the city which was accessible from land could be surrounded in the same way with a wall and towers, so that it would be impossible even for them to stand their ground on their own defences, since our army seemed to have built its walls practically on the walls of the town and we were near enough to throw missiles. Besides, they were unable to make use of their ballistic engines, in which they had placed great hopes, because we were too near; and they were aware that, given the chance of fighting on equal terms from walls and towers, they could not match the valour of our men. They therefore had recourse again to surrender on the same terms as before.

2. Spain – the surrender of Varro

17. In Further Spain, Marcus Varro, hearing initially about events in Italy and doubting Pompey's chances of success, spoke about Caesar in very friendly terms. He said that he was under an existing bond of duty, owing to his previous appointment as Pompey's lieutenant; no less strong, indeed, were the ties of friendship between himself and Caesar; and he was aware of the duties of an officer who held a charge of trust. He also knew the extent of his own resources and of the good-will of the whole province towards Caesar. He took this line in everything he said, but made no move

in any direction. Later, however, he learned that Caesar was being detained at Massilia; he heard that Petreius had joined forces with Afranius, that large numbers of auxiliaries had mustered and that others were hoped for and awaited, while the whole of Hither Spain was of one mind; he heard of the later developments at Ilerda, i.e. Caesar's difficulties over the corn supply, about which indeed he was receiving detailed and exaggerated accounts in dispatches from Afranius. Then Varro too began to move in step with Fortune.

18. He held a levy all through the province, made up two legions to full strength, and added about thirty auxiliary cohorts. He collected a large quantity of corn for dispatch to the Massiliotes and to Afranius and Petreius, ordered the people of Gades to build twelve warships, and had several more built at Hispalis. He took all the money and ornaments out of the shrine of Hercules into the town of Gades, sent six cohorts there from the province as a garrison and put in charge of the town Gaius Gallonius, a Roman knight and friend of Domitius, who had been sent there by Domitius to administer an inheritance. All weapons, whether private or public property, were collected in Gallonius's house. Varro himself held public assemblies at which he inveighed against Caesar. He frequently announced from his official dais that Caesar had suffered reverses, that large numbers of troops had deserted him and gone over to Afranius, and that he had this news on good authority and by reliable messengers. These reports alarmed the Roman citizens in the province and he compelled them to guarantee to give him, for the conduct of government, eighteen million sesterces, 20,000 pounds of silver and 120,000 pecks of wheat. If he judged any communities to be friendly to Caesar, he imposed heavier burdens on them, installed garrisons and arranged for the trial of private individuals; if anyone was alleged to have spoken against the Roman State, that person's property was confiscated. He forced the whole province to swear allegiance to himself and Pompey.

On learning of the events in Hither Spain, he prepared for war. Now, his plan of campaign was simply to go to Gades with two legions and keep there the ships and all the corn; for he knew that the whole province supported Caesar. He thought that once he had collected the corn on the island[32] and had the ships there too, it would not be difficult to carry on the war.

Caesar had many urgent reasons for returning to Italy, but he had decided not to leave any part of the Spanish war unfinished, because he knew that Pompey had conferred great benefits[33] on the Hither province and had large numbers of clients there.

19. Accordingly, Caesar sent two legions to Further Spain with Quintus Cassius, a tribune of the people, and he himself with six hundred cavalry proceeded there by long stages. He sent an edict ahead specifying a day on which he wished the magistrates and chieftains of all the tribes to meet him at Corduba. This edict was published throughout the province and no tribe failed to send part of its ruling body to Corduba by the stated time, nor was there any Roman citizen of any repute who did not come there too. At the same time, the community of Roman citizens in Corduba on their own initiative closed the gates against Varro, put guards and watches on the towers and the wall, and kept with them, to guard the town, two cohorts known as the 'Colonials'[34] who chanced to have come there. During the same period, the people of Carmo, by far the strongest tribe in the whole province, spontaneously drove out three cohorts which had been installed as a garrison in the town's citadel by Varro, and shut the gates.

20. Varro therefore made all the more haste to reach Gades with his legions as soon as possible, in case he should be cut off by land or sea; so strong and so enthusiastic was the support for Caesar which was being revealed all over the province. When he advanced a little farther he received a dispatch from Gades. This informed him that as soon as word was received of Caesar's edict the leading men of Gades had agreed with the tribunes of the cohorts in garrison there to drive Gallonius out and hold the city and the island for Caesar. Thus resolved, they warned Gallonius to leave Gades of his own accord, while he could safely do so; if he did not, they would take action. This frightened Gallonius into leaving Gades. Hearing of this, the men of one of the two legions (the one known as the 'Homebred'[35]) removed their standards from Varro's camp while he himself stood by and looked on. They withdrew to Hispalis where they installed themselves in the forum and the colonnades without doing any damage. The

community of Roman citizens there so strongly approved of their action that they all eagerly received the soldiers into their homes. Varro was thoroughly frightened by these events; he altered his route and sent word ahead that he was coming to Italica, but was informed that the gates had been closed against him. Then, finding every way barred, he sent word to Caesar that he was willing to hand over his legion to anyone Caesar should designate. Caesar sent Sextus Caesar and ordered Varro to hand over to him. Varro did so and came to Corduba to see Caesar; he gave faithful account of his public monies, handed over what money he had and indicated the whereabouts of all his ships and corn.

21. Caesar held a public meeting at Corduba and thanked the various sections of the people. He thanked the Roman citizens for their zeal in taking the town into their own hands; the Spaniards, for having driven out the garrisons; the people of Gades for having foiled the attempts of his adversaries and asserted their own right to independence; the military tribunes and centurions who had come there as a garrison, for having lent their strength to support the townsfolk's decisions. He remitted to the Roman citizens the money which they had promised Varro to pay into the treasury. He restored their property to those whom he heard had suffered confiscation for having spoken too freely. He bestowed rewards on certain communities and individuals and filled the rest with hopes for the future. After spending two days at Corduba, he went on to Gades. There he gave orders that money and offerings which had been taken from the shrine of Hercules and stored in a private house should be brought back to the temple. He put Quintus Cassius in charge of the province and assigned four legions to him. He himself took the ships which Varro and the people of Gades under Varro's orders had built, and arrived within a few days at Tarraco, where deputations from practically the whole of Hither Spain were awaiting his arrival. As before, he bestowed honours on certain tribes, both at large and to individuals, then left Tarraco and proceeded by land to Narbo and from there to Massilia. There he learned that a law had been passed to create a dictator and he himself had been nominated by the praetor Marcus Lepidus.

3. Massilia capitulates

22. The Massiliotes were worn down by all sorts of trouble. They had begun to suffer from an extreme shortage of grain; they had twice been defeated in a naval battle; their frequent sallies had been routed; besides, they were assailed by severe pestilence, the result of long confinement and abnormal diet – for they were all subsisting on old stocks of millet and rotten barley, which they had long ago obtained and stored as a public reserve for just such an emergency; a bastion had been thrown down and a large part of the wall undermined; and they had given up hope of help from the provinces and the armies, which they learned had come into Caesar's power. They decided therefore to surrender, in earnest. However, a few days before, Lucius Domitius had learned the intentions of the Massiliotes and had got together three ships, two of which he assigned to his adherents; he embarked on one himself and set off, as soon as he got stormy weather. He was observed by ships which had been sent out by Brutus, according to daily routine, and were keeping watch by the harbour. They lifted anchor and began following. Domitius's own ship held steadily on its course in flight and with the help of the storm soon went out of sight, but the other two, alarmed at meeting our ships, went back into harbour. The Massiliotes, obeying orders, brought their weapons and catapults out of the town, took the ships out of the harbour and dockyards, and handed over the money from their treasury. After this Caesar, sparing them rather because of the age and fame of the city than because of any services to himself, left two legions there as a garrison and sent the rest to Italy. He himself set off for Rome.

4. Africa – Curio's campaign

23. At about the same time, Gaius Curio was on his way from Sicily to Africa. Scorning from the very outset the forces of Publius Attius Varus, he was transporting only two of the four

legions which he had received from Caesar and five hundred cavalry. After spending two days and three nights on the voyage he put in at the place called Anquillaria. This is about twenty-two miles from Clupea; it has fairly good anchorage in summer and is contained between two projecting headlands. Lucius Caesar, the younger, had been awaiting Curio's arrival off Clupea with ten warships which had been beached at Utica after the Pirate War and which Publius Attius had had repaired for this war. However, he was frightened by the size of Curio's fleet; he had fled back from the high seas and, urging his trireme to the nearest shore he had run it aground and left it there, while he fled on foot to Hadrumetum*. On Lucius's flight, the rest of his ships went to Hadrumetum. He was pursued by the quaestor Marcius Rufus with twelve ships which Curio had brought from Sicily as a guard for the transports. When Marcius saw the ship abandoned on the beach he hauled it off with a rope and then returned with his fleet to Gaius Curio.

24. Curio sent Marcius ahead to Utica with the fleet; he himself began to make his way there with the army and after two days' march reached the river Bagradas. There he left the lieutenant Gaius Caninius Rebilus with the legions while he himself went ahead with the cavalry to reconnoitre Castra Cornelia[36], since that place was thought highly suitable for a camp. Now, it consists in a straight ridge jutting out to sea, very steep and rough on either side, but with a slightly gentler slope on the side towards Utica. As the crow flies, it is a little more than a mile from Utica, but in between there is a stream, up which the sea flows for some distance, and the ground around it is marshy for a long way. Anyone wishing to avoid the marsh has to make a detour of six miles to reach the town.

25. Exploring the area, Curio caught sight of Varus's camp, adjoining the town wall near the gate known as 'War-gate', on a site with strong natural defences – on one side it had the town of Utica itself, and on the other the enormous substructure of the theatre, which is in front of the town, and which left only a narrow and difficult passage by which to approach the camp. At

* This town was under the protection of Gaius Considius Longus with a garrison of one legion.

the same time he observed that the roads were crowded with people carrying goods and driving beasts, which they were conveying from the countryside into the town in their alarm at the sudden disturbances. He set his cavalry on them, to despoil them and treat them as booty; at the same time, Varus sent to their aid from the town 600 Numidian cavalry and 400 infantry which King Juba had sent as reinforcements to Utica a few days before. Juba had a traditional bond of friendship with Pompey's family; he also had a grudge against Curio, because the latter as tribune had proposed a bill making Juba's kingdom State property[37]. The cavalry engaged; and the Numidians were unable to withstand the very first impact of our men, but withdrew to their camp by the town with the loss of about 120 men. Meanwhile the warships arrived and Curio ordered a proclamation to be made to the supply ships, about 200 in number, which were lying off Utica, that he would consider as enemies any who did not at once take their vessels over to Castra Cornelia. Instantly they all lifted anchor, left Utica, and went where they were bid. This secured supplies of all sorts for the army.

26. Curio then returned to his camp by the Bagradas, where he was hailed as *imperator*[38] by the whole army; on the following day he led them to Utica and camped near the town. Before the fortifications of the camp were completed, the cavalry on guard reported that large reinforcements of cavalry and infantry sent by the king were approaching Utica; at the same time a great cloud of dust came into view and in a moment the head of the column was in sight. Startled by this unexpected development, Curio sent out cavalry to bear the brunt of the initial onset and hold them up, while he himself quickly withdrew the legions from the defence-works and drew them up for battle. The king's forces had been marching along without apprehension, not troubling to keep in order, and being in consequence unable to manoeuvre and in disarray, they were routed when our cavalry engaged, before our legions had even time to deploy and take up their positions. The royal cavalry escaped almost unharmed, since they raced along the shore and took refuge in the town, but a great many of the infantry were killed.

27. On the following night two Marsian centurions deserted

from Curio's camp with twenty-two men from their companies and went over to Attius Varus. Whether they were expressing their real opinion to Varus, or whether they were saying what he would like to hear (for we readily believe what we wish were so, and we hope that others feel as we do), at any rate they told him that the whole of Curio's army was disaffected, and that it was highly necessary that Varus should come face to face with the army and give them a chance to talk with him. Varus was convinced, and on the following morning he led his legions out of camp. Curio did the same, and each drew up his own forces, with only a narrow valley between them.

28. With Varus's army was Sextus Quintilius Varus, who, as shown above*, had been at Corfinium. After his release by Caesar he had come to Africa. Now, Curio had brought over with him those legions which Caesar had previously taken over at Corfinium. They were still in the same ranks and companies, although a few of the centurions were different. Taking this opportunity of talking to them, Quintilius began to ride around Curio's lines, pleading with the men not to forget the first military oath[39], which they had sworn to Domitius and to himself, as quaestor; not to bear arms against those who had endured the same fortunes as themselves and suffered the same siege, nor to fight on behalf of those who insultingly called them deserters. He also held out some hopes of financial reward, which they might expect from his own generosity if they followed him and Attius. There was no response of any kind from Curio's army to this speech; nothing more occurred and both leaders took their forces back to camp.

29. However, in Curio's camp everyone was seized with a powerful fear, and this was rapidly intensified by the various remarks that were passed. Everyone, in fact, was forming personal opinions, adding to what he had heard from others something of his own fear. When one of these views had passed from one source to several other people and each had passed it on to someone else, there would seem to be several authorities for the story. It was a civil war; the men involved were of a type to indulge readily in gossip and follow the version they preferred; these were legions

[* C.W.I.23]

95

which a little time before had been on the opposing side. For even Caesar's kindness had lost some of its effect from the frequency with which it was offered. Men from different townships were thrown together, for they were equally made up of Marsi and Paelignians. And concerning those who on the previous night had left their tents and gone over to the other side, there were various unpleasant stories going about. Uncertainty was ill received and some reports were actually invented by men who wished to appear better informed[40].

30. Curio therefore held a council of war and began to discuss the conduct of the campaign. Some were of the opinion that they should at all costs make an effort and attack Varus's camp, because they believed that when the troops were in this sort of mood idleness was most dangerous. Finally, they said, it was better to show courage and try the fortunes of war in battle, than to be deserted and betrayed by their own men and suffer the ultimate agony. Others thought that they ought to withdraw to Castra Cornelia in the small hours of the morning, to give the soldiers more time to come to their senses; besides, if they should come to any harm, they would be able, thanks to their large fleet, to withdraw more quickly and safely from there and to take refuge in Sicily.

31. Curio was against both plans. He said that one was as faint-hearted as the other was foolhardy. One side was contemplating a shameful flight, the other was for fighting even in an unfavourable position. 'How,' he said, 'can we reasonably hope to take a camp which has been well fortified and is in a strong position besides? What do we gain, if we sustain severe losses and then withdraw from the attack? You should know that while success wins for commanders the good-will of their men, failure earns their hatred. If, however, we move camp, what does that amount to but an ignominious retreat, a complete abandoning of hope, which moreover will antagonize our army? No man with a sense of honour should be made to suspect that he is not fully trusted, for that diminishes his zeal; nor should a ruffian be allowed to know that he is feared, for our fear will merely increase his insolence. Now, if we had already established the truth of the allegations about the disaffection of the army – which I am sure

are either utterly false or at any rate less serious than they are made out to be – would it not be much better to keep this concealed and covered up, rather than to provide confirmation of it? Should we not rather keep the troubles of the army hidden, like physical wounds, so as not to raise the hopes of the enemy? Some suggest, further, that we should depart in the middle of the night. The purpose of this, I suppose, is to provide more scope for misdemeanour; for such behaviour is usually held in check by fear or a sense of shame, and these feelings lose much of their effectiveness in the dark.

'Therefore, I am neither so sanguine as to think we should make a hopeless attack on the camp, nor so timorous as to give up hope altogether. I think that we should try every means possible, and I am confident that presently you and I will find that our judgements in the main coincide.'

32. He dismissed the council and summoned an assembly of the troops. He reminded them how their zeal had helped Caesar at Corfinium and how thanks to their good-will and their example he had won over the greater part of Italy. 'You and your action,' he said, 'were subsequently copied by all the townships, and it was with good reason that Caesar entertained the most friendly feelings towards you, while his opponents thought very ill of you. For Pompey suffered no reverse in battle; what dislodged him and made him leave Italy was your action, which foreshadowed what was to come. Caesar has entrusted to your faithful keeping myself, whom he held very dearly, and the provinces of Sicily and Africa [41], without which Rome and Italy cannot be preserved. There are some here who urge you to desert us; obviously, their chief desire is simultaneously to betray us and to make you bear the guilt of a heinous crime. What worse fate can they conceive for you in their wrath, than that you should betray those who believe they owe you everything, and fall into the power of those who believe that you were the cause of their ruin? Have you not heard about Caesar's successes in Spain? He has routed two armies, defeated two generals, and taken over two provinces; and all this was done within forty days of coming within reach of his opponents. Are those who could not resist when they were unharmed likely to resist now that they are ruined? You followed

Caesar when victory was uncertain; now that the issue is settled, are you going to follow the loser when you should be reaping the reward of your good service?

'They say that you have deserted and betrayed them and they mention your first oath. Did you really desert Lucius Domitius, or did Domitius desert you? Was it not he who abandoned men who were ready to endure all that fortune might bring? Did he not try to save himself by running away, without your knowledge? You were betrayed by him; and was it not by Caesar's kindness that you were spared? How could you be held by an oath, when the general himself threw away his symbols of office [42], abandoned his command and became a private individual – and was then himself captured and came under the power of another? We are left with a new theory of obligation, that you should ignore the oath by which you are bound and uphold the one which was cancelled by the surrender and loss of rights [43] of the general.

'But perhaps you are satisfied with Caesar, and your grievances are against me. I do not intend to recount the services I have done you; they do not as yet come up to my intention and your expectation. However, soldiers always look to the outcome of a war for the reward of their labours; and even you have no doubt what the outcome will be. Indeed, why should I omit mention of my own conscientiousness or, as far as things have gone, my fortune? I brought the army over safe and sound without the loss of a single ship; do you have any complaint about that? On the way I scattered the enemy fleet at the first encounter. Twice in two days I won a cavalry battle. I took two hundred vessels and their cargoes right out of the harbour, out of the very grasp of the enemy, and so robbed them of the ability to get supplies either by land or in ships. Scorn such good fortune and such leaders; choose instead the disgrace at Corfinium, the flight from Italy, the surrender of Spain, which foreshadow the result of the war in Africa. I indeed chose to call myself a soldier of Caesar's; you have hailed me as *imperator*. If you have changed your minds, I return your gift. Give me back my own name, in case you should seem to have bestowed the honour on me in mockery.'

33. This speech upset the soldiers; they interrupted him fre-

quently while he was actually speaking, and were apparently very hurt at being suspected of disloyalty; and as he left the meeting they all urged him to be bold and not to hesitate to put their courage and loyalty to the test by joining battle. Since he had thus managed to sway the feelings and ideas of his men, Curio decided, with their unanimous agreement, to entrust the issue to a battle at the earliest opportunity. On the following day he led them out and drew them up for battle in the same place where they had taken up position previously. Attius Varus did not hesitate to lead out his men likewise, so as not to lose any opportunity either of trying to suborn the troops, or of fighting in a favourable position.

34. There was, as shown above*, a valley between the two armies. It was not very big, but the sides were difficult and steep to climb. Each waited for the forces of the other to attempt to cross, so that they themselves might join battle in the more favourable position. All at once, on the left wing of Publius Attius, all the cavalry, mingled with a good many light-armed infantry, came into view, going down into the valley. Curio sent the cavalry and two cohorts of Marrucini to meet them. The enemy cavalry failed to withstand the first onset, but gave their horses rein and fled to their own forces; abandoned, the light-armed troops who had charged along with them were surrounded and killed by our men. All Varus's army turned to watch, and saw them fleeing and being cut down. Then Rebilus, one of Caesar's lieutenants, whom Curio had brought with him from Sicily because of his extensive military experience, said, 'You see the enemy terrified, Curio; why hesitate to make use of your opportunity?' Curio paused only to tell his soldiers to remember their avowals of the previous day, then ordered them to follow him and charged at their head. The going in the valley was so difficult that those in front could not clamber out easily without help from their comrades below. However, the minds of Attius's men were taken up with their own fear, and with the rout and the slaughter of their comrades, and they had no thought of resisting; indeed, they all believed that they themselves were already being surrounded by the cavalry. And so, before a javelin

[* Ch. 27.]

could be hurled or our men could get any nearer, the whole of Varus's army turned tail and fled back to camp.

35. During this retreat, a certain Fabius, a Paelignian from the lowest ranks of Curio's army, caught up with the head of the retreating column and began looking around for Varus, calling for him loudly by name, so as to appear to be one of his own men who had something to tell him. Varus, hearing his name called several times, stopped and asked the man who he was and what he wanted; Fabius then aimed a blow with his sword at his exposed arm and very nearly killed him; Varus, however, escaped by lifting his shield to parry the blow. Fabius was then surrounded and killed by the troops who were nearest.

The fleeing troops were so numerous and so disordered that they blocked the gates of the camp and obstructed the way. More men died there, without being wounded, than perished in the actual battle or the retreat, and they were very nearly driven out of the camp as well. Some of them carried straight on into the town. However, the nature of the ground and the fortifications of the camp denied Curio's men access, and besides they had marched out to give battle, and did not have with them the necessary equipment for an assault on a camp. Curio therefore led them back to camp. His only casualty was Fabius; on the other side, about six hundred were killed and a thousand wounded. On Curio's departure, all these wounded and many others pretending to be wounded left the camp in fear and withdrew to the town. Varus observed this and realized that his men were thoroughly demoralized; and so, leaving a trumpeter and a few tents for appearance's sake he led the rest of the army into the town in silence in the small hours of the morning.

36. On the following day Curio opened the siege of Utica by starting a circumvallation. In Utica, the populace were unused to war, as the result of a lasting period of peace. The inhabitants were very well disposed towards Caesar because of certain benefactions he had conferred on them; the community of Roman citizens was made up of diverse elements; and there was considerable panic because of the previous battles. Therefore they all openly began to talk of surrender, and to urge Publius Attius not to insist on jeopardizing the fortunes of them all through his own obstinacy.

Meanwhile, advance messengers arrived from King Juba, announcing that he was approaching with large forces and urging them to guard and defend the city. This news gave their demoralized spirits fresh resolution.

5. Curio's last stand

37. The same news was brought to Curio, but it was some time before he could be induced to believe it, such was his confidence in his own resources. Besides news was now arriving by messengers and dispatches of Caesar's successes in Spain. Curio was carried away by all this, and thought that the king would not make any efforts against him. When, however, he learned on reliable authority that the king's forces were less than twenty-five miles from Utica, he abandoned the siege-works and withdrew to Castra Cornelia, where he began to gather stores of corn, to strengthen the camp and to collect timber. He sent orders at once to Sicily for the other two legions and the rest of the cavalry to be sent to him. The camp was highly suitable for the conduct of a campaign, thanks to the nature of the site, its fortifications, its nearness to the sea and the availability of water and salt*. As the district was well-wooded, there could be no lack of timber and the well-filled fields ensured an ample supply of grain. Therefore Curio had the full approval of all his men for his decision to await the rest of his forces and prolong the campaign.

38. Then he heard from some deserters from the town that Juba had been recalled by a border war and troubles with the people of Leptis and had stayed in his kingdom, and that instead his officer Saburra had been dispatched with a moderately large force and was approaching Utica. He accepted this story without question, changed his plans, and decided to offer battle.

His decision was strongly influenced by his youthful audacity, his earlier progress and his confidence in success. So, at nightfall he sent all his cavalry towards the enemy camp by the river Bagradas, where Saburra, of whom news had come previously,

* Large quantities of salt had already been gathered from the near-by salt-pits.

was in command. (The king, however, was following on with all his forces and had halted six miles away from Saburra.) The cavalry covered the distance in the night and made a surprise attack on the unsuspecting Numidians, who, following a barbarian habit, had not halted in formation but were spread about. While they were dispersed like this and heavy with sleep, the cavalry attacked them, killed a great number of them and made many flee in panic; then they returned to Curio, bringing prisoners with them.

39. Curio, leaving five cohorts to guard the camp, had marched out with all his forces towards three o'clock in the morning, and he met the cavalry and learned of their success after he had advanced about six miles. He asked the prisoners who was in command of the camp at the Bagradas and they replied that it was Saburra. In his eagerness to finish the march he did not enquire further, and looking towards the companies nearest him, 'You see, men,' he said, 'how the prisoners' story tallies with that of the deserters? They both say that the king is away and has sent small forces, which failed to be a match for a few cavalry. Hasten on, then, to win spoils and renown, so that we may begin at once to think of rewarding you and rendering due gratitude.'

The exploit of the cavalry was in itself notable, especially in that a small number had encountered so large a host of Numidians; however, they themselves gave an embroidered account of the incident, with the usual readiness of men to sound their own praises. They also displayed large quantities of spoil and captured men and horses, so that any further lapse of time seemed merely to delay ultimate victory. Curio's hopes, therefore, were matched by the zeal of his troops. He ordered the cavalry to follow and speeded up the march in order to attack the enemy while they were still actually fleeing in panic. The cavalry, however, were wearied as a result of their all-night journey; they were unable to keep up, and kept straggling behind. Even this, however, did not impair Curio's confidence.

40. When Juba was informed by Saburra of the battle during the night he sent him as reinforcements two thousand Spanish and Gallic cavalry, whom he was accustomed to keep by him as a personal bodyguard, together with the most reliable part of the

infantry. He himself followed on more slowly with the rest of his forces and sixty elephants. Saburra, suspecting that the cavalry had been merely an advance party and that Curio himself would soon arrive, drew up his cavalry and infantry and gave them orders to pretend to be frightened and to give ground and retreat gradually; he himself would give the signal for battle when necessary, and would give such commands as he saw the situation required. Curio's earlier confidence was increased by his interpretation of the present situation; thinking that the enemy were in retreat, he brought his forces down from the higher ground on to the plain.

41. He then advanced a fairly long way. After about sixteen miles, since his army were worn out with their exertions, he halted. Saburra gave his forces the signal; he marshalled the battle-line and began going around the ranks encouraging the men. He kept the infantry at a distance for the time being, using them merely for display, and put his cavalry into the actual battle-line. Curio rose to the occasion; he addressed his men, and called on them to place all their reliance on their own bravery. There was no lack of courage or enthusiasm for battle, either among the infantry, tired as they were, or among the cavalry, although they were few in number and exhausted. There were, however, only two hundred cavalry, the rest having stopped on the way. Wherever they attacked the enemy line they did, indeed, force the enemy to give ground, but they were unable to pursue them far or spur their horses on strongly. The enemy cavalry, on the other hand, began to outflank our line on both sides and trample our men down from behind. When some of our cohorts detached themselves from the line and charged, the Numidians, being fresh, would get away thanks to their speed; then, as our men were returning to their lines, the Numidians would encircle them and cut them off. As a result, it did not appear safe for our men either to stand their ground and keep in their ranks or to charge forward and try their fortune. The enemy's forces kept growing, as frequent reinforcements arrived from the king; our men's strength was sapped by exhaustion; and besides the wounded could neither leave the line nor be conveyed to a place of safety, since the whole army was surrounded and penned in

by the enemy cavalry. They abandoned hope of survival, and, as men are wont to do in their last hours, either lapsed into self-pity or asked for their relatives to be looked after, if fortune could rescue anyone from this peril. Fear and grief filled the whole army.

42. Curio, seeing their terror and realizing that neither his exhortations nor his pleas were being heeded, decided that in their wretched situation there was only one hope of safety left. He ordered them to occupy, in a body, the near-by hill and to convey the standards there. Saburra sent his cavalry there too and forestalled them. Then indeed our men fell into utter despair; some were killed by the cavalry as they attempted to flee, others threw themselves down, even though they were unhurt. Gnaeus Domitius, a cavalry officer, gathered a few horsemen round Curio and urged him to flee and save himself, and to make for the camp, promising that he himself would stay with him. Curio, however, declared that he would never go and face Caesar again after losing the army that Caesar had entrusted to him; and so he fought on and was killed. A very few of the cavalry got away from the battle; but those who had halted at the tail of the column, as mentioned above*, to rest their horses, seeing at a distance the rout of the entire army, retired safely to the camp. Every one of the infantry was killed.

43. On hearing the news, the quaestor Marcus Rufus, who had been left in camp by Curio, exhorted his men not to lose heart. They begged and entreated to be taken back by ship to Sicily. He promised to do this, and ordered the captains to have all the boats inshore at nightfall. Nevertheless there was general panic. Some were saying that Juba's forces were approaching, others that Varus was coming after them with his legions and that they could already see the dust of their approach, although none of this was so at all. Others again suspected that the enemy fleet was going to swoop on them. And so in the general terror everyone tried to fend for himself. Those on board the fleet were hurrying to set off. Their flight spurred the captains of the transport vessels to follow suit, and only a few small boats assembled to obey orders and carry out their task. The shores, however, were crowded and

[*Ch. 39.]

there was such controversy about who, among so many, should have priority of embarking, that some ships were sunk by the weight of the numbers on board, and the rest were deterred from getting too close by the fear that this might happen to them.

44. As a result only a few soldiers and fathers of families succeeded in getting on board, either by personal influence or appeals to compassion or by swimming out to the ships, and reached Sicily safely. The rest sent some centurions as envoys to Varus during the night and surrendered to him. Juba, seeing cohorts of these troops in front of the town on the following day, declared that they were his spoils and ordered the majority of them to be killed, choosing out a few whom he sent back to his kingdom. Varus protested that he had broken faith with him, but did not dare to resist. Juba himself rode into the town, escorted by a number of senators, including Servius Sulpicius and Licinius Damasippus, and within a few days he decided what he wanted done at Utica and gave orders accordingly; then he returned with all his forces to his kingdom.

PART III: THE GREAT CONFRONTATION

1. Caesar in Italy – Pompey's preparations

1. Caesar as dictator held the elections, and the consuls elected were Publius Servilius and Julius Caesar, this being the year in which Caesar could legally become consul[44].

Credit was rather tight throughout Italy and debts were not being paid. Caesar therefore decided to appoint arbitrators to evaluate property, movable and otherwise, at pre-war values, to be handed over to the creditors. He took this step because he thought it the most effective way to remove or lessen the fear of a total abolition of debts which usually accompanies wars or civil wars, and to preserve the credit of debtors. Further, by means of bills put to the people by the praetors and tribunes, he restored to their former status several persons convicted of corruption under a law of Pompey's[45] during the period in which Pompey had had a legionary garrison in the city. (Their trials had been completed in a single day, and sentences were pronounced by jurymen different from those who heard the evidence. Those condemned had offered their services to Caesar, if he wished to make use of them, at the beginning of the Civil War; since they had given him the chance, he now treated them as if he had actually availed himself of the offer.) He had decided that the credit for their restoration ought to appear to rest with the people, rather than with his good nature; while he did not wish to appear ungrateful in rendering due thanks, he did not want to be accused of arrogance in forestalling the generosity of the people.

2. He spent eleven days in the transaction of this business and in holding all the elections and the Latin holidays[46]. He then abdicated from the dictatorship, left Rome and went to Brundisium, where he had ordered twelve legions[47] and all the cavalry to muster. However, he found only enough ships to transport, at a pinch, 15,000 legionaries and 500 cavalry. This one thing, shortage of ships, hindered Caesar from bringing the war to a speedy end. But in fact the forces embarked were themselves rather depleted;

many had been lost during all the campaigns in Gaul, the long march from Spain had removed a great many, and the unhealthy autumn weather in Apulia and around Brundisium, after the wholesome regions of Gaul and Spain, had seriously affected the health of the whole army.

3. Pompey had gained a whole year, free from war and unharassed by enemies, for the collecting of forces. He had gathered a large fleet from Asia, the Cyclades, Corcyra, Athens, Pontus, Bithynia, Syria, Cilicia, Phoenicia and Egypt; he had had ships for a large fleet constructed in all these places; he had demanded and exacted a large quantity of money from Asia, Syria and all the kings and tetrarchs and dynasts and the free peoples of Achaea; and he had compelled the tax-farming companies in the provinces under his control to pay out large sums to him.

4. He had made up nine legions of Roman citizens – five which he had brought across from Italy; one of veterans, from Cilicia*; one from Crete and Macedonia, of veterans who had settled in these provinces after their discharge by their previous commanders; and two from Asia, which Lentulus when consul had ordered to be enrolled. Besides these he had distributed among the legions, as so-called 'supplements', large numbers of men from Thessaly, Boeotia, Achaea and Epirus, mixed with some of Antonius's old troops [48]. Over and above these legions, he was waiting for two to come from Syria with Scipio. He had 3,000 archers from Crete, Lacedaemon, Pontus, Syria and other states, two cohorts of slingers, of 600 men each, and 7,000 cavalry. Of these last, 600 were Galatians, whom Deiotarus had brought, and Ariobarzanes had brought 500 from Cappadocia; Cotys had supplied about the same number from Thrace and had sent his son Sadala; there were 200, of outstanding valour, from Macedonia, under the command of Rhascypolis; 500 from the troops of Gabinius at Alexandria†, brought over on the fleet by Pompey's son; 800 he had collected among his own slaves and herdsmen. Tarcondarius Castor and Domnilaus had supplied 300 from Gallograecia, and Castor had come in person, while Domnilaus had sent his son; 200, mostly mounted archers, had been sent from Syria by

* He made this up from two legions and called it 'the Twin'.

† Aulus Gabinius had left these as a garrison with King Ptolemy.

Antiochus of Commagene, to whom Pompey gave a large reward.
He added also Dardanians and Bessi, some of them mercenaries,
others conscripted or volunteers, as well as men from Macedonia,
Thessaly and other peoples and states; and so he made up the
number mentioned above.

5. He had obtained a large quantity of corn from Thessaly, Asia,
Egypt, Crete, Cyrene and elsewhere. He had decided to winter in
Dyrrachium and Apollonia and all the towns along the coast, so
as to prevent Caesar's crossing the sea, and to this end he had
stationed his fleet all along the coast. The Egyptian ships were
under the command of his son Pompeius; the Asiatic under Decimus Laelius and Gaius Triarius; the Syrian under Gaius Cassius;
the Rhodian under Gaius Marcellus with Gaius Coponius; the
Liburnian and Achaean fleet under Scribonius Libo and Marcus
Octavius. The control of the navy as a whole, however, he put in
the hands of Marcus Bibulus, who was in sole charge of the
organization; the supreme command rested with him.

6. On arrival at Brundisium, Caesar addressed his troops. 'We
have come almost to the end of our toils and dangers; you may
therefore leave your slaves and baggage behind in Italy with easy
minds. You must embark with only basic kit, to allow a greater
number of troops to be put on board. When we win, my
generosity in reward will answer all your hopes.' They all called
out to him, bidding him give what orders he liked; they would
carry them out cheerfully. They set sail on the fourth of January.
Seven legions were embarked[49], as indicated above. On the following day they reached land, at Acroceraunia. Mistrusting the harbours, because he believed them to be in the hands of the enemy,
he found a quiet anchorage in a rocky and dangerous stretch of
the shore, and without damaging a single ship he disembarked his
men, near a place called Palaeste.

2. Negotiations in Epirus

7. Lucretius Vespillo and Minucius Rufus were at Oricum with
eighteen Asiatic ships, of which they had been put in command
by Decimus Laelius; however, they lacked the confidence to ven-

ture out of harbour. Marcus Bibulus was at Corcyra with 110 ships; but Caesar was sighted off the coast before any word at all of his approach had been brought to that area, and as the ships were not ready to sail and the rowers were dispersed, Bibulus was not quick enough in coming out.

8. After disembarking the men, Caesar sent the ships back to Brundisium the same night, so that the rest of the legions and the cavalry could be brought across. His lieutenant Fufius Calenus was assigned to this mission, with orders to transport the legions with all possible speed; but the ships left land too late and, failing to avail themselves of the night breeze, they were intercepted during this return journey. Bibulus at Corcyra had received word of Caesar's arrival, and hoped to intercept some of the ships while they were loaded; in fact, he met them empty and captured about thirty. He vented on these his exasperation at his own negligence and his chagrin; he set fire to them all, burning the crews and captains as well, in the hope that the severity of the reprisals would be a deterrent to the rest. That job done, he put ships in every anchorage all along the coast from Sason to the harbour of Corcyra. He manned the guard-posts with extra care; although it was severe winter weather, he himself slept out on board ship, shirking no task or duty and expecting no help; his one aim was to get to grips with Caesar.

9. After the departure of the Liburnian ships from Illyricum, Marcus Octavius and his ships went to Salonae. There he stirred up the Dalmatians and other native peoples and persuaded Issa to cease supporting Caesar; at Salonae, he found the Roman community were not to be moved either by promises or by threats of danger, and so he embarked on a siege. The town is, indeed, protected by its position and its hill; but the Roman citizens quickly made wooden towers for their further protection. Since their small numbers made them incapable of effective resistance, when they themselves succumbed to numerous wounds they resorted to extreme measures to get help; they set free all their adult male slaves, and cut off the hair of all the women, to make ropes for the catapults. Seeing their determination, Octavius put five camps in a ring round the town, and began trying to reduce them both by a blockade and by attacks. They were prepared to endure

anything, but were particularly hard-pressed by lack of corn. They
sent a deputation to Caesar asking for his help in this; their other
hardships they sustained by themselves as best they could. After
a long time had elapsed, and the dragging on of the blockade had
made Octavius's men rather careless, the besieged took their
chance one midday, the time at which the Pompeians withdrew
from the walls. They stationed their boys and women-folk along
the walls, so that there should be no apparent departure from
their daily routine; they themselves formed into a body together
with the men they had recently set free and broke into the
nearest of Octavius's camps. They stormed it, then went straight
on to attack a second, then the third and fourth and finally the
remaining one; they drove the Pompeians out of all the camps,
killed a great many of them and forced the remainder, including
Octavius himself, to flee to their ships. Winter was now approaching[50], and after receiving such severe losses Octavius decided to
give up the siege and went to join Pompey at Dyrrachium.

10. We have told how Lucius Vibullius Rufus, an officer of
Pompey's, twice came into Caesar's power* and was released by
him. Caesar thought his own generosity to Vibullius would make
the latter a suitable person to send on a mission to Pompey.
Besides, he knew that Vibullius had influence with Pompey. The
substance of the message to be conveyed was this: 'Both of us
ought to stop being obstinate, disarm, and not tempt fortune
further. We have both suffered enough damage to serve as a
lesson and a warning, and make us fear the ills that still remain.
You have been driven from Italy, you have lost Sicily, Sardinia
and both the Spanish provinces, and 130 cohorts of Roman citizens in Italy and Spain. I have suffered the death of Curio, the
loss of the African army and the surrender of Antonius and his
men at Corcyra Nigra. Let us therefore spare both ourselves and
Rome; our own losses have given us enough proof of the power
of fortune in war. This is the best time of all to discuss peace,
while we are both confident and appear equally matched; but if
fortune should favour one, only a little, the one who seems the
better off will have nothing to do with terms of peace, nor will
he be satisfied with an equal share, when he believes he can have

* Once at Corfinium and a second time in Spain [C.W. I. 15, 38].

everything. As for the conditions of peace, since we ourselves have been unable to reach a settlement up till now, we should ask the Senate and people at Rome to frame terms. Meanwhile, it should content the State and ourselves if we at once swear publicly to dismiss our armies within three days. When we have laid down our arms and the support on which we now rely, then we shall perforce be content with the decision of the Senate and people. So that you can agree to this the more readily, I undertake to dismiss all my forces on land and in the various cities.'

11. Vibullius was put ashore at Corcyra. He thought it no less urgent to inform Pompey of Caesar's sudden arrival, so that the former could decide on the appropriate action to take, before he began to discuss peace terms. Accordingly, he travelled day and night, changing horses at every town for the sake of speed, in his haste to reach Pompey and inform him that Caesar was on his way. Pompey was at that time in Candavia, on the journey from Macedonia to winter quarters at Apollonia and Dyrrachium. The news alarmed him, and he began to press on towards Apollonia by forced marches, in case Caesar should occupy the coastal towns. Caesar, for his part, disembarked his men and set off the same day for Oricum; on his arrival, Lucius Torquatus, who was holding the town under Pompey's orders and had a garrison of Parthini there, closed the gates and tried to defend the town. He ordered the Greeks to get up on the wall and arm themselves, but they refused to fight against someone who had an official command from the Roman people, and the townsfolk actually attempted on their own initiative to let Caesar in. Torquatus had no hope of help; he opened the gates and surrendered himself and the town to Caesar, who let him go unharmed.

12. Once he had taken Oricum, Caesar went on without stopping to Apollonia. Lucius Staberius, the commander there, on hearing of his arrival began to have water conveyed into the citadel, to prepare its defences, and to demand hostages from the people of Apollonia. They refused to give them; further, they said they would not close the gates against a consul, nor would they take it upon themselves to judge differently from the whole of Italy and the Roman people. When he learned of their feelings, Staberius fled from Apollonia secretly. The citizens sent a

111

deputation to Caesar and admitted him to the town. Their example was followed by the people of Byllis and of Amantia and the rest of the neighbouring communities and the whole of Epirus, all of whom sent deputations to Caesar promising to obey his orders.

13. However, when Pompey learned what had happened at Oricum and Apollonia, he was afraid for Dyrrachium, and pressed on, travelling night and day. At the same time reports were coming in that Caesar was approaching. Pompey's army had been hurrying on without pause, making no difference between night and day, and such panic now seized them that almost all those from Epirus and the neighbouring regions deserted the standards, while a good many threw away their weapons and the march took on the appearance of a rout. Pompey halted near Dyrrachium and gave the order to mark out a camp site; since the army was still terror-stricken, Labienus took the initiative in coming forward and swearing that he would not desert Pompey, and would undergo the same fate as he, whatever fortune should dole out to them. The rest of the officers swore likewise; they were followed by the military tribunes and centurions, and the whole army took the same oath.

Since he had been forestalled in reaching Dyrrachium, Caesar stopped hurrying and made camp by the river Apsus in the territory of Apollonia, so that the communities which had behaved well towards him should have the security of the protection given by fortresses and watch-posts. He decided to wait there for the arrival of the rest of the legions from Italy, and to spend the winter in tents. Pompey did the same, and setting up camp across the river he brought all his troops and auxiliaries there.

14. At Brundisium, Calenus embarked the cavalry and the legions on such ships as he had, according to Caesar's orders, and set sail. When he had proceeded a short way from the harbour, he received a dispatch from Caesar warning him that the harbours and all the coastal area were commanded by their adversaries' ships. At this news Calenus turned back towards harbour and recalled all the vessels. One of these, as it was under private command and carried no troops, persisted on its way and did not obey his orders. It was carried down to Oricum and there overpowered by Bibulus. He took his vengeance on everyone aboard,

slaves and free, even the youngsters, killing every one of them. In this way the safety of the whole army turned on a brief space of time and a sheer coincidence[51].

15. Bibulus, as shown above, was with the fleet off Oricum; but while he was keeping Caesar away from the harbours and the sea, he himself was entirely debarred from the land in that region; for Caesar had stationed forces on guard, commanding all the coastal area, and there was no chance of getting wood and water or of mooring ships to the land. Bibulus and his men were in great difficulties and suffering serious shortages of necessary supplies, so much so that they were compelled to fetch wood and water, like their other provisions, by boat from Corcyra. It even happened on one occasion, when they had rather severe storms, that the men were forced to collect the dew which had formed in the night on the skins covering the ships. These hardships, however, they bore with endurance and calm, and were convinced that they must not leave the shores bare nor abandon the harbours.

They were, then, in the difficulties I have described; but after Libo had joined Bibulus, the two of them talked, from their ships, with the officers Manius Acilius and Statius Murcus, one of whom was in command on the town walls, the other in charge of the guards on land. They told them that they wished to speak to Caesar on matters of the highest importance, if they were afforded an opportunity, adding a few words to back this up and give the impression that they wanted to discuss a settlement. They asked for a truce in the meantime; this was granted, as they appeared to have something important to offer, and the Caesarians knew that Caesar was very anxious for a settlement. It was thought that Vibullius's mission had done some good.

16. Caesar at that time was near Buthrotum, a town opposite Corcyra. He had gone out with one legion to obtain supplies of corn, of which he was rather short, and to secure the communities farther inland. At Buthrotum, he received a dispatch from Acilius and Murcus informing him of the requests of Libo and Bibulus, and leaving his legion he himself returned to Oricum. On arrival, he summoned the Pompeians to a conference. Libo appeared and apologized for the absence of Bibulus. He was, he said, a very

hot-tempered man and had besides certain private quarrels with Caesar[52], dating from the time of his aedile-ship and praetor-ship; for these reasons he had avoided a meeting in case his temper should be a hindrance in such important and salutary negotiations. As for Pompey, he was and always had been very eager for a settlement and an armistice. They themselves had no power in the matter, as a decision of the council of war had entrusted supreme command of the war and everything connected with it to Pompey; however, once they were informed of Caesar's demands, they would transmit them to Pompey, who would, if they asked him, carry on the rest of the negotiations through them. Libo asked that the truce should be maintained in the meantime, until a messenger could return from Pompey, and that neither side should harm the other. He added a few words about his cause and his troops and allies. 17. To these last words Caesar did not see fit to reply at the time, nor do we consider there is sufficient reason for putting them on record now.

Caesar demanded safe conduct for envoys from himself to Pompey; Libo and Bibulus must either guarantee this or else personally receive the envoys and have them taken to Pompey. As for the truce, the spheres of operation were so divided between them that while they with their fleet were preventing his ships and reinforcements from reaching him, he was barring them from land and fresh water. If they wanted his blockade to be relaxed, they must themselves relax their own naval blockade; if they kept it up, he would maintain his. They could none the less discuss a settlement, even supposing the blockade was not dropped; it was no hindrance to discussion. Libo refused either to accept Caesar's envoys or to guarantee their safe conduct; he referred the whole matter to Pompey. The one thing he insisted on and pressed for most strongly was a truce. Caesar realized that Libo had entered on the entire discussion simply to escape from his immediate danger and privation, and that he had no real hope of a settlement to offer. He therefore returned to considering the conduct of the campaign.

18. After being prevented from landing for many days, Bibulus contracted a serious illness as a result of cold and hardship. As he could not have it attended to and would not abandon the com-

mission he had undertaken, he succumbed to the severity of the illness. On his death, there was no one person on whom supreme command devolved; each officer controlled his own squadron separately as he thought fit.

Once the flurry caused by Caesar's sudden arrival had subsided, Vibullius, as soon as appeared practicable, called in Libo and Lucceius and Theophanes[53], Pompey's principal confidential advisers, and began to discuss Caesar's proposals. He had barely started when Pompey interrupted and forbade him to say any more. 'What do I want,' he said, 'with life or citizenship which I shall appear to possess by Caesar's good grace? And that will be the ineradicable impression, if people think that I have been brought back to Italy, which I left voluntarily.' Caesar learned of this after the end of the war from persons who were present at the conversation. None the less he went on trying by other means to have conferences to discuss peace.

19. Between the two camps, Caesar's and Pompey's, there was only a single river, the Apsus, and the soldiers used frequently to talk together; those doing so had agreements that no missiles would be thrown across in the meantime. Caesar sent his lieutenant Publius Vatinius right up to the bank of the river, with orders to do whatever seemed most conducive to bringing about a peace, and to shout out frequently, asking whether, as between citizens, they might send two envoys to discuss peace – a privilege which had been granted even to the fugitives from the Pyrenean mountains[54] and to the pirates, and which ought especially to be granted as the aim was to stop citizens from bearing arms against each other. Vatinius said a good deal in a suppliant vein, as was fitting for his safety and that of them all, and was heard in silence by the troops on both sides. A reply came from the other side that Aulus Varro undertook to come the next day to talk and at the same time to see how they could arrange for envoys to come in safety and state their case; and a time was fixed for the meeting. When they met on the following day, a great crowd gathered on both sides and there was keen anticipation of the outcome; everyone appeared to be bent on peace. From the crowd, Titus Labienus stepped forward. He began to talk, in a very haughty manner, about peace, and to argue with

Vatinius. He was interrupted in the middle of his harangue by a shower of missiles from all directions. He himself was protected by the men's shields and avoided hurt, but several men were wounded, including Cornelius Balbus, Marcus Plotius, Lucius Tiburtius, and a good many centurions and ordinary soldiers. Then Labienus said : 'Now then, stop talking about an agreement. Until Caesar's head is delivered to us, there can be no peace.'

3. Trouble in Italy

20. During the same period, the praetor Marcus Caelius Rufus, at the start of his term of office, took up the cause of the debtors. He set up his official dais next to the seat of Gaius Trebonius, the urban praetor[55], and promised his help, if anyone should appeal against the evaluation of property and the payments decided on by arbitration, according to the procedure established by Caesar during his stay in Rome. However, Caesar's decree was equitable, and Trebonius was administering it humanely, holding the view that in the present times judgement should be given with clemency and moderation; the result was that no one could be found to initiate an appeal. For someone of even average audacity might plead poverty as an excuse or complain of misfortune, either his own in particular or the badness of the times in general, and dilate on the difficulties of auctioning goods; but among confessed debtors, who would have the brazen effrontery to try to keep his property intact? So no one was found to make this demand, and Caelius turned out to be more exacting than the interested parties themselves. After this start, so as not to appear to have embarked in vain on a discreditable crusade, Caelius proposed a bill to the effect that payment of debts could be deferred for six years, free of interest.

21. The consul Servilius and the other magistrates were against him, and Caelius was not getting the results he had hoped for. In an attempt to whip up popular enthusiasm, he abandoned the earlier proposal and introduced two bills, one remitting a year's rent on dwellings to tenants, the other proposing cancellation of existing debts. Trebonius was mobbed by a crowd and driven from

his dais; several persons were wounded. The consul Servilius raised the matter in the Senate, and they voted that Caelius should be debarred from political life[56]. In accordance with this decree the consul banned him from the Senate and made him leave the rostrum when he attempted to address an assembly. Caelius was smarting with indignation at his disgrace; he made a feint of going off to join Caesar, but secretly sent messengers to Milo[57], who had killed Clodius and been condemned on that count. He recalled Milo to Italy, because the latter still had the remains of a troop of gladiators from the games he had given, joined forces with him, and sent him to the district around Thurii to incite the herdsmen[58] to revolt. Caelius himself went to Casilinum; however, his standards and arms at Capua were seized, at the same time as the gladiators at Naples were discovered to be planning the betrayal of the town. His plans were revealed and he was shut out of Capua. The Roman community had taken up arms and considered that he must be treated as an enemy; so, afraid that he might be in danger, he abandoned his design and went off elsewhere.

22. Meanwhile, Milo was sending letters around to the towns saying that he was acting on the instructions and with the authority of Pompey, from whom he had received orders through Vibullius; he was trying also to win over those whom he judged to be in difficulties from debts. Making no progress with these people, he broke open some slave barracks and began an assault on Cosa in the territory of Thurii. There, when he attempted to win over some of the townsfolk and offered money to Caesar's Gallic and Spanish cavalry who had been put in as a garrison, they killed him. So an enterprise which had a great beginning and had made all Italy anxious, the magistrates being preoccupied and the times troubled, had a quick and easy ending.

4. Antony runs the gauntlet

23. Libo left Oricum with the fleet of fifty ships of which he was in command and sailed to Brundisium. There he occupied the island opposite the harbour, since he thought it preferable to

blockade and keep watch on the one place from which our forces must set out, rather than the whole coast-line and its harbours. Arriving suddenly, he seized and burned some transport vessels, taking away one that was loaded with grain, and causing great alarm among our men. He disembarked soldiers and archers by night, dislodged a garrison of cavalry, and, thanks to the favourable terrain, he had such success that he sent a dispatch to Pompey telling him to have the rest of the ships beached and repaired, if he liked, as he himself with his fleet would keep back Caesar's reinforcements.

24. At that time, Antony was at Brundisium. Trusting in the courage of his men, he took about sixty ships' boats, fitted them with wicker hurdles and screens and put picked men on board. He stationed these severally at various points along the shore and ordered two triremes which he had had built at Brundisium to advance to the mouth of the harbour, as though to allow the rowers to exercise. Libo observed that they had advanced rather too boldly, and he sent five quadriremes against them, hoping to cut them off. When these came near our ships, our veterans began withdrawing towards the harbour, while the Pompeians, in the flush of excitement, pressed after them without sufficient caution. Then a signal was given and Antony's boats suddenly bore down on the enemy from all directions. At the first encounter they took one of the quadriremes, complete with its rowers and marines, and forced the rest to flee ignominiously. A further source of distress was that Antony had stationed cavalry all along the sea shore, so that the Pompeians were unable to get water. This difficulty, together with his shameful rout, so distressed Libo that he left Brundisium and abandoned the blockade of our men.

25. Many months had now passed and winter was well advanced[59], and still the ships and legions did not come from Brundisium to Caesar. To Caesar, it seemed as if several opportunities had been missed, because certainly winds had often blown to which he thought they must surely entrust themselves. The more time passed, the keener was the watch kept by the commanders of the Pompeian fleets and the more confident they were that they could keep our men back. They were goaded on by frequent dispatches from Pompey, rebuking them for not having stopped

Caesar crossing in the first place, and urging them to stop the rest of his army; and they were awaiting a season which, as the winds dropped, became every day more difficult for transports. This situation made Caesar anxious, and he wrote sharply to his men at Brundisium, ordering them, when they got a suitable wind, not to miss the chance of sailing, if they could hold a course even for the coast near Apollonia and land there. This region was the most clear from watch by ships, since the Pompeians did not dare to venture too far away from the harbours.

26. The Caesarians responded by summoning up their courage and boldness; under the direction of Mark Antony and Fufius Calenus, with the men themselves expressing eagerness and ready to face any danger to save Caesar, they set sail with a south wind and on the following day sailed past Apollonia and Dyrrachium. They were observed from land, and Gaius Coponius, who was in charge of the Rhodian fleet at Dyrrachium, led his vessels out of harbour. The wind having dropped, they had already drawn near our ships, when the same south wind freshened again and saved us. For all that, Coponius did not give up trying; in the hope that the persistent efforts of his sailors could overcome even the violence of the gale, he kept on pursuing none the less, even when our men had been carried by the extreme force of the wind past Dyrrachium. They took advantage of the kindness of fortune, but were still afraid of an attack from the fleet, if the wind should happen to drop. When they came to a harbour called Nymphaeum, about three miles past Lissus, they put the ships in there, thinking less of danger from the wind* than of danger from the enemy fleet. As soon as they entered harbour, by an unbelievable stroke of luck the wind, which had been blowing from the south for the past two days, veered round to the south-west.

27. This could be regarded as a sudden reversal of fortune. Those who had just been alarmed for themselves, were being received into a secure harbour; those who had menaced our fleet were forced to feel alarm at their own danger. And so, with the change of circumstances, the storm protected our ships while battering the Rhodian ships, so much so that all the decked ships, sixteen

---

* This harbour had protection from the south-west wind, but not from the south.

in number, were dashed to pieces and wrecked, and of the large numbers of rowers and marines on board some were dashed on the rocks and killed, and some were hauled off by our men. All the latter Caesar spared and sent home.

28. Two of our ships which had sailed more slowly were overtaken by night and not knowing where the rest had landed they halted at anchor off Lissus. Otacilius Crassus, who was in charge at Lissus, sent a number of skiffs and small boats and made ready to attack them; at the same time, he began negotiations for the surrender of the men and promised that they would not be harmed. One of the ships had on board 220 men from a newly-recruited legion, and the other had just under 200 veterans. This incident showed the extent to which a courageous spirit preserves its possessor; for the recruits were terrified by the number of ships and worn out by sea-sickness, and on receiving an assurance that the enemy would do them no harm, they gave themselves up to Otacilius; they were all brought before him and, in violation of the oath, were brutally put to death in his presence. The veterans, on the other hand, who had also suffered the hardships of the storm and confinement in the hold, had no thought of falling short of that degree of bravery they had always displayed. By discussing terms and pretending to negotiate a surrender they spun out the time during the first part of the night, then they forced the steersman to run the ship aground and, finding themselves a suitable place, they spent the rest of the night there. At dawn, Otacilius sent against them about 400 cavalry, who were guarding that part of the coast, together with men-at-arms from the garrison. The Caesarians defended themselves and after killing several of the enemy they reached our forces safely.

29. Meanwhile, the community of Roman citizens occupying Lissus* admitted Antony and gave him all manner of aid. Otacilius, fearing for his own safety, fled from the town and went to Pompey. Antony disembarked his forces, which consisted of three legions of veterans, one of recruits and 800 cavalry. He sent most of the ships back to Italy to bring across the rest of the troops and the cavalry. He left the 'punts' (a kind of Gallic craft) at

* Caesar had previously assigned the town to them and had had it fortified[60].

Lissus, with the idea that if Pompey, thinking Italy was deserted as was the widespread belief, should take his army across there, Caesar would have some means of following him. He quickly sent messengers to Caesar with details of where he had landed and how many men he had brought.

30. Caesar and Pompey received the news at about the same time; for they had seen the ships sailing past Apollonia and Dyrrachium and had themselves made their way overland after them, but for the first few days they did not know where they had put in. Once the facts were known, each adopted a different policy. Caesar's aim was to join up with Antony as soon as possible; Pompey intended to place himself in Antony's line of advance and, if possible, make a surprise attack from ambush. Both led out their armies on the same day from their camps by the Apsus. Pompey had no obstacles to his march as he did not have to cross the river, and he hurried on by forced marches towards Antony. When he knew that Antony was near, he found a suitable spot and halted his forces there. He kept them all within camp and forbade them to light fires, in order to keep their arrival the more secret. Word of this was immediately brought to Antony by some Greeks. He sent messengers off to Caesar and stayed in camp for a day; on the day after that, Caesar arrived. On learning of Caesar's approach, Pompey withdrew from his position, in case he should be hemmed in between the two armies, and went with all his forces to Asparagium in the territory of Dyrrachium where he pitched camp in a suitable spot.

5. The lieutenants in Macedon

31. During this period Scipio, after sustaining some setbacks around Mount Amanus, had adopted the title *imperator*[61] and had then proceeded to demand large sums of money from local communities and rulers. He also exacted from the tax-farmers of his province the arrears of money for the last two years as well as an advance on the next year's payments, and he required the whole province to supply cavalry. These were mustered; and leaving behind him on the borders the hostile Parthians, who a short time

before had killed the general Marcus Crassus[62] and had held Marcus Bibulus[63] to siege, he led the legions and cavalry out of Syria. The province had reached a state of extreme apprehension and fear of a war with Parthia, and not a few of the troops were heard to say that they would go against the enemy if they were led, but they would not take arms against a citizen and a consul. Scipio took his legions to Pergamum and distributed them to billets among the wealthiest citizens as their winter quarters; then he gave them large amounts of cash and, to secure their good-will, turned the towns over to them for plunder.

32. Meanwhile the sums of money demanded were being extorted with the utmost harshness all over the province[64]. Moreover, many different kinds of devices were thought up to satisfy avarice. A poll-tax was imposed on slaves and free men; there were taxes on pillars and on doors; there were requisitions of grain, troops, weapons, rowers, missile engines, transport. So long as a name could be found for the object, this was held to justify the exaction. Not only in cities, but practically in hamlets and in single little fortresses, men were put in command with independent authority, and any extremes of cruelty or atrocity on their part earned them the name of being good men and good citizens. The province was full of official attendants and official commands, it was packed with officers and collectors, who filled their own pockets as well as exacting the money that was demanded. They would allege that they had been driven from home and country and lacked all the necessities of life, so as to cover their dishonourable exactions with a fair-seeming excuse. A further source of distress was that interest rates had risen very high, as generally happens in wartime, when all the available money is in demand. In these circumstances, they said that postponement for a day was as good as a present. In this way, the debts of the province were multiplied during these two years. In spite of all this, the Roman citizens in the province were not spared; fixed sums of money were demanded from separate citizen communities and cities, and it was alleged that these were being exacted as loans, in accordance with a decree of the Senate. The tax-collectors, as in Syria, were made to give advances on the following year's taxes.

33. Further, Scipio ordered the monies which had for a long

time past been stored up in the temple of Diana at Ephesus to be removed. He fixed a day for this to be done; when he arrived at the temple, accompanied by several of the senatorial order, whom he had summoned to be there, he was given a dispatch from Pompey with the news that Caesar had crossed the sea with his legions, and orders to hurry with his army to join Pompey, and postpone everything else. He then dismissed those he had summoned; he himself began to prepare to travel to Macedonia, and set out after a few days. This event saved the money of Ephesus.

34. Caesar joined up with Antony's army and withdrew from Oricum the legion he had put there to guard the sea coast. He decided that he must test the feelings of the provinces and advance farther. Since he had received deputations from Thessaly and Aetolia promising that if he sent in forces the communities there would obey his orders, he sent to Thessaly Lucius Cassius Longinus, with a newly-recruited legion, called the Twenty-Seventh, and 200 cavalry, and to Aetolia Gaius Calvisius Sabinus with five cohorts and a few cavalry. Since these regions were not far away, he strongly urged these officers to try to secure a corn supply. He ordered Gnaeus Domitius Calvinus to proceed to Macedonia with two legions, the Eleventh and the Twelfth, and 500 cavalry. From that part of the province which had the title of 'free', the local ruler, Menedemus, had been sent as an envoy. He guaranteed the zealous support of all his people.

35. Calvisius, on his arrival, was received with the utmost cordiality by all the Aetolians. He expelled the Pompeian garrisons from Calydon and Naupactus and took possession of the whole of Aetolia. Cassius arrived in Thessaly with his legion. He met a varying reception in different communities as there were two factions there. Hegesaretos, a man whose influence was long established, favoured Pompey's cause, while Petraeus, a young man of very high rank, was energetically supporting Caesar with his own resources and those of his people.

36. At the same time Domitius arrived in Macedonia, and numerous deputations from the local communities began coming to him. Then word came that Scipio was close at hand with his legions. This gave rise to universal speculation and rumour; for in general when something unexpected happens rumour goes

beyond the facts. Scipio wasted no time in Macedonia but hurried on towards Domitius; then when he was about twenty miles away he suddenly turned aside to go after Cassius Longinus in Thessaly. This he did so quickly that his approach and his arrival were reported simultaneously. To expedite his journey, he left Marcus Favonius at the river Haliacmon, which separates Macedonia from Thessaly, with a force of eight cohorts to guard the legions' baggage, and ordered him to build a fortress there. At the same time the cavalry of King Cotys, which habitually hovered on the frontiers of Thessaly, swooped down on Cassius's camp. Cassius was terrified. He had heard of Scipio's approach and seeing the cavalry, which he thought were Scipio's, he made for the mountains around Thessaly, and from there began to journey towards Ambracia.

However, as Scipio was hastening in pursuit a dispatch overtook him from Marcus Favonius, saying that Domitius was approaching with his legions and that he could not maintain the position where he had been stationed without help from Scipio. At this, Scipio changed his mind and his route. He gave up the pursuit of Cassius and hurried to help Favonius. And so by dint of marching on without stopping day and night he arrived in the nick of time; for the first of his advance-guard were seen at the same time as the dust of Domitius's army came into view. Thus Cassius was saved by the energy of Domitius and Favonius by the speed of Scipio.

37. Scipio stayed two days in the base camp near the river Haliacmon, which flowed between his own camp and that of Domitius, and at dawn on the third day he led his army across a ford, pitched camp, and on the following morning drew up his forces in front of the camp. Then also Domitius decided that he ought to bring out his legions without hesitation and engage battle. There was a plain about six miles long between the two camps, but while Domitius brought his own lines close up to Scipio's camp, the latter persisted in staying close by the rampart. Domitius's troops were restrained from engaging, although with difficulty; but they were most effectively deterred by the fact that a stream with very steep banks flowed just beneath Scipio's camp and hampered their advance. Scipio saw how keen and eager they

were to fight; he suspected that on the following day he would either be forced against his will to fight or, if he stayed in camp, he would be utterly disgraced, as he had raised high hopes with his arrival; and so he followed his reckless advance with an ignominious withdrawal. During the night, without even giving the order to strike camp, he crossed the river, went back to the same area as he had come from and there pitched camp on a natural eminence near the river. A few days later, he placed some cavalry in ambush by night in the place where our men had been in the habit of coming for fodder during the preceding days; and when Quintus Varus, Domitius's cavalry commander, came according to daily routine, they suddenly rose up out of ambush. Our men, however, stood up to their attack bravely. Each man quickly went to his own place in the ranks and then they all, on their part, charged the enemy. They killed about 800 of them and put the rest to flight, then returned to camp with the loss of two of their own men.

38. Then Domitius, hoping that Scipio could be enticed into a battle, pretended to be forced by shortage of corn to move. The order to strike camp was given, and after advancing three miles he stationed the whole of the infantry and cavalry in a suitable concealed spot. Scipio made ready to follow and sent a large part of the cavalry ahead to reconnoitre and find out the route taken by Domitius. They advanced, and the leading squadrons had already entered the ambush when their suspicions were aroused by the neighing of horses. They began to turn back, while those following them, seeing their sudden return, halted. Since the ambush was discovered, our men, so as not to waste time waiting for the rest, cut off the two squadrons which they had caught. The only one who escaped was an officer, Marcus Opimius; all the rest of these squadrons they either killed or brought as prisoners to Domitius.

6. Stalemate at Dyrrachium

39. Caesar, after withdrawing the guards from the sea coast, as related above*, left three cohorts at Oricum to protect the town,

[* Ch. 34.]

and also to guard the warships which he had brought across from Italy. This commission, and the town, were in the charge of Manius Acilius, a lieutenant, who brought the ships into the inner harbour behind the town and moored them to land. He sank a transport ship in the mouth of the harbour and fastened another to it. On top of these he built a tower commanding the actual entry to the harbour and manned it with soldiers who were charged to protect it against any sudden mishaps.

40. News of this reached Pompey's son Gnaeus, who was in command of the Egyptian fleet, and he came to Oricum. Using large numbers of cables, he hauled up the scuttled ship; the other ship which had been posted on guard by Acilius he attacked with several vessels, on which he had built towers all up to the same height. He therefore had the advantage of fighting from a loftier position; he kept sending fresh men in to replace those who were tired; and at other points he was making assaults on the walls of the town, both with scaling ladders from land and also from the fleet, with the object of splitting up the enemy's forces. As a result, his opponents were overcome by exhaustion and by the sheer numbers of his missiles; he dislodged the defenders, all of whom fled in the ship's boats, and captured the ship. At the same time he captured a natural reef which lay on the other side of the town and made the site a peninsula; he then put rollers under four biremes and dragged them across the bank with winches into the inner harbour. This enabled him to attack from both sides the warships which were lying moored to the land, empty, and he seized four and burned the rest. On completing these operations, he left there Decimus Laelius, whom he had withdrawn from the Asiatic fleet, and who was preventing supplies from Byllis and Amantia from being brought into the town. He himself proceeded to Lissus, attacked the thirty transport ships left by Mark Antony in the harbour and burned them all. He attempted to storm Lissus, which was defended by the Roman citizens of the community there and by the soldiers whom Caesar had sent as a garrison, and after spending three days and losing a few men in the assault he retired without achieving his aim.

41. When Caesar learned that Pompey was near Asparagium he set off there with his army. On the way he stormed the town of

the Parthini, where Pompey had a garrison, and after two days he reached Pompey and camped near him. On the following day he led out all his forces, formed them up in line of battle, and offered Pompey an opportunity of settling the issue. When he observed that Pompey did not stir from his position, he led the army back to camp and decided he must try a different course. And so on the following day he set off with all his forces for Dyrrachium, making a long detour and going by a difficult and narrow track, hoping either to force Pompey towards Dyrrachium or to cut him off from the town, as he had gathered all his food supplies and war materials there. He succeeded in doing the latter. Pompey at first did not realize Caesar's intention, seeing him going off in a different direction, and thought he had been forced to withdraw by lack of corn; later, he learned the truth from scouts, and on the following day he struck camp, hoping that he could get ahead of Caesar by a shorter route. Caesar had suspected this would happen; exhorting his men to endure fatigue cheerfully, he stopped for only a small part of the night; he reached Dyrrachium in the morning, just as the head of Pompey's column came into view in the distance, and pitched camp.

42. Pompey, being cut off from Dyrrachium and having failed to obtain his objective, adopted an alternative plan. He built a strong camp on a height called Petra, which was fairly accessible by ship and afforded vessels protection from certain winds. He ordered part of the war fleet to muster there, and supplies of corn and foodstuffs to be conveyed there from Asia and all the other regions which he controlled. Caesar judged that the war was going to be protracted for rather a long time and he despaired of getting supplies from Italy. Pompey's forces were in possession of the entire coast and his own fleets, which had been wintering in Sicily, Gaul and Italy, were a long time in coming. He therefore sent Quintus Tillius and the lieutenant Lucius Canuleius to Epirus to get corn, and as that district was rather far away he had granaries built in certain spots and assigned to the neighbouring communities the task of providing transport for the corn. He also gave orders that what corn there was should be collected from Lissus, the Parthini and all the forts. This corn was very scanty in amount. The reason was partly the nature of the countryside

itself, since it is a rugged, mountainous area and the inhabitants mostly use imported corn; but there was also the fact that Pompey had foreseen this and during the preceding days had plundered the Parthini. He had pillaged and ransacked their houses and had his cavalry carry off to Petra all the grain they had gathered.

43. On learning this, Caesar planned a strategy in accordance with the nature of the terrain. Around Pompey's camp were several high, rugged hills. First he sent forces to occupy these hills, and built forts on them; then he began constructing a line of entrenchments, as the nature of the ground allowed in each case, from one fort to another, to surround Pompey. His aims, taking into consideration his own difficulties over the corn supply and Pompey's great cavalry strength, were to reduce the danger involved in bringing in corn and supplies for the army and at the same time to prevent Pompey from getting fodder and make his cavalry ineffective. He had also a third aim – to diminish the high degree of prestige which Pompey appeared to have among foreign peoples; this would be attained once the word should have spread around the world that Pompey was blockaded by Caesar and did not dare to join battle.

44. Pompey was reluctant to leave the sea, because supplies for the army were being brought in by ship, and Dyrrachium, because he had stored there all his war equipment – missiles, weapons, ballistic engines; but he could not stop Caesar's entrenchments without consenting to fight, which he had decided he must not do at that time. The only course remaining was, as a last resort, to occupy as many hills and hold as wide an area with his troops as possible, so as to spread out Caesar's forces as far as he could; and this he did. He built twenty-four forts embracing a circuit of fifteen miles and got fodder within this area, which also included a number of places sown with crops, on which for the time being he could graze the beasts. And so, while our men were seeing to it that their own line of entrenchments went continuously from one fortress to the next, with no place where the Pompeians could break out and attack them from the rear, the latter, in the area within, were constructing a continuous line of entrenchments in order to prevent our men penetrating anywhere and surrounding their rear. The Pompeians were winning, both

because they had more men and because the inner area had a smaller perimeter. Pompey had decided against using his entire forces to check Caesar and so becoming involved in a regular battle; but wherever there was a position that Caesar wanted to occupy, Pompey sent in his archers and slingers, of which he had a large number. Many of our men were being wounded; they had become very much afraid of the archers and had made themselves tunics or coverings of wadding, patchwork or hides to ward off the missiles.

45. Both sides put all their efforts into securing strategic positions. Caesar was trying to confine Pompey in as small an area as possible, Pompey to occupy as many heights as possible and enclose the largest possible area. As a result, there were constant skirmishes. In one of these, when Caesar's Ninth legion had occupied a certain position and begun to fortify it, Pompey occupied a near-by hill, just opposite, and began to hamper our men at work. As there was almost level ground affording access to our position on one side, he first of all threw round it a cordon of archers and slingers and then sent in large numbers of light infantry and brought up missile engines, thus hindering our work of fortification; for it was not easy for our men simultaneously to defend themselves and to work at the fortifications. When Caesar saw that his men were exposed to injury on all sides, he ordered them to withdraw and abandon the position. The withdrawal route was down a slope. The enemy pressed on them all the more hotly and harassed their withdrawal, because they appeared to have abandoned the position out of fear. It is said that on that occasion Pompey boastfully remarked to his men that he would not object to being called an incompetent general if Caesar's legions withdrew without severe damage from the position into which they had imprudently advanced.

46. Caesar, fearing for the safe withdrawal of his men, ordered screens to be brought up to the edge of the hill as a protection against the enemy and set up facing them, and behind these he ordered soldiers, in concealment, to dig a fairly wide trench and create as many obstacles as possible all over the ground. He himself stationed slingers at suitable points to give covering fire to our men as they withdrew. On completing these preparations he

ordered the legion to be withdrawn. At this, the Pompeians began pressing hard after our men, with more insolence and daring than ever, and they threw down the screens in front of the entrenchments, so as to cross the trenches. Caesar observed this, and was afraid that his men might appear to have been routed rather than withdrawn and that some worse setback might be sustained. When they had gone about half-way he made Antony, who was in charge of that legion, urge them to the attack, and gave the order for a trumpet signal and a charge at the enemy. The men of the Ninth suddenly launched their javelins in unison, charged at a run from lower ground up the slope, drove the Pompeians headlong, and made them turn tail. The latter were seriously hampered in their retreat by the upright hurdles, the poles planted in their way and the uncompleted trenches. Our men, however, were satisfied to get away without disaster. After killing several men and losing five of their own in all, they retired and, occupying other hills a little behind this one, completed their entrenchments.

47. This was a new and unusual kind of warfare, in the number of forts, in the extent of the area and of the entrenchments, in the whole nature of the blockade, and in various other respects as well. For, when one side tries to blockade another, it is usually when they have attacked and hemmed in a routed and weakened enemy, or one overcome in battle or demoralized by some setback, and when they themselves have the superiority in numbers of cavalry and infantry; and the motive of the blockade is usually to cut the enemy off from corn supplies. On this occasion, however, Caesar was hemming in fresh and unharmed forces with a smaller number of troops. The enemy had plentiful supplies of everything – for every day large numbers of ships were coming in from all directions to bring supplies, and no wind could blow without their having a favourable course from some direction or other. Caesar himself, on the other hand, had used up all the available corn supplies for a long way around and was suffering extreme shortage. His troops were putting up with this with remarkable endurance; for they recollected that when they suffered the same hardships the previous year in Spain, by their efforts and their fortitude they had brought to an end a great war. They remembered that they endured severe privation at Alesia and even

more at Avaricum, and had come off victorious over very powerful tribes. They did not refuse barley when it was offered, nor vegetables; and meat, of which there was a large supply from Epirus, they held in great esteem[65].

48. Those who had been in the valleys had also found a kind of root, called 'chara', and this when mixed with milk greatly alleviated their need. They made it into something resembling bread. There was a large quantity of it; they made this into loaves and when the Pompeians, talking to our men, taunted them with famine, they used frequently to throw these loaves at them, to dash their hopes.

49. The corn crops were now beginning to ripen and the mere hope helped them to bear their want, since they trusted that they would soon have plenty. Remarks could frequently be heard from the soldiers talking while on guard, saying that they would live on the bark of trees sooner than let Pompey slip out of their grasp. They were also pleased to hear from deserters that the Pompeians were maintaining their cavalry horses, but that the rest of their animals had been killed, and that the men themselves were finding their health affected by their cramped conditions, the foul smell from the large number of corpses, and the daily toil, as they were not accustomed to construction work. Their health also suffered from the extreme shortage of water, for Caesar had either diverted or blocked with great dams all the rivers and streams running down to the sea; the district was mountainous, with valleys so narrow as to form canyons, and these he had blocked up by driving piles into the ground and heaping up earth against them to hold back the water. The Pompeians were therefore obliged to look for low-lying, marshy spots and dig wells there, thus having a further toil added to their daily tasks; and in any case these springs were rather a long way from some of their forts and soon dried up in the heat. Caesar's army, on the other hand, was in excellent health and had plentiful supplies of water, as well as abundance of all kinds of foodstuffs except corn. However, they saw a better season daily approaching and greater hopes held out, as the corn ripened.

50. In this new fashion of campaigning, new methods of fighting were being devised by both sides. When the Pompeians

131

observed from the fires that cohorts of our men were sleeping out at night beside the fortifications, they attacked in silence, all shot arrows into the throng and then hastily retreated. Our men learned from their experience and devised a remedy; they built their fires elsewhere....[66]

51. Meanwhile Publius Sulla, whom Caesar had put in charge of the camp in his absence, learned of this and came to the help of the cohort with two legions. As a result of their arrival, the Pompeians were easily repulsed. They did not even withstand the sight of our charge; as soon as the front ranks were dislodged the rest turned and gave ground. When our men were following up, however, Sulla called them back, to prevent their pursuing too far. Most people, indeed, think that if he had been willing to pursue more keenly the war might have been concluded on that day; but his decision does not appear to deserve censure, for the functions of a lieutenant are different from those of a general. One has to act entirely according to orders, the other must take important decisions independently. Sulla had been left by Caesar in the camp, and when he had freed his own men he was content with this. He did not wish to fight a full-scale battle (a proceeding which might in any case result in some misfortune) in case he should seem to have usurped the rôle of the general.

The circumstances of the retreat gave the Pompeians great difficulty; for they had advanced from an unfavourable position and halted at the top of a hill. If they were to withdraw down the slope, they were afraid that our men might press them hard from higher ground. Nor was there much time left before sunset, for in hopes of bringing matters to a conclusion they had prolonged the encounter almost until night. Pompey therefore took the course forced on him by circumstances and occupied a certain hillock which was so far from our lines that no missiles shot from engines could reach it. Here he took up his position, fortifying it and keeping all his forces there.

52. At the same time there was fighting in another two places. Pompey had made assaults on several forts so as to draw our forces apart and prevent help being brought from the neighbouring garrisons. In one place, Volcatius Tullus withstood with three cohorts the attack of a legion and beat it down from there. In

another, Germans attacked our fortifications, killed several men and retired unharmed.

53. Thus on one day there were six engagements[67], three at Dyrrachium and three at the fortifications; and when all these were reckoned up, we discovered that the Pompeians had lost about 2,000 men, including several recalled veterans and centurions. Among these was Valerius Flaccus, son of that Valerius Flaccus who had been assigned Asia as propraetor; and six military standards were captured. Not more than twenty of our men were lost in all the skirmishes put together. In the fort, however, not a single soldier escaped being wounded, and four centurions from one cohort lost their eyes. Wishing to bring proof of their exertions and the danger they had undergone, the men picked up about 30,000 arrows that had been fired into the fort and counted them out before Caesar, and they brought him the shield of the centurion Scaeva[68], in which were found 120 holes. In return for Scaeva's services to himself and to the State, Caesar gave him 200,000 sesterces and announced he was promoting him from the eighth rank up to the first centurionate – for it was certain that it was largely thanks to him that the fortress had been saved; and later he lavishly rewarded the cohort with double wages, corn, clothes, food allowances and military decorations.

54. During the night Pompey built large additional fortifications. In the ensuing days he built towers and, raising the defence-works to a height of fifteen feet, he shielded that part of the camp with screens. After five days, he got another cloudy night and barricaded all the gates of the camp, putting obstacles in front. Then in the small hours of the morning he led his army out in silence and returned to his old lines.

55. Every day after that Caesar led his army out on to level ground and drew it up in formation, to see if Pompey would be willing to give battle, bringing his legions almost up to Pompey's camp; his first line was only just out of range of a javelin or catapult-shot from Pompey's rampart. Pompey, to keep up his reputation, drew up his forces in front of the camp – in such a way, however, that the third line was right against the rampart, while the whole army was drawn up within range of covering fire.

56. When Cassius Longinus and Calvisius Sabinus had, as shown above[69], received the submission of Aetolia, Acarnania and Amphilochia, Caesar decided that he must advance a little farther and try Achaea. He therefore sent Quintus Calenus there and attached to him Sabinus and Calvisius with their cohorts. On word of their approach, Rutilius Lupus, who had been sent into Achaea by Pompey and was in control there, began to fortify the Isthmus to keep Fufius out. Calenus received the voluntary submission of Delphi, Thebes and Orchomenus, and took several cities by storm. He sent envoys round to the rest to try to persuade them to be friends with Caesar. Such were the tasks occupying Fufius.

57. These events were going on in Achaea and near Dyrrachium. Meanwhile, it was known that Scipio had arrived in Macedonia, and Caesar sent to him Aulus Clodius, a friend of both. Caesar had begun to count him among his own intimates after having in the first place had him introduced with recommendations by Scipio. He gave Clodius a letter and a verbal message, of which the gist was this: he had tried in every way to secure peace; he thought that the fact that nothing had yet been decided was the fault of those whom he had chosen to be his agents in this matter, because they had been afraid of carrying his proposals to Pompey at an inopportune time. Now, Scipio's personal authority was such that he could not only state his own views freely but he could even to a large extent control Pompey and direct him when he went astray; moreover, Scipio had command of an army in his own right, so that over and above his personal influence he had the power to exercise compulsion. If he were to use this power, then his alone would be the credit of securing a respite for Italy, peace for the provinces and salvation for the empire. Clodius went with this message to Scipio. During the first few days he was apparently given a ready hearing but on the succeeding days he was not admitted to discussion. We learned later after the war was over that Scipio was severely taken to task by Favonius, and Clodius returned to Caesar without accomplishing his mission.

58. To make it easier to hem in Pompey's cavalry near Dyrrachium and prevent them getting fodder, Caesar constructed large

fortifications across the two approaches to the town, which as we said [70] were narrow, and set fortresses there. After a few days, when Pompey realized that his cavalry were useless, he brought them back by ship to within his own lines. There was a severe shortage of fodder, so much so that they were feeding the horses with leaves stripped from trees and with the tender roots of reeds, which they pounded up; for they had consumed all the crops of sown corn within their lines. They were being obliged to bring fodder up from Corcyra and Acarnania, a long voyage away, and as the supply of this became less, to supplement it with barley and so to maintain the horses. Eventually, however, supplies began to fail everywhere, not only barley and fodder and cut grass but even leaves from the trees, and the horses were wasted with hunger. Pompey decided he must make some attempt to break out.

7. Setbacks for Caesar

59. Caesar had in his cavalry two brothers, Allobroges. These were Roucillus and Egus, the sons of Adbucillus, who had been chieftain of his tribe for many years. They were men of outstanding courage, of whose excellent and stalwart service Caesar had availed himself in all his campaigns in Gaul. For these reasons, he had assigned to them the highest magistracies among their own people, and had had them exceptionally enrolled in the Senate [71]. He had given them lands in Gaul captured from the enemy and large monetary rewards and had turned them from poor men into men of substance. Their valour not only earned them Caesar's esteem but also made them popular in the army; however, relying on Caesar's friendship and carried away by stupid, barbarian vanity they began to look down on their own people, to cheat the cavalry of their pay, and to appropriate all the plunder for themselves. All the cavalry, very upset at this, came to Caesar and complained publicly of the wrongdoings of these two. Amongst other charges, they said that by making a false return of the numbers of cavalry they were embezzling the pay of several men.

60. Caesar did not think that this was a suitable occasion for taking cognizance of the matter. Making large allowances because of their valour he postponed the whole business. He reproved them in private for using the cavalry for their profit. He told them that they should look to his friendship for everything and base their hopes for the future on his kindness in the past. However, these events brought them into general disrepute and contempt, as they gathered not only from the gibes of others but also from the private judgement of their own consciences. Impelled therefore by shame, and thinking perhaps that they were not being let off scot-free but were merely being reserved for a future occasion, they decided to leave us and try new fortune and new friends. They talked with a few of their adherents, together with whom they dared to undertake such a crime, and first of all they attempted, as we learned after the war, to kill the cavalry commander Gaius Volusenus, so as to have some token of their support to show when they deserted to Pompey. This enterprise, however, appeared rather difficult and no opportunity was afforded for its accomplishment; and so they borrowed as much money as they could, as if they wanted to make amends to their men and make good the money they had embezzled, and then they bought large numbers of horses and deserted, with their accomplices, to Pompey.

61. Pompey led them all round his army and displayed them; for they were of noble birth, richly appointed, and had come with a large retinue and with many mounts, and besides, they had a reputation for bravery and had been held in esteem by Caesar. Moreover, their desertion was an occurrence of a new and unusual kind, for up till then no one, either from the infantry or the cavalry, had deserted Caesar for Pompey, although almost every day men were deserting Pompey for Caesar, as indeed did the whole of those conscripted in Epirus and Aetolia and all the regions now in Caesar's power. These two, however, knew everything. They knew where parts of the fortifications were not complete, they knew where military experts might find deficiencies, they had observed the timetable of routine, the distances between positions and the varying degrees of conscientiousness at different guard-posts, according to the temperament or enthusiasm

of the officers in charge. All this they reported to Pompey.

62. Armed with this information, Pompey, who as shown above had already decided to try to break out, ordered his men to make wicker coverings for their helmets and to collect materials for a rampart. Once these preparations were complete, he embarked a large number of the light infantry and archers and all the materials by night on dinghies and fast boats. Just after midnight he led sixty cohorts from his main camp and from the outposts to that part of the fortifications nearest the sea and farthest from Caesar's camp. He also dispatched there the ships mentioned above, with the light infantry and materials as well as the warships which he had at Dyrrachium, and issued instructions for each man. Near this part of the fortifications Caesar had the quaestor Lentulus Marcellinus stationed with the Ninth legion, and he had sent Fulvius Postumus to help him, since Marcellinus was suffering from an indisposition.

63. There was a fifteen-foot ditch there and, facing the enemy, a ten-foot rampart the earth-works of which were also ten feet in width. About five furlongs away there was another rampart, facing in the opposite direction and not built up quite so high. Caesar had made the double wall there during the preceding days, fearing that our men might be surrounded by the fleet. His aim was to make resistance possible for us, if there should be fighting on two sides. However, the extent of the works and the continual daily toil required – for he had embraced a circuit of some seventeen miles with his lines – did not give him a chance to finish. As a result, he had not yet completed the cross wall by the sea, which was to join these two lines of fortification together. Pompey knew this, from the information given by the Allobroges, and it was a circumstance which brought our men a good deal of trouble. Our cohorts of the Ninth had camped out by the sea, and suddenly at dawn the Pompeians arrived; at the same time some soldiers sailed round and began throwing missiles at the outer wall and filling the ditches with earth and brushwood; the legionaries brought up scaling ladders and frightened the defenders of the inner rampart with ballistic engines and missiles of every kind while large numbers of archers surrounded us on both sides. Moreover, the only kind of missile we had was stones, and

the wicker coverings on their helmets gave the enemy a large measure of protection against blows from these. When, therefore, our men were beginning to have the worst of it on every count and were having difficulty in maintaining their resistance, the deficiency in the fortifications mentioned above was noticed; men disembarked between the two ramparts, where the work had not been completed, and coming through the water they attacked our men from behind, beat them away from both walls and forced them to turn tail.

64. When this mêlée was reported, Marcellinus sent some cohorts up from the camp to help our men in distress; but these cohorts, seeing the men fleeing, failed either to give them heart by their arrival or themselves to withstand the onset of the enemy. The result was that any reinforcements that came up, being infected with the panic of those fleeing, merely increased the alarm, and the danger too – for the withdrawal was being hampered by the large numbers of men there. In this battle a legionary standard-bearer who had been seriously wounded and was growing weak said, on seeing our cavalry, 'I have faithfully guarded this eagle for many years in my lifetime and now, dying, I restore it, with equal faithfulness, to Caesar. I beg you, do not allow our military honour to be disgraced – something which has never happened before in Caesar's army – and bear the eagle to him safely.' So it chanced that the eagle was preserved, though all the centurions of the first cohort were killed except the senior centurion of the second line.

65. Pompey, after great slaughter of our men, was now approaching Marcellinus's camp, striking no small degree of alarm into the remaining cohorts, when Mark Antony, who was in the nearest outpost and had received a report, was observed coming down from the high ground with twelve cohorts. His arrival checked the Pompeians and gave our men heart, so that they rallied from their panic. Word was sent to Caesar by smoke signal from fort to fort, as had been the habit previously, and not long afterwards he himself came there too with cohorts drawn from some of the outposts. He learned of our defeat and saw that Pompey had got out of the lines, so that he could get fodder freely along by the sea and had free access by ship. Since Caesar had

failed to attain his object, he altered his strategy and ordered a camp to be built alongside Pompey's.

66. When this was completed Caesar's scouts observed that some cohorts, apparently about as many as would make up a legion, were behind the wood, being led towards the old camp. The situation of this camp was as follows. During the preceding days, when Caesar's Ninth legion had opposed itself to Pompey's forces and, as we said, was building lines of fortifications around them, it placed a camp there. This camp bordered on a certain wood, and was only about a quarter of a mile from the sea. Then, changing his plans for certain reasons, Caesar moved the camp a little farther forward, and after a few days Pompey occupied the place and, since he intended to have a greater number of legions there, he built a second, larger wall, while leaving the inner rampart. In this way the smaller camp enclosed in the larger served as a fort and citadel. He had, moreover, built a side-wall from the left corner of the camp to the river, rather less than half a mile away, to allow the troops to fetch water more freely and without danger. Pompey, however, also changed his strategy, for reasons unnecessary to discuss, and left the site. The camp stayed thus for several days; all the fortifications, indeed, were still intact.

67. The scouts reported to Caesar that the standards of a legion had been conveyed in there. This was also observed and confirmed from several of the forts. The place was about half a mile from Pompey's new camp. Caesar, hoping that he could overpower this legion, and eager to make good the losses of the day, left two cohorts on the lines to give the appearance of being engaged in work on fortifications. He himself went off by an indirect route, as covertly as possible, with the rest of the cohorts, numbering thirty-three, including the Ninth legion, which had lost many of its centurions and had its troops depleted in number. He led these in a double line to Pompey's legion in the smaller camp. His original supposition proved not to be mistaken; for he reached the place before Pompey could observe him and, although the defence-works of the camp were large, on attacking quickly with the left wing, where he himself was, he drove the Pompeians down from the rampart. The gates were blocked with a 'hedgehog' [72]. Fighting went on here for a short time, our men trying to break in and the

enemy defending the camp. In particular, a gallant resistance was put up by Titus Puleio (who, as we saw[73], was responsible for the betrayal of the army of Gaius Antonius). However, the courage of our men prevailed. Hacking apart the 'hedgehog' they burst into the larger camp, and then also into the fort enclosed in it, since the routed legion had taken refuge there, and killed a good many fighting.

68. But fortune, whose power is very great in all spheres, but particularly in warfare, often brings about great reversals by a slight tilt of the balance; and so it happened on this occasion. The cohorts on Caesar's right wing, not knowing the area, followed the line of fortifications which, as shown above, led from the camp to the river; they kept looking for a gate, thinking that this was the wall of the camp. When they discovered that it went right down to the river, they knocked down the wall, which no one was defending, and crossed over, followed by all our cavalry.

69. Meanwhile the news reached Pompey, after a fairly long interval. He withdrew five legions from the work of fortification and led them to help his men. His cavalry was approaching ours at the same time as his army in battle formation was coming into the view of our men who had seized the camp; everything was suddenly changed. Pompey's legion was encouraged by hope of speedy relief and began attempting resistance at the rear gate; they actually charged our men. Caesar's cavalry, fearing for their line of retreat (for they were going up along the entrenchments by a narrow passage) began to flee. The right wing, which was cut off from the left, observed the panic of the cavalry, and to avoid being overpowered inside the fortifications began withdrawing by the breach they had made. Most of these men threw themselves head-first from a ten-foot rampart into the trench, in case they should be caught in the confined space, and the first to do so were trampled down, while the rest escaped to safety by treading over their bodies. On the left wing, the troops observed that Pompey was close at hand and that their own men were running away. Since they had the enemy on the outside as well as the inside, they were afraid of being hemmed in, and began in self-preservation to go back the way they had come. Everywhere was full of turmoil, panic and rout; so much so that, when Caesar

grabbed the standards of the men fleeing and ordered them to halt, some gave their horses rein and continued in their course of flight, while others in their fear actually let the standards drop, but no one halted at all.

70. In the midst of these troubles, certain circumstances saved us from the destruction of our entire army. First, Pompey, I believe, feared an ambush because the situation was so contrary to his expectations, in that only a little while before he had seen his own men fleeing from the camp. He therefore did not venture for some time to go near the entrenchments. Secondly, the cavalry were hindered in their pursuit because the gates were narrow and, besides, they were blocked by Caesar's men. In this way trivial circumstances had important effects for both sides. For instance: when Pompey's camp had already been stormed, the fortifications running down from the camp to the river prevented the achievement of the victory that was already in Caesar's grasp; on the other hand, the same factor, by slowing down the pursuers, saved our men.

71. In these two battles on one day Caesar lost 960 soldiers and some notable Roman knights, Tuticanus Gallus, a senator's son, Gaius Fleginas from Placentia, Aulus Granius from Puteoli and Marcus Sacrativir from Capua, as well as thirty-two military tribunes and centurions. Of all these, however, the majority did not receive a single wound, but were crushed in the entrenchments and on the river-banks in the panic-stricken flight of their own comrades. Thirty-two military standards were lost. Pompey was hailed as *imperator* after this battle. He kept this title and afterwards allowed himself to be addressed by it, but he was never in the habit of using it to head his dispatches nor did he have the badge of the laurel wreath [74] on his *fasces*. Labienus, for his part, prevailed on Pompey to have the prisoners handed over to him. He then brought them out, apparently for display, and addressing them as fellow-soldiers and asking them in insulting terms whether veteran troops were in the habit of running away, he killed them in the sight of all. This he did to strengthen the Pompeians' trust in himself as a deserter.

72. These events put such confidence and spirit into the Pompeians that they no longer paid attention to the strategy of the

war but thought they had as good as won it. They did not reflect that the reasons for their success were the small numbers of our men, the difficulty of the terrain, the confined space (the camp being already occupied), the two-fold fear of attack both from inside and outside and the fact that our army was split in two and one part could not help the other. They did not consider, further, that there had been no decisive encounter, no battle, and that our men, owing to their numbers and the confined space, had inflicted more damage on themselves than they had received from the enemy. Finally, they did not recall how things commonly happen in war, how small causes – false alarm or sudden panic or religious scruple – had often inflicted great damage, how often through the inadequacy of a commander or the fault of a tribune an army had come to grief. They broadcast that day's victory through the world by word of mouth and by dispatches just as if they had conquered by their own valour and as if no reversal could occur.

73. Since he had been forced to abandon his earlier plans, Caesar decided that he must alter his entire strategy. Accordingly, all at once he withdrew all the garrisons and abandoned the blockade. He then mustered all his army in one place and addressed the troops. He urged them not to be disheartened or afraid at what had happened, but to balance against this one setback, and not a serious one at that, all the many successful engagements they had had. 'Thank fortune,' he said, 'that we took Italy without bloodshed; we pacified the two Spanish provinces, where there were the most warlike of men under experienced and practised generals; we have brought into our control the neighbouring provinces[75], which supply us with corn. Finally, consider how lucky we have been in that, when all the harbours and the whole coast as well were infested with enemy fleets, we were conveyed across safely right through the midst of them. If everything does not turn out favourably, we must help fortune by some efforts of our own. The setback we have sustained is anyone's fault rather than my own. I gave an opportunity for battle on favourable ground; I took possession of the enemy camp; I drove them out and overcame them in fighting. But, whether through your own agitation, or from some mistake, or by some stroke of fate, the

victory that was as good as in our grasp was lost; so you must all make an effort to repair the damage by your valour. If you do, you will turn our loss to gain, as happened at Gergovia[76]; and those who were afraid to fight before will actually offer themselves for battle.'

74. He went on to censure and demote several standard-bearers. Indeed, the whole army, as a result of its setback, was so chagrined and so eager to make good the damage to its reputation that no one needed orders from tribune or centurion; everyone, as punishment, imposed on himself heavier toils. The common soldiers were unanimously eager to fight, while some of the officers as well, moved by considerations of strategy, thought they ought to stay on the spot and offer battle. Caesar, on the other hand, had little confidence in his demoralized troops and thought they should be given time to rally their spirits; and he was seriously concerned about the supply of corn, now that they had abandoned the fortifications.

8. Caesar moves to Thessaly

75. And so, pausing only to have the sick and wounded taken care of, he sent all the baggage train ahead in silence after nightfall from the camp to Apollonia, with orders not to stop for rest until the journey was completed. He sent one legion to escort them. These arrangements were completed, and then, keeping two legions in the camp, he had the rest led out in the last hours of the night by several gates and then on by the same route; then, a little later, in order both to observe military procedure and to keep his departure secret as long as possible, he gave the order to strike camp, and leaving at once he caught up with the rear of the column and was soon out of sight of the camp. Pompey, on learning of his plans, made no delay in starting the pursuit. Heading in the same direction, in hopes of catching our men on the march encumbered and frightened, he led the army out of camp and sent the cavalry ahead to delay the end of the column. He failed to catch up, as Caesar, by marching light, had got a long way ahead. However, when they reached the river Genusus,

whose banks formed an obstacle, the cavalry caught up with the rear of the column and delayed them by skirmishing. Caesar sent his own cavalry against them, together with 400 light-armed front-line men, who were so successful that when the cavalry engaged they drove them all back, killed a good many and themselves returned unharmed to the column.

76. After completing the full distance that he had intended to march that day and taking the army across the river Genusus, Caesar took up quarters in his old camp opposite Asparagium. He kept all the troops inside the rampart and sent out the cavalry to fetch fodder with orders to come back to camp quickly by the rear gate. Pompey likewise, after completing that day's march, took up quarters in his old camp near Asparagium. His troops were not required for construction work, the fortifications being intact, and so some went out quite far to fetch fodder and wood while others, as the decision to start had been sudden and the great part of the baggage and animals had been left behind, were tempted by the nearness of their earlier camp to go back and fetch them. Putting their weapons in their tents, they left the entrenchments. They were thus rendered unable to pursue. Caesar had foreseen this, and about midday he gave the signal to set out. Doubling that day's march he advanced about eight miles farther; this Pompey could not do, as his men had gone off.

77. On the following day Caesar followed the same procedure; he sent the baggage ahead at nightfall and himself left in the last hours of the night so that, if they should be forced to fight, he might meet the emergency with his army unencumbered for action. He did the same on the succeeding days. As a result, although the rivers were running very high and it was difficult to proceed, he came to no harm. Pompey had been held up on the first day and exerted himself in vain on the succeeding days, straining to make long marches in his eagerness to catch up the forces ahead; on the fourth day he gave up the pursuit and decided to adopt some other strategy.

78. Caesar had to get to Apollonia in order to leave the wounded, pay the army, make sure of the allies, and leave a force to protect the cities. However, he allowed only so much time for attending to these matters as his haste permitted; he was afraid

that Pompey might get to Domitius first; this served as an incentive to spur him on towards Domitius with all speed. His whole strategy was based on the following considerations: if Pompey took the same route, then, once he had drawn him away from the sea and from those resources he had collected at Dyrrachium and had cut him off from his supplies of corn and provisions, he could force him to fight on equal terms; if Pompey should cross to Italy, then he could join forces with Domitius and march through Illyricum to rescue Italy; if Pompey attempted to attack Apollonia and Oricum and cut him off entirely from the sea coast, then by besieging Scipio he could force Pompey to bring help to his own side. Caesar therefore sent messengers ahead to Domitius with dispatches giving him instructions. He left garrisons – four cohorts at Apollonia, one at Lissus, three at Oricum – left those who were disabled by wounds at various places in Epirus and Athamania, then began his march. Pompey also, guessing at Caesar's intentions, judged that he should hurry towards Scipio, in order either to help him, if Caesar should direct his march that way, or, if Caesar should refuse to leave Oricum and the coast because he was waiting for legions from Italy, then himself to attack Domitius with all his forces.

79. For these reasons, each of them was in a hurry, both in order to help his own forces and not to miss an opportunity of overpowering his adversaries; but Caesar had been obliged to make a detour in order to go to Apollonia, whereas Pompey going through Candavia had an easy route into Macedonia. A further unexpected difficulty arose, as Domitius for several days had had his camp next to Scipio's, and then had left to get corn and had marched to Heraclia, which is close to Candavia, so that fortune itself seemed to be putting him in Pompey's way. Caesar, so far, was unaware of this. At the same time Pompey had sent dispatches round all the provinces and states describing the encounter at Dyrrachium in far more inflated and exaggerated terms than the events justified, and the word had spread about that Caesar had been routed, had lost almost all his forces, and was fleeing. This had endangered Caesar's march, and had caused several communities to defect from their friendly relations with him. The result was that men sent by several different routes from Caesar

to Domitius and from Domitius to Caesar were totally unable to complete the journey. However, the Allobroges, friends of Roucillus and Egus, who as related above * had deserted to Pompey, saw some of Domitius's scouts on the road and told them everything that had happened, either because of their old acquaintance, as they had campaigned together in Gaul, or because they were puffed up with vainglory. They told them of Caesar's setting out and of the approach of Pompey. The news was passed on to Domitius; and so, thanks to his enemies, with barely four hours to spare he escaped from danger and met Caesar on the march near Aeginium, which commands the way into Thessaly.

80. They combined forces and Caesar went on to Gomphi, which is the first town in Thessaly on the route from Epirus. The people there had on their own initiative sent a deputation to Caesar a few months previously, saying that all their resources were at his disposal, and asking for a garrison of soldiers. However, the rumour described above about the engagement at Dyrrachium had already reached them, with exaggeration on numerous points. As a result Androsthenes, the ruler of Thessaly [77], preferring to be Pompey's adherent in victory rather than Caesar's ally in adversity, gathered into the town all the large population of slaves and free men from the countryside, closed the gates, and sent messengers to Scipio and Pompey asking them to come to his aid. He said that he could rely on the fortifications of the town, provided he were relieved quickly, but he could not sustain a protracted siege. Scipio had taken his legions to Larissa on learning of the departure from Dyrrachium. Pompey was not yet near Thessaly. Caesar pitched camp, and ordered scaling ladders and huts to be made and screens got ready for an immediate attack. He then exhorted his soldiers, telling them how their general shortage of supplies would be relieved by getting possession of a well stocked and rich town, and at the same time how they might strike terror into the other communities by making an example of this one, especially when this happened before help could hurry in. And so, taking advantage of the singular enthusiasm of his men, before mid-afternoon on the day of his arrival he began to attack the town. Although its walls were very high, he took it before

[* Ch. 59–60.]

sunset and gave it to the troops to plunder. Then he moved camp from the town at once and went to Metropolis, so that he reached there before any word had arrived, by messenger or rumour, of the storming of Gomphi.

81. The people of Metropolis at first had followed the same policy; influenced by the same rumours they closed the gates and posted armed men on the walls; but later, when they learned of the fate of Gomphi from some prisoners whom Caesar had had led up to the wall, they opened the gate. Caesar was very careful to preserve them from harm; and so, when the other States in Thessaly compared the fortune of the people of Metropolis with the fate of the people of Gomphi, there was none except Larissa, which was in the hands of large forces of Scipio's, which did not obey Caesar and carry out his orders. Caesar, finding a suitable place in the countryside, where the crops were now almost ripe, decided to wait there for Pompey's arrival and make that the sole theatre of operations.

9. Pompey follows

82. Pompey arrived in Thessaly a few days later. He delivered an address to the whole army, thanking his own men and encouraging those of Scipio, now that victory was in their grasp, to earn a share in the booty and the rewards. He gathered all the legions into one camp; then, sharing the honour of command[78] with Scipio, he ordered the trumpet calls to be made before Scipio's tent and a second commander's tent to be pitched for him. Now that Pompey's forces had been increased by the combination of two large armies, everyone's original opinion was reinforced and hopes of victory grew, so much so that any further lapse of time seemed merely to delay their return to Italy. If at any time Pompey acted with particular slowness or deliberation, they would say that the business need keep them only a single day, and that Pompey took pleasure from being in command and was treating ex-consuls and ex-praetors as if they were his slaves. They were already starting to squabble openly among themselves about rewards and priest-hoods and were assigning the consulships for years to come, while

some were claiming the houses and property[79] of people in Caesar's camp. In the council of war there was great controversy as to whether Lucilius Hirrus should be allowed to stand in absence at the next election of praetors, as he had been sent by Pompey to Parthia. His friends asked Pompey for an assurance that he would fulfil the undertaking he had made on Hirrus's departure, so that the latter should not appear to be cheated through the exercise of Pompey's personal authority; the rest, however, were insisting that where all underwent the same toils and dangers one man should not be allowed to take precedence of the rest.

83. Over Caesar's priesthood, Domitius, Scipio and Lentulus Spinther were already quarrelling daily, and had descended to the most virulent insults. Lentulus claimed the respect due to age; Domitius boasted of his popularity in Rome and his prestige; Scipio was relying on his relationship with Pompey. Acutius Rufus even indicted Lucius Afranius before Pompey for the alleged betrayal of the army in Spain. Lucius Domitius said in the council that his view was that when the war was over three tablets should be given to each of the senators who had taken part in the fighting with them, and that they should pass judgement on each of those who had remained in Rome and on those who had been with Pompey's forces but had taken no active part in military action. One tablet should be for those voting that they should be allowed to go scot-free; one for those wishing them to be disfranchised; and one for those who wished to fine them[80]. In short, everyone was busily securing office for himself, or financial reward, or pursuing private grudges, and they were thinking not of how to win but of how to exploit the victory.

84. Once Caesar had secured the corn supply and strengthened the troops' morale, and once sufficient time had elapsed since the engagements at Dyrrachium for him to believe that he had properly gauged the spirit of his men, he decided that he must find out to what extent Pompey had any intention or wish to join battle. He therefore led the army out of camp and drew them up for battle, first on his own ground and rather farther away from Pompey's camp, but on succeeding days moving out from his own camp and bringing the lines close up under the hills occupied by

Pompey. This manoeuvre raised the men's morale higher every day. For the cavalry, however, he followed the earlier tactics described above.* Since they were very much inferior in numbers, he ordered young light-armed infantry from a picked corps of front-line men, specially selected for agility, to fight among the cavalry, and by daily practice acquire the technique of this kind of fighting also. The result was that 1,000 cavalry were able, even on rather open ground, to venture to withstand the attack of 7,000 Pompeians, when necessary, without being greatly dismayed by their numbers. Indeed, during those days Caesar fought a successful cavalry battle and killed several men, including one of the two Allobroges who, as related above, had deserted to Pompey.

10. The battle of Pharsalus

85. Pompey, whose camp was on a hill, kept drawing up his line of battle by the lower spurs of the mountain, always, as it seemed, waiting to see if Caesar would offer battle on unfavourable ground. Caesar, judging that Pompey could in no way be enticed out to battle, decided to move his camp from there and keep constantly on the march. His aim was, by moving camp and going to various places, to make it easier to get corn and at the same time to try to get some opportunity *en route* for battle, as well as to tire out Pompey's army, which was unaccustomed to exertion, by daily marches. Having taken this decision, he gave the signal for departure, and the tents were already struck when he observed that Pompey's line had advanced a little farther forward from the rampart than was its daily habit, so that it appeared possible to fight without being in an unfavourable position. Caesar then said to his men, when the column was already going through the gates, 'We must postpone our march for the time being and think of battle, just as we have always desired. Our spirits are ready for battle; we shall not easily find another chance.' Then he led the troops out quickly, without kit.

86. Pompey also, as was learned later, had decided at the insistence of all his men to settle the issue by battle. Indeed he had

[* Ch. 75.]

even said in the council of war during the preceding days that
Caesar's army would be routed before the two lines came to grips.
The majority were surprised at this. 'I know that what I promise
is almost incredible,' he said, 'but listen to my tactical plan, so
that you may go to battle with the more confidence. I have advised
the cavalry, when the armies come within fairly close range, to
attack Caesar's right wing on its exposed flank, surround the line
in the rear and thus throw his army into confusion and rout it
before a missile is thrown from our side at the enemy. They have
undertaken to do so, and in this way we shall bring the war to an
end without danger to the legions and almost without bloodshed.
It is not difficult, in view of our superiority in cavalry.' He exhorted them also to be prepared in spirit for what was to come
and, since the opportunity for battle, which had often been in
their thoughts, was being offered, not to let their conduct and
prowess belie the expectations of the rest.

87. Labienus spoke next. He belittled Caesar's forces and ex-
tolled Pompey's plan to the skies, saying: 'Do not think, Pompey,
that this is the army which conquered Gaul and Germany. I took
part in all the battles and I am not giving an unconsidered opinion
on something I know nothing about. A very small part of that
army survives; the greater part has perished, as it must needs have
done in so many battles; the unhealthiness of the autumn in Italy
carried off a good many; many have gone home; many were left
behind on the mainland of Italy. Have you not heard that cohorts
were formed out of those who stayed behind at Brundisium because of sickness? These forces you see were made up to strength
from the levies of the last few years[81] in Cisalpine Gaul and most
of them are from the colonies in Transpadane Gaul. Besides, such
good men as the army contained perished in the two battles at
Dyrrachium.' He then swore that he would not re-enter the camp
except as a victor and he urged the others to swear likewise.
Pompey praised him and took the same oath; and none of the rest
hesitated to swear. After this, the council broke up, with everyone
full of joy and hope; and they were already mentally anticipating
victory, since it seemed that the assurance given by so experienced
a general on a matter of such moment could not be mistaken.

88. When Caesar approached Pompey's army, he observed his

line drawn up as follows. On the left wing were the two legions which had been handed over by Caesar in accordance with the decree of the Senate at the beginning of the troubles. One was named the First, the other the Third[82]. Pompey himself was there. Scipio was holding the centre of the line with his legions from Syria. The legion from Cilicia[83] together with the Spanish cohorts which, as we said[84], were brought over by Afranius, was stationed on the right wing. Pompey believed that these were his strongest troops. The rest he had stationed between the centre and the wings and had made up 110 cohorts. There were 45,000 men, plus about 2,000 time-expired veterans from the special-duty corps[85] of the earlier armies who had come to join him. These he dispersed throughout the battle-line. The remaining seven cohorts he had posted to guard the camp and the near-by forts. His right wing was protected by a stream with steep banks*, and he had therefore put all the cavalry, archers and slingers on the left wing.

89. Caesar, keeping his previous order of battle, had stationed the Tenth legion on the right wing and the Ninth on the left, although the latter had been sorely depleted by the battle at Dyrrachium. To it he added the Eighth legion, so as almost to make one legion out of two, and ordered them to cooperate. He had eighty cohorts stationed in the line, totalling 22,000[86] men. He had left two cohorts to guard the camp. He had put Antony on the left wing, Sulla on the right and Gnaeus Domitius in the centre. He himself took up his position opposite Pompey. At the same time, he observed the dispositions described above, and fearing that his right wing might be surrounded by the large numbers of the Pompeian cavalry, he quickly took one cohort from each legion from his third line and formed them into a fourth line, which he stationed opposite the cavalry. He gave them their instructions[87], and warned them that that day's victory would depend on the valour of those cohorts. He also ordered the third line and the army as a whole not to charge without his command, saying that he would give a signal with his flag[88] when he wished them to do so.

90. In giving the usual address of encouragement to the troops, in which he related the good service they had done him at all

[* The Enipeus.]

times, he recalled above all that he could call the troops to witness the earnestness with which he had sought peace, his attempts to negotiate through Vatinius by personal interviews and, through Aulus Clodius, with Scipio, and his efforts at Oricum to negotiate with Libo for the sending of envoys. It had never been his wish to expose his troops to bloodshed, nor to deprive the State of either army. After this speech, at the insistence of his troops, who were afire with enthusiasm, he gave the signal by trumpet.

91. In Caesar's army there was a recalled veteran named Crastinus, who in the previous year had been chief centurion of the Tenth legion in his service, a man of outstanding valour. When the signal was given, he said : 'Follow me, you who were formerly in my company, and give your general the service you have promised. Only this one battle remains; after it, he will recover his position, and we our freedom.' Looking at Caesar, 'General,' he said, 'today I shall earn your gratitude, either dead or alive.' So saying, he ran out first from the right wing, followed by about 120 crack troops, volunteers from the same century.

92. Between the two armies there was just enough space left for them to advance and engage each other. Pompey, however, had told his men to wait for Caesar's onset, and not to move from their positions or allow the line to be split up. He was said to have done this on the advice of Gaius Triarius, with the intention of breaking the force of the first impact of the enemy and stretching out their line, so that his own men, who were still in formation, could attack them while they were scattered. He also thought that the falling javelins would do less damage if the men stood still than if they were running forward while the missiles were discharged. Moreover, Caesar's troops, having to run twice the distance, would be out of breath and exhausted. It appears to us that he did this without sound reason, for there is a certain eagerness of spirit and an innate keenness in everyone which is inflamed by desire for battle. Generals ought to encourage this, not repress it; nor was it for nothing that the practice began in antiquity of giving the signal on both sides and everyone's raising a war-cry; this was believed both to frighten the enemy and to stimulate one's own men.

93. Our men, on the signal, ran forward with javelins levelled;

but when they observed that Pompey's men were not running to meet them, thanks to the practical experience and training they had had in earlier battles they checked their charge and halted about half-way, so as not to approach worn out. Then after a short interval they renewed the charge, threw their javelins and, as ordered by Caesar, quickly drew their swords. Nor indeed did the Pompeians fail to meet the occasion. They stood up to the hail of missiles and bore the onset of the legions; they kept their ranks, threw their javelins, and then resorted to their swords. At the same time the cavalry all charged forward, as instructed, from Pompey's left wing, and the whole horde of archers rushed out. Our cavalry failed to withstand their onslaught; they were dislodged from their position and gave ground a little. Pompey's cavalry thereupon pressed on the more hotly and began to deploy in squadrons and surround our line on its exposed flank. Observing this, Caesar gave the signal to the fourth line which he had formed of single cohorts. They ran forward swiftly to the attack with their standards and charged at Pompey's cavalry with such force that none of them could hold ground. They all turned, and not only gave ground but fled precipitately to the hilltops. Their withdrawal left all the archers and slingers exposed, and, unarmed and unprotected, they were killed. In the same charge the cohorts surrounded the Pompeians who were still fighting and putting up a resistance on the left wing, and attacked them in the rear.

94. At the same time Caesar gave the order to advance to the third line, which had done nothing and had stayed in its position up till then. As a result, when fresh and unscathed troops took the place of the weary, while others were attacking from the rear, the Pompeians could not hold out, and every one of them turned tail and fled. Caesar was not wrong in thinking that the victory would originate from those cohorts which had been stationed in a fourth line to counteract the cavalry, as he had declared in cheering on his men; for it was by these first that the cavalry were repulsed, it was by these that the slingers and archers were massacred, and it was by these that the Pompeian left wing was surrounded and the rout started. When Pompey, however, saw his cavalry routed, and observed that part of his forces on which he most relied in a state of panic, having no

confidence in the rest he left the field; he rode straight to the camp and said to the centurions he had posted on guard at the prae- torian gate, loudly, so that the soldiers could hear: 'Watch the camp and defend it strenuously, if there should be any reverse. I am going round to the other gates to make sure of the guard on the camp.' So saying, he went to his tent, doubting his chances of success and yet awaiting the outcome.

95. The Pompeians were driven back in their retreat inside the rampart. Caesar, thinking that they should be given no respite in their panic, urged his men to take advantage of the generosity of fortune and storm the camp. Even though it was extremely hot – for the engagement had gone on until midday – his men were ready to undertake any toil, and obeyed his order. The camp was being zealously defended by the cohorts left to guard it, and more fiercely still by the Thracian and native auxiliaries. For the troops who had fled from the field, terrified and exhausted, mostly dropped their weapons and military standards and had more thought for continuing their flight than for the defence of the camp. Nor indeed could those who had taken up their position on the rampart hold out any longer against the hail of missiles. Overcome by their wounds, they abandoned their posts and at once, led by their centurions and tribunes, fled to the hilltops near the camp.

96. In Pompey's camp could be seen artificial arbours, a great weight of silver plate laid out, tents spread with fresh turf, those of Lucius Lentulus and several others covered with ivy, and many other indications of extravagant indulgence and confidence in victory; so that it could readily be judged that they had had no fears for the outcome of the day, in that they were procuring unnecessary comforts for themselves. Yet these were the men who taunted Caesar's wretched and long-suffering army with self- indulgence, although the latter had always been short of all kinds of necessities. When our men were already inside the rampart, Pompey got a horse, removed his general's insignia, rushed out of the camp by the rear gate and galloped off to Larissa. He did not stop there, but with a few of his men whom he had picked up in his flight he went on through the night without stopping, accom- panied by thirty cavalrymen, until he reached the sea. There he

embarked on a grain-ship, with, it was said, frequent laments that he should have been so grossly mistaken, that he appeared almost to have been betrayed by the very group of men whom he had hoped would secure victory but who had in fact started the flight.

97. Once Caesar had taken possession of the camp, he urged the soldiers not to let preoccupation with plundering render them incapable of attending to the tasks that remained. They obeyed, and he began building fortifications round the hill. Since the hill had no water, Pompey's men had no confidence in this position and leaving the mountain they all began retreating towards Larissa over its foothills. Caesar observed what they intended to do, and dividing his own forces he ordered part of the legions to stay behind in Pompey's camp and sent part back to his own camp; he took four legions with him and started along a more convenient route, to intercept the Pompeians. After advancing six miles he drew up his battle line. Observing this, the Pompeians halted on a hill, close under which ran a river. Caesar spoke encouragingly to his troops and though they were tired with continual exertion all during the day, and night was already approaching, he constructed a fortification cutting off the river from the hill, so that Pompey's men should not be able to get water during the night. When this was complete, the Pompeians sent a deputation and began to negotiate a surrender. A few of the senatorial order who had joined them sought to save themselves by fleeing during the night.

98. At dawn Caesar ordered all those who had settled on the hill to come down from the higher ground on to the plain and throw down their weapons. They did this without demur; then they threw themselves to the ground with their hands outstretched, weeping, and begged him for their lives. He reassured them, told them to get up, and spoke briefly to them about his own leniency, to alleviate their fears. He spared them all and charged his own soldiers to see to it that none of them suffered any physical violence or lost any part of his property. These matters taken care of, he ordered the other legions to come from the camp to join him, and the ones which he brought with him to go back to camp and rest in their turn. He arrived at Larissa on the same day.

99. In this battle he lost not more than 200 troops, but about thirty centurions, stout men. Crastinus also, whom we mentioned above, was killed, fighting staunchly, by a sword thrust full in the face. Nor did his words on setting out to battle prove false; for Caesar judged that Crastinus's valour in that battle had been outstanding and that he had rendered most excellent service. From the Pompeian army about 15,000 appeared to have fallen, but more than 24,000 surrendered – for the cohorts which had been on guard in the fortresses gave themselves up as well to Sulla. Many besides fled for refuge to the neighbouring communities, and from this battle 180 military standards were brought to Caesar, and nine eagles. Lucius Domitius collapsed from exhaustion while fleeing out of the camp to the mountain and was killed by cavalrymen.

100. At the same time Decimus Laelius arrived with his fleet at Brundisium, and with the same intentions as Libo (as we described above*), he occupied an island opposite the harbour. Likewise Vatinius, who was in command at Brundisium, decked and equipped some light boats, enticed Laelius's ships out and took one of them, a quinquereme, which was brought out too far, as well as two smaller vessels, at the narrow entrances to the harbour; he also proceeded to cut off the men with the fleet from water supplies by stationing cavalry in various places. Laelius, however, had the advantage of a more convenient season for sailing, and he brought up water from Corcyra and Dyrrachium on cargo boats. He refused to be deterred from his mission and he could not be driven away from the island and the harbour, either by the disgrace of losing his ships or by shortage of necessities, until news came of the battle in Thessaly.

101. At about the same time Gaius Cassius came to Sicily with a fleet of Syrians, Phoenicians and Cilicians. Caesar's fleet was divided into two parts, the Praetor Publius Sulpicius being in charge of one half at Vibo by the strait, and Marcus Pomponius of the other at Messana. Cassius swooped down on Messana with his ships before Pomponius could be informed of his approach, and taking him by surprise with no guards posted and the vessels in no proper ranks, he sent down against Pomponius's fleet, on a

[* Ch. 23.]

[III.102.3] THE GREAT CONFRONTATION

strong following wind, transports filled with wood and pitch and
tow and other incendiary materials. He burned all the vessels,
thirty-five of them, of which twenty were decked. This raised
such a panic that, although there was a legion stationed at
Messana, the town could scarcely be defended and if word of
Caesar's victory had not been brought at that very time by
mounted relays, the general opinion was that it would have been
lost. However, the message came in the nick of time and the town
was defended. Cassius went off then to Sulpicius's fleet at Vibo,
where our ships had put in to land because of the same fear, and
events followed the same pattern as before. Cassius, with a following wind, sent in about forty transport boats ready for fire-raising;
the flames caught hold on either wing and five ships were consumed. When, however, the fire began creeping over a wider area
because of the force of the wind, the troops among the sick in the
veteran legions who had been left on guard over the ships found
the disgrace intolerable. Of their own initiative they embarked
and cast off; they attacked Cassius's fleet and captured two quinqueremes, on one of which was Cassius himself. He, however, was
taken off in a dinghy and escaped. Two triremes also were captured. Not long after, the news came of the battle of Thessaly, so
that even the Pompeians were convinced; for up till that time
they thought it was a story invented by Caesar's officers and
friends. At the news, Cassius left this region with his fleet.

11. The death of Pompey

102. Caesar judged that he must drop everything else and pursue
Pompey where he had betaken himself after his flight, so that he
should not be able to gather more forces and renew the war; and
he advanced daily as far as he could go with the cavalry and
ordered a legion to follow by shorter stages. An edict had been
published in Pompey's name that all the younger men in the
province, both Greeks and Roman citizens, should assemble to
take an oath. But whether Pompey had published this to divert
suspicion, so as to keep his intention of further flight secret as
long as possible, or whether he was attempting to hold Macedonia

with fresh levies, if no one stopped him, could not be gauged. He himself stayed at anchor for one night. He summoned his hosts in Amphipolis to him, asked for money for necessary expenses, and then on learning of Caesar's approach left the place and arrived in a few days at Mytilene. He was delayed by a storm for two days and then, with the addition to the fleet of further fast boats, reached Cilicia and then Cyprus. There he learned that by the agreement of all the people of Antioch and of the Roman citizens who had business concerns there, the citadel had been seized with the object of shutting him out, and messages had been sent to those who were said to have fled to neighbouring communities telling them not to come to Antioch; if they did, they would be in great danger of their lives. The same thing had happened at Rhodes to Lucius Lentulus, consul the previous year, Publius Lentulus, a former consul, and various others. They were following Pompey after flight from the battle, but when they reached the island they were refused admittance to the town and its harbour. Messengers were sent telling them to go away, and so they reluctantly set sail. Moreover, word of Caesar's approach was by now spreading among the cities.

103. Learning this, Pompey abandoned his project of going to Syria; he raised money from the company of tax-farmers and from some private individuals. He loaded on the ships a great quantity of bronze coin for military purposes, armed two thousand men, whom he had partly selected from the households of the tax-farmers and partly exacted from businessmen, and those of their own people whom particular individuals offered as suitable for the enterprise, and came to Pelusium. As it happened, King Ptolemy[89] was there, a mere boy, who was waging war with large forces against his sister Cleopatra. A few months ago, by means of his intimates and favourites he had expelled her from the kingdom. Cleopatra's camp was not far away from his. Pompey sent to him, asking to be received in Alexandria for the sake of the hospitality and friendship he had shown his father, and to receive protection in his trouble from the king's resources. However, the men he had sent, after they had finished their mission, began to talk rather freely with the king's soldiers and to urge them to give Pompey their services and not to despise his ill-fortune. Among the latter

were several of Pompey's own troops, whom Gabinius had taken over from the army in Syria, brought to Alexandria and left there, after the end of the war, with the boy's father, Ptolemy.

104. Then the favourites of the king, who were administering the kingdom for him on account of his youth, learned this. Either (as they alleged later) swayed by the fear that Pompey might suborn the royal army and seize Alexandria and Egypt, or from contempt of him in his misfortune (it is usually the case that friends become enemies in adversity), they gave to all appearances a very generous response to the envoys he had sent and bade him come to the king; but they themselves conferred together secretly and then sent Achillas, an officer of the king, a man of singular audacity, and Lucius Septimius, a military tribune, to kill Pompey. Pompey was addressed by them courteously and was induced to approach by some acquaintance with Septimius, who had led a century under him in the war against the pirates. So he boarded a little boat, with a few of his companions; and there he was killed by Achillas and Septimius. Lucius Lentulus was also seized by the king and put to death in captivity.

105. When Caesar reached Asia, he gradually discovered that Titus Ampius had attempted to remove money from the temple of Diana at Ephesus and for that purpose had summoned all the senators from the province to act as witnesses to the amount of money, but he had been interrupted by Caesar's approach and had fled. So Caesar twice saved the money of Ephesus. It was also established, by going back and counting the days, that at Elis, in the temple of Minerva, on the day on which Caesar had his victorious battle, the image of Victory placed before that of Minerva herself, which hitherto had looked towards Minerva, turned round towards the door and the threshold of the temple. On the same day at Antioch in Syria there was twice heard such a great noise of an army and so loud a sound of trumpet signals that the population armed themselves and ran to their various posts on the walls. This also happened at Ptolemais. At Pergamum, in secret and hidden temples, to which it is lawful for none but priests to go, and which the Greeks call the *adyta*, there was the sound of drums. Again, at Tralles, in the temple of Victory, where

they had consecrated a statue of Caesar, during those days a palm was displayed which had grown up inside the building out of the pavement, in the join of the paving stones.

12. Caesar at Alexandria

106. Caesar stayed on a few days in Asia. Then he heard that Pompey had been seen at Cyprus, and thinking that the latter was making for Egypt because of his connexion with the kingdom and the other conveniences of that place, he went to Alexandria with the legion which he had ordered to follow him from Thessaly, and a second which he had summoned from the lieutenant Quintus Fufius in Achaea, with about 800 cavalry, and ten warships from Rhodes and a few from the Asiatic fleet. In these legions there were about 3,200 men. The rest had been overcome by wounds received in battle and by the toil of a long march, and had not managed to follow. Caesar, however, relying on the fame of his exploits, had not hesitated to set out with weak forces, thinking that all places would be safe for him. At Alexandria he learned of Pompey's death. Just as he was disembarking he heard the shouting of the troops whom the king had left to guard the town and saw them rushing towards him. This was because the *fasces* were being carried before him, a circumstance which the whole host thought was a slight on the royal dignity. The disturbance was quelled, but for several days on end there were frequent outbreaks when mobs gathered, and several troops were killed, in all parts of this city.

107. Caesar therefore ordered the other legions, which he had formed from Pompey's troops, to be fetched from Asia, since he himself was detained perforce at Alexandria by the etesian winds[90], which are most adverse for those sailing from there. Meanwhile, thinking that the quarrels of the royal family concerned both the Roman people and himself as consul, and that he had all the more a duty to act because it was in his earlier consulship that an alliance had been formed with Ptolemy, the present king's father, by a law and a decree of the Senate, he announced that he had decided that King Ptolemy and his sister Cleopatra

should dismiss the armies they had and settle their quarrels by submitting them to him for judgement rather than by force of arms between themselves.

108. Because of the king's youth, the kingdom was being administered by his tutor, a eunuch named Pothinus. He began first of all to complain among his adherents and express indignation that the king should be summoned to plead his case; then he found some accomplices for his design among the king's favourites, secretly summoned the army from Pelusium to Alexandria and put in charge of all the forces that same Achillas whom we mentioned above*. This man was egged on and puffed up by promises from Pothinus himself and from the king. Pothinus gave him instructions by messenger and dispatch.

In the will of Ptolemy the elder, the older of his two sons and the older of his two daughters had been entered as heirs. In this same will, Ptolemy called on the Roman people, by all the gods and by the treaties he had made at Rome, to see that it was carried out. One copy of the will had been taken to Rome by his emissaries to be placed in the treasury, but since, owing to the political troubles, this had proved impossible, the will had been deposited instead with Pompey; a duplicate copy had been kept under seal at Alexandria and was now produced.

109. While the matter was under discussion before Caesar, who was particularly anxious as a friend of both sides and as arbitrator to settle the disputes in the royal family, it was suddenly reported that the royal army and all the cavalry were approaching Alexandria. Caesar's forces were by no means so great that he could rely on them if there had to be fighting outside the town. The alternative course was to stay where he was in the town and try to discover Achillas's plans. He issued orders, however, for all the troops to stand by under arms, and urged the king to send the most influential of his intimates as envoys to Achillas and notify him of his wishes. The king chose Dioscorides and Serapion, who had both been on missions to Rome and had had great influence in Ptolemy the elder's court, and sent them to Achillas. When they came into his presence, without listening to them or inquiring why they had been sent, he ordered them to be arrested

[* Ch. 104.]

and put to death. One of them was wounded, and was promptly seized by his friends and carried off for dead; the other was killed. Thereupon, Caesar took steps to have control of the king's person, both from the consideration that the king's name carried great weight among his people and also in order that the war might appear to have been undertaken rather on the private initiative of a few ruffians than by royal design.

110. Achillas had forces which appeared by no means contemptible either in numbers or in the quality of men or in their military experience. He had 20,000 men-at-arms. These included Gabinius's men, who by now had grown accustomed to the lax way of life at Alexandria. They had ceased to think of themselves as Roman, forgotten the standards of discipline of the Roman people, and had married and mostly had children by the marriages. Added to these were men collected among the brigands and pirates of Syria and the province of Cilicia and the neighbouring areas; and many condemned criminals and exiles had joined them. All our runaway slaves had found a safe refuge and an assured livelihood, if they enrolled as soldiers. If any of them was arrested by his master, his comrades would unite to rescue him, resisting violence to any one of their number inasmuch as it was a threat to themselves, since they were all in a similar situation. These men had been accustomed to demand the execution of royal favourites, to plunder the property of the wealthy, to besiege the palace for a rise in pay, to drive some from the throne and summon others to fill it, according to some ancient tradition of the Alexandrian army. There were besides 2,000 cavalry. All these were veterans of numerous wars at Alexandria; they had restored the elder Ptolemy to the throne, they had killed the two sons of Bibulus, they had made war on the Egyptians. Such was their military experience.

111. Relying on these forces and despising Caesar's small numbers, Achillas was occupying Alexandria with the exception of that quarter of the town which Caesar was holding with his troops. At the first onslaught he had tried to break into Caesar's house, but Caesar had posted cohorts about the streets and held off the attack. At the same time there was fighting at the harbour, and this produced by far the most serious struggle. For simultane-

ously there was a battle going on among scattered forces in a number of streets, and the enemy were attempting by force of numbers to seize the warships, of which fifty had been sent to help Pompey and had returned home after the battle in Thessaly, all of them four- and five-banked ships, fully equipped and fitted out for battle. There were another twenty-two besides, which had usually been on guard at Alexandria, all decked. If they seized these, then by taking Caesar's fleet they would have the harbour and the whole sea in their power and could prevent Caesar from obtaining supplies and reinforcements. The contest therefore was as keen as one would expect, since one side saw that a swift victory, the other that their very salvation depended on the result. Caesar, however, prevailed. He burned all these vessels[91] and those in the dockyards, since he could not protect so wide an area with his small force, and he hastily disembarked his men by the Pharos[92].

112. The Pharos is a tower of great height, a work of marvellous construction, standing on an island from which it takes its name. This island lies off Alexandria and forms a harbour. Earlier kings built out into the sea a bar stretching about 1,500 yards, and this joins the island to the town by a narrow causeway. On the island are dwellings of Egyptians and a suburb the size of a town; and if any vessels ever turn aside a little from their course as a result of carelessness or bad weather the inhabitants are in the habit of plundering them, like pirates. Now, because of the narrowness of the strait there can be no access by ship to the harbour without the consent of those who hold the Pharos. In view of this, Caesar took the precaution of landing his troops while the enemy was preoccupied with fighting, seized the Pharos and posted a garrison there. The result was that safe access was secured for his corn supplies and reinforcements*. In the other parts of the town they parted after indecisive fighting and neither side was beaten – the reason being the confined space. After a few had been killed on either side, Caesar drew a cordon round the most vital positions and constructed defences during the night. In this area of the town there was a small part of the palace, into which he himself

* He had sent round to all the near-by provinces and summoned reinforcements.

had initially been admitted to live, and there was a theatre adjacent to the house which served as a citadel and had access to the harbour and to the dockyards as well. He augmented these defences on subsequent days, so that they could serve as a barrier in place of a wall, and he would not be obliged to fight against his will.

Meanwhile the younger daughter of Ptolemy[93], hoping to take possession of the throne while it was untenanted, left the palace, joined Achillas, and began to wage war jointly with him. However, a quarrel soon arose between them about the leadership; this increased the bounties to the troops, for each tried separately to win their support by lavish largesse. While this was going on among the enemy, Pothinus, the king's tutor and regent, who was in Caesar's part of the town, was sending messengers to Achillas urging him not to slacken in his efforts or lose heart. His intermediaries were betrayed and arrested, and Pothinus was put to death by Caesar. These events were the beginning of the Alexandrian war.

THE ALEXANDRIAN WAR

I. EVENTS IN EGYPT

1. Military preparations

1. When the Alexandrian war flared up, Caesar sent for all the
ships from Rhodes, Syria and Cilicia; he sent for archers from
Crete and cavalry from Malchus, king of the Nabataeans[1]. He
gave orders for ballistic machines to be collected from all quarters,
corn to be dispatched and auxiliary troops brought in. Meanwhile,
the fortifications were worked on and enlarged every day, and all
parts of the town which appeared insufficiently strong were
equipped with protective sheds and screens. Battering rams were
applied through apertures in some buildings against the buildings
adjoining, and the defence works were extended into such space
as was thus created by demolition or was captured by force.
Alexandria is almost entirely secure against fire; the buildings
have no carpentry or timber, and are composed of masonry constructed in arches and roofed with rough-cast or flag-stones.
Caesar took special pains, by extending his works and bringing up
screens, to shut off from the rest of the city that part which was
rendered most cramped by the marsh that formed a barrier to the
south of it. His aims were: firstly, once the city had been divided
into two, to have his forces under the control of one authority
with a single strategy; secondly, to enable help to be brought from
one part of the town to the other to support his men if they were
in difficulties; thirdly and most important, to secure a plentiful
supply of water and fodder, as he had only a scanty supply of one
and none at all of the other, whereas the marshland could provide
plenty of both.

2. This did not cause the Alexandrians, for their part, to hesitate
or delay in carrying out their preparations. They had in fact already dispatched to all parts of Egyptian territory, as far as the
royal power extended, envoys and recruiting officers to hold a
levy; they had conveyed into the town a large quantity of missiles and ballistic machines and had gathered a vast horde of troops.
Moreover, huge workshops had been set up inside the city. They

had also armed the adult male slaves, to whom the wealthier owners supplied daily food and pay. This numerous force they stationed at various points to guard the outlying districts; the veteran cohorts they kept in the most densely populated parts of the town and relieved them of ordinary duties, so that they could act as a reserve force to bring reinforcements to any part of the city where there should be fighting. Every street and alleyway they had blocked with a triple barrier, built of dressed blocks of stone and no less than forty feet high. The lower-lying parts of the city they had fortified with tall towers, ten storeys high. They had, besides, built some more towers of the same height which were moveable; and putting wheels under these they used horses and ropes to tow them along the straight streets[2] to wherever they wanted them.

3. The city, being very productive and possessing abundant stores, furnished equipment of all kinds. The inhabitants themselves were intelligent and sharp-witted; and they showed such smartness in copying what they observed our men doing that it seemed almost as if our men were imitating their operations; they also devised many expedients for themselves. They were attacking our lines, while simultaneously defending their own. Both in councils of war and in public assemblies their leaders kept repeating that the Roman people were gradually getting into the habit of taking over the kingdom. 'A few years ago,' they said, 'Aulus Gabinius was in Egypt with an army. Pompey, in his flight, betook himself here. Caesar has come with his armies and the death of Pompey has done nothing to prevent Caesar from lingering here. If we do not drive him out, the kingdom will be turned into a province. We must act quickly; for while he is cut off by storms owing to the season of the year he cannot receive reinforcements from overseas.'

4. Meanwhile, as mentioned above*, a disagreement had arisen between Achillas, the commander of the veteran forces, and Arsinoe, the younger daughter of Ptolemy. Each was laying plots against the other and trying to seize the supreme command. Arsinoe, with the help of her tutor, the eunuch Ganymede, stole a march on Achillas and killed him. After his murder she herself,

[* C.W. III. 112.]

with no colleague and no guardian, held the supreme command; the army was put in the charge of Ganymede, who on taking over increased the bounties to the troops and carried out the rest of his duties with invariable thoroughness.

2. *The water supply poisoned*

5. Almost the whole of Alexandria is riddled with underground channels connected with the Nile, by which water is conveyed to private houses. This water in course of time settles down and grows clear and it is this which householders and their establishments are in the habit of using; for the water brought down by the Nile is so muddy and turbid that it gives rise to many different illnesses; but the common people must perforce be content with it, since there is not a single public fountain in the whole city. However, the main channel was in that part of the city which was in the hands of the Alexandrians, and this circumstance suggested to Ganymede the possibility of cutting off our men's water supply. (Being dispersed in various districts to guard the defence-works, they were making use of water drawn from channels and wells in private houses.)

6. Ganymede's plan was adopted and he embarked on this large and difficult task. He blocked up the channels and cut off all those parts of the city held by himself; then, using wheels and machinery, he proceeded to pump large quantities of water up from the sea, and kept pouring this continuously down from the higher ground towards Caesar's part of the city. As a result, the water drawn from the nearest houses was a little more salty than usual, and this aroused great speculation among our men as to how it could have come about. They could scarcely credit their own senses, since those lower down said that the water they were getting was of the same quality and taste as usual. They all began comparing, and discovered by tasting how much the water differed. In a short time, indeed, the water from the nearest region was completely undrinkable, while the water from lower down was gradually found to be more and more spoilt and brackish.

7. This removed their doubts; and they were seized with such

panic that they all believed themselves in extreme jeopardy. Some said that Caesar was delaying the order to embark, while others were much more concerned at the impossibility, as they thought, of keeping their preparations for withdrawal secret from the Alexandrians, as they were such a short distance away, or of making their escape to the ships, with the Alexandrians pursuing hotly on their heels. Now, there were a great many townsfolk in Caesar's part of the city, whom he had not moved from their dwellings because they made a show of being loyal to our men and appeared to have broken away from their own people; but if I had to defend the Alexandrians as being neither deceitful nor foolhardy, I should merely be wasting a lot of words; indeed, when one gets to know both the nation and its nature, no one can doubt that this breed is most apt to be treacherous.

8. Caesar used both coaxing and reasoning to allay his men's fears. He declared that if they dug wells fresh water could be found, because every coastal district naturally had veins of fresh water. Even if the nature of the Egyptian coast should be different from all the rest, none the less, since they had unhindered control of the sea and the enemy had no fleet, they could not be stopped from fetching water every day by ship, either from Paraetonium to the left or the island[3] to the right, since these two trips were never simultaneously prevented by adverse winds. As for flight, it was out of the question, not merely for those for whom their reputation came first, but even for those who thought of nothing but their lives. It was only with great effort that they could beat back the direct onslaughts of the enemy from the fortifications; if they abandoned these, they would be no match for the enemy either in numbers or in position. Besides, embarkation, especially from small boats, involved difficulty and delay, while the Alexandrians had on their side extreme speed and familiarity with the area and the buildings. Their victory would make them more insolent than ever; they would dash ahead seizing the higher ground and the buildings, and so prevent our men from withdrawing and reaching the ships. So, he said, they should put that idea out of their heads and concentrate on the necessity of conquering at all costs.

9. After rousing his men's spirits with this speech, Caesar in-

structed the centurions to suspend all other operations and have the men devote themselves to digging wells, working continuously through the night. The task was undertaken, with everyone setting to enthusiastically, and in one night a great quantity of fresh water was found. Thus the laborious contrivances and mighty efforts of the Alexandrians were counteracted by a short period of work. Two days later the Thirty-seventh legion, part of Pompey's surrendered troops[4], which had been embarked by Domitius Calvinus together with corn, weapons, missiles and ballistic engines, put in to the coast of Africa a little above Alexandria. This fleet was prevented from making harbour by an east wind, which blew continually for many days; but in all that area there are excellent places for anchorage. As they were detained there a long time and were suffering from shortage of water, they sent a fast boat to inform Caesar.

3. Naval engagements

10. To decide for himself what action appeared necessary, Caesar went on board ship, and ordered all the fleet to follow. He did not embark any of the troops, because he did not wish to leave the fortifications unmanned, as he was going rather far away. When he reached a place called Chersonesus, he put some of the rowers ashore to fetch water. Some of their number went too far away from the ships in search of plunder and were caught by enemy cavalry. From them the enemy learned that Caesar himself had come with the fleet and that he had no troops on board. This information made them believe that fortune had offered them a chance of victory. They therefore manned with marines all the ships they had ready[5] for sailing and met Caesar on his return with the fleet. Caesar did not wish to fight that day, for two reasons: firstly, he had no troops on board; secondly, it was late afternoon, and night was likely to give increased confidence to those who could rely on their familiarity with the place. Besides, he would not have the advantage of exhorting his men, since no exhortation was quite appropriate which could not single out individual instances of courage or slackness. Caesar therefore

withdrew such of the ships as he could to land at a place where he thought the enemy would not be able to follow.

11. There was one ship from Rhodes on Caesar's right wing, moored a long way from the rest. Seeing this, the enemy could not restrain themselves; four decked ships and several open ones bore down on it at speed. Caesar was impelled to go to the rescue, to avoid the disgrace of suffering an ignominious trouncing in full view of the enemy, although his opinion was that if anything untoward should happen to the men on board, they would deserve it. Battle was joined and the Rhodians fought energetically. In all their engagements they had been outstanding for military skill and courage, and on this occasion in particular they did not hesitate to bear the whole brunt of the attack, in case it should seem their fault if a defeat was sustained. They fought, therefore, with marked success. One enemy quadrireme was captured, a second sunk and two stripped of all their combatants, while a great number of the combatants on the remaining ships as well were killed. If the battle had not been cut short by nightfall, Caesar would have secured the whole enemy fleet. This disaster completely broke the enemy's spirit, and Caesar returned to Alexandria with his own victorious vessels, towing the merchant ships against a gentle breeze.

12. When the Alexandrians saw themselves now worsted not by the courage of combat troops but by the skill of naval crews, they were so demoralized at this reverse that they began to lose confidence in their ability to defend themselves from the buildings which, together with their high position, had been of help to them. They used all the timber they had to build a barrier, as they feared that our fleet might even come right up to the land and attack. However, after Ganymede declared in the council that he would replace the lost ships and increase the size of the fleet as well, they were filled with renewed optimism and confidence and began to repair the old ships, applying themselves to the work with energy and enthusiasm. They had lost more than 110 warships in the dockyards and the harbour, but even so they did not abandon the idea of restoring the fleet. They saw that if they had a strong fleet reinforcements and supplies could not be got in to Caesar. Besides, they were seafaring men whose city and native

district were by the sea, and they had been trained in sailing from childhood by daily practice; and so they were eager to avail themselves of a resource that was natural to them and part of their daily lives; and they knew how effective small boats could be. Therefore they went to work with a will to make up the fleet[6].

13. There were guard-ships stationed at all the mouths of the Nile[7] to exact customs duties; these they recalled to Alexandria. There were, tucked away in dockyards belonging to the palace, old ships which had not been used for sailing for many years. These they repaired. They were short of oars; they stripped the roofs off colonnades[8], gymnasia and public buildings, and the planks served as oars. Their native intelligence and the resources of the city both supplied their needs. Anyway, they were not preparing for a long voyage, but attending only to the requirements of the immediate present; they saw that they would have to engage in the harbour itself. And so in a few days, against all expectations, they completed twenty-two quadriremes, and five quinqueremes, to which they added a number of smaller, undecked ships. After rowing trials in the harbour to test the capabilities of each vessel, they put suitable troops on board and made all preparations for battle. Caesar had nine ships from Rhodes*, eight from the Pontus, five from Lycia and twelve from Asia[9]. Ten of these were quinqueremes or quadriremes, the rest smaller and mostly undecked. However, relying on the valour of his troops, and knowing the nature of the enemy forces, he made ready to fight.

14. Both sides were now in a mood of self-confidence. Caesar sailed around Pharos and drew up his ships opposite those of the enemy. He posted the Rhodian ships on the right wing and the Pontic on the left. Between these he left a space of rather less than half a mile, which seemed sufficient for deploying the ships. Behind this line he posted the rest of the ships in reserve, each with orders to follow and assist a designated vessel. Without hesitation the Alexandrians brought out their fleet and drew it up. They placed twenty-two ships in the front line and stationed the rest in a second line as reserves. They also brought out a great number

* Ten had been sent but one had been wrecked on the voyage on the coast of Egypt.

of smaller boats and dinghies, armed with fire-darts, in hopes that their sheer numbers, together with the noise and the flames, could strike terror into our men. Between the two fleets, leaving only a narrow passage, were shoals which belong to the territory of Africa (for they say that half of Alexandria is in Africa). They waited a fairly long time to see which side would take the initiative in crossing over, because they saw that those who got into the narrow passage would find it more awkward both to deploy the fleet and to withdraw in the event of a reverse.

15. The Rhodian ships were under the command of Euphranor, whose nobility of spirit and courage challenged comparison with our own people rather than merely with the Greeks. It was because of his reputation for skill and this spirit of his that he had been chosen by the Rhodians to hold the command of the fleet. Observing Caesar's hesitation, he said, 'It seems to me, Caesar, that you are afraid that if you enter the shoals with your leading ships you may be compelled to fight before you can deploy the rest of the fleet. Leave it to us; we shall bear the brunt of the fighting while the rest are following up. We shan't let you down. We feel ashamed and indignant to watch those people flaunting themselves in front of us any longer.'

Caesar gave him some words of encouragement, praised him warmly and gave the signal for battle. When four of the Rhodian ships had advanced beyond the shoals the Alexandrians surrounded them and attacked. The Rhodians withstood them and deployed shrewdly and skilfully[10], to such effect that in spite of the inequality of numbers none of their ships offered a broadside to the enemy, and none had its oars swept off; they met the enemy's onset head-on every time. Meanwhile the rest of the ships came up after them. Then the confined space forced them to cease relying on skill; the whole contest began to turn on valour. Everyone in Alexandria, both of our people and of the townsfolk, whether occupied on the defence-works or in fighting, made for the highest rooftops, found a place with a view of the whole scene and sent up prayers and vows each to his own immortal gods for victory.

16. The stakes in the contest were by no means equal. If our men were repulsed and defeated, then neither sea nor land offered

them a way of escape, and if they were victorious, the whole
future course of events was still doubtful; whereas if the Alexandrians won the naval battle, they would have complete mastery,
but if they came off worse they could still try their fortune in
other ways. At the same time it seemed a hard and pitiful state
of affairs that a mere handful should be struggling for decisive
victory and the safety of all; if any one of them failed in spirit or
courage, the remainder too would have to look out for themselves,
without having had the opportunity of fighting on their own behalf. Caesar had repeatedly expounded all this during the preceding days to his men, to make them fight with the greater courage
seeing that the safety of all was in their keeping. The same points
had been made to each one by his comrades, friends and acquaintances, who urged them to live up to their own self-esteem and
the good opinion entertained of them by all the others, whose
judgement had selected them to go out to battle.

They fought, therefore, with such determination that this seafaring, sailorly people found no protection in their cleverness and
skill, the larger fleet derived no benefit from its superior numbers,
and the men chosen for their valour out of such a host nevertheless did not equal the courage of our men. In this battle one quinquereme was captured and a bireme with the marines and rowers,
and three were sunk, while our side suffered no losses. The rest
of the Alexandrian ships fled by the shortest way to the town; the
enemy covered their retreat from the piers and buildings over-
looking the water, and prevented our men from coming close.

17. To prevent a recurrence of this situation, Caesar judged that
he must use all possible means to get into his power the island[11]
and the causeway[12] leading to it. He believed that he could attack
the city and the island simultaneously, since the fortifications in
the town were for the most part complete. With this determination he embarked on small craft and dinghies ten cohorts, a picked
body of light infantry and such of the Gallic cavalry as he thought
suitable. He sent decked ships to attack the other side of the
island, in order to split the enemy forces, promising large rewards
for the first to take the island.

At first the enemy sustained our attack on both sides; for there
were simultaneously men fighting defensively from the rooftops

and men-at-arms guarding the shore, where the rugged ground prevented our men from having easy access, and besides these, others were skilfully manoeuvring with light craft and five warships, protecting the straits. However, a few of our men, after making reconnaissance and sounding the shallows, landed on the shore, and were followed by others; and when these made a determined attack on those who had stationed themselves on the level part of the shore, all the people of Pharos turned and fled. Seeing them routed and the harbour left unguarded, those on the ships put in to the shore by the town and disembarked hastily to defend the buildings.

18. They were unable, however, to maintain themselves long within these defences, even though the buildings were not unlike those in Alexandria (though on a smaller scale), with tall towers connected together acting as a wall, and although our men had not come prepared with scaling ladders or hurdles or the other equipment for an assault. Terror robs men of their powers of reason and judgement and impairs their physical capacity; and so it happened on this occasion. Those who had thought themselves a match for us when fighting on equal terms on level ground were now so terrified by the rout of their own men and the killing of a few that they did not dare to make a stand on thirty-foot-high buildings but threw themselves into the sea and swam the distance of about three-quarters of a mile to the town. A good many of these, nevertheless, were captured or killed; the number of prisoners in all was 6,000.

19. Caesar allowed the men to plunder. He gave them orders to demolish the buildings, construct a fort by the arch nearer the Pharos and put a guard there. The people of Pharos had fled and abandoned this arch; the Alexandrians were guarding the other, which was narrower and nearer the town. However, Caesar made a similar attack on this second arch on the following day, since he saw that once he had possession of both, the enemy would be deprived of all chance of sailing out and making sudden raids. He had already dislodged the garrison there by volleys of arrows and missiles from the ships and driven them back into the town and had disembarked the equivalent of three cohorts, which was as many as could form up in the cramped space, while the rest of his

forces were stationed on board ship. Next, he ordered a barricade
to be put up on the side of the bridge facing the enemy, and
ordered the arch[13] sustaining the bridge, which provided a way
out for ships, to be filled up and blocked with stones. When this
had been done, so that no vessel at all could get out, and the
barricade had been begun, all the Alexandrian forces rushed out
of the town and took up position on open ground opposite the
fortifications of the bridge. At the same time they stationed beside
the causeway the fire-boats which they were in the habit of sending through the arches to fire the transports. Our men were fighting from the bridge and from the boats by the causeway.

20. While Caesar was occupied with this situation and urging
on the troops, a large number of our rowers and seamen disembarked from our warships on to the causeway, some impelled by
a desire to watch, others to take part in the fighting. These at first
began driving the enemy boats away from the causeway with
stones and sling-shot, and appeared to be having considerable
success thanks to the number of their missiles; when, however, a
few of the Alexandrians ventured to disembark beyond that spot,
catching them on their exposed side, then they began pelting back
in confusion to the ships, just as they had emerged, with no fixed
order or formation and no discipline. Their flight encouraged
more of the Alexandrians to disembark and they pursued our
flustered troops the more hotly. At the same time those who had
stayed on board began hastily hauling in the gangways and pushing the boats off, in case the enemy should seize them. Our men
in the three cohorts which had taken up position on the bridge
and at the end of the causeway were thrown into confusion by all
this. They heard shouting behind them and saw their comrades
fleeing, and they were meeting a hail of missiles in front. Fearing
that they might be surrounded in the rear and that the ships
might go away and cut off their retreat entirely, they abandoned
the unfinished fortification by the bridge and rushed at top speed
towards the ships. Some of them got on to the nearest ships, only
for them to sink under the weight of so many men. Others were
killed by the Alexandrians while they hung back wondering what
to do. Some were luckier; they reached some ships lying at anchor
ready for action and got away safely, while a few, lifting up their

shields and making determined efforts, swam out to the nearest vessels.

21. Caesar, so long as he was able by exhortation to keep his men by the bridge and the fortification, was exposed to the same danger; when he saw that they were all giving ground, he withdrew to his own vessel. He was followed by a crowd of men who began forcing their way on board and made it impossible to steer the ship or push it off from land; whereupon Caesar, who had guessed that this would happen, jumped overboard and swam out to the ships standing farther off. From there, he sent small boats back to pick up his men in difficulties and saved a considerable number. As for his own ship, it sank under the pressure of numbers and was lost, with all the men on board. In this battle the losses were about 400 legionary troops and a little over that number of seamen and rowers. The Alexandrians strengthened the fort with stout defence-works and numerous missile engines. They hauled up the stones out of the sea and thereafter made free use of the channel for sending out ships.

22. Our men were far from being demoralized by this set-back. Their resentment stimulated them to make sallies in force to attack the enemy fortifications. In the daily skirmishes, whenever an opportunity offered for the Alexandrians to make a sortie and charge they were prevented from coming to grips both by our fortifications and by the ardent spirit of our men. Caesar's exhortations to all and sundry were outstripped by the efforts of the legions and their keenness to fight; indeed, it was necessary rather to restrain them and prevent them from engaging in dangerous encounters, than to urge them on to fight.

23. The Alexandrians, either, as we may conjecture, because they saw that success increased the morale of our men while failure spurred them on, and they knew of no third alternative situation which could give them the superiority in the fighting; or on the advice of supporters of the king among Caesar's forces; or else acting on a plan conceived by themselves and for which a secret mission had obtained the king's approval – the Alexandrians sent a deputation to Caesar asking him to release the king and let him join his own people. They said that the whole people was ready to obey the king's commands; they were weary of a girl who

ruled by proxy and of the cruel despotism of Ganymede. If, with
the king at their head, they entered into relations of trust and
friendship with Caesar, there would be no danger to frighten the
populace and prevent them from submitting.

24. Caesar was very well aware that this was a deceitful nation,
always given to dissimulating their real intentions; nevertheless
he decided that it would be politic to grant their request for pardon. For, if their requests were at all in earnest, then he thought
that the king, if released, would stay loyal; or – an alternative
more in accordance with their nature – if they wanted the king to
be their leader in war, he thought it would be more dignified and
honourable for him to wage war against a king than against a
horde of foreigners and runaway slaves[14]. He urged the king,
therefore, to look to the interests of his ancestral realm, to have
mercy on his renowned country, which had been scarred shame-
fully by fire and destruction, and, firstly, to bring his people back
to their senses and then to keep them sensible; and to show good
faith towards himself and the Roman people, since he trusted him
so much that he was sending him to his own armed foes. Then he
shook hands with the lad, and was about to dismiss him. But the
king, though almost grown-up, began weeping – so as to live up
to the character of his countrymen, for he was well-trained in
wiles. He begged Caesar not to send him away, saying that his
own kingdom was not dearer to him than the sight of Caesar.
Checking the boy's tears, and somewhat moved himself, Caesar
declared that, if those were his sentiments, they would soon be
together again, and he sent him to his people. The king, like a
horse released from the starting box[15] and given its head, began
to wage war against Caesar with such energy that it appeared
that the tears he had shed at their meeting had been tears of joy.
A good many of Caesar's officers, his friends, centurions and common soldiers were pleased that this had happened, since his excessive generosity, as they thought, had been made ridiculous by the
trickery of a boy. As if Caesar's sole motive had been generosity,
and not the most shrewd calculation!

25. The Alexandrians observed that, although they had acquired
a leader, their own morale was no better and that of the Romans
no worse; they were distressed by the jibes of the soldiers at the

king's youth and weakness; and there were rumours, not yet
heard by Caesar, that forces were being brought to him overland
from Syria and Cilicia. Accordingly, they decided to cut off the
food supplies which were being brought in to our forces by sea,
and they stationed vessels ready for action in suitable places near
Canopus to lie in wait for our supply convoys. When this was
reported to Caesar, he ordered the whole fleet to be prepared for
action and mustered. He put Tiberius Nero in command. The
Rhodian ships sailed with this fleet, and with them went Euphranor, without whom no naval engagement had ever been fought,
and none that was not successful. But Fortune is wont to reserve
for a harsher fate those on whom she has heaped most blessings,
and she now accompanied Euphranor in a different aspect from
that she had formerly worn. For when they reached Canopus,
both fleets formed up and engaged, and Euphranor, as usual, was
the first into battle. He holed and sank an enemy quadrireme.
Then he followed its neighbour too far; his comrades did not
follow up fast enough and he was surrounded by the Alexandrians. No one brought him help, either because they thought he
was sufficiently well protected by his courage and good fortune, or
because they were afraid for their own safety. And so the one man
who acquitted himself with success in that engagement was the
only one to die, going down with his victorious battleship.

4. The last stages

26. Meanwhile, Mithridates of Pergamum, a man of high standing at home, skilled and courageous in war, and a loyal and
esteemed friend of Caesar's, had been sent to Syria and Cilicia at
the start of the Alexandrian war to fetch reinforcements. At
about this time he arrived at Pelusium, by the overland route between Egypt and Syria, with the large forces which he had been
able to collect quickly thanks both to his own conscientious efforts
and to the extreme good-will of the states.

Pelusium had been given a strong garrison by Achillas because
of its strategic position – for the whole of Egypt is thought to be
protected as it were by barriers, on the seaward approach by Pharos

and on the landward by Pelusium. Mithridates suddenly surrounded it with large forces. The substantial garrison put up a
stubborn resistance; but thanks to the large numbers of fresh
troops which he kept sending in to relieve the wounded or tired,
and thanks to his persistence and determination in attack, he re-
duced the town on the same day as he first attacked it, and installed a garrison of his own. After this success he pressed on
towards Caesar in Alexandria, peacefully subduing and bringing
over to Caesar's side all the regions which lay on his line of
march, thanks to the prestige which normally attends a victor.

27. There is a place not very far from Alexandria which is perhaps the best known in those parts. It is called Delta, a name
derived from its resemblance to the letter. A certain part of the
river Nile is split and follows two paths which gradually diverge
and are widely separated at the coast, where the river flows into
the sea. When the king learned that Mithridates was approaching this place, knowing that he would have to cross the river, he
sent against him a large force which he thought could certainly
overpower and annihilate Mithridates, or at the least hold him
back. While he hoped that Mithridates would be defeated, he
would be satisfied to hold him back and cut him off from Caesar.
Those troops who managed to cross the river from the Delta and
meet Mithridates first engaged battle, in their hurry to steal a
march on those following and get the sole credit for the victory.
Mithridates met their onset with great prudence, setting up a
fortified camp according to our custom; but when he saw the
enemy rashly and boldly coming right up to the defence-works, he
made a sally all around the camp, and killed a large number of
them. If the rest had not taken advantage of their knowledge of
the district to find cover, and, some of them, withdrawn to the
ships in which they had crossed the river, they would have been
utterly destroyed. When they had recovered a little from their
fright they joined up with those who were following and began
to attack Mithridates again.

28. Mithridates sent a messenger to inform Caesar of these
events, while the king was informed of them by his own men. As
a result the king set out to check Mithridates and Caesar to meet
him at about the same time. The king took the faster route, sailing

down the Nile on which he had a large fleet ready. Caesar did not wish to take this route, to avoid having a naval battle on the river; instead, he sailed round by the sea, which, as shown above *, is said to belong to Africa. However, he met the king's forces before the latter could attack Mithridates and joined the victorious Mithridates with his army intact. The king had halted with his forces in a naturally strong position. The place itself was elevated above the plain which lay beneath it all around, and it was protected on three sides by defences of various types; one side adjoined the river Nile, the second ran along the highest part of the terrain, so as to contain part of the camp, and the third was surrounded by marshland.

29. Between the camp and Caesar's line of march was a narrow river with very high banks, which was a tributary of the Nile and was about seven miles away from the king's camp. When the king learned that Caesar was approaching by this route he sent all his cavalry and some picked light infantry to this river, to prevent Caesar from crossing and to open battle from a distance, high up on the banks. This position would be to their advantage, since courage could confer no benefit nor would cowardice incur any risk. Our cavalry and infantry were thereby stung to resentment at the thought that they had been fighting so long against the Alexandrians without getting the better of them. Therefore the German cavalry scattered, looking for fords in the river, and some of them swam across, where the banks were less high; and meanwhile the legionaries cut down great trees, long enough to reach from one bank to the other, threw these across, and hastily pitching earth on top they crossed over. The enemy were so frightened by their attack that they put all their hopes of safety in flight; but this was in vain, for very few came back from the rout to the king and almost all the rest were killed.

30. After this signal success, the victorious Caesar pressed straight on to the king's camp, judging that his sudden arrival would strike terror into the Alexandrians. When, however, he saw that the camp was protected by a large defence-work, as well as by the nature of the site, and saw the close-packed mass of armed men stationed on the walls, he refused to let his troops,

[* Ch. 14.]

wearied with travelling and fighting, go up to assault it, and he himself pitched camp not far from the enemy. The king had built a fort in a near-by village not far from his camp and had connected it to the camp by walls so as to contain the village. Caesar attacked this fort on the following day and took it. He used all his forces, not because he thought it would be a difficult enterprise with a smaller force, but in order to go straight on and attack the king's camp while the Alexandrians were still in alarm at his success. Therefore, in pursuing the fleeing Alexandrians from the fort to the camp, his troops carried right on up to the fortifications and began to fight fiercely at long range. There was access for an attack by our men in two places, on one side where as we showed there was an unimpeded approach and the other where there was a small gap between the camp and the river Nile. A very large, specially picked force of Alexandrians was defending the side where the approach was easiest; but those who were defending on the side of the river Nile were the most successful in repelling and wounding our men, for the latter were being hit by missiles from two directions, in front from the rampart of the camp, and in the rear from the river, in which a large number of ships were drawn up, harassing our troops with fire from slingers and archers.

31. Caesar saw that his men were fighting as keenly as they could and yet were not making much progress because of the difficulty of the position. He noticed that the Alexandrians had left the highest-lying part of the camp unguarded, both because it had natural protection, and because the men had run down to the scene of the fighting, partly to watch, partly to take part. He ordered some cohorts to go round the camp and attack the highest point. He put in command of these Carfulenus, a man outstanding both for dauntlessness and for military skill. When they reached the place, our men found only a few guards on the fortifications, and they engaged fiercely. The Alexandrians fell into a panic at the noise of fighting coming from different directions, and began running about all over the camp in confusion. Their panic stimulated our men to such a degree that they captured the camp almost simultaneously on all sides, though those on the highest ground were first, and, running down from there, killed large numbers

of the enemy in the camp. In an attempt to escape from this danger, a great many of the Alexandrians threw themselves down in crowds from the rampart on the side adjoining the river. The first of these were overwhelmed in the ditch itself by the collapse of a large part of the wall, while the rest were able to escape more easily. It is known that the king himself fled from the camp and was taken on board a ship, but the vessel was capsized by the crowds of men swimming for the nearest ships and he perished.

32. After this signal and speedy success Caesar was confident of a resounding victory. He hastened with his cavalry by the shortest route to Alexandria and entered victoriously that part of the town occupied by the enemy forces. His expectations were fulfilled; for the enemy, on news of the battle, had no further thought of fighting. On his arrival he reaped the deserved reward of his courage and undaunted spirit; the entire populace of the town threw down their weapons and abandoned the fortifications. They adopted the garb usually worn by suppliants attempting to turn the wrath of despots, brought out all the sacred objects to the sanctity of which they were accustomed to appeal in trying to placate the enmity and wrath of their kings, and coming to meet Caesar they surrendered to him. Caesar received their submission, reassured them, and then proceeded through the enemy lines to his own part of the town; where he received the congratulations of his own men, who were delighted not only at the successful outcome of this great war with all its fighting but also at the happy nature of his arrival.

33. Caesar thus gained possession of Egypt and Alexandria. He appointed as rulers those whom Ptolemy had designated in his will, with appeals to the Roman people not to allow them to be changed. The older of the two boys, the king, being dead, Caesar handed over the rule to his younger brother[16] and to the elder of the two daughters, Cleopatra, who had remained loyal and stayed with his forces. The younger, Arsinoe, in whose name, as we described, Ganymede had for a long time ruled as a despot, he decided to banish from the kingdom, so that no fresh quarrel should be started by trouble-makers before the power of the rulers had become established by passage of time. Taking the Sixth legion of veterans with him, he left the rest[17] there, to give support to

the power of kings who could have neither the affection of their own people, because they had remained loyal supporters of Caesar, nor the authority of long usage, since they had been made rulers only a few days before. At the same time he thought it important for the prestige of our empire and for the common good, if the rulers were to remain loyal, that they should have the protection of our forces, while if they proved ungrateful, these same forces could constrain them. When he had finished making all these arrangements, he set off by land for Syria.

II. EVENTS IN ASIA

34. Meanwhile, King Deiotarus had come to Domitius Calvinus, to whom Caesar had assigned the administration of Asia and the neighbouring provinces, to beg him not to allow his own kingdom, Armenia Minor, nor Cappadocia, the kingdom of Ariobarzanes, to be occupied and ravaged by Pharnaces. Unless they were freed from this menace, he said, they could not carry out orders and pay the money promised to Caesar. Domitius knew that the money was necessary for paying military expenses; he also reflected that it was a disgrace to the Roman people, and brought dishonour both on himself and on the victorious Caesar, for the kingdoms of their allies and friends to be occupied by a foreign king. He hastily sent messengers to Pharnaces, ordering him to withdraw from Armenia and Cappadocia and not to try to take advantage of the Roman people's preoccupation with a civil war to make inroads on its rights and authority. Thinking that his injunction would be more effective if he took an army nearer the region, he went to the legions and took one of the three, the Thirty-sixth, with him, sending the other two to Caesar in Egypt in response to a dispatch summoning them. (One of the two did not take part in the campaign of Alexandria, as it had been sent by the overland route through Syria.)

To the Thirty-sixth Domitius added two native legions which Deiotarus had had for several years, established in accordance with our methods of training and armament, and 100 cavalry, and he took the same number from Ariobarzanes. He sent Publius Sestius to the quaestor Gaius Plaetorius to fetch the legion which had been made up of troops hastily levied in Pontus, and Quintus Patisius to Cilicia for auxiliary troops. All these forces mustered quickly at Comana under the orders of Domitius.

35. Meanwhile the envoys brought back a reply from Pharnaces. He had withdrawn from Cappadocia, but had retained Armenia Minor, on the plea that he had a right to hold it by ancestral title. Moreover, he was keeping the case of this kingdom open, to be settled by Caesar, and was ready to submit to his decision. Gnaeus Domitius saw that Pharnaces had withdrawn from Cappadocia

perforce and not voluntarily. It was easier for him to defend
Armenia, which was adjacent to his own kingdom, than Cappadocia, which was more remote; and he had thought that Domitius
was going to bring all three Roman legions and had remained the
more boldly in Armenia when he heard that he had sent two of
them to Caesar. Domitius therefore began to insist that he should
withdraw from this kingdom likewise. The legal position of
Armenia was just the same as that of Cappadocia, he said, and
Pharnaces was not within his rights in demanding that the
question be left open to be settled on Caesar's arrival, for the
question would be 'open' only if the original *status quo* were
preserved. With this reply, he set off with the forces described
above for Armenia. He decided to march over the uplands; from
Comana in Pontus there is a high wooded ridge stretching as far
as Armenia Minor and separating Armenia from Cappadocia. He
observed that this route had the definite advantages that on the
heights there could be no surprise attacks by the enemy, and
that Cappadocia, which lay below the ridge, would supply plenty
of foodstuffs.

36. Meanwhile, Pharnaces sent several embassies to Domitius to
treat for peace, bearing him royal gifts. Domitius steadfastly
spurned all the gifts and replied that nothing was more important
to him than the recovery of the prestige of the Roman people and
the realms of her allies. Approaching Nicopolis* by a series of
long marches he pitched camp about seven miles from the town.
Proceeding from this camp, he had to go through a very narrow
and difficult defile. Pharnaces posted in ambush a picked body of
infantry and the whole of his cavalry; he also gave orders for a
large herd of cattle to be spread about in this pass and country
folk and townsfolk to be about in the area, so that, if Domitius
came through the pass as a friend, he would have no suspicions
of an ambush seeing men and animals going about in the fields as
if friends were arriving, while if he came as an enemy, his
soldiers would scatter to seize the booty and could be cut down
while they were dispersed.

[* A town in Armenia Minor. The town itself stands on a plain, but
has a barrier of high mountains on two sides some distance from the
town.]

37. While making these preparations, Pharnaces kept on none the less sending embassies to Domitius to treat for peace and friendly relations. He thought that in this way Domitius could the more readily be deceived. On the contrary, however, the hope of peace gave Domitius a reason for prolonging his stay in the same camp. Pharnaces therefore recalled his men to camp, since he had failed to get an immediate opportunity for ambush and was afraid that it might be discovered.

On the following day Domitius moved nearer Nicopolis and brought his camp up closer to the town. While our men were busy constructing the new camp, Pharnaces marshalled his battle line according to his customary method. His front was a single straight line, with three lines of reserves strengthening either wing, and the same in the centre, while in the gaps between centre and wings to right and left there was a single line. Domitius stationed part of his forces in front of the rampart and completed work on the camp.

38. On the following night Pharnaces intercepted couriers bringing dispatches for Domitius about the situation in Alexandria. From these he learned that Caesar was in extreme danger and that Domitius was commanded to send reinforcements to him as soon as possible and to move nearer Alexandria himself, through Syria. This news made Pharnaces think that he would virtually win the victory if he could spin out the time, since he believed that Domitius would have to depart quickly. He therefore drove two straight trenches, four feet deep and not far apart, from that part of the town where he saw our men would have the easiest access and most favourable position for fighting, to the point which he had determined as the limit for deploying his forces. He drew up his battle line always between these two trenches, but posted all the cavalry on the flanks, outside the trenches, since this was the only way in which they could be of use. They greatly outnumbered our cavalry.

39. Domitius was more alarmed at Caesar's danger than his own; but he thought he could not safely depart if he were either to try to secure the terms which he had already rejected or were to leave after being refused terms. Accordingly, he formed his men up for battle not far from the camp. He stationed the Thirty-sixth

legion on the right wing, the Pontic on the left and Deiotarus's legions in the centre, forming up the latter on a very narrow front and posting the remaining cohorts[18] as reserves. The two armies then proceeded to battle, arranged as described.

40. Both sides received the signal and charged almost simultaneously. The fighting was fierce and accompanied with varying success. The Thirty-sixth charged the royal cavalry outside the trench and was so successful that it went right up to the town walls, crossed the ditch, and began attacking the enemy in the rear. The Pontic legion, however, on the other wing, drew back a little way from the enemy and attempted to go round and cross over the trench in order to attack the enemy on their exposed flank, but were pinned down and overpowered while engaged in crossing. As for Deiotarus's legions, they scarcely withstood the enemy charge. And so the king's forces, being victorious on the right wing and in the centre, all turned against the Thirty-sixth. The latter bore the onset of the winning forces bravely, and when they were surrounded by the large numbers of the enemy, with extreme presence of mind they formed a circle and so withdrew towards the foothills of the mountains, where Pharnaces was unwilling to follow because the position would be to his disadvantage. Almost the whole of the Pontic legion was lost and the greater part of Deiotarus's troops killed. The Thirty-sixth, however, withdrew to the high ground with the loss of no more than 250. In that battle fell several men of distinction and renown, Roman knights. After this defeat, Domitius rallied the remains of his army and retired by a safe route through Cappadocia into Asia.

41. Pharnaces was delighted at his success. Hoping to get what he wanted from Caesar, he occupied Pontus in full force. There he behaved as a conqueror and a cruel despot; promising himself his father's fortune but with a happier outcome, he stormed many towns, plundered the property both of Roman citizens and of Pontic subjects, and inflicted on those men whose beauty or youth at all recommended them a punishment more wretched than death itself[19]. So, meeting with no resistance, he took possession of Pontus, congratulating himself on the recovery of his hereditary kingdom.

III. EVENTS IN ILLYRICUM

42. About the same time a setback was suffered in Illyricum[20], a province which in the preceding months had been held not only without disgrace but actually with credit. For in that summer Quintus Cornificius, Caesar's quaestor, was sent there as propraetor with two legions. The province had very little resources for feeding armies and had been exhausted and ravaged by the neighbouring wars and by rebellions. Nevertheless, Cornificius both recovered and held on to the province, thanks to his own good sense and conscientiousness, for he took good care not to make any rash advances. Fortresses had been established in several places on high ground, and their favourable position encouraged the garrisons to come down and make raids. Cornificius stormed these and allowed the soldiers to plunder them. Although they provided lean pickings, nevertheless the loot was welcome, in view of the general bareness of the province, and especially welcome as the reward of bravery. When Octavius, in his flight from the battle of Pharsalus, put in with a large fleet on that coast, Cornificius, with a few vessels belonging to the Iadertini, who had always displayed outstanding loyalty to Rome, seized some of Octavius's shattered ships. As a result, by adding the captured ships to those of his allies he was capable of undertaking naval warfare too.

The victorious Caesar now in pursuit of Gnaeus Pompeius in a totally remote part of the world, heard that several of his opponents had collected the remnants of their forces and gone to Illyricum, as the nearest place to Macedonia. He sent orders to Gabinius to take the legions of newly-levied troops and go to Illyricum. There he was to join forces with Quintus Cornificius and repel any danger that menaced the province. If, however, the province did not need large forces for its protection, he was to take the legions into Macedonia. Caesar ordered this in the belief that the whole of that area would be ready to renew warfare while Gnaeus Pompeius was alive.

43. When Gabinius arrived in Illyricum it was the difficult

winter season. He may have overestimated the resources of the province, or he may have been expecting a lot from the good fortune of the victorious Caesar, or relying on his own courage and skill, thanks to which he had often, in the perils of war, achieved outstanding successes as an independent commander under his own auspices[21]. Anyhow, he received no help from the resources of the province, which was in part exhausted and in part disloyal, and it was impossible for him to bring in supplies by sea because of stormy weather. And so, constrained by serious difficulties, he conducted the campaign not as he wished but as he had to. The result was that when he was forced through lack of supplies to try to storm fortresses or towns in extremely severe weather, he was frequently worsted, and became such an object of contempt to the enemy that as he was withdrawing to Salonae, a sea-coast town inhabited by staunch and loyal Roman citizens, he was forced to fight while on the march. In this battle he lost more than 2,000 soldiers, thirty-eight centurions and four tribunes. He made his way to Salonae with the remainder of his forces and there, overcome by all manner of difficulties, he died of an illness within a few months. His ill-luck while alive and his sudden death raised Octavius's hopes of securing possession of the province. However, the conscientiousness of Cornificius and the courage of Vatinius, as well as the influence of fortune, which is a very powerful factor in war, put a stop to his success.

44. While Vatinius was at Brundisium he learned what had happened in Illyricum. He received frequent dispatches from Cornificius summoning him to come to the aid of the province and he heard that Marcus Octavius had made a treaty with the natives and was attacking our garrisons in several places, partly by sea using his own forces, and partly on land using those of the natives. Vatinius was in bad health and had barely the bodily strength to carry out his projects; nevertheless by sheer courage he overcame his physical handicap as well as the difficulties involved in the season and the haste of the preparations. He himself had only a few warships in the harbour, and so he wrote to Quintus Calenus in Achaea asking him to send a fleet. As this was not forthcoming quickly enough – for our forces were in great danger, and unable to withstand the assault of Octavius –

Vatinius fitted beaks on a number of light vessels. He had a considerable quantity of these although the vessels were not big enough for engaging in battle. With these boats he augmented his fleet and embarked veterans, of whom he had large numbers from all the legions, who had been left behind at Brundisium on the sick-list when the army was being conveyed across to Greece. He then proceeded to Illyricum. Among the coastal tribes, he recovered some who had defected and gone over to Octavius; others, who had refused to change their minds, he passed by, since he felt bound to allow nothing to delay him in catching Octavius as speedily as possible. Octavius in the meantime was assailing Epidaurus, where we had a garrison, both by land and by sea. The arrival of Vatinius forced him to abandon the siege and Vatinius rescued the garrison.

45. Octavius knew that Vatinius's fleet consisted in large part of light boats, and relying on the strength of his own fleet he moored by the island of Tauris. Vatinius sailed there after him, not because he knew that he had stopped there in particular, but because he had decided to pursue him farther. He was approaching Tauris with his ships widely separated because of the stormy weather and as he had no suspicion of the presence of the enemy, when he saw a vessel coming towards him, manned with troops and with its yards lowered to the middle of the mast. Observing this he quickly ordered the sails to be lowered[22], the yards let down and the troops armed. Then he hoisted the flag he used for giving the battle signal and ordered the foremost of the ships following to do the same. Vatinius's men began preparing to meet the sudden emergency; then Octavius's force, already prepared, began coming out of the harbour. Both sides formed up. Octavius's were better ordered, but Vatinius's were readier in spirit.

46. Vatinius observed that his ships were neither large enough nor numerous enough to fight a chance engagement; accordingly he decided to leave the issue to fortune, and was himself the first to attack Octavius's quadrireme with his own quinquereme. Octavius on his part had his vessel rowed swiftly and strongly against Vatinius's, and the two ships collided head-on with their beaks so hard that Octavius's ship had its beak knocked off and was held entangled by its woodwork. Battle was joined fiercely

in other parts of the area and the ships flocked in particular to the support of the two commanders; as a result, as each vessel came to help its own side, there was a large-scale battle at close quarters over a confined area of sea. The more closely-packed they could get the ships in the battle, the more Vatinius's men had the advantage. Displaying remarkable courage, they did not hesitate to jump across from their own vessels into those of the enemy, and, the terms of the fighting being thus equalized, they began to carry the day by their marked superiority in valour. Octavius's own galley was sunk and a number of others were captured or pierced with beaks and sunk. Some of his marines were slain on the ships, others knocked into the sea. Octavius himself took to a small boat; this, however, sank under the numbers who tried to take refuge in it. Thereupon, despite his wounds, he swam to his escort vessel and was received on board. Night was falling and putting an end to the fighting and a great wind sprang up, so that he was able to flee under sail, followed by several of his ships, which happened to have survived the danger.

47. After this success, Vatinius sounded the retreat and returned victoriously with his forces completely unscathed to the harbour from which Octavius had come out to fight. In the battle he captured from Octavius one pentereme, two triremes, eight two-banked ships and a good many rowers. He spent the following day repairing his own vessels and the captured ones and set off two days later for the island of Issa, where he believed Octavius had fled after the defeat. This island contained the most notable town in that region and the most loyal to Octavius. On his arrival the townsfolk came as suppliants and surrendered to him, and he learned that Octavius with a few small boats had gone off towards Greece with a following wind, and intended to go on from there to Sicily and thence to Africa.

So in a short space of time Vatinius won a resounding victory, recovered the province and returned it to Cornificius, and drove the enemy fleet out of the entire gulf. He then returned to Brundisium with his fleet and his army intact.

IV. EVENTS IN SPAIN

48. Now, during the period in which Caesar was blockading Pompey near Dyrrachium, then winning his victory at Palae-pharsalus and fighting at Alexandria amid great dangers (which rumour made out to be even greater), Quintus Cassius Longinus who had been left in Spain as propraetor to hold the Further province had made himself extremely unpopular. This may have been the effect of his own habitual disposition, or of the hatred he had conceived for the province when as quaestor he was wounded there in an ambush. He was aware of his unpopularity, either from a consciousness on his part that the province returned his dislike, or from many signs and evidences on the part of people who found it difficult to conceal their hatred, and he was anxious to compensate for his unpopularity in the province by winning the affection of the army. He therefore concentrated his army in one place, and immediately promised them a hundred sesterces apiece. Not long afterwards, after storming the town of Medo-brega and Mount Herminius in Lusitania, where the townsfolk had taken refuge, and being acclaimed *imperator* he awarded the men a hundred sesterces each. He also gave numerous large rewards to individual soldiers. All this produced an appearance of affection for the time being from the troops but gradually and imperceptibly undermined the strictness of military discipline.

49. Cassius posted his legions in their winter quarters and went to Corduba to hold his legal sessions. He had previously incurred large debts and these he determined to settle by imposing heavy tax burdens on the province; besides, as is the usual consequence of habitual largesse, greater benefactions were expected of the giver, to maintain the reputation of open-handedness. Rich men were forced to pay sums of money which Longinus not only allowed but actually insisted should be accredited personally to him. People of slender means were lumped in with the rich because of personal quarrels, and no source of gain, whether large and manifest or small and mean, was overlooked by the governor, both in his official capacity and in private. Everyone who had

anything to lose was made to give bail or put on the list of accused. As a result, men had the fear of prosecution to worry them, as well as the losses and damage to their personal estates.

50. The outcome was that, as Longinus as governor was behaving just as he had done as quaestor, the provincials for the second time began laying the same sort of plot to encompass his death. Their hatred was intensified by some of his retinue who, although they were his partners in the business of extortion, none the less detested the man in whose name they did wrong; whatever booty they got they put down to their own credit, while whatever they missed or had difficulty in getting they ascribed to Cassius. He enrolled a new legion, the Fifth[23], and this still further increased his unpopularity, both because of the levy itself and because of the extra expense. A force of 3,000 cavalry was made up and equipped at enormous expense. The province was given no respite.

51. Meanwhile, a dispatch arrived from Caesar, ordering Cassius to bring his army across to Africa and march through Mauretania to the border of Numidia, because Juba had sent large reinforcements to Gnaeus Pompeius and was expected to send still greater ones. This dispatch sent Cassius into raptures of delight at the thought that he was being given such a chance of getting his hands on new provinces and an extremely productive kingdom. Accordingly, he himself went to Lusitania to muster the legions and round up auxiliary forces. He commissioned certain individuals to prepare a supply of corn and 100 ships, and to assess and levy monetary contributions, so that there should be no delay on his return. He was back sooner than anyone expected; for Cassius was not deficient in energy or alertness, especially when he wanted something.

52. The army were mustered and encamped at Corduba. Cassius held an assembly and informed them of Caesar's orders. He promised them 100 sesterces each on arrival in Mauretania. The Fifth legion would stay in Spain. He then went to Corduba. On the afternoon of the same day he was entering the court-house when a certain Minucius Silo, a client of Lucius Racilius, handed him a petition, as though he were a soldier making some request. He then fell in behind Racilius, who was at Cassius's side, as though

waiting for a reply, and, when he got an opportunity, quickly slipped in between them, seized Cassius from behind with his left hand and with his right stabbed him twice with a dagger. The cry was raised and all the conspirators ran to the attack. Munatius Flaccus ran his sword through the attendant nearest him and killed him, then wounded an officer, Quintus Cassius. Thereupon Titus Vasius and Lucius Mercello with similar boldness gave help to Flaccus, their fellow-townsman. (They were all from Italica.) Lucius Licinius Squillus dashed at Longinus himself as he lay there and inflicted slight wounds.

53. There was a rush to protect Cassius, for he was in the habit of being attended at all times by a large armed bodyguard of Beronians and time-expired soldiers. These kept off the rest who were coming up to join in the assassination, including Calpurnius Salvianus and Manilius Tusculus. Minucius's attempt to run away was hampered by stones lying in the street, and he was over-powered and brought before Cassius, who had been carried home. Racilius fled into a friend's house near by and waited to find out for certain whether Cassius had been killed. Lucius Laterensis was quite positive that he had been killed and rushed joyfully to the camp, where he congratulated the native-born troops and those of the Second legion, whom he knew particularly detested Cassius. The mob hoisted him up on to the platform and acclaimed him as praetor; for there was no one either born in the province – like the men of the native legion – or else virtually a provincial as the result of long residence there – like the men of the Second – who did not share in the hatred felt by the entire province for Cassius. As for the Thirtieth and Twenty-first legions, they had been en-rolled in Italy only a few months before and assigned to Cassius by Caesar, and the Fifth had only recently been raised in the province.

54. Meanwhile it was reported to Laterensis that Cassius was alive. He received this news with more chagrin than alarm, but quickly recovered himself and went to see Cassius. When the Thirtieth legion learned what had happened, they marched into Corduba to help their commander. The Twenty-first did likewise and were followed by the Fifth. There were now two legions left in camp. The Second were afraid that they might be left alone

and as a result their true feelings might be inferred; and so they followed the example of the others. The native legion stuck by its convictions and could not be budged by any kind of intimidation.

55. Cassius ordered the arrests of those who were named as privy to the plot. He sent the legions back to camp, retaining five cohorts of the Thirtieth. On the evidence of Minucius he learned of the involvement in the conspiracy of Lucius Racilius, Lucius Laterensis and Annius Scapula – the last a man of very high position and influence in the province and as close a friend of his as Laterensis and Racilius – and he promptly vented his indignation by ordering them to be executed. He handed Minucius over to his freedmen to be tortured, and likewise Calpurnius Salvianus. Salvianus had made a statement in evidence in which he cited even more people as conspirators – some believe truthfully, others protest that he was under duress. The same punishment was inflicted on Lucius Mercello. Squillus named more conspirators; Cassius ordered them to be executed unless they bought themselves off; for instance, he openly settled with Calpurnius for 60,000 sesterces and with Quintus Sestius for 50,000. Even if their fines were justified by extreme guilt, nevertheless the fact that the danger to his life and the pain of his wounds were compounded for cash shows that in Cassius there was a struggle between cruelty and avarice.

56. Several days later he received a dispatch from Caesar, informing him that Pompey had been defeated in battle, had lost his forces and fled. Cassius received the news with mixed feelings. The news of victory compelled him to feel happy, but the end of the war would put an end to his present licence; and so he could not decide whether he preferred to be free from all fears or free from all restraint. When his wounds were healed, he summoned all those in whose books he was entered as a debtor for various sums and ordered them to enter him as a creditor for those sums; if he thought anyone was getting off too lightly, he demanded still more money from him. He also held a levy of Roman knights, conscripting men in all the colonies and citizen communities; and as they were terrified of having to serve overseas, he ordered them to purchase their discharge from their military oath. This was

a large source of revenue, but a still larger source of hatred. After this, he held a review of the entire army and sent the legions and auxiliaries he intended to take with him to Africa to the point of embarkation. He himself went to Hispalis to inspect the fleet which he was having prepared and waited there, because he had issued an edict to the entire province ordering those who had not paid up the monies demanded to come to him personally. This summons seriously disturbed them all.

57. Meanwhile he received a report from Lucius Titius, who had been a tribune in the native legion, that that legion while encamped at Ilipa had mutinied and killed several centurions who refused to let them strike camp. The legion had then left the Thirtieth (the two of them were jointly under the command of the lieutenant Quintus Cassius) and hurried to join the Second, which was being taken to the strait by a different route. Thereupon Cassius set out by night with five cohorts of the Twenty-first and in the morning reached Naeva. He waited there that day, to observe what was happening, and then proceeded to Carmo. The Thirtieth, the Twenty-first, four cohorts of the Fifth and all the cavalry then gathered there, and he heard that four cohorts had been overpowered by the native troops near Obucula and had then accompanied them to join the Second legion; and they had all joined forces and chosen Titus Thorius of Italica as their commander. He hastily held a council of war and sent his quaestor Marcus Marcellus to keep control of Corduba, and the lieutenant Quintus Cassius to Hispalis.

A few days later word arrived that the Roman community at Corduba had revolted and that Marcellus, either voluntarily or under compulsion (reports varied on this), was taking their side, and that the two cohorts of the Fifth legion which had been the garrison force at Corduba were doing likewise. Cassius was furious; he struck camp and on the following day reached Segovia on the river Singilis. There he held an assembly of the troops and tried to find out their feelings. He discovered that they were loyal to him, not for his own sake but for that of the absent Caesar, and would flinch from no danger, so long as the province was rescued for Caesar through their efforts.

58. Meanwhile Thorius led the veteran legions to Corduba. So

that the dispute should not appear to have its origin in any
naturally mutinous spirit either in the soldiers or in himself, and
at the same time in order to oppose an authority of equal weight
to Cassius, who appeared the stronger because he was acting in
Caesar's name, Thorius publicly declared that he intended to recover the province of Gnaeus Pompey. It may be that he did this
also out of hatred for Caesar and support for Pompey, whose name
carried a great deal of weight among those legions which had
been commanded by Marcus Varro. What his real motive was,
however, was a matter of general speculation; certainly, this was
his professed motive, and the troops bore it out so far as to have
the name of Gnaeus Pompey written on their shields. The Roman
community, not merely the menfolk but mothers and young boys
as well, came in a body to meet the legions, and begged them not
to come as enemies and sack Corduba. 'We are with you all,' they
said, 'in opposing Cassius; but please do not force us to act against
Caesar.'

59. The army was touched by the tears and entreaties of so
great a throng. They saw that they had no need of the name and
memory of Pompey in their campaign against Cassius; that
Longinus was as hateful to all the Caesarians as to the Pompeians
and that they could not induce either the Roman community or
Marcus Marcellus to oppose Caesar's cause. And so, they took
Pompey's name off their shields; they adopted Marcus Marcellus
as their leader and gave him the title of praetor, although he
declared he would go on defending Caesar's cause. Then, lending
their support to the Roman community, they encamped near
Corduba. Within two days Cassius camped about four miles
away, on high ground across the river Baetis, in sight of the
town. He wrote to King Bogus in Mauretania and to Marcus
Lepidus the proconsul in Hither Spain, asking them for Caesar's
sake to send help as quickly as possible to the province and
himself. Meanwhile he ravaged the territory of Corduba like an
enemy and set fire to buildings.

60. This shameful outrage made the legions which had chosen
Marcellus as their leader come running to him with entreaties
that he should lead them out to fight. They begged Marcellus
to grant them an opportunity of battle before they witnessed the

shameful destruction of the notable treasures of the people of
Corduba by rapine, sword and fire. Marcellus thought it would
be a very great pity to join battle, since the losses sustained by
both the victors and the losers would alike fall on Caesar, and this
was something he could not help. However, he led his legions
across the Baetis and drew them up for battle. When he observed
that Cassius had drawn up his line in front of his camp, on
higher ground, Marcellus took advantage of the excuse that the
enemy was not coming down into the plain and persuaded his
men to return to camp. And so he began to withdraw his forces.
Cassius knew that Marcellus was weak where his own army was
strong – that is, in cavalry. He therefore sent in his cavalry to
attack the legions as they were withdrawing and killed a good
many of the rearguard on the banks of the river. These losses made
Marcellus realize the snags and difficulties involved in crossing
the river, and he transferred his camp to the other side of the
Baetis. Both leaders brought their armies out in battle formation
frequently, but because of the difficulties of the terrain battle
was never joined.

61. Marcellus was by far the stronger in infantry, since he had
veteran legions which had experience of many battles. Cassius was
relying on the loyalty rather than the valour of his legions.
Accordingly, once the two camps had been brought closer together and Marcellus had seized a position suitable for a fortified
post with which he might prevent Cassius's men from getting
water, Longinus was afraid that he might virtually be put to siege
in territory which was not in his control and was, besides, hostile.
He therefore withdrew from the camp silently by night and
marched quickly to Ulia, a town which he believed to be loyal
to him. Here he pitched camp so close to the town walls as to have
protection from attack on all sides, thanks both to the nature of
the site (Ulia is situated on a high hill) and to the fortifications of
the city itself. Marcellus followed him and pitched camp close by,
as near to Ulia as possible. He then reconnoitred the area and
found that he was compelled to adopt those tactics which he most
wished to follow, i.e. not to have a battle (which he knew would
be impossible to avoid if there were an opportunity, given the
excited feelings of his men), and to prevent Cassius from roaming

too far afield, so that other communities should not suffer the same fate as the people of Corduba. By setting up forts at strategic points and linking these with entrenchments forming a continuous ring he penned in both Cassius and Ulia. Before these works were complete, Cassius sent out all his cavalry, thinking that these would be very useful to him if they prevented Marcellus from collecting fodder and corn, while they would be a severe liability if shut up by a blockade and rendered useless, while consuming his own essential supply of corn.

62. A few days later King Bogus, who had received Cassius's dispatch, arrived with his forces. He joined to the legion he had brought with him several auxiliary cohorts of Spaniards; for, as generally happens in civil wars, while at that time most of the Spanish communities favoured Marcellus, a number took Cassius's side. Bogus arrived with his forces at Marcellus's outer lines. There was fierce fighting on both sides and this was repeated frequently, with fortune assigning victory sometimes to one side and sometimes to the other; however, Marcellus was not dislodged from his lines.

63. Meanwhile, Lepidus arrived at Ulia from the Hither province with thirty-five legionary cohorts and a large number of cavalry and other auxiliaries. His intention was to settle impartially the quarrel between Marcellus and Cassius. On his arrival Marcellus without hesitation voluntarily entrusted himself to Lepidus. Cassius, on the other hand, stayed within his defences, either because he thought he had a better legal claim to power than Marcellus or because he was afraid that Lepidus's mind might already have been influenced by the advances of his opponent. Lepidus pitched camp near Ulia and proceeded to act totally in concert with Marcellus. He refused to allow fighting; he invited Cassius to visit him, giving his personal assurance of his entire safety. Cassius hesitated for a long time, wondering what he should do and how far he should trust Lepidus; but, seeing that he would never achieve anything if he stuck to his present attitude, he demanded that the entrenchments should be dismantled and that he should be allowed to depart freely.

They had not only made a truce but had practically reached a peace settlement, the fortifications were being razed and the guards had been withdrawn, when the king's forces made an attack on the fort of Marcellus nearest to the king's camp and overpowered a number of troops there. This came as a surprise to everyone – if, indeed, 'everyone' included Cassius, for there was some doubt as to whether he knew about it. If Lepidus had not angrily come quickly to the rescue and broken up the fight, there would have been greater losses.

64. Since the way was now open to Cassius, Marcellus joined camps with Lepidus, and they set off with their forces to Corduba, at the same time as Cassius started towards Carmo. About the same time Trebonius arrived to take over the province as proconsul[24]. On learning of his arrival, Cassius distributed the legions and cavalry he had with him into winter quarters, then he himself hastily gathered his possessions and hurried to Malaga, where he boarded ship, although it was a bad season for sailing. He himself alleged that he did not wish to trust himself to Lepidus, Trebonius and Marcellus; his friends said that he did not wish to make an undignified progress through the province, the greater part of which had revolted against him; others said that he did not wish the money he had amassed by his unbounded extortions to fall into the hands of anyone else. He set off in what, for winter, was good weather; but after he had put in at the river Ebro to avoid a night voyage, the weather became somewhat stormier. However, believing that there would be no greater danger in sailing, he set off. But there were billows rolling in against him at the river mouth; he could not turn the ship because of the force of the river current, nor could he hold course straight ahead because of the size of the waves. The ship sank right in the river mouth, and he perished.

V. CAESAR CHASTENS PHARNACES: ZELA

65. Caesar came from Egypt to Syria. There he learned from persons who had come to him from Rome and from information in dispatches from the city that there was a great deal that was bad and harmful in the administration at Rome and that no part of the government was being properly conducted; for quarrels among the tribunes were giving rise to dangerous disturbances[25] and the corruption and indulgence of military tribunes and legionary commanders were allowing a great many breaches of military practice, which were bound to undermine strict discipline[26]. All this seemed to demand his presence; nevertheless he thought priority must be given to organizing the provinces and districts into which he had just come so that they would be free from internal disturbances, would adopt laws and judicial procedures, and would cease to fear external enemies. He hoped that this could quickly be accomplished in Syria, Cilicia and Asia, since these provinces were not being harassed by any hostilities; he saw that there was a weightier task in front of him in Bithynia and Pontus. He was receiving reports that Pharnaces had not withdrawn from Pontus, and he did not think it likely that he would withdraw, since his successful battle against Domitius Calvinus had inflated him with self-confidence. He spent some time in most of the communities of standing, gave rewards to those communities and individuals who had merited them, and heard and gave judgement on long-standing disputes. He formally received under his protection the kings, tyrants and dynasts of the neighbouring province, who had all come flocking to him, on condition that they would accept responsibility for guarding and defending the province, then sent them away as firm friends of himself and of the Roman people.

66. He remained a few days in the province and appointed as commander of the legions and governor of Syria Sextus Caesar, his friend and relative. He himself went to Cilicia on the fleet by which he had come. He summoned an assembly from all the

communities of this province of Tarsus, which is perhaps the best-known and strongest town in the whole of Cilicia. There he settled all the affairs of the province and of the neighbouring states. Then in his eagerness to get the campaign started, he went off without further delay, and proceeded by forced marches to Cappadocia. He spent two days at Mazaca and then came to Comana, the site of the most ancient and sacred shrine of Bellona[27] in Cappadocia. This place is held in such reverence that the priest of the goddess is considered by the entire people to come second in dignity, authority and power to the king. This priesthood he assigned to a very noble Bithynian, Lycomedes. He was of royal descent and his right to the priesthood which he was now reclaiming was incontestable, although during the long passage of time, owing to the vicissitudes of fortune of his ancestors and a change in the royal dynasty, the continuity had been broken.

Ariobarzanes and his brother Ariarathes had both served Rome well. So that Ariarathes should not be tempted by the prospect of succession to the throne, nor, as heir to the throne, intimidate Ariobarzanes, Caesar gave Ariarathes part of Lesser Armenia and put him under the suzerainty and authority of Ariobarzanes. Then he proceeded on his journey as swiftly as before.

67. As he approached Pontus and the territory of Gallograecia, he was met as a suppliant by Deiotarus. The latter at this time was tetrarch of almost the whole of Gallograecia, though the other tetrarchs insisted that he had no right to it, either in law or by custom. At any rate, he had certainly been styled king of Lesser Armenia by the Senate. He laid aside his royal insignia and came to Caesar in the dress, not merely of a private person, but actually of someone on trial in court[28], and begged his forgiveness; he said that he had supported Pompey under the constraint of commands backed by the menace of military force, situated as he was in a region where there were no forces of Caesar's to protect him; it had been none of his concern to pass judgement on the disputes of the Roman people, but merely to obey present commands.

68. In reply, Caesar recalled the many benefits he had conferred on Deiotarus by public decree when he was consul.[29] He pointed out that his excuses could not forgive his folly, as a man of such conscientiousness and intelligence could have known who was

master of Italy and Rome, on which side the Senate and Roman people and the government were, and who, in short, was consul after Lentulus and Marcellus[30]. However, he was willing to make allowances, in view of Deiotarus's past services, of the old bonds of hospitality and friendship between them, of Deiotarus's age and standing, and of the entreaties of all the guests and friends of Deiotarus who had come flocking in crowds to beg forgiveness for him. He therefore told Deiotarus to resume his royal dress, and said he would consider the disputes among the tetrarchs later. As for the legion which Deiotarus had raised among his own subjects and had equipped and trained in our fashion, he ordered him to bring it, and all his cavalry, to take part in the campaign.

69. On arrival in Pontus, Caesar mustered all his forces at one place. Their numbers were modest and their military experience not extensive. There was the Sixth legion, which he had brought with him from Alexandria and which was a veteran legion which had undergone many toils and dangers; but it had lost many men, owing partly to the difficulties of journeys by land and sea and partly to its numerous campaigns, and it was now so depleted that it consisted of less than 1,000 men. Apart from this, there were three other legions – one that of Deiotarus, and two which had been in the battle which, as described above*, Gnaeus Domitius fought against Pharnaces.

Envoys came to Caesar from Pharnaces asking him above all not to come to their country as an enemy; for Pharnaces would carry out all his commands. They reminded him particularly that Pharnaces had not consented to give Pompey any auxiliary forces to use against Caesar, while Deiotarus, who had given troops, had nevertheless made his peace with Caesar.

70. Caesar replied that he would be absolutely fair to Pharnaces, if he was in fact going to fulfil his promises. However, he warned the envoys, in mild terms as was his habit, not to cite the case of Deiotarus nor to be too pleased with themselves for their good deed in not sending help to Pompey. 'I myself,' he said, 'am never happier than when pardoning suppliants; but I cannot overlook public outrages against the provinces on the part of those who may have done me service. In any case, as for this good deed you

[* Ch. 40–41.]

speak of, it was far more profitable for Pharnaces, who avoided being defeated, than it was for me, to whom the immortal gods granted the victory. As for the great and dreadful wrongs done to the Roman citizens trading in Pontus, I cannot put these right, and so I am prepared to forgive Pharnaces for them. I cannot restore life to the slain nor manhood to the castrated – the torture, worse than death, which Roman citizens have undergone. But Pharnaces must withdraw from Pontus; he must make speed to release the slaves belonging to the tax-gatherers and restore to the allies and to the Roman citizens the rest of the property in his possession. When he has done this, then he may send me the gifts and presents which generals are accustomed to receive from their friends after victory.' (For Pharnaces had sent him a golden crown.) With this reply he sent the envoys back.

71. Pharnaces readily pledged his word for everything. He hoped that Caesar, in his haste to get on, would believe his promises more readily than the facts warranted, in order to proceed more quickly and with a clear conscience to deal with more urgent matters (for no one was unaware that many reasons summoned Caesar back to Rome). Pharnaces therefore began to be dilatory, to demand a more remote date for withdrawal, to propose terms for agreement, in order to create delay, and in short to cheat. Caesar, realizing the fellow's wiliness, did now from necessity what on other occasions he had naturally been accustomed to do: he joined battle before anyone expected it.

72. Zela is a town in Pontus, fairly well defended considering its situation in a plain; for its wall is on a natural hillock, which has almost the appearance of an artificial construction and raises it to a considerable height on all sides. Round this town are many high hills, cut into by valleys. The highest of these, which is very well known in those parts because of the victory of Mithridates[31] and the misfortune of Triarius and defeat of our army, is almost joined to the city by tracks over high ground and is not much more than three miles away. Pharnaces installed himself here with all his forces, after repairing the fortifications of the old camp where his father had been successful.

73. Caesar pitched camp five miles from the enemy. He observed that the valley which protected the king's camp would likewise

by its width protect his own, provided that the enemy did not forestall him in occupying the positions concerned, which were much nearer the king's camp. He ordered materials for a rampart to be conveyed within his lines. These were quickly collected, and on the following night, towards the end of the night, he set out with all his legions in light order, leaving the baggage in the camp. At dawn, surprising the enemy, he captured the very place in which Mithridates had fought his successful battle against Triarius. He ordered the slaves to bring here all the collected materials from the camp, so that none of the soldiers should have to leave the work of fortification since the intervening valley separated the enemy camp from the camp-works which Caesar had begun by no more than a mile.

74. Pharnaces suddenly observed the move at dawn and drew up all his forces in front of the camp. However, the ground between was so uneven that Caesar presumed they were being drawn up mainly in accord with the usual military practice, either to slow up his work by making him keep greater numbers of men under arms, or to demonstrate the royal confidence, so that Pharnaces might give the appearance of maintaining his position as much by armed force as by fortifications. Therefore Caesar was not deterred from going on with the construction, merely drawing up the first line in front of the rampart and letting the rest go on with the work.

Pharnaces, however, decided to engage battle. He may have been tempted by the lucky associations of the place; or perhaps he was influenced by the auspices and omens which, as we heard later, he followed; or perhaps it was because he gathered that we had only a few soldiers under arms – he had believed at first that the large number of slaves who were carrying materials, as though it was their daily task, were soldiers; or perhaps he was relying on his own veteran army, which his envoys boasted had engaged in battle and won forty-two times, while despising our army, which he knew he had repulsed when it was under Domitius's command. Anyhow, whatever the reason, he began to descend the steep side of the valley. Caesar for some time was amused at his vainglorious display and at the way in which his men were crowded together in a position into which no sane enemy would advance. Meanwhile Pharnaces began to climb up the steep hill opposite at the same speed as he had made the sharp descent, and with his troops in order.

75. Caesar was startled by this incredible rashness – or self-confidence. He was caught off-guard and unprepared; he was simultaneously calling the troops away from the fortification work, ordering them to arm, deploying the legions and forming the battle-line; and the sudden bustle that this occasioned caused great alarm among our men. While the ranks were still not drawn up and our men were in disorder, royal chariots armed with scythes threw them into confusion; however, large numbers of missiles were launched at the chariots and they were soon over-powered. They were followed by the enemy in battle formation. The battle-cry was raised and they came to grips. We were greatly helped by the nature of the ground, and greatly also by the kind-ness of the immortal gods[32], who participate in all the fortunes of war, but particularly where it has proved impossible to conduct the battle by reasoned tactics.

76. After hard, bitter fighting at close quarters, the first signs of victory appeared on the right wing, where the veteran Sixth legion was stationed. On that side the enemy were being pushed down the slope; meanwhile on the left wing and in the centre all the king's forces were being routed, much more slowly, but nevertheless by the same divine aid. The ease with which they had come up over the uneven ground was now counterbalanced by the speed with which, once they were dislodged, they were driven down, thanks to the same slope. Many soldiers were lost – some slain, some overwhelmed by their comrades falling on top of them. Those who had the fleetness to escape crossed the valley; but as they had thrown away their weapons they were unable, being unarmed, to take advantage of their position. Our men, however, were exhilarated by their success and did not hesitate to clamber up the slope and attack the fortifications, and despite the resistance of the cohorts left on guard by Pharnaces they soon took the camp. The whole of Pharnaces' host was either killed or captured; he fled with a few horsemen, and if the assault on the camp had not made it easier for him to escape he would have fallen alive into Caesar's hands.

77. At such a victory, Caesar, though many times victorious, was filled with incredible joy, because he had finished a great war so quickly; and he was made the more joyful by the recollection of the peril in which he had suddenly been placed. An easy victory had befallen him in very difficult circumstances. Pontus was recovered and all the royal booty presented to the soldiers. On the following day he ordered the Sixth legion to return to Italy to receive rewards and honours, sent Deiotarus's auxiliaries back home, and left two legions in Pontus with Caelius Vinicianus. He himself set off with the cavalry in light order.

78. So he travelled through Gallograecia and Bithynia to Asia, and heard and judged all the disputes in those provinces. He also assigned powers to kings, tetrarchs and states. He appointed Mithridates[33] of Pergamum, whose swift and successful campaign in Egypt we described above, king of Bosphorus, which had been under the rule of Pharnaces – for Mithridates was of royal descent and had received a royal upbringing. Mithridates, king of the whole of Asia, had on account of his noble origin taken him, when he was small, from Pergamum into his own camp and kept him many years. Also, by interposing a friendly king, Caesar was protecting the provinces of the Roman people against barbarian and hostile kings. He also assigned to Mithridates, by virtue of his race and kinship, the tetrarchy of Gallograecia which Deiotarus had seized and held a few years before. However, he stayed nowhere longer than the needs of the troubles at Rome seemed to warrant. After accomplishing all his business with great success and great speed, he arrived in Italy sooner than anyone expected.

TRANSLATOR'S NOTE

After the death of Pompey, the Pompeians rallied in Africa, where they received support from King Juba. Scipio took over command of the Roman forces.

Caesar, on his arrival in Italy, quelled the mutiny in Campania. At Rome, he passed some interim measures for the relief of debtors. Rewards, for example, governorships and priesthoods, were bestowed on some of his followers, and some were enrolled in the Senate to fill vacancies. Clemency was shown to repentant Pompeians. Caesar was elected consul for 46 B.C., and sailed for Africa.

THE AFRICAN WAR

1. Initial landings in Africa

1. After travelling several days, doing a full day's journey every day without exception, Caesar arrived on 17 December at Lily-baeum, and made it plain that he intended to embark at once, although he was accompanied by no more than a single legion of new recruits and scarcely 600 cavalry. He had his tent set up right on the beach, so that the waves almost broke against it. He did this so that there should be no expectation of any intermission, but everyone should be in a state of readiness, whatever the hour or the day. During this time, as it happened, he did not get any weather suitable for sailing. None the less, he kept the rowers and troops on board ship and kept on the alert for any opportunity of setting off. Meanwhile reports were coming in from the inhabitants of the provinces about the strength of the enemy – it was said that there were innumerable cavalry, four legions belonging to the king, a great force of light infantry, ten legions under Scipio, 120 elephants and several fleets; but in spite of this he was undaunted and remained steadfastly optimistic.

Meanwhile the numbers of his warships grew from day to day; more transports assembled there; and he was joined by four newly-recruited legions, a fifth of veterans, and about 2,000 cavalry.

2. In all, six legions and 2,000 cavalry were gathered; as each legion arrived it was put on board the warships, and the cavalry on the transports. So, he ordered the greater part of the ships to go ahead and make for the island of Aponiana, which is ten miles from Lilybaeum; he himself stayed behind a few days. He confiscated and sold for the State the property of a few individuals, and gave the praetor Alienus, who was governor of Sicily, comprehensive instructions, and in particular orders for the quick embarkation of the rest of the army. Then he himself embarked on 25 December and at once followed the rest of the ships. And so, sailing with a steady wind and in a fast vessel he came in sight of Africa three days later. A few warships were with him; as for the rest of the fleet, i.e. the transports, all but a few had been scattered by the wind and wandering off course made for various

places. He sailed past Clupea with his fleet, and then Neapolis; he also passed by a number of forts and towns not far from the sea.

3. He reached Hadrumetum, where his opponents had a garrison under the command of Gaius Considius. Then Gnaeus Piso came into view, coming along the coast with his cavalry towards Hadrumetum and accompanied by about 3,000 Moors. Caesar waited briefly outside the harbour for the rest of his ships to assemble, then disembarked his army. The forces present numbered 3,000 infantry and 150 cavalry. He pitched camp in front of the town and installed himself without molesting anyone; all his men were restrained from looting. Meanwhile those in the town packed the walls with armed men and massed in front of the gate to defend themselves. Their numbers amounted to the equivalent of two legions. Caesar rode around the town and made a thorough survey of the terrain, then returned to camp. Some blamed him for lack of foresight in not having previously instructed the pilots and captains what places in the area they were to make for, and not having given them sealed orders, as had been his own usual practice on previous occasions, so that after reading these at a specified time they might all make for a designated spot. This had by no means slipped Caesar's mind; but in fact he guessed that there would be no port on African territory to which the fleets could put in which would afford sure protection against enemy forces. Instead, he was watching for any opportunity for disembarking that chance might offer.

4. Meanwhile, an officer, Lucius Plancus, asked Caesar for authority to negotiate with Considius and see if somehow he could be brought to his senses. The request was granted, and accordingly he wrote a letter and gave it to a prisoner to take to Considius in the town. As soon as the prisoner arrived, when he was just about to hand over the letter, as instructed, to Considius, the latter inquired before taking it, 'Where did you get this from?' The prisoner replied, 'From the commander, Caesar.' Considius retorted, 'There is one commander of the Roman people at the present time, and that is Scipio.' Then he ordered the prisoner to be put to death at once in his presence and gave the letter, still unread and sealed as before, to a reliable man to take to Scipio.

5. Caesar spent a day and a night in the vicinity of the town and there was no sign of a reply from Considius. Moreover, the rest of his forces still did not arrive to reinforce him, he was short of cavalry and had insufficient forces to attack the town, and what he had were raw recruits. He did not want his army to suffer serious losses as soon as it arrived; and besides, the defences of the town were exceptionally good and the slope up towards it made it difficult to attack. There were also reports that large reinforcements of cavalry were on their way to help the towns-folk. He decided therefore that it would not be sensible to linger there in order to attack the town, since while he was so occupied he might be taken in the rear by the cavalry and so find himself in difficulties.

6. Accordingly, Caesar was thinking of moving camp; then suddenly a large crowd made a sally from the town and were re-inforced just then, as it happened, by the arrival of a force of cavalry, sent by Juba, to collect their pay. They seized the camp, which Caesar had just left in beginning his march, and then they began to pursue the rear of his column. Observing this, the legionaries suddenly halted and the cavalry, despite their small numbers, joined battle most courageously against heavy odds. An incredible thing happened; less than thirty Gallic cavalry beat off 2,000 Moorish cavalry, and drove them into the town. Once these had been repulsed and driven within the fortifications, Caesar continued his march. As this was repeated several times – the enemy would attack, and then be driven back into the town by the cavalry – Caesar posted at the rear of the column a few co-horts of the veteran troops he had with him, and some of the cavalry, then began to march on at an easy pace with the rest of his forces. In consequence, the farther they went from the town, the slower the Numidians were in pursuing them. Meanwhile he was met on the march by deputations from towns and strongholds who promised to supply corn and declared themselves ready to obey orders. And so on that day he camped at the town of Ruspina; that was 1 January.

7. From there he proceeded to the town of Leptis, a free com-munity with exemption from taxes. A deputation from the town came to meet him, expressing their complete readiness to carry out

his wishes. Accordingly he stationed centurions and guards at the town gates to prevent any troops entering the town and harming any of the inhabitants, while he pitched camp by the shore not far from the town. As it happened, some of his transports and warships put in at this same place. As for the rest, according to reports, it appeared that, not knowing the area, they were heading in the direction of Utica. For the time being Caesar did not leave the coast and strike inland, on account of the missing ships, and he kept all his cavalry on board, with the object, I suppose, of preventing devastation of the countryside. He ordered supplies of water to be conveyed to the ships. Meanwhile some rowers who had disembarked to fetch water were suddenly caught in a surprise attack by Moorish cavalry*, and many received javelin wounds, while several were killed.

8. Meanwhile Caesar sent out messengers to Sardinia and the other neighbouring provinces, with dispatches ordering them to arrange, immediately on receipt, for the sending of reinforcements, supplies and corn. He also unloaded some of the warships and sent Rabirius Postumus to Sicily to fetch a second convoy of troops. Meanwhile he ordered ten warships to be detailed to search for the rest of the transports and also to give protection by sea against enemy raids. He also ordered the praetor Gaius Sallustius Crispus to proceed with some ships towards the island of Cercina, which was in enemy hands, because he had heard that there were large quantities of corn there. He gave orders and instructions to each individual in such a way that there could be no room for excuses on the grounds of impracticability, and no hesitations to cause delay. Meanwhile, he learned from deserters and from local inhabitants of the terms agreed to by Scipio and those who were campaigning with him against Caesar – in fact, Scipio was maintaining a force of cavalry belonging to the king at the expense of the province of Africa. Caesar declared that he felt sorry for men who were so crazy as to prefer to pay tax to a king rather than live with their fellow citizens in their own country in secure possession of their own fortunes.

* The Moors lie concealed in ambush in hollows with their horses, then suddenly show themselves; they avoid battles at close quarters in the plain.

9. On 3 January Caesar moved camp. Leaving six cohorts under Saserna to garrison Leptis he himself returned to Ruspina, from which he had come the day before, with the remainder of his forces. The army's baggage was left there, and then with a force in light marching order he set off round the villages to fetch corn. The townsfolk were ordered to send all the wagons and pack-animals after them. And so, after finding a large quantity of corn, he returned to Ruspina. His object in returning there was, I suppose, to avoid leaving the coastal towns in his rear unprotected, but instead to secure them with garrisons and so make them strongholds for the reception of the fleet.

10. There he left Publius Saserna (brother of the man whom he had installed at the neighbouring town, Leptis) with a legion, under instructions to convey as much wood as possible into the town. He himself took seven cohorts from the veteran legions, who had served on board the fleet with Sulpicius and Vatinius, left Ruspina and went to the harbour, which is about two miles from the town; there, towards evening, he embarked with these forces. The entire army were ignorant of their commander's intentions and anxious to find them out; and in their distress they were tormented by fear and unhappiness. For they saw themselves set down in Africa with a small force, and a newly recruited one at that and not all of them disembarked, to face large forces, including the countless cavalry of a treacherous nation; they could find no comfort in their present situation and no help in the advice of their comrades; their one comfort was in the bearing of their commander himself, in his energy and his remarkable cheerfulness – for he displayed an exalted and alert spirit. The men found reassurance in this, and they all hoped that his experience and foresight would make everything plain sailing for them.

11. Caesar spent a night on board ship, and was about to set off just as it was growing light when suddenly the part of the fleet which had caused him concern by going astray put in at that very place. At this news, Caesar ordered all his men to disembark and to wait on the shore under arms for the arrival of the rest of the soldiers. Accordingly, as soon as these ships had been brought into harbour with their cargo of infantry and cavalry, he returned to Ruspina, set up camp there, and then set off personally with

thirty cohorts in light order to get corn. This showed that Caesar's intention had been to go to the aid of the transports which had gone astray, without the knowledge of the enemy, in case his own ships should fall in unawares with the enemy fleet; nor had he wanted the troops who were left behind on guard to know of this, in case their fears at their own small numbers as compared with the enemy should lower their morale.

12. When Caesar had advanced about three miles from the camp, scouts and advance patrols of horsemen brought word that they had seen the enemy's forces not far away. Sure enough – no sooner did the message come than a great cloud of dust became visible. At this news Caesar quickly ordered the whole of his cavalry, of which he had only a small force available, and the few archers he had to be summoned from the camp, and the standards to follow him slowly in regular order; he himself went ahead with a few armed men. Once the enemy became visible in the distance, he ordered his men to don their helmets and prepare for battle on the plain; in all, his forces numbered thirty cohorts, 400 cavalry and 150 archers.

13. Meanwhile the enemy, led by Labienus and the two Pacidei, drew up a line of remarkable length, closely packed, consisting not of infantry but of cavalry; these they had interspersed with Numidian light infantry and unmounted archers, and massed them so closely that from a distance Caesar's men thought they were all infantry forces. Caesar, meanwhile, deployed a single line as best he could in view of his small numbers; he posted the archers in front of the line and stationed the cavalry to cover the right and left wings, with instructions to see to it that they were not outflanked by the superior numbers of the enemy cavalry – for he thought that in the main battle line he would be encountering the infantry.

14. Both sides waited; Caesar made no move, and saw that in putting his own scant numbers against the great host of the enemy he would have to employ strategy rather than force. Suddenly the enemy cavalry began to spread out towards the flanks and take in the high ground, thus causing Caesar's cavalry to spread out thinly and at the same time threatening them with encirclement. Caesar's cavalry had difficulty in standing up to their numbers.

Meanwhile the two lines were about to engage in the centre when suddenly the Numidian light infantry ran forward alongside the cavalry out of the close formation and threw javelins into the ranks of the legionary infantry. Caesar's men thereupon attacked them, and the cavalry fled; but the infantry withstood them for the time being, until the cavalry should charge again and come to their assistance.

15. Caesar observed that he was presented with a new type of tactics and that the ranks of his men fell into disorder in the charge; for the infantry, in pursuing the enemy cavalry too far from the standards exposed their flanks and received javelin wounds from the Numidians nearest them, while the speed of the cavalry enabled them easily to evade the soldiers' pikes. He therefore sent the order along the ranks that no soldier was to advance more than four feet ahead of the standards. Meanwhile Labienus's cavalry, relying on the superiority of numbers on their side, lost no time in surrounding Caesar's small force, while the few Julian cavalry, as they were worn out by the weight of the enemy attack and their horses were wounded, gradually gave way; the enemy, meanwhile, pressed harder and harder. So in a moment all the legionaries were surrounded by the enemy cavalry. Caesar's troops were driven into a circle and so were penned in, as it were, and compelled to fight in a confined space.

16. Labienus was riding up and down in the front line bareheaded, cheering on his own men as he did so, and occasionally addressing Caesar's legionaries like this: 'What do you think you're doing, rookie? Little fire-eater aren't you? Are you another one who's had his wits fuddled by his nibs's fine talk? I tell you, he's brought you into a desperate situation. I'm sorry for you.'

Then a soldier said, 'I'm no raw recruit, Labienus; I'm a veteran of the Tenth.' 'I don't recognize the standards of the Tenth,' Labienus replied. 'You'll soon be aware what sort of man I am,' said the soldier. As he spoke, he threw off his helmet, so that he could be recognized by Labienus, then aimed his javelin at him and flung it with all his might. He drove it hard full into the chest of Labienus's horse and said, 'Let that show you, Labienus, that it's a soldier of the Tenth who attacks you.'

However, the soldiers in general had lost heart, especially the

219

recruits; for they kept looking around for Caesar and did nothing beyond dodging the enemy javelins.

17. Meanwhile Caesar, conscious of the enemy's tactics, ordered the line to be extended as far as possible; then he ordered alternate cohorts to face about, so that one was drawn up behind the standards, the next in front. By this manoeuvre, he split the enemy cordon in two on the right and left wings. He then cut one half off from the other by means of his cavalry and proceeded to launch an attack from inside with his infantry, who hurled volleys of missiles and put the enemy to flight. Not going too far forward, for fear of ambush, he returned to his own lines, while the other half of his infantry and cavalry did likewise. After this engagement, in which the enemy had been routed with heavy casualties, he began to fall back within his own defences, still keeping formation.

18. Meanwhile, Marcus Petreius and Gnaeus Piso, with 1,600 picked Numidian cavalry and a fairly large force of infantry (also Numidians) arrived, and hurried straight to the aid of their comrades. And so the enemy, rallying their spirits again and taking fresh courage, wheeled the cavalry round and began to attack the rearmost of the legionaries as they were withdrawing to try to hinder them from retiring into their camp. Observing this, Caesar ordered the standards to face about and battle to be renewed out in the plain. The enemy were employing the same tactics as before and not coming to close quarters. Moreover, Caesar's cavalrymen found that their horses were worn out as a result of recent sea-sickness, thirst, fatigue, wounds and fighting against odds, and lacked the speed to keep up a steady pursuit of the enemy. There was only a small part of the day left. Caesar went round all the cavalry and infantry cohorts and urged them to make one great effort and not let up until they had driven the enemy back beyond the farthest high ground and taken possession of it themselves. And so, once the enemy began to throw their missiles carelessly and with the appearance of fatigue, he gave the signal and launched a sudden attack with his cohorts and cavalry squadrons. In a moment, with no trouble, they pushed the enemy back off the plain and behind the hill, which they seized themselves. They remained in occupation for a short time and then withdrew at an

easy pace, still in formation, to their own defence-works. The enemy, for their part, after this check withdrew at last to their own positions[1].

19. Meanwhile after the action had been broken off a large number of men of all classes deserted from the enemy; numerous enemy cavalry and infantrymen were captured as well. From these the enemy plans were learned; they had come with the intention of repeating their victory over Curio. They hoped that Caesar's legionaries, being few in number and raw recruits, would be thrown into confusion by their novel and unfamiliar style of fighting and would be surrounded and overpowered by the cavalry. Labienus was reported to have said before the assembled troops that he would supply such large quantities of auxiliaries to reinforce Caesar's opponents that Caesar's men would be exhausted merely with killing, and even in the very moment of victory would be overcome by his men. His self-confidence was based on the superior numbers of his forces; for, in the first place, he had heard that the three veteran legions at Rome were mutinous and refused to cross over to Africa; secondly, he had commanded these troops in Africa for three years and they now knew him well and were thoroughly loyal to him; and besides he had large auxiliary forces of Numidian cavalry and light infantry, as well as the forces he had brought over with him from Buthrotum after Pompey's final battle and flight, namely the German and Gallic cavalry. He had also levied forces in Africa among half-castes, freedmen and slaves. He had, moreover, auxiliary forces from the king, 120 elephants and countless cavalry and, finally, legions enrolled from men – 12,000 of them – of all sorts. With this basis for his bold self-confidence, Labienus, with 1,600 Gallic and German cavalry, with 7,000 Numidians riding without bridles, reinforced besides by the 1,600 cavalry of Petreius, and four times as many infantry, both heavy and light, and numerous archers, mounted and unmounted and slingers – with these forces on 4 January on the sixth day after Caesar's landing in Africa battle was engaged on an absolutely flat and unimpeded plain from about eleven o'clock until sunset. In this encounter Petreius was seriously wounded and withdrew from the field.

2. *Waiting at Ruspina*

20. Meanwhile Caesar devoted still more care to fortifying his camp. He strengthened the guard-posts by increasing their garrisons. He led an entrenchment from the town of Ruspina to the sea and a second one from the camp, likewise to the sea, to secure communications back and forth and permit reinforcements to come to his aid without danger. He had missiles and missile engines brought up from the ships and armed some of the Gallic and Rhodian rowers and marines from the fleet and installed them in the camp so that, if possible, he might follow the example of his opponents and intersperse his cavalry with light infantry. He also fetched large numbers of archers – Ityreans, Syrians and men of every nationality – from the fleet and filled out his forces with these. The reason for these measures was that he had heard two days after the battle that Scipio was approaching and joining forces with Labienus and Petreius. His forces were said to number eight legions and 3,000 cavalry.

Caesar also set up smithies, saw to the manufacture of large quantities of arrows and missiles and the casting of sling-shot, and had wooden stakes collected. He sent messengers and dispatches to Sicily to collect supplies of hurdles and timber for rams, timber being scarce in Africa, and also to send him iron and lead. He further observed that he could not have any supply of grain in Africa unless it was imported; for the harvest had not been gathered in the previous year on account of his opponents' troop-levies, since the farmers who were tributaries[2] of Rome were enlisted. Moreover, his opponents had collected corn from all over Africa into a few well-fortified towns so that the whole territory of Africa was exhausted of corn; they were also razing and abandoning all the towns except those few which they could hold with garrisons of their own forces, and had forced the inhabitants to move into the garrisons, so that the fields were now deserted and laid waste.

21. To meet this pressing need Caesar had managed to collect a certain quantity of corn in his garrisons by soliciting and coaxing private individuals, and was using it very sparingly. Meanwhile

he made a personal tour of the defence-works every day and
doubled the number of cohorts on guard, because of the numbers
of the enemy. Labienus ordered his wounded, of whom there were
a great many, to be bandaged and conveyed in wagons to Hadrumetum. In the meantime, Caesar's transports were straying badly
off course, because of their unfamiliarity with the area and the
situation of the camp. When this was reported, Caesar stationed
vessels round the islands and harbours so that supplies could be
brought in in greater safety.

22. Meanwhile Cato, who was in command at Utica, never
stopped haranguing Gnaeus Pompeius the younger, at length and
often. 'When your father was your age,' he said, 'he saw the State
oppressed by wicked and criminal citizens, and good men either
killed or punished by exile and so deprived of their homeland and
their civic rights. And so, in the enthusiasm engendered by his
desire for renown and his nobility of spirit, though merely a private citizen and barely out of his childhood, he collected the
remnants of his father's army and restored the independence of
Italy and of the city of Rome, when they were all but overwhelmed and destroyed. He also recovered by force of arms, with
amazing speed, Sicily, Africa, Numidia and Mauretania. By these
feats he won for himself that repute which is unmatched for
glory and renown throughout the world, and though still only a
youth and a knight, he celebrated a triumph. And he entered life
without the advantages of a father who had achieved such noble
exploits, such an eminent position won for him by his forebears,
such large numbers of dependants and so famous a name. You, on
the other hand, have your father's rank and prestige, and you
are in yourself sufficiently endowed with nobility of spirit and
conscientiousness. Will you not, then, make an effort? Go to
your father's clients and demand aid for yourself, for the State,
and for all right-thinking men.'

23. These words, coming from so respected a man, stimulated
the youth. He set off from Utica with thirty vessels of various
sorts, some of them armed with beaks, and invaded Mauretania
and the kingdom of Bogus. With an army of slaves and free men,
about 2,000 in number, some with weapons, some not, he began
to make for the town of Ascurum, in which there was a royal

garrison. As Pompeius approached, the townsfolk allowed him to draw closer until he was actually approaching the gates and wall of the town; then they sallied out, crushed the Pompeians and drove them back in wholesale panic to the sea and their ships. After this failure Gnaeus Pompeius the younger set sail and without putting in to shore again made for the Balearic Islands.

24. Meanwhile Scipio, with the forces detailed above, left a large garrison at Utica and proceeded first to Hadrumetum, where he pitched camp. He stayed there a few days, then made a march by night and joined forces with Labienus and Petreius, and they took up position in a single camp about three miles from Caesar. Meanwhile their cavalry kept roving around Caesar's defence-works, picking off men who had gone outside the entrenchment to fetch water or fodder; as a result, they penned all their opponents within their lines. Caesar's men were therefore in serious difficulty over the corn supply, because no consignments had as yet been brought from Sicily or Sardinia and the season of the year made it impossible for vessels to rove about on the sea without danger; nor did they hold more than six miles of African territory in any direction and they were troubled by lack of fodder. Under stress of this emergency, the veteran infantry and cavalrymen, who had completed many campaigns by land and sea and had often been hard-pressed by dangers and privations of this sort, collected sea-weed from the beach, washed it in fresh water, and by giving this to their hungry beasts kept them alive.

25. While this was occurring King Juba, learning of Caesar's difficulties and shortage of supplies, decided that he should not allow Caesar time to recover his strength and increase his resources. He therefore collected large forces of cavalry and infantry and leaving his kingdom hastened to the help of his friends. Meanwhile Publius Sittius and King Bogus had joined forces; learning of King Juba's departure they moved their troops nearer his kingdom. Sittius attacked Cirta, the richest town in the kingdom, and stormed it within a few days, as well as two other Gaetulian towns. He offered them terms, namely that they should evacuate the town and hand it over to him; they refused and were subsequently all captured and killed. He moved on from there, continually ravaging the countryside and the towns. Juba was

informed of this when he was not far away from Scipio and his officers, and decided that it was better to go to the rescue of his kingdom and himself than to go off to help others and find himself driven out of his own kingdom and perhaps repulsed on both fronts. He began, therefore, to return and even withdrew his auxiliary forces from Scipio, in his fear for himself and his kingdom. He left thirty elephants and went off to rescue his territory and towns.

26. Meanwhile, there was some doubt in the province about Caesar's arrival. No one believed that he had come to Africa with the troops himself; they thought it was merely some lieutenant of his. He therefore wrote dispatches and sent them round all the communities informing them of his arrival. Meanwhile some nobles began to flee from their towns and come to Caesar's camp where they recounted the cruelty and harshness of his opponents. Caesar was moved by their tears and complaints; although he had previously decided to summon all his troops and auxiliaries from their base camps at the beginning of summer to fight a campaign against the enemy, he now decided to launch his campaign that winter, and hastily wrote to Alienus and Rabirius Postumus in Sicily and sent them off by a fast boat, ordering them to have the army conveyed across to him as quickly as possible, without making winter or stormy weather any excuse for delay. 'The province of Africa,' he told them, 'is perishing and being utterly overthrown at the hands of our enemies. Unless we help our allies quickly, our foes' wickedness and treachery will leave nothing except the bare soil of Africa itself, not even a roof to shelter us.' He himself was in such a state of impatience and anticipation that the day after he sent the messenger and dispatches to Sicily he kept saying that the fleet and the army were delaying, and day and night he kept his eyes and thoughts fixed steadfastly on the sea. This was not surprising; for he saw that farm-houses were being burned down, fields devastated, flocks plundered and killed, towns and forts razed and abandoned, and the leading citizens slain or kept in chains while their children were carried off, ostensibly as hostages, and enslaved; and because of the smallness of his forces he could be of no assistance to the people when they appealed to him in their wretchedness for his protection. Meanwhile he kept

the troops continuously busy on the defence-works, strengthening the camp, constructing redoubts and forts, and building causeways out into the sea.

27. Scipio meanwhile began to train the elephants in the following way. He drew up two battle-lines. One was of slingers, to face the elephants in the rôle of the enemy and fire small stones against the front line formed by the beasts. Then he drew up the elephants in a line and posted his own battle-line behind them, so that when the fire of stones began from the enemy side and the elephants wheeled round in terror towards their own side, his men should throw stones at them and drive them back again towards the enemy. This was a slow and painful process; for elephants are unruly beasts who can be trained only with difficulty, by dint of many years of teaching and prolonged practice; and even then, when they are brought out into the battle-line they are a menace to both sides.

28. While both commanders were employed in this way in the neighbourhood of Ruspina, the ex-praetor Gaius Vergilius, who was in command at the coastal town of Thapsus, observed Caesar's troop-carriers, sailing not in convoy or on any set course, because of their unfamiliarity with the region and the situation of the camp. Seizing the opportunity, he manned a fast vessel he had on the spot with troops and archers and, taking also the ships' dinghies, he began to pursue the straggling vessels. He attacked several, but was beaten off and forced to withdraw; nevertheless he persisted in his attempts, until he chanced to fall in with a vessel on board which were the brothers Titius, Spanish youths, tribunes of the Fifth, whose father Caesar had enrolled in the Senate[3]. With them was Titus Salienus, a centurion in the same legion. This latter had virtually blockaded Caesar's lieutenant Marcus Messalla[4] in a house at Messana and expressed mutinous sentiments in his hearing; he had also been responsible for withholding, under guard, some money and trappings required for Caesar's triumph. For these reasons, Salienus feared for his own safety; and so, because of his own consciousness of guilt he persuaded the young men not to offer resistance and to surrender to Vergilius. The result was that they were taken by Vergilius to Scipio, placed under guard and put to death three days later. As

they were being led to execution, the elder Titius is said to have asked the centurions to kill him before his brother; this request was readily granted and so they were put to death.

29. Meanwhile the cavalry squadrons which both commanders kept posted on guard in front of the entrenchments were engaging daily in constant skirmishes with each other; and sometimes Labienus's Gauls and Germans and Caesar's cavalry would even exchange pledges of truce and talk to each other. Meanwhile Labienus with part of his cavalry was attempting to force his way into the town of Leptis, which was garrisoned by six cohorts under the command of Saserna. The town was exceptionally well fortified and well supplied with missile engines, so that the task of the defenders was easy and free from danger. Labienus's cavalry persisted repeatedly in their efforts, and on one occasion a squadron had positioned itself in close formation just outside the gates when a carefully aimed dart from a scorpion struck their commanding officer and pinned him to his horse, whereupon the rest fled back to camp in terror. This event deterred them thereafter from making assaults on the town.

30. In the meantime Scipio practically every day drew up his forces for battle not far from the camp, at about a quarter of a mile's distance; he would spend the greater part of the day there and then go back to camp. This was repeated several times, but no one emerged from Caesar's camp or approached Scipio's forces. This forbearance on the part of Caesar and his army finally roused Scipio to scorn; he led out his entire force, with thirty elephants carrying turrets drawn up in front of the line; then advancing and deploying as he did so his large numbers of cavalry and infantry over as wide a front as possible, he halted on the plain, not so very far from Caesar's camp.

31. On being informed of this, Caesar gave orders that the troops who had advanced in front of the defences to fetch fodder or timber, or even had gone in search of stakes or other materials for the fortifications, should all withdraw within the defences in an orderly and gradual fashion, without any confusion or panic, and take up their posts on the defence works. As for the cavalry on guard, he ordered them to remain at their stations until the enemy came within javelin-range; if they approached any nearer,

then they were to withdraw with as little loss of face as possible within the defence works. He ordered the rest of the cavalry likewise to stand by under arms at their posts. Of course, he did not go up on to the rampart and personally supervise the execution of these orders; with his remarkable skill and expertise in warfare he remained in his tent and issued orders through scouts and messengers. For he observed that, although the enemy could draw on vast numbers of men, he had frequently routed and repulsed them, broken their spirit, spared their lives and overlooked their transgressions; as a result, their own incompetence and their uneasy consciences would prevent their becoming so confident of victory as to venture to attack his camp. Besides, the very weight of his name had no inconsiderable effect in depressing the courage of the enemy army. Further factors were the excellence of his defence works, the height of the rampart and the concealed stakes, skilfully planted outside the rampart, all of which circumstances, even without men to defend the camp, would keep the enemy from approaching. He had also large supplies of scorpions, catapults and other customary defensive machines.

Caesar had made all these preparations on account of the lack of numbers and experience of his army, not from any alarm at the strength of the enemy, though his actions had given the enemy the impression that he was lacking in assertiveness and confidence. His reason for not leading out his forces to battle – few and inexperienced though they were – was not any misgiving about his prospects of victory, but his conviction that it mattered *how* the victory was won. After so many achievements, the defeat of enormous armies, the winning of brilliant victories, he thought it would be a stain on his reputation if he should be thought to have caused a lot of bloodshed merely in winning a victory over the remnants of his enemies, rallying after their rout. He had decided therefore to put up with their swaggering and insolence until some part of his veteran legions should arrive with the second convoy.

32. Meanwhile Scipio, as I said earlier, lingered there for a short time, to demonstrate his contempt for Caesar, then gradually
⌐ his troops back to camp. There he assembled them and spoke
⌐ about their fears. He told them that Caesar's army was

utterly demoralized, and in encouragement he promised that he
would soon afford them the victory that was their due. Caesar
ordered his troops back to the defence-works and kept the recruits
working constantly till they were exhausted in order to complete
the fortifications. Meanwhile Numidians and Gaetulians were
deserting every day from Scipio's camp. Some went back to the
king's territory, while others came streaming incessantly into
Caesar's camp, because they and their ancestors, they knew, had
benefited by the kindness of Gaius Marius[5] and they heard that
Caesar was a relative of his. Caesar selected the more distinguished
of these, gave them letters to take back to their countrymen and
sent them off, urging them to band together to defend themselves
and their people, and not to submit to the orders of his enemies
and opponents.

33. During these events near Ruspina, a deputation came to
Caesar from Acylla, an independent community exempt from
taxation, saying that they were ready and willing to carry out
whatever commands he might give. Their one earnest request was
that he would grant them a garrison, so that they could carry out
his orders under protection and without running into danger.
They undertook to supply corn and anything else they possessed
for the sake of the common good. Caesar readily acceded to their
request and gave them a garrison; he instructed Gaius Messius, an
ex-aedile, to proceed to Acylla.

On learning of this, Considius Longus, who was in command at
Hadrumetum with two legions and 700 cavalry, left part of his
force there as a garrison and moved towards Acylla with seven
cohorts. Messius completed the march first, and forestalled Considius in reaching Acylla with his cohorts. Then, when Considius
reached Acylla with his troops and found a Caesarian garrison
already installed, he did not venture to hazard his men but retired
to Hadrumetum without attempting any action such as the size
of his force might have led one to expect. A few days later, when
Labienus brought up some cavalry, he went back and pitched
camp and began to invest Acylla.

34. During this period Gaius Sallustius Crispus, who, as mentioned above, was sent out a few days previously by Caesar with
a detachment of ships, reached Cercina. On his arrival the

ex-quaestor, Gaius Decimius, who was in charge of supplies there and had a large guard made up of his own slaves, got hold of a small boat, embarked and took to flight. Meanwhile the praetor Sallustius was welcomed by the people of Cercina, and finding a large quantity of corn there he loaded up the cargo boats, of which there were a good many, and sent them to Caesar's camp. Meantime at Lilybaeum the proconsul Alienus embarked the Thirteenth and Fourteenth legions, 800 Gallic cavalry and 1,000 archers and slingers on transport ships and sent this second convoy to Caesar in Africa. The vessels had a following wind, and all arrived safely in harbour three days later near Ruspina, where Caesar was encamped. So Caesar had two occasions for delight at once, the arrival of the corn and of the reinforcements; and now that his men's cheerfulness was restored and the corn problem eased, he was at last freed from the burden of his anxiety. He ordered the legionaries and cavalry who had just disembarked to rest and recover from their fatigue and sea-sickness, and assigned them to various posts in the forts and on the defences.

35. The course of events surprised Scipio and his companions and made them seek for an explanation. Gaius Caesar was usually in the habit of taking the initiative and provoking battle, and they suspected that his altered behaviour concealed some important stratagem. His forbearance therefore had the effect of dismaying them; they chose two of the Gaetulians who appeared to be most sympathetic to their cause, and making them lavish promises and offers of rewards they sent them into Caesar's camp to spy, in the guise of deserters.

As soon as the two were led before Caesar, they asked for an assurance that they could speak out frankly without danger. This was given, and they proceeded: 'Commander, sir: many times a lot of us Gaetulians, who are clients of Gaius Marius, as well as nearly all the Roman citizens[6] in the Fourth and Sixth legions, have wanted to desert to you and seek your protection; but guards of Numidian cavalry prevented us from doing this without danger. Now we have been given the chance, and we are only too glad to come to you. Scipio sent us out as spies to find out whether ~v trenches or traps for elephants had been made in front of the · of the gateways in the rampart, and at the same time to discover what tactics you proposed to use against these beasts and your plan of battle, and to report back.' They were commended and rewarded by Caesar and taken to join the rest of the deserters. The truth of their story was soon confirmed; for on the following day a great many legionaries from the legions named by the Gaetulians deserted from Scipio and came to Caesar's camp.

36. While these events were taking place at Ruspina, Marcus Cato, who was in charge of Utica, was enlisting troops every day, without exception, from among freedmen, Africans, even slaves and men of all descriptions, and sending them to Scipio's camp for his disposal. Meanwhile a deputation arrived at Caesar's camp from the town of Thysdra, into which 300,000 measures of wheat had been conveyed by Italian businessmen and farmers. They informed Caesar how much corn they had, and requested him to send them a garrison to help to keep safe both the corn and their own supplies. Caesar thanked them there and then and said that he would be sending a garrison shortly, then dismissed them with words of encouragement to rejoin their fellow-countrymen. Meantime Publius Sittius invaded Numidian territory with his forces and stormed and captured a fort situated on a strong point on a hill, into which Juba had conveyed corn and other usual military supplies for the conduct of the war.

3. Consolidation

37. When Caesar had augmented his forces with the two veteran legions, and the cavalry and light infantry from the second convoy, he ordered the empty vessels to return at once to Lilybaeum to bring over the rest of the army. He himself, on the night of 25–6 January, towards midnight, ordered all his scouts and aides to stand by. In this way, in total secrecy and without anyone suspecting, he gave orders in the small hours for all the legions to be led out of camp and to follow him in the direction of Ruspina (where he had a garrison), which had been the first town to come over to his side. From there he descended a short slope and led the legions along the left-hand edge of the plain, near the sea. The plain here is remarkably flat and extends for some twelve miles;

it is surrounded by a ridge, not very high, rising up close by the
sea, which gives it something of the appearance of a theatre. On
this ridge there were a few eminences, on each of which stood
some very old turrets and look-out posts; in the last of these
Scipio had an outpost with some troops.

38. Caesar then climbed the ridge described and proceeded to
march from one hill, with its turret and fort, to another, completing the manoeuvre in less than half an hour. Then he came fairly
near the last fortified hill, the one nearest to the enemy camp, on
which, as I have shown, there was an outpost manned by Numidians. He halted briefly and surveyed the terrain; he then posted
the cavalry on guard and set the legions to work constructing
fortifications along the middle of the ridge from the point where
he had now arrived to his original starting-place. Observing this,
Scipio and Labienus led all the cavalry out of their camp and
formed them up in battle formation, advancing them about a
mile from their defences; they then drew up the infantry as a
second line rather less than half a mile from the camp.

39. Caesar urged his troops to keep on with their work and not
to be perturbed by the enemy forces. When he observed that the
enemy line was now only just over half a mile from his fortifications and realized that they were approaching with the intention
of stopping the work of his soldiers and driving them off, he saw
that he would have to withdraw the troops from the fortification.
He therefore ordered a squadron of Spanish cavalry to gallop to
the near-by hill, dislodge the garrison there and occupy the position, and commanded a few light infantry to follow them up and
reinforce them. These duly attacked the Numidians, captured
some alive, wounded several of the cavalrymen as they fled, and
occupied the height. Labienus observed this, and in order to bring
help to his men more quickly he detached almost the whole of
the right wing of his cavalry line and hurried to support his retreating forces. When Caesar saw that Labienus had got a good
distance away from his main force, he sent the left wing of his
own cavalry in to cut off the enemy.

40. In the plain where these movements were taking place there
was a very large farm house, with four towers. This blocked
Labienus's view, so that he was unable to see that he was being

cut off by Caesar's cavalry. As a result, he first realized the presence of the Julian squadrons when he found that his own men were being cut down in the rear. This threw the Numidian cavalry into a sudden panic and they fled straight back to camp. The Gauls and Germans, who had stood fast, were surrounded by troops coming from the higher ground and in their rear, and though they offered stout resistance they were all cut down. When this was seen by Scipio's legions drawn up in front of the camp, they all fell into a blind panic and began rushing back into camp by every gate.

Once Scipio and his forces had been swept away from the hills and plain and driven back into camp, Caesar ordered the retreat to be sounded and conducted all the cavalry back within his defences. When the plain was cleared, he saw the bodies of the Gauls and Germans, a remarkable sight. Some of these men had been won over by Labienus's personal prestige so as to follow him from Gaul; others had been persuaded to join him by money and promises of gain, while others again had been captured after Curio's last battle, and as their lives had been spared they had been anxious to demonstrate their gratitude by displaying complete loyalty. These were the men whose bodies, remarkable for size and comeliness, now lay hacked and limp all over the plain.

41. On the day after this engagement, Caesar withdrew his cohorts from all his strong-points and drew up his entire force on the plain. Scipio, after the disaster to his men and his heavy losses in dead and wounded, remained without moving within his defences. Caesar deployed his battle line along the lowest spurs of the ridge and gradually advanced towards the camp. His legions were within a mile of Uzitta, which was in Scipio's hands, when the latter, fearing that he might lose the town, from which he was in the habit of obtaining water and other necessary supplies for his army, led out all his forces to the rescue. His army was deployed in a four-fold line, according to his usual practice, with the front line made up of cavalry drawn up by squadrons, interspersed with armoured elephants bearing towers. Now, Caesar interpreted Scipio's move as meaning that he was coming with the determination to engage in battle, and he halted in the place mentioned just above. Scipio used the town to cover the centre

of his line. He drew up the right and left wings, where his elephants were, in full view of his opponents.

42. Caesar waited until almost sunset and saw that Scipio was making no attempt to advance from the point where he had halted and was rather preparing to defend himself on the spot, if necessary, than to venture to engage in hand-to-hand fighting on the plain; he therefore decided against advancing any nearer the town on that day. He had learned that there was a large garrison of Numidians there, and besides, since the enemy had screened the centre of his line with the town, he knew that it would be difficult for him simultaneously to make an assault on the town and to fight a pitched battle on unfavourable ground on the right and left wings, especially as his men had been standing under arms since morning without food and were tired. He therefore led his troops back to camp, and on the following day began to extend the fortifications nearer the enemy line.

43. Meanwhile Considius, with eight cohorts and Numidian and Gaetulian mercenaries, was besieging Acylla, where Gaius Messius commanded a garrison of some cohorts. Considius made prolonged and repeated efforts, frequently constructing large siege-works, which were burned by the townsfolk. His efforts were meeting with no success, and when he received the startling news of the cavalry engagement, he burned the corn, of which he had a quantity in the camp, spoiled the oil and other basic food supplies, abandoned the siege of Acylla, and marching through Juba's territory he gave Scipio part of his forces and then withdrew to Hadrumetum.

44. Meanwhile one of the vessels from the second convoy dispatched by Alienus from Sicily, with Quintus Cominius and Lucius Ticida, a Roman knight, on board, went astray from the rest and was carried by the wind down to Thapsus, where Vergilius used dinghies and fast boats to capture it and bring it in to shore. Another ship, a trireme, from the same convoy went off course and was driven by a storm to Aegimurus, where it was captured by the fleet of Varus and Marcus Octavius. It contained veteran troops with one centurion and a number of recruits. Varus spared their lives, saving them from ill-treatment, and had them taken to Scipio. When they came before the latter and halted in

front of his dais, 'I know full well,' he said, 'that it is not of your own free will but at the instigation and command of that accursed general of yours that you are engaged in this wicked vendetta against your fellow-citizens and all right-thinking men. Since fortune has placed you in my hands, if you are willing – as you certainly ought – to join all right-thinking men in defending the State, I have resolved to grant you your lives and to pay you. So let me hear your views.'

45. After this speech, Scipio, under the impression that they would undoubtedly express gratitude to him for his kindness, afforded them an opportunity to speak. One of them, a centurion of the Fourteenth legion, spoke up. 'Thank you for your extreme kindness, Scipio – I will not call you general – in promising me my life and safety, even although I am, properly, a prisoner of war; and I might perhaps avail myself of your kindness, if this did not involve utterly criminal conduct. Do you really expect me to take arms and oppose Caesar, my own general, under whom I have commanded a company, and his army, for whose victorious reputation I have fought for more than thirty-six years[7]? I will not; and what is more, I strongly urge you to abandon your enterprise. For if you have not realized yet whose forces you are opposing you may learn now. Choose out of your army what you judge to be your strongest cohort and pit it against me; I shall choose from my comrades who are now in your hands no more than ten men. Then you may judge, from our valour, what fate you may expect for your forces.'

46. The ready courage of this retort was quite unexpected by Scipio. He was furious and, stung with indignation, he indicated his wishes to his centurions by a nod. He had the centurion put to death at his feet and ordered the rest of the veterans to be segregated from the recruits. 'Take away those fellows,' he said, 'befouled with unspeakable crimes and glutted with the blood of their fellow-citizens.' Accordingly they were led outside the rampart and tortured to death. He ordered the recruits to be distributed among the legions and refused to allow Cominius and Ticida to be brought before him.

Caesar was distressed at news of this. He had ordered men to stand on guard out at sea off Thapsus with warships, to protect his transports and warships; these men he now discharged from the army with ignominy, and published a communiqué censuring them severely.

47. Round about this time something utterly incredible happened to Caesar's army. Although the Pleiades had set[8], there was a huge rainstorm some time after midnight along with hail stones. The inconvenience occasioned by this was increased by the fact that Caesar was not following his earlier practice of keeping his army in winter quarters, but was advancing every two or three days, getting close to the enemy and building a camp, and his troops were kept busy in this work and had no opportunity to look after themselves. Besides, in his eagerness to get the troops over from Sicily, he had been refusing to allow any baggage or slaves or any of the usual military comforts to be put on board, but only the troops themselves and their weapons. In Africa itself, not only had no one either acquired or bought anything, but they had used up what they had previously saved, because of the high price of food. As a result, they were in extremely straitened circumstances. Only a very few men were sleeping under proper tents; the rest were camping under makeshift shelters made out of clothes or reeds and branches woven together. And so these tents were weighed down by the sudden rain and the hail that succeeded it; they were ripped to shreds by the force of the water. It was the dead of night, and the fires had been put out. All the foodstuffs were spoiled; and the men went wandering about the camp holding their shields over their heads. On this same night the tips of the pikes of the Fifth legion caught fire.

48. Meanwhile King Juba had been informed of Scipio's cavalry engagement and had received a dispatch from the latter summoning him. He therefore left his officer Saburra with part of his army to deal with Sittius, and leaving his kingdom proceeded personally to join Scipio, in order to give his army additional impressiveness and to strike fear into Caesar. With him he took three legions, 800 cavalry with bridles and a large force of Numidians without bridles, a great many light infantry, and thirty elephants. On arrival, he pitched the royal camp, with the forces detailed, separately but not far from Scipio.

In Caesar's camp there had previously been considerable alarm, and the suspense of waiting for the royal forces had been more upsetting for his army before Juba arrived; but after he established his camp beside the other, they thought little of his forces and abandoned all their fears. And so the awe he had inspired in his absence was utterly dispelled by his presence.

It was obvious to anyone that the king's arrival had given Scipio fresh spirit and confidence; for on the following day he led out all his own forces and those of the king, with the sixty elephants, and deployed them for battle in as impressive a manner as possible. He then advanced a little farther than usual from his own defences, waited – not very long – then withdrew to camp.

4. Caesar takes the offensive

49. Caesar observed that Scipio had received pretty well all the reinforcements he had been expecting, and knew that battle would not be long delayed. He therefore began to advance with his forces along the top of the ridge, and hastened to extend lines of fortification, build forts and seize and occupy the heights nearer Scipio, in case his opponents, relying on the size of their forces, would occupy the hill nearest them and so prevent his advancing any farther. Labienus had also decided to occupy this particular hill, and as he was nearer to it, he managed to reach it more rapidly.

50. There was a valley of considerable width, with high, steep sides, running back in several places to form cave-like hollows. This valley Caesar had to cross before the hill which was his objective could be reached. On the far side of the valley was an old olive-grove, with trees closely set together. Labienus saw that if Caesar wished to take the hill he must first cross the valley and the olive-grove, and was able, thanks to his acquaintance with the terrain, to station himself here in ambush with part of the cavalry and some light infantry. He had posted a further detachment of cavalry in hiding behind the heights so that, after he himself had made his surprise attack on the legionaries, the cavalry should suddenly come out from behind the hill and reveal itself; Caesar and his army would then be thrown into confusion

by this double assault and, finding it impossible either to advance or to retreat, would be surrounded and cut down. Caesar sent some cavalry out ahead, but came right up to the place without being aware of the ambush. Labienus's men, however, either because they misunderstood or forgot his instructions, or because they were afraid of being caught in the hollow by Caesar's men, began coming out in ones and twos from the rocks and making for the crest of the hill. Caesar's cavalry pursued them, killed some and captured some alive; they then pushed straight on towards the hill, dislodged Labienus's holding force, and occupied the position. Labienus and part of his force managed with difficulty to escape.

51. After this exploit by the cavalry, Caesar assigned the work of fortification among the legions and built a camp on the height he had taken. Then he began to construct two containing walls from his main camp across the plain in the direction of the town of Uzitta, which lay on the level ground between his own camp and that of Scipio and was in Scipio's hands; he oriented these walls so that they ran towards the right and left corners of the town. His intention in constructing these walls was to protect his flanks when he advanced his forces nearer the town to begin the assault, so that he should not be surrounded by cavalry and forced to abandon the attack; he also hoped to make it easier to confer with the enemy and, if any persons should wish to desert (as had often happened before, but with extreme hazard to those who did so) then this could be done easily and without danger. He also wished to find out, when he came nearer the enemy, whether the latter intended to fight. To these reasons was added the further consideration that the ground there had a slight depression and a number of wells could be dug; his source of water was scanty and at some distance. While the works of construction mentioned were being carried out by the legions, part of the force stood in front of them in battle array close to the enemy, while the barbarian cavalry and light infantry engaged in hand-to-hand skirmishes.

52. Towards evening, as Caesar was leading his men back from this work to their camp, Juba, Scipio and Labienus made a violent attack on the legionaries, using all their cavalry and light infantry. Caesar's cavalry were beaten back by this sudden mass attack of

the enemy and gave ground for a time. However, their opponents derived no advantage from this, for Caesar halted the march, and brought his forces back to the aid of the cavalry. The latter took fresh heart at the arrival of the legions, and wheeling round they charged the Numidians, who had fallen into disarray in the heat of their pursuit, and drove them right back to the royal camp with severe casualties, and many killed. But for the facts that nightfall overtook them during this engagement and a dust-storm blew up and completely destroyed visibility for both sides, Juba, and Labienus as well, would have fallen into Caesar's hands, while the cavalry and light infantry would have been annihilated. As it was, an incredible number of Scipio's troops from the Fourth and Sixth legions deserted, some of them going to Caesar's camp, and some making off wherever they could. Moreover a good many of Curio's former cavalry, feeling no confidence in Scipio and his forces, likewise deserted to Caesar.

53. While the leaders on both sides were engaged in this way in the neighbourhood of Uzitta, two legions, the Tenth and the Eighth, which had sailed in transports from Sicily, had been approaching the harbour of Ruspina when they caught sight of some of Caesar's ships standing guard off Thapsus. Fearing that they were on the point of falling unawares among an enemy fleet waiting to ambush them, they put out to sea again, and it was only after a long and stormy voyage that, many days later, worn out with thirst and privation, they reached Caesar.

54. These legions disembarked. Caesar well remembered the lack of discipline previously existing in Italy among the troops and the plundering done by certain individuals; he now found an excuse, albeit a slender one, for making an example. Gaius Avienus, a tribune of the Tenth, had taken over one of the ships in the convoy, filled it with his own slaves and horses, and brought not a single soldier over from Sicily. On the following day, Caesar assembled the tribunes and centurions of all the legions and addressed them from his dais.

'I should have wished above all,' he said, 'that people might at long last have put an end to their impertinence and insubordination and ceased to take advantage of my leniency, moderation and forbearance. But since they will not of themselves set any bounds or limits, then I shall myself make an example, in accordance with military practice, to teach the rest to amend their behaviour.

'Gaius Avienus: whereas you did in Italy incite the troops of the Roman people to action against the State and did plunder various municipalities, and whereas you have been of no service either to myself or to the State, but have, instead of troops, embarked your own slaves and livestock, and have thereby caused the State to be short of troops at a time of crisis – for these reasons I discharge you with ignominy from my army and order you to remove yourself today from Africa and to do so with all possible speed.

'Further, you, Aulus Fonteius: whereas you have, as a tribune, incited to mutiny, and, as a citizen, have been disloyal, I dismiss you from my army.

'Titus Salienus, Marcus Tiro, Gaius Clusinas: whereas you, having attained your ranks in my army by favour, and not through merit, have nevertheless shown yourselves neither brave in warfare nor loyal and serviceable in peace, and have directed yourselves towards inciting the men to mutiny against their commander rather than to respectful and obedient conduct – I judge you unfit to hold rank in my army. I dismiss you and order you to leave Africa as soon as possible.'

He then handed them over to the centurions, and had them put on board ship with no more than one slave each.

55. Meanwhile the Gaetulian deserters, whom Caesar, as mentioned above, had dispatched with letters and verbal messages, reached their own people. Thanks to their personal influence, added to the weight of Caesar's name, they readily persuaded the Gaetulians to revolt from Juba. They all immediately seized arms and unhesitatingly opposed the king. News of this was brought to Juba; and as he was now compelled to divide his forces between three fronts, he took six of the cohorts he had brought to oppose Caesar and sent them to the territory of his kingdom as a protection against the Gaetulians.

56. Caesar's lines of fortification were now complete, and stretched to a point just outside the range of missiles from the town. He set up a camp there and put catapults and scorpions close together in line in front of it, training them on the town

and using them constantly to harry the defenders. He also brought up five legions from his earlier camp.

Now that they were within access, certain of the more prominent and distinguished persons began clamouring to see their acquaintances and relatives and held conversations with them. Caesar was fully aware of the advantage to be gained from this; and in fact some of the nobler Gaetulians among the royal cavalry, including several cavalry captains (whose fathers had, in earlier days, served under Marius and been rewarded by him with grants of territory, but after Sulla's victory had been made subject to King Hiempsal) deserted to Caesar. They numbered about 1,000; seizing their opportunity at nightfall, when the torches had already been lit, they came over with their horses and grooms to Caesar's camp, which was situated in the plain near Uzitta.

57. Scipio and his associates were informed of this, and while they were still in a state of consternation at this setback, they happened to observe Marcus Aquinus holding a conversation with Gaius Saserna. Scipio sent a message to Aquinus that he had no business to fraternize with the enemy. The messenger reported Scipio's words; but as Aquinus none the less stayed to complete his conversation, Juba sent a courier as well to tell him, in Saserna's hearing : 'The king forbids you to fraternize.' Aquinus was overawed by this message and obeyed the king. To think that things should have come to such a pass ! that a Roman citizen, a man who had been elected to office by the Roman people, whose country and whose personal fortunes were still intact, should prefer to obey a barbarian, Juba, rather than comply with the orders of Scipio or, while his companions were killed in civil war, himself return unharmed. Indeed, arrogant as was Juba's behaviour towards Marcus Aquinus, a man of humble antecedents who had attained no very elevated rank in the Senate, his behaviour towards Scipio, a man of such distinction by his birth, his prestige and the offices he had held, was even more outrageous. Before the king's arrival Scipio had been in the habit of wearing a red cloak; and it is said that Juba took him to task for this, saying that he should not affect the same dress as himself. Scipio therefore changed to white garments, and submitted to the insolence and uncouthness of a Juba.

58. On the following day the enemy led all their forces out of their camps, and taking possession of a certain high ridge not far from Caesar's camp, they formed up in battle line and waited. Caesar, for his part, led out his forces and quickly deployed them in front of his defence-works on the plain. Doubtless he assumed that the enemy, in view of the size of their forces, augmented with those of the king, and their previous readiness in sallying out, would take the initiative in approaching and engaging. He rode around encouraging the legions, then gave the signal and began to wait for the enemy to advance. He himself had good reason for not advancing too far from his defences. There were several armed enemy cohorts in the town of Uzitta, which was in Scipio's hands; and as his right wing was opposite the town, he was afraid that if he advanced past it, the enemy would make a sally from the town and attack him on the flank. He was further deterred by the existence of an area of rough ground in front of Scipio's line, which he thought would hinder his men in a charge.

59. I think I ought not to omit a description of the manner of deployment of the forces on either side[9]. Scipio arranged his line as follows. In the front line he posted his own legions and those of Juba; behind these he had a reserve of Numidians drawn out in so long and thin a line that from a distance it looked as if the centre was a single line. On the right and left wings he had stationed elephants at equal intervals and behind them light-armed infantry and Numidian auxiliaries. He had put all his bridled cavalry on the right wing, as the left was covered by the town of Uzitta and there was no room there to deploy cavalry. In addition he had stationed some Numidians and a huge force of light infantry on the right of his line, at a distance of at least a mile, forcing them hard up against the lower slopes of the hill, a manoeuvre which took them some distance away both from his own forces and from those of the enemy. His intention was that, after the two lines engaged, in the first stages of the battle the cavalry would extend their flanking movement slightly, then thanks to their numbers they could surprise and surround Caesar's army, thus throwing it into confusion, and overpower it with volleys of javelins. This was Scipio's plan of battle for the day.

60. Caesar's order of battle was as follows, starting from the left wing and proceeding to the right. On the left wing, he had the Tenth and Ninth legions, in the centre the Twenty-fifth, Twenty-ninth, Thirteenth, Fourteenth, Twenty-eighth and Twenty-sixth. On the right wing, he had two lines, and stationed there some cohorts from the veteran legions, together with a few cohorts of the new recruits. His third line he had posted on the left wing, extending from there as far as the central legion of the line, so that his left wing had a treble line. His reason for these dispositions was that his right wing was covered by his fortifications, while he would have difficulty in holding back the vast numbers of the enemy cavalry with his left. He also concentrated his cavalry on the left wing and, as he lacked confidence in them, he sent up the Fifth legion to support them and interspersed the cavalry with light infantry. He put detachments of archers in various formations at specific parts of the line, and especially on the wings.

61. These were the dispositions on either side. They were formed up not more than a quarter of a mile apart. There was perhaps no occasion previously on which such proximity did not lead to a battle; yet they stood there from morning until late afternoon. Finally Caesar had begun to withdraw his forces inside his fortifications – when suddenly the entire force of Numidian and Gaetulian cavalry without bridles (which had been stationed at a distance) began to move to the right and advance on Caesar's camp, which was on high ground, while Labienus's bridled cavalry stayed where it was and tried to draw off the legions. Then suddenly part of Caesar's cavalry together with the light infantry advanced against the Gaetulians, recklessly and without orders, went too far, and after crossing the marshy ground proved incapable of withstanding the superior numbers of the enemy. The cavalry were deserted by the light infantry and sustained severe damage before fleeing back to their own forces. One horse was lost and many wounded, and twenty-seven of the light infantry killed. Scipio was delighted with his cavalry's success; and night had already fallen when he led his forces back to camp.

Fortune, however, did not allow Scipio's soldiers to continue in the enjoyment of their success. On the following day, a

detachment of cavalry which Caesar had sent to Leptis to get grain
met on the way about 100 marauding Gaetulian and Numidian
cavalry, whom they attacked, capturing some alive and killing
the others. Meantime, Caesar continued his daily routine; the
legions were led down into the plain and continued to work on
the fortifications, extending a ditch and rampart across the plain
and so blocking the enemy's sallies. Scipio for his part likewise
built counter-defences, in great haste in case Caesar should cut
him off from the high ground. Both generals, then, were busy
with defence-works, but none the less their cavalry engaged in
skirmishes every day.

62. Meanwhile Varus, learning of the approach of the Seventh
and Eighth legions from Sicily, quickly put out with the fleet,
which he had already docked at Utica for the winter. He manned
some fifty-five ships with Gaetulian rowers and marines and sailed
from Utica to Hadrumetum, to lie in wait. Unaware of this
manoeuvre, Caesar sent Lucius Cispius with a detachment of
twenty-seven ships in the direction of Thapsus, to give cover to his
convoy, and sent Quintus Aquila for the same purpose to Hadrumetum with thirteen warships. Cispius quickly reached his
destination; Aquila being caught in a storm and unable to round
the point found a sheltered bay in which he and his fleet could
find both refuge and concealment. The rest of the fleet lay out at
sea off Leptis. The rowers had disembarked and dispersed on dry
land, some making their way to the town to purchase food, and
so the vessels were left unguarded. Varus was informed of this
by a deserter. Seizing his opportunity he came out of the inner
harbour at Hadrumetum before midnight; he arrived at Leptis
early in the morning with his whole fleet, set fire to the transports
which were standing rather far out to sea, outside the harbour,
and seized two five-banked ships, meeting with no resistance as
there were no defenders on board.

63. Meanwhile information of these events was brought to
Caesar as he was touring the defence-works in his camp, about
six miles away from the harbour. He dropped everything and
went off on horseback at full speed to Leptis, and there he ordered
all the ships to follow him. He himself embarked on a small craft
and went off in pursuit of the enemy fleet. On the way he met

Aquila, who was in a state of panic and confusion at the numbers of the enemy.

Meantime Varus, thrown into consternation at Caesar's speed and daring, had wheeled the fleet round and was making off with his entire force towards Hadrumetum. Caesar caught up with him in four hours' sailing and recovered one of his own quinqueremes with all its crew and a crew of enemy guards, numbering 130, besides. He captured the nearest enemy trireme, which had lagged behind to offer resistance, together with all its crew.

The rest of the enemy ships rounded the headland and took refuge in the inner harbour at Hadrumetum. The wind did not hold long enough for Caesar likewise to round the point; he therefore spent the night at anchor off shore; at dawn he approached Hadrumetum and set fire to all the transports outside the harbour. Then, as the rest had either been beached by the enemy or collected in the inner harbour, he waited for a while to see if the enemy would offer battle, then returned to camp.

64. The men taken prisoner with the ship included Publius Vestrius, a Roman knight, and Publius Ligarius, one of Afranius's men. The latter had been released by Caesar, with the rest, in Spain and had afterwards gone to join Pompey; then in his flight after Pharsalus he had gone to Varus in Africa. For his faithlessness and treachery, Caesar ordered him to be killed. However, he pardoned Publius Vestrius, both because his brother had paid over money on request to Caesar at Rome, and because he himself made good his case before Caesar, explaining that he had been captured by Nasidius's squadron and was on the point of being led to execution when he was saved by the kindness of Varus, but had afterwards found no opportunity of desertion.

65. The natives of Africa customarily have secret underground cellars for the storage of corn, both in the open fields and in most of the farmhouses. They make this provision principally against war and the sudden appearance of an enemy. Caesar learned of this through an informer; and he sent two legions with some cavalry out of camp in the small hours of the morning, to a distance of about ten miles from the camp, and later admitted them again, loaded with corn. Learning this, Labienus advanced about seven miles from camp along the ridge of high ground by which

Caesar had made his way the previous day, and there made a camp large enough for two legions. Under the impression that Caesar would make the same trip frequently to get corn, Labienus established himself daily, with a large force of cavalry and light infantry, in positions suitable for ambush.

66. In the meanwhile some deserters had informed Caesar about Labienus's ambushes. He therefore waited a few days, until daily repetition of the same routine should make the enemy lax, then suddenly one morning ordered three veteran legions and part of the cavalry to follow him out by the rear gate. Sending the cavalry ahead, he suddenly surprised the ambushers hiding in the gulleys, cut down about 500 of the light infantry, and forced the rest to flee ignominiously. Labienus meanwhile hurried up with all his cavalry to help his fleeing troops. Since Caesar's small force of cavalry could not stand against the weight of numbers on Labienus's side, Caesar deployed his legions for battle and displayed them to the enemy. By so doing he frightened Labienus and checked his attack, and so was able to withdraw all his cavalry unharmed. On the following day Juba crucified all those Numidians who had abandoned their posts and fled back to camp.

5. The Pompeians lose the initiative

67. Meanwhile Caesar was having difficulty in maintaining a supply of corn; he therefore collected all his forces in camp; he assigned garrisons to Leptis, Ruspina and Acylla, and put Cispius and Aquila in charge of the fleet with instructions that one should blockade Hadrumetum, the other Thapsus. Then he set fire to his camp and left towards the end of the night, with his forces in battle formation and the baggage on the left wing. He came to the town of Aggar, which had previously suffered frequent attacks by the Gaetulians and had been stalwartly defended by the inhabitants. There he set up a single camp in the plain, and went out personally with part of his army around the farms in search of corn. He found a great quantity of barley, oil, wine and figs, and a small amount of wheat, and having thus provided for his army he returned to camp. Meanwhile Scipio learned of Caesar's

departure, proceeded to follow him, with all his forces, over the heights, and installed his troops in three camps about six miles from Caesar's camp.

68. There was a town called Zeta, which lay about ten miles from Scipio, but in a direction fairly accessible from his camp, whereas it was remote and distant from Caesar, being some fourteen miles from him. To this town Scipio sent two legions to collect corn. A deserter informed Caesar, who moved his camp from the plain to a safer position on high ground, and leaving a garrison there, set out towards the end of the night, marched past the enemy camp, and took the town. He learned that Scipio's legions were out in the countryside collecting food, and was just going to march against them when he observed enemy forces hurrying up to help the legions. This restrained him from attacking. And so, after taking prisoner Gaius Minucius Reginus, a Roman knight and a close friend of Scipio, who was in command of the town, and Publius Atrius, a Roman knight from the Roman community at Utica, and commandeering twenty-two royal camels, he left a garrison under his lieutenant Oppius and himself returned to camp.

69. He had to pass Scipio's camp; and when he was not far from there, Labienus and Afranius attacked the rear of his column, revealing themselves from among the near-by hills where they had been lying in ambush with all their cavalry and light infantry. Seeing them, Caesar ordered his cavalry to meet the enemy attack, while the legionaries were to stack their kit and charge quickly with their standards. They began to carry out these commands; and, as soon as the legions charged, the enemy cavalry and light infantry were dislodged and driven off the hill with no difficulty. Caesar, judging that the enemy were now routed and cowed and would not give any further trouble, resumed his march; whereupon the enemy sallied out again from the near-by hills and attacked Caesar's legionaries in the same way as described above. The enemy troops were Numidians and light infantry, endowed with remarkable quickness and used to fighting alongside the cavalry and keeping pace with them as they advanced or retreated. This was repeated several times; the enemy pursued Caesar's forces if he resumed the march, but fled if he made a stand; they

refused to come close but contented themselves with wounding the horses with javelins – an unusual tactic. Caesar realized that their object was simply to force him to make camp in a place where there was no water, so that his fasting army, who had tasted nothing from the last hours of the night to the late afternoon, and his beasts should alike perish of thirst.

70. It was drawing towards sunset and he had advanced less than 100 yards in four hours. Caesar withdrew his cavalry from the rear of the column, because of the losses among the horses, and called on the legions to take their place. By using the legionaries in this way and advancing calmly and slowly he was able to withstand the enemy's onslaughts without too much difficulty. Meantime the Numidian cavalry kept rushing ahead over the high ground to his left and right and using their numbers to throw a kind of cordon round his army, while some of them attacked the rear of the column. On Caesar's side, meanwhile, if only three or four of his veterans turned round and launched their javelins at the attacking Numidians, more than 2,000 of the latter fled as one man; then they would rally and wheel round for the attack again, follow at a distance, and throw javelins at the legionaries. In this manner, alternately advancing and making a stand, Caesar completed the march, although slowly, bringing his men back into camp in the first hour of the night, with no losses and only ten wounded. Labienus retired to his camp with 300 missing and many wounded or exhausted with constant attacking. Meanwhile Scipio had deployed his legions with the elephants in front of the camp where Caesar could see them, hoping to terrify him; he now took them back to camp.

71. Faced with an enemy of this kind, Caesar now proceeded to train his men, not as a general does veterans who have fought many successful campaigns, but as a trainer does inexperienced gladiators; he told them how many feet they should retire, how they should wheel round against the enemy, how to put up a resistance in a limited space, how to advance and retire alternately and make feint attacks; he almost went so far as to tell them where and how to throw their javelins. For it was remarkable to what extent the enemy light infantry had occasioned worry and anxiety among our men. Their constant javelin

fire caused casualties among the horses and kept the cavalry from
engaging, while their speediness wore out the legionaries; for as
soon as any of the heavy infantry, under pursuit, halted and
attacked them, they easily ran out of danger.

72. Consequently, Caesar was seriously worried; for whenever
there was an engagement he found himself totally unable to
match the enemy cavalry and light infantry with his own cavalry,
unsupported by legionaries. A further disquieting circumstance
was that he had as yet no experience of the enemy legions; he did
not know how he could withstand the combined forces of the
enemy cavalry and their truly remarkable light infantry, once
these were joined by the legions as well. And yet another source
of anxiety was the persistent feeling of panic engendered in his
men by the size and numbers of the elephants.

For this last problem at least, however, he had found a solution.
He had ordered a number of elephants to be transported from
Italy so that our men might familiarize themselves with the
appearance and characteristics of the beast, and learn which parts
of its body were readily vulnerable to missiles and, when it was
fully equipped and armoured, which part was left exposed and
unprotected, and so was a suitable target for missiles. Further, he
hoped that through familiarity the horses would lose their fear
of the smell, sound and appearance of the beasts. He very largely
succeeded in achieving these aims. The troops handled the beasts
and observed how slow-moving they were, the cavalry used them
for javelin practice, with untipped darts, and the passivity of the
beasts had made the horses grow accustomed to them.

73. Such, then, were Caesar's sources of anxiety; and their
effect was that his former rapid style of campaigning had given
place to a more cautious and deliberate policy. This was not surprising; the forces he had were accustomed to fighting in Gaul, on
level terrain, and against the Gauls, an open-natured people and
not at all given to guile, who were accustomed in warfare to rely
on their valour, not on trickery. Now, however, he had to try to
accustom his men to recognize the guiles, traps and ruses of the
enemy, and know when they should pursue and when to give
them a wide berth. To help them to learn this more quickly, he
saw to it that the legions were not retained in one spot, but were

kept constantly on the move from place to place, ostensibly to get food-supplies. His calculation was that the enemy would be sure to follow in his tracks. And two days later he deployed his forces and led them out, with extreme care, passing close by the enemy camp, and then offered battle on level ground. Seeing that the enemy shrank from accepting, he led the legions back to camp towards evening.

74. Meanwhile a deputation came from the town of Vaga, near Zeta, which as we said had been taken over by Caesar. They earnestly entreated him to send them a garrison, and promised to help him with numerous essential military supplies. About this time, thanks to the good-will of the gods and their favour towards Caesar, a refugee arrived and told his fellow citizens that King Juba had hurried to the town with his forces to forestall the arrival of Caesar's garrison, and on his arrival he had invested the town with a large force, stormed it, killed every single one of the inhabitants and abandoned the town itself to his soldiers to plunder and destroy.

75. Meanwhile Caesar held a ceremonial purification[10] of the army on 21 March. On the following day, he advanced with his entire force some five miles from camp and halted in battle formation about two miles from Scipio's camp. When he observed that, despite this clear and prolonged challenge, the enemy were reluctant to fight, he led his troops back. On the following day he struck camp and began to march towards Sarsura, where Scipio had installed a garrison of Numidians and amassed a stock of corn. Observing this move, Labienus began harassing the rear of the column with his cavalry and light infantry. He succeeded in cutting off the baggage trains of camp-followers and traders who were carrying their goods in wagons, and this encouraged him to venture to come up closer to the legions, under the impression that they would be tired with carrying their kit and incapable of fighting. Caesar had taken this into account, in fact, and had ordered 300 men in each legion to march without packs. These he sent to counter Labienus's cavalry, with squadrons of his own cavalry in support; and Labienus promptly panicked at the sight of their standards, wheeled his cavalry round, and fled ignominiously. After killing a number of Labienus's men and

wounding a great many more, our legionaries returned to their standards and resumed the march. Labienus continued in pursuit at a distance, moving along the crest of a ridge of hills on our right.

76. On arrival at Sarsura, Caesar slaughtered Scipio's garrison while his adversaries looked on, not daring to come to the rescue of their allies. The garrison commander, Publius Cornelius, a veteran recalled to the colours by Scipio, put up a stout resistance, but was finally surrounded by overpowering numbers and killed. Caesar took over the town, issued the corn there to his army, and proceeded to Thysdra, where he arrived on the following day. Thysdra was at the time occupied by Considius with a large garrison and his personal guard of gladiators. Caesar made a reconnaissance of the town, but was discouraged from attempting a siege by the lack of a water supply. He went on about four miles farther and camped by water, then set out not long before dawn and returned to his previous camp near Aggar. Scipio likewise led his force back to their former camp.

77. Meanwhile the people of Thabena, who lived at the extreme edge of Juba's kingdom, by the coast, and were by tradition subject to his jurisdiction, massacred the royal garrison and sent a deputation to Caesar informing him of their exploit, earnestly begging the Roman people to reward them by coming to their aid. Caesar approved their attitude and sent a tribune, Marcius Crispus, with a cohort and some archers and missile engines to protect Thabena. Just at this time, the troops who, for reasons of sickness or leave, had been unable to sail to Africa previously with the standards, arrived in a single convoy. There were about 4,000 infantry, from all the legions, 400 cavalry and 1,000 slingers and archers. And so Caesar led out all the legions and these forces, and halted in battle formation on the plain five miles from his own camp and two from that of Scipio.

78. Below Scipio's camp was a town named Tegea, where he kept a regular garrison of some 2,000 cavalry. This cavalry he drew up in line to flank the town to the right and left, while he himself led his legions out of camp and, after advancing no more than about a mile from his defences, halted in battle formation on the lower slopes of the ridge. A considerable time elapsed

without Scipio's making any further move, and the day was wasting away in inaction; finally Caesar ordered some of his cavalry squadrons to charge the enemy cavalry posted beside the town, and sent in light infantry, archers and slingers to support them. This manoeuvre got under way and the Julian forces charged at a gallop; but Pacideius began extending his line, to allow his cavalry to outflank the Julian squadrons, and still put up a stubborn and spirited fight. Observing this, Caesar ordered the 300 soldiers without packs (he had customarily kept that number from each legion in light order) from the legion stationed nearest in the line to the site of the engagement to go to the aid of the cavalry. Labienus meanwhile began sending in further cavalry as reinforcements, and replaced the wounded and exhausted cavalry with fresh, energetic men. Caesar's 400 cavalry proved unable to withstand the onset of the enemy, who numbered some 3,000; they were suffering casualties at the hands of the Numidian light infantry and they began gradually to give ground. Caesar sent in another wing of cavalry to hurry to support the others, who had their hands full. This relieved his forces; they made a massed charge on the enemy and routed them, killing many and wounding a great number. They pursued the enemy for three miles, driving them as far as the hills, and then returned to their own lines. Caesar remained in battle line until about four p.m., then returned to camp, with no casualties. In this engagement Pacideius was seriously wounded in the head by a pike which pierced his helmet, and a number of officers and all the most gallant troops were killed or wounded.

79. He found it impossible by any means to force the enemy to come down on to the plain and hazard their legions; he observed that he could not pitch camp any closer to the enemy because of the lack of an adequate water supply; he realized that his opponents were not actuated by any confidence in their own superiority, but simply believed that the difficulty of getting a water-supply rendered him no danger to them; and so, on the fourth of April, in the small hours, he left the camp by Aggar, marched sixteen miles by night, and camped near Thapsus, which Vergilius was holding with a large garrison. On the same day he began to construct lines of investment. He seized several suitable

strategic points and established guard-posts at these, to prevent
the enemy's breaking in on him and taking any positions inside
the lines. Meanwhile, Scipio was informed of Caesar's strategy;
and he was now forced to offer battle, to avoid the humiliation
of losing his devoted supporters, the men of Thapsus, and Vergilius as well. He therefore hurried in pursuit of Caesar, keeping
to the high ground, and halted with his forces in two camps,
about eight miles from Thapsus.

6. Thapsus

80. There was a salt lake, and between it and the sea a narrow
isthmus, no more than a mile and a half wide. Scipio attempted
to enter this passage and bring help to the people of Thapsus.
Caesar had anticipated this; for on the previous day he had constructed a fort there and installed a garrison of three cohorts,
while he himself with the rest of his forces invested Thapsus
with a line of siege-works which, together with his camp, formed
a crescent[11]. Meanwhile Scipio, finding himself debarred from his
intended route, spent the day and night marching round on the
far side of the lake and then, as it was growing light, he took up
his position near the sea at no great distance – about a mile and
a half – from the camp and fortification mentioned above, and
began to build a camp. When this was reported to Caesar, he
withdrew his troops from the construction work, left Asprenas in
command with two legions to guard the camp and hurried off
himself to the spot with a force in light order. He left part of the
fleet at Thapsus and ordered the rest to sail round behind the
enemy, come as close in to shore as possible, and watch for his
signal. On this signal, they were to raise a sudden shout, taking
the enemy by surprise in their rear, so that in their alarm and confusion they would be obliged to look behind them.

81. When Caesar arrived and saw that Scipio had his line
drawn up in front of the rampart, with elephants stationed on
both wings, while none the less some of the troops were still
actively engaged in constructing defences, he himself drew up a
three-fold line; he posted his Tenth and Second legions on the

right wing, the Eighth and Ninth on the left, and stationed five cohorts from the Fifth legion on each wing as a fourth line, opposite the elephants. On both wings he had archers, slingers and cavalry interspersed with light infantry. He himself hurried around the ranks on foot, recalling the prowess of the veterans in previous battles and greeting them affably, to raise their morale. As for the recruits who had never fought in a battle, he urged them to try to match the valour of the veterans and to strive to attain, through winning a victory, the same level of respect and renown.

82. As he was making his tour of the army, he observed the enemy in frantic movement around the rampart, running here and there in confusion and sometimes withdrawing inside the gates, sometimes coming out in a disorderly and reckless fashion. A number of other people began to notice the same thing; then all of a sudden there was an outcry from the officers and recalled veterans. They urged Caesar to give the signal without further ado, since the gods were clearly indicating that the victory was destined to be theirs. Caesar still hesitated and refused to be budged by their eager insistence. He was bawling out constantly that he did not approve of engaging in battle by an impromptu sally, and repeatedly checking the line from advancing, when suddenly a trumpeter on the right wing, yielding to pressure from the troops and without Caesar's orders, began to sound the call to charge. This was taken up by all the cohorts and they began to advance on the enemy; but the centurions faced about and vainly attempted to restrain their men, urging them not to engage without their commander's orders.

83. Caesar realized that it was impossible to resist his troops' impetuosity; he gave the word, 'Good Luck', and set his horse at a gallop against the enemy front line. Meanwhile the slingers and archers on the right wing hurled rapid volleys of missiles at the dense mass of elephants, with the result that the beasts, terrified by the whistling of the sling-shot and the showering stones and lead bullets, turned round and began to trample down their fellows, who were close-packed behind them, and to rush in through the unfinished gateways in the rampart, while the front ranks of the Moorish cavalry on the same wing as the elephants

also deserted their posts and fled. So our legions quickly got round the elephants and seized the rampart of the enemy; a few of the latter put up a fierce resistance and were killed, but the rest rushed off in flight to the camp they had left the day before.

84. Mention must be made of the gallantry of a veteran of the Fifth legion. On the left wing, an elephant, maddened by the pain of a wound, had attacked an unarmed camp-follower. The beast first trampled him underfoot then, kneeling on him, lifting its trunk and trumpeting loudly, was crushing him to death. The soldier could not forbear to challenge the creature, fully armed as he was. When the elephant saw the soldier coming at it with his lance at the ready, it abandoned the corpse, wrapped its trunk round the soldier and lifted him up into the air. The soldier, realizing that in this kind of desperate situation resolute action was called for, kept hacking with his sword at the trunk wrapped round him. The pain forced the elephant to let the soldier drop, and trumpeting loudly it turned round and ran back to join the other beasts.

85. Meanwhile the garrison of Thapsus sallied out by the sea-ward gate and, whether their intention was to help their own men, or to abandon the town and save themselves by flight, they came out and, wading waist-high through the water, made for land. The slaves and attendants in the camp threw stones and javelins at them and so prevented them getting out on to land. They therefore returned to the town.

Meanwhile, Scipio's forces were routed and in flight all over the field, with Caesar's legions in hot pursuit and giving them no chance to rally. When they reached the camp for which they had been making, with the object of repairing it, renewing their defence and finding themselves a commander – someone they could look to and under whose commanding authority they could campaign – and realized there was no one on guard there, they threw away their weapons and made straight for the king's camp. On arrival there, they found that this too was in the hands of Caesar's men. Abandoning hope of reaching safety, they halted on a hill and saluted in military fashion by lowering their arms. This stood the unhappy fellows in little stead; for our veterans were in such a blaze of indignation that not only could they not be induced to spare their enemies, but they even wounded or killed several refined and distinguished Romans on their own side, calling them agitators. These included Tullius Rufus, who died when a soldier deliberately ran him through with a javelin; Pompeius Rufus, likewise, received a sword wound on the arm and would have been killed had he not quickly fled to Caesar. As a result, several Roman knights and senators withdrew in alarm from the battle, in case they too might be killed by the troops, whose great victory had emboldened them to overstep all limits in licentious behaviour, in the expectation that their successes would earn them pardon. Accordingly, though all these soldiers of Scipio begged Caesar for protection, they were killed to a man, under Caesar's very eyes and despite his entreaties to the troops to spare them.

86. The three camps were captured, 5,000 of the enemy killed and a good many put to flight. Caesar then returned to camp, with the loss of fifty of his own men and a few wounded. On arrival, he at once halted in front of the town of Thapsus. He captured sixty-four elephants, completely accoutred with their howdahs and trappings, and lined them up in front of the town. His intention was to try to break down the resolution of Vergilius and those besieged with him by a demonstration of the defeat of their fellows. He then called Vergilius himself by name, inviting him to surrender and promising to show mercy and clemency towards him. Seeing that there was no reply, he went away from the town. On the following day, after taking the auspices, he assembled the troops within sight of the townsfolk. He praised them, gave cash gratuities to all the veterans and from his tribunal issued decorations to all who had rendered conspicuously good service. Then, leaving Rebilus in command at Thapsus with three legions and Gnaeus Domitius at Thysdra (which was in the hands of Considius) with two to continue the siege, he himself made his way to Utica, to which he had previously sent on Marcus Messalla with the cavalry.

7. The settlement of Africa

87. Meanwhile Scipio's cavalry who had fled from the battle-field arrived at the town of Parada on their way to Utica. The news of Caesar's victory had arrived before them and they were refused admission by the inhabitants; they therefore stormed the town and wreaked a cruel vengeance by piling up logs in the forum, heaping on top all the goods of the townsfolk and setting fire to them, then tying up the townsfolk themselves of all ages and descriptions and throwing them into the flames. They then pro-ceeded to Utica.

Some time before, Marcus Cato, judging that the support of the people of Utica was half-hearted, because of the benefits conveyed by the Julian law[12], had expelled the unarmed populace from the town; he had had a camp constructed in front of the War-gate, complete with a trench, albeit a small one, and had forced the people to live there, inside a cordon of guards. The town senate, however, he kept under surveillance inside the town. The cavalry, then, proceeded to attack and to attempt to storm the camp, just because they knew that the detainees had favoured Caesar's cause. They hoped to kill them, and so avenge by their destruction the painful smart of their own defeat. The people of Utica, heartened by Caesar's victory, beat off the cavalry with stones and cudgels. Accordingly, failing to gain possession of the camp, the cavalry burst into Utica, and there murdered many of the people and broke into and plundered their houses.

Cato was totally unable to persuade them to join him in the defence of the town and to give up the killing and looting; and, as he knew their intentions, in order to appease their greed he gave them 100 sesterces each. Faustus Sulla did likewise and bribed them out of his own pocket; he then left Utica along with them and made towards the king's territory.

88. Meanwhile a considerable number of fugitives arrived at Utica. Cato assembled them together with the Three Hundred[13], who had contributed money to Scipio's war effort, and urged them to set free their slaves and defend the town. Since it was apparent

to him that only some of them agreed, while the others were in a state of utter terror and bent on flight, he abandoned any further efforts, and put ships at the disposal of the intending fugitives, to go off wherever they wished. He himself made all his arrangements with the utmost care. He put his children in the charge of Lucius Caesar, who at the time was acting as his quaestor. Then he retired to bed without rousing any suspicions, behaving and talking just as usual, but secretly took a sword into his bedroom and ran himself through. As he collapsed, still breathing, his doctor and his slaves suspected something and rushed into the room. They began to staunch and tie up his wound, but he ruthlessly pulled it open with his own hands and so deliberately put an end to himself. The people of Utica had hated him for the side he took; but they had been so impressed by his integrity, by his difference from the other leaders and by the remarkable way in which he fortified the town and equipped it with bastions, that they gave him a funeral.

After his death, Lucius Caesar, hoping to turn the situation to his own advantage in some way, assembled the people and made a speech urging them to open the gates, saying that he entertained great hopes of Caesar's mercifulness. And so the gates were opened and Lucius left Utica and went to meet the general Caesar. Messalla made his way to Utica, as ordered, and put guards on all the gates.

89. Meanwhile Caesar proceeded from Thapsus to Usseta, where Scipio had stored a great quantity of corn, armour, missiles and other commodities, with only a small guard. On arrival, he took possession of the place, then went on to Hadrumetum. Entering the town without hindrance, he took an inventory of the arms, corn and money, and spared the lives of Quintus Ligarius and Gaius Considius the younger, who were there at the time. He went on from Hadrumetum the same day, leaving Livineius Regulus there with a legion, and made for Utica. On the way he was met by Lucius Caesar, who suddenly fell at his feet and begged him for one favour alone – to spare his life. Caesar readily assented, as both his inclination and his general policy dictated, and he followed his normal practice in sparing the lives likewise of Caecina, Gaius Ateius, Publius Atrius, Lucius Cella and his

son, Marcus Eppius, Marcus Aquinus, the son of Cato, and the
children of Damasippus. He arrived at Utica as it was getting dark
and spent the night outside the town.

90. He entered the town on the following morning and, summoning an assembly, delivered a rousing speech in which he
thanked the inhabitants of Utica for their efforts on his behalf.
As for the Roman citizens – the businessmen and those of the
Three Hundred who had donated money to Varus and Scipio –
after accusing them at considerable length and dilating upon their
misdeeds he finally ordered them to come out without apprehension. He undertook to grant them their lives at least; but he intended to sell their property, with the proviso that if anyone
bought back his own property he would record the sale and note
the money paid as a fine, so that the owner would be secure. The
Romans, pallid with fear and thinking that through their guilt
they had forfeited their lives, eagerly clutched at this unexpected
offer of salvation. They accepted his terms and asked Caesar to
exact a fixed sum of money from the Three Hundred as a whole.
Accordingly he imposed a fine of 200,000,000 sesterces, to be paid
in six instalments over three years to the Roman people. They
accepted this without demur and thanked him, declaring that
this day marked the start of life for them.

91. Meanwhile King Juba, in his flight from the battle, had
been hiding with Petreius in farmhouses during the day and
travelling by night. He reached his kingdom and went to the
town of Zama, where his residence was and his wives and
children. He had also collected here all the money and treasure
from the entire kingdom, and had strongly fortified the town at
the outset of the war. The townsfolk had already heard the welcome news of Caesar's victory and consequently refused to admit
Juba; for at the beginning of his war against the Roman people,
he built a huge pyre of logs in the centre of the forum in Zama,
with the intention that, should he be defeated, he would pile all
his property on top, massacre the citizens and throw them on as
well, then set fire to it, and lastly commit suicide on top of it, so
that he, together with his children, his wives, his subjects and all
the royal treasure, might be burned.

Juba waited a long time before the gates, trying to influence the people of Zama. First he tried threats, in virtue of his authority; then, realizing that he was making no headway, he turned to entreaties, and begged them to give him access to the gods of his own home. When he saw that their resolve was unshaken and that neither threats nor entreaties could persuade them to let him in, he made a third approach, asking them to hand over his wives and children so that he could take them away with him. When he found that the townsfolk vouchsafed no reply at all, he went away from Zama after these fruitless efforts and retired with Marcus Petreius and a few cavalrymen to his country residence.

92. Meanwhile the people of Zama sent a deputation to Caesar at Utica about this and asked him to send them help before the king should raise a force and launch an attack on them; even without help, they said, they were ready to preserve themselves and the town, while they remained alive, for Caesar. Caesar commended the envoys and told them to go home in advance of him and report that he was coming. He himself left Utica the following day with the cavalry and set out for the royal territory. On the way several officers from the royal forces met him and begged for pardon, which he accorded.

The news of his mercifulness spread, and when he reached Zama pretty well all the cavalry of the kingdom came to him and were released from their fears and danger.

93. While these events were taking place on either side, Considius, who was guarding Thysdra with his own household slaves, a troop of gladiators and some Gaetulians, heard of the slaughter of his comrades. Stricken with terror at the approach of Domitius and the legions and despairing of saving himself he abandoned the town, slipped away secretly laden with gold and accompanied by a few barbarians, and began to flee towards royal territory. On the way the Gaetulians accompanying him, in their greed for booty, cut him down and made their escape where they could.

Meanwhile Gaius Vergilius realized that, hemmed in both on land and by sea, he could do nothing; he knew that his comrades were either slain or fled, that Cato had made away with himself at Utica, that the king had been abandoned by his followers and was wandering about, an object of scorn to his own people, that Saburra and his forces had been destroyed by Sittius, that Caesar had been admitted without hesitation to Utica and that there was nothing left of their enormous forces. Accordingly, he obtained an assurance of safety for himself and his children from Caninius, who was in command of the siege, and surrendered himself, and all that he had, and the town.

94. Meanwhile the king, finding every town closed to him, gave up hope. He dined with Petreius, and so that they might make a show of dying courageously they had a sword fight. Juba, who was the stronger, easily dispatched the feebler Petreius. Then, after trying in vain to run a sword through his chest, he succeeded in persuading a slave to kill him[14].

95. Meanwhile Publius Sittius, after routing the army of Juba's general, Saburra, and killing the general himself, was marching with a small force through Mauretania when, as it happened, he encountered Faustus and Afranius, together with the force with which they had sacked Utica. They numbered about 1,000 and were on their way to Spain. He quickly laid an ambush by night and at dawn he attacked and either killed or received the surrender of all of them, except a few cavalry at the head of the column, who escaped. He captured alive Afranius and Faustus, with the latter's wife and children. A few days later there was some disturbance in the army and Faustus and Sulla were killed. Caesar granted Pompeia and Faustus's children their lives and allowed them to retain their property.

96. Meanwhile Scipio, together with Damasippus, Torquatus and Plaetorius, was on his way to Spain in a convoy of warships. After a long voyage in stormy weather they were driven in to land at Hippo Regius, where Sittius's fleet was at the time. Scipio's fleet, outnumbered by the latter, was surrounded and sunk, and Scipio perished there, together with the others I have just mentioned.

97. Meanwhile[15] Caesar at Zama held an auction of the royal property and sold the possessions of those Roman citizens who had borne arms against the Roman people. He bestowed rewards on the people of Zama, who had taken the course of barring their gates against the king, let contracts for the collection of the royal

taxes, declared the kingdom a province[16] and installing Gaius Sallustius there as proconsul he left Zama and went to Utica.

There he sold the property of those who had commanded companies under Juba and Petreius. He imposed a fine of 2,000,000 sesterces on the people of Thapsus and 3,000,000 on their Roman community, 3,000,000 again on the people of Hadrumetum and 5,000,000 on their Roman community, but took steps to safeguard their towns and property from being sacked and plundered. The people of Leptis had in former years been despoiled of their property by Juba, but after a formal complaint to the Senate through an embassy arbitrators had been appointed and the property recovered; they were now compelled to pay a fine of 3,000,000 pounds of oil a year, because at the outset, in consequence of disagreement among their leaders, they had allied themselves with Juba and had supplied him with arms, troops and money. The fine on Thysdra, because of the insignificance of the place, was merely a quantity of corn.

98. Caesar then embarked at Utica on 13 June and arrived two days later at Caralis in Sardinia. There he imposed a fine of 10,000,000 sesterces on the people of Sulci and ordered them to pay one eighth of their produce instead of the usual tithes. He sold the property of a few of their number; then he embarked on 27 June and sailed along the coast of Italy. He was delayed in harbours by bad weather, and so took twenty-eight days to reach Rome.

THE SPANISH WAR

1. Caesar pursues the Pompeians

1. Pharnaces had been defeated, Africa taken over, and the survivors of these campaigns fled to the young Gnaeus Pompeius. While Caesar was detained in Italy by the celebration of his triumphs[1], Pompeius had put in at the Balearic Islands and had gained control of Further Spain. To make it easier to gather forces against Caesar, Pompeius began to appeal for protection to each community separately, and in this way, partly by persuasion and partly by intimidation, he got together a fairly large force and began to ravage the province. In these circumstances, some communities voluntarily sent him help, while others shut their gates against him. When he seized any of the latter towns by force, if there was any rich citizen there who had been of outstanding service to Pompey, the size of his fortune would ensure that some other charge was laid against him, so that he could be put out of the way and his money used to reward the spoilers. In this way a few were enriched on the enemy side and their forces grew larger. As a result the communities which were opposed to Pompeius sent frequent messages to Italy clamouring for help.

2. Caesar was now dictator for the third time and had been designated for a fourth term. He completed a great deal of business[2] before making the journey, then rushed to Spain at top speed to finish off the war. He was met by a deputation from the people of Corduba, who had turned against Gnaeus Pompeius, and informed that the town could be captured by night. They explained that it was only as a result of taking his rivals by surprise that Pompeius had managed to seize the province; and besides, Pompeius was now displaying his own alarm at the prospect of Caesar's arrival by the fact that he had stationed scouts everywhere to inform him of Caesar's approach. They also advanced many other plausible arguments. Caesar's hopes were raised. He sent word of his arrival to his lieutenants, Quintus Pedius and Quintus Fabius Maximus, whom he had previously put in command of the army, and instructed them to send any cavalry raised in the province to serve as his own guard. However, he came up with them sooner than they themselves expected;

and he did not, as he had wished, get cavalry to protect him. 3. At the same time it was Gnaeus's brother, Sextus Pompeius, who was holding Corduba with a garrison, that town being considered the capital of the province, while young Gnaeus himself was besieging the town of Ulia and had already been delayed there for some months. When news of Caesar's arrival reached Ulia a deputation was sent out without Gnaeus's knowledge, and once in Caesar's presence began begging him to send help as soon as possible. Since the town had, as Caesar knew, at all times been utterly loyal to the Roman people, he promptly ordered that six cohorts and a corresponding number of cavalry should set out at about nine o'clock that night. He put in command of these a man well known in the province and not lacking in military expertise, Lucius Vibius Paciaecus.

It so happened that just as Vibius reached Pompey's guard-posts he was caught in a storm, with a violent gale blowing; and the violence of the storm made the approaches to the town so dark that each man could hardly recognize his neighbour. This difficulty proved of the greatest usefulness to them. So, when they got there, he ordered the cavalry to take up the infantry on their pillions, and they advanced rapidly, right through the enemy outposts, to the town. When they were still among the guard-posts, they were challenged and one of our men told the questioner to hold his tongue, as they were trying at that moment to reach the walls and take the town. The guards were disconcerted by this reply; and this, coupled with the violence of the storm, prevented them from exercising proper care in the execution of their duties. When our men came up to the gate, they gave a password and were admitted by the townsfolk. The infantry were assigned to posts in various parts of the town and stayed inside, while the cavalry raised a shout and sallied out against the enemy camp. The result was that in this operation, inasmuch as it had taken the enemy unawares, pretty well the majority of the men in camp there thought they were on the point of capture.

4. Caesar dispatched this force to Ulia and then, in order to draw Pompeius away from the siege there, advanced rapidly on Corduba. On his way, he sent ahead some stalwart heavy infantry, with a detachment of cavalry. As soon as they came within sight of the

town, the infantry were taken up pillion, a manoeuvre which the people of Corduba were unable to observe. As they approached the town, a large force came out to mow down the cavalry; whereupon the heavy infantry previously mentioned dismounted. They then fought a vigorous battle, with the result that out of those vast numbers only a few got back into the town. Sextus Pompeius was dismayed at this, and wrote to his brother asking him to come quickly to the rescue, in case Caesar should capture Corduba before he got there. Gnaeus was on the point of taking Ulia; but, alarmed by his brother's dispatch, he began to march with his troops towards Corduba.

5. Caesar reached the river Baetis and was unable to cross because of the depth. He lowered into the water wicker baskets filled with stones, laid timbers on top, and so made a bridge by which he brought his troops across, and then installed them in a camp divided into three. He encamped opposite the town, near the bridge, with his forces, as we have just said, in three sections. When Pompeius and his forces arrived, he encamped in the same way on the opposite side of the river. In order to cut off Pompeius from the town and the supplies there, Caesar began carrying a line of fortifications towards the permanent bridge; Pompeius did likewise. Thereupon, it became a race between the two generals to reach the bridge first, and this occasioned daily skirmishes, in which sometimes our men had the better of it, and sometimes theirs[3].

The struggle grew more intense; both sides began to engage in hand-to-hand fighting, in their determination to hold the position, and became massed together near the bridge; and as, closely jammed together, they came near the banks, they would fall in. By this stage, the two sides were vying, not merely in piling one death on another, but in matching mound with mound of corpses. Caesar spent several days in this way, and was anxious to bring the enemy down on to level ground, if at all possible, and settle the issue at the earliest opportunity.

6. He saw that this was by no means the wish of his opponents. In order to entice them on to the plain in the same way as he had drawn them away from Ulia, he led his forces across the river, and ordered large fires to be lit at night; and so he set off for

Pompeius's strongest garrison, Ategua. Pompeius was informed of this movement by deserters. On the earliest possible day he abandoned the mountains and their passes and retired to Corduba, taking a great train of wagons and loaded mules with him.

Caesar began to invest Ategua with siege-works and construct lines of fortifications round it. He received word that Pompeius was setting out that day, and he prepared his defences against the latter's arrival by occupying several forts, in some of which he could station cavalry and in some infantry to keep constant guard day and night on his camp. Now it so happened that Pompeius arrived in the early morning, when there was a thick mist; and thanks to the poor visibility he surrounded Caesar's cavalry with several infantry cohorts and squadrons of cavalry, and cut them to pieces, so thoroughly that only a few escaped the slaughter.

7. On the following night Pompeius set fire to his camp, and proceeding through the passes on the far side of the river Salsum he encamped on a hill between the two towns of Ategua and Ucubi. Caesar meanwhile had finished work on the fortifications and began to take the necessary measures for assault, building an earth-work and bringing up screens. This region is mountainous and presents obstacles to military operations. It is divided by a plain, the basin of the Salsum, this being nearer to Ategua, about two miles away. It was in the direction of Ategua that Pompeius had pitched camp on the hills, within sight of both towns, but he did not venture to come to the help of his own side. He had the eagles and standards of thirteen legions; but of those which he considered gave him any solid support, two were legions which had deserted from Trebonius, i.e. the Homebred[4] legion and the Second, and there was one raised among the Roman colonists in those parts; a fourth was one of Afranius's old legions, which he had brought with him from Africa; the rest were made up of runaway slaves and auxiliaries[5]. As for light infantry and cavalry, our men were vastly superior both in courage and in numbers.

8. In addition, Pompeius was inclined to protract hostilities, because the district was hilly and not unsuitable for the construction of fortified camps. For practically the whole of Further Spain is fertile and correspondingly well-watered, so that a blockade is difficult and stands little chance of success. In addition, because

of the frequent raids by the natives, all places remote from towns are protected by towers and fortifications, roofed over, as in Africa, with rough-cast, not with tiles. They also contain look-out points, commanding a wide prospect because of their altitude. Moreover, most of the towns in this province are pretty well protected by the mountains, and are situated on natural eminences, so that one has to climb up to reach them, and the approach is thereby made difficult. The natural situation of the Spanish towns makes them so difficult to besiege that they are not easily captured by an enemy; as proved to be the case in this war. In this particular case, Pompeius had established his camp between the towns already mentioned, Ategua and Ucubi, within sight of both. About four miles from his camp there is a natural hillock, called the Camp of Postumius[6], and there Caesar had set up a fort for defence.

9. Pompeius observed that the position of this fort on the same ridge of hills and its distance from Caesar's camp concealed it from the latter; he also observed that, as it was cut off by the river Salsum, Caesar was unlikely to let himself in for sending help, in view of the difficulty of the terrain. Confident, therefore, in his own judgement, Pompeius set out after midnight and began to make an assault on the fort. His men approached, raised a sudden shout, and began to hurl showers of missiles, wounding a great many of the defenders. Thereupon, the latter began to fight back, and word was taken to Caesar in his main camp. He proceeded with three legions to rescue our men; on his approach, the enemy began to flee in panic. Many of them were killed and several captured, including two [?] centurions*. Many besides threw away their weapons in their flight, and eighty of their shields were collected.

10. On the following day, Arguetius arrived from Italy with the cavalry. He brought five standards which he had taken from the townsfolk of Saguntum. (Mention was omitted at the proper place of the fact that cavalry had come to Caesar from Italy under Asprenas.) That night, Pompeius set fire to his camp and began to march towards Corduba. A king named Indo, who had brought troops of his own to accompany the cavalry, was too reckless in

[* Lacuna in text.]

his pursuit of the enemy column, and was cut off and killed by the native legionaries.

11. On the following day our cavalry went out rather far in the direction of Corduba in pursuit of those who were conveying supplies from the town to Pompeius's camp. They captured fifty of these and brought them back to our camp with their pack-animals. On the same day Quintus Marcius, who was one of Pompeius's military tribunes, deserted to us. In the small hours of the night there was fierce fighting in the town and large quantities of firebrands were thrown. Previous to this, Gaius Fundanius, a Roman knight, deserted from the enemy camp to us.

12. On the following day, our cavalry captured two soldiers from the native legion, who said they were slaves. On arrival, they were recognized by the troops who had previously served with Fabius and Pedius and had deserted from Trebonius. They were given no chance of securing pardon, and were put to death by our troops. At the same time, two messengers were captured who had been sent from Corduba to Pompeius and had come to our camp in mistake; their hands were cut off and they were released. Starting towards midnight, the enemy as usual spent a long time hurling large quantities of firebrands and missiles, and wounded several men. When the night was over, they made a sally against the Sixth legion, while our men were dispersed at their work on the fortifications, and then began fighting fiercely. However, our men sustained this violent attack, even though the townsfolk had some protection from their more elevated position. Although the latter had taken the initiative in making a sally, they were nevertheless beaten back thanks to the valour of our men, who, despite their position of disadvantage on lower ground, succeeded in repelling the enemy, wounding a good many and forcing them back into the town.

13. On the following day Pompeius began to construct a line of fortifications from his camp to the river Salsum. There were a few of our cavalry in a guard-post; the enemy came on them in superior strength, drove them out, and killed three. On the same day, Aulus Valgius, who was son of a senator and had a brother in Pompeius's camp, left all his belongings behind, mounted a horse and deserted.

A scout from Pompeius's Second legion was captured by our troops and put to death; at the same time, a lead bullet was thrown, with the inscription, 'On the day when you approach to take the town, I shall lay down my shield.' This encouraged some of our men, and in the confident belief that they could scale the wall and take possession of the town without hazard, they began on the following day to construct a siege-work close to the town wall. A large section of the first wall being knocked down*. ... After this, they were spared by the townsfolk, as if they had been on their own side*. ... [The townsfolk] begged Caesar to get rid of the heavy infantry who had been installed in the town by Pompeius as a garrison. Caesar replied that he was in the habit of issuing terms, not of accepting them. The deputation returned to the town and reported Caesar's reply; thereupon the inhabitants raised a shout, hurled all sorts of missiles and began fighting all around the battlements. As a result, pretty well all the men in our camp were positive that the townsfolk were going to make a sally that day. A cordon was accordingly thrown round the walls and violent fighting went on for some time; moreover, a missile shot by our men from an engine knocked down a turret, throwing down five of the enemy who had been in it, together with a lad whose duty it was to keep an eye on our engine.

14. Earlier on that day Pompeius had succeeded in establishing a fort across the Salsum without any hindrance from our men, and was filled with unjustified self-confidence at having been able to seize a position almost in our lines. Likewise on the following day he pursued his usual practice and went fairly far afield. At one place where we had a cavalry guard-post, several of our cavalry squadrons, together with some light infantry, were dislodged from their position; and because of their inferiority in numbers, both the cavalry squadrons and the light infantry were completely overpowered by the enemy squadrons. This took place within sight of both camps, and the Pompeians were congratulating themselves, because they had begun to push ahead and force our men to fall back. When, however, our men made a stand against them at a certain point, with their usual outstanding bravery, and raised a cry, then the enemy refused battle.

[* Text defective.]

15. With most armies, the nature of a cavalry engagement is usually as follows: when a cavalryman dismounts to fight with an infantryman, he is considered by no means a match for him – as happened in this engagement. Some picked light infantry came up to engage our cavalrymen, taking them by surprise; and when their advance was observed in the course of the fighting, several of the cavalrymen dismounted. As a result, the cavalry soon began to fight an infantry action, so effectively that they were slaughtering their opponents right up close to the rampart. In the engagement, 123 of the enemy fell; and among those who were forced back to camp, several had lost their weapons and many were wounded. Three of our men fell; the wounded numbered twelve infantry and five cavalry. Later on the same day the usual fighting along the battlements broke out. The enemy shot a large number of missiles and firebrands at our troops, who were on the defensive, and then proceeded to an impious and cruel deed; under our very eyes they cut the throats of some of their hostages in the town and began to throw the bodies down from the walls – a barbarous deed and one which has no parallel in recorded history.

16. At the end of this day the Pompeians sent a messenger without our men's knowledge, with instructions to the men in the town to set fire to our towers and earth-work during the night and make a sally in the small hours. And so, after spending a great part of the night hurling missiles and firebrands, they opened a gateway, on the side towards and in sight of Pompeius's camp, and their entire force sallied out. They brought with them brushwood and hurdles to fill the ditches, as well as hooks to pull apart the thatched huts built by our men as winter quarters, so that they could burn them. They also brought silverware and clothes, with the idea that, while our men were preoccupied with looting it, they could kill some of them and so take refuge with Pompeius's forces; for in anticipation of their succeeding in their attempt Pompeius spent the whole night moving his forces up and down by the Salsum in battle formation. Although the sally took our men by surprise, thanks to their valour they succeeded in beating off the enemy and driving them back into the town with many casualties. They seized their booty and weapons and captured

some of them alive; these they killed on the following day. At the same time a deserter from the town reported that after the massacre of the townsfolk one Junius, who had been in a mine, cried out that his people had committed a heinous crime; their hosts had done nothing to deserve such cruel treatment; they had admitted them to the shelter of their temples and their homes, and they in return had violated hospitality with a crime. He had said a great deal more besides, so that the others were overawed by his speech and put a stop to the massacre.

17. So, on the following day Tullius came as an envoy with Cato and Antonius[7] and spoke before Caesar. 'I wish the immortal gods had vouchsafed that I should be a soldier of yours rather than of Gnaeus Pompeius, and that I might be displaying my constancy and courage as a participant in your victory, and not in his defeat. His reputation, already doomed to disaster, has slumped so low that we, Roman citizens, are in want of protection and on account of the disastrous calamity of our country are accounted public enemies. We had no good fortune, either at the first when he was successful, nor later when he was worsted. After withstanding so many legionary assaults and parrying, in engagements by night and day, the blows of swords and missiles, we now find ourselves abandoned and deserted by Pompeius. Therefore we now admit ourselves overcome by your valour and we beg you in your clemency to spare us and ask you to grant us our lives.'

Caesar's reply was: 'As I have behaved to foreign peoples, so I shall behave to citizens who surrender.'

18. The deputation was sent back. When it reached the gate Tiberius Tullius went in; and when Antonius failed to follow Cato as he went in, the latter turned back to the gate and seized him. Observing these happenings, Tiberius at once drew his dagger and stabbed Cato's hand; then he and Antonius fled to Caesar. At the same time a standard-bearer from the First legion deserted and gave information that on the day of the cavalry battle thirty-five men from his detachment had been lost, and that they had not been allowed to say so in Gnaeus Pompeius's camp, or even to say that anyone at all had died. A slave, whose master was in Caesar's camp (he had left his wife and sons in the town)

murdered his mistress and so managed to escape into Pompeius's camp without detection by Caesar's guards. From there, he sent information written on a lead shot, telling Caesar of the preparations for defence in the town. So the message was received, and when the man who usually discharged the shot returned to the town*. . . . Later on two brothers, Lusitanians, deserted and reported a public speech made by Pompeius. He had said that, since he could not come to the help of the town, they should withdraw by night out of sight of their opponents, in the direction of the sea. One man, they said, had objected, saying that they ought to go into battle rather than give the signal for flight; the man who said this had his throat cut. At the same time, some of Pompeius's messengers were captured on their way to the town. Caesar passed on their dispatches to the townsfolk, but informed the couriers that if any one of them wanted his life spared he should set fire to a wooden tower belonging to the townspeople, and he promised him a total pardon if he did so. It was a difficult task for anyone to set fire to that tower without risk; and so, at the end of the day, when one man did come rather close to the wooden tower, he was killed by the men in the town. On the same night a deserter reported that Pompeius and Labienus had expressed their displeasure at the massacre of the townsfolk.

19. Towards midnight, a wooden tower belonging to us suffered damage which extended from the base up as far as the second and third storeys. At the same time there was fierce fighting from the battlements, and the townsfolk set fire to our tower mentioned earlier, since they were able to take advantage of a favourable wind. On the following day a mother threw herself down from the battlements and slipped across to us. She said that she and her household had agreed to desert to Caesar, but that the others had been seized and killed. At this time also, a set of tablets was thrown down from the wall, on which was found written: 'Lucius Munatius to Caesar. If you grant me life, since I have been deserted by Gnaeus Pompeius, I shall display the same courage and constancy in support of you as I did for him.' At the same time the same deputation of townsfolk as had come out before came to Caesar, saying that if he granted them their lives

[* Lacuna in text.]

they would surrender the town the following day. He replied that he was Caesar and would keep his word. And so on 19 February he took the town and was acclaimed as *imperator*.

20. On learning from deserters of the surrender of the town, Pompeius moved camp in the direction of Ucubi, established forts around that area and proceeded to keep within his lines. Caesar struck [camp*] and moved nearer to Pompeius's camp. At the same time, one morning one of the heavy infantry from the native legion deserted to us and reported that Pompeius had assembled the people of Ucubi and ordered them to conduct a careful search to find out who were his supporters and who favoured the victory of his opponents. Previously to this, the slave who, as mentioned above, murdered his mistress, was caught in a mine in the captured town; he was burned alive. About the same time eight men of the heavy infantry of the Eighth legion deserted to Caesar, and our cavalry had an engagement with the enemy cavalry and a number of the light infantry were fatally wounded. The same night some scouts were caught – three slaves and a man from the native legion. The slaves were crucified and the soldier was beheaded.

21. On the following day some cavalry and light infantry deserted to us from the enemy camp. At that time also about forty of their cavalry made a sortie against a watering party of ours, killed several, and carried some off alive; eight of their cavalrymen were captured. On the following day, Pompeius beheaded seventy-four men, who were said to be in favour of a victory for Caesar, and ordered the rest to be taken back into the town; 120 of these escaped and came over to Caesar.

22. Previous to this, the envoys from Urso who had been captured in the town of Ategua set out, accompanied by some of our men, to report to the people of Urso what had happened and to ask them what hopes they could entertain of Gnaeus Pompeius when they saw hosts massacred – especially as many other crimes besides were being committed by those whom the citizens had admitted for their protection. On arrival at the town, our party, which consisted of knights and senators, did not venture to go inside, except for such as were members of that community. After

[* Text defective.]

discussion, the envoys were on their way back to our men outside the town when the townsfolk pursued them with a force and cut them down from behind. There were two survivors, who escaped to Caesar with news of what had happened. The townsfolk sent scouts to the town of Ategua. When they established for certain that the events had been just as the envoys had reported, the townsfolk began to mob the man responsible for murdering the envoys, throwing stones at him and shaking their fists; they cried that he had brought about their ruin. Escaping with difficulty from this perilous situation, he asked the townsfolk to send him to plead with Caesar, undertaking that he would satisfy him. Permission was granted and he left the town. Then he got together a pretty large force, secured admission to the town by treachery at night and carried out a large-scale massacre. He put to death those of the leading citizens who had been opposed to him, and took over control of the town. Previous to this, runaway slaves reported that the property of the townsfolk was being sold, and that no one was allowed to go outside the ramparts wearing a belt[8]. The reason for these restrictions was that, since the day when Ategua was captured, a great many had fled in panic to Baeturia. They entertained no hope of victory, and if anyone deserted from our side he was forced into the light infantry and got only seven denarii a month[9].

23. In the following period, Caesar brought his camp up closer and began to carry a line of fortification towards the river Salsum. Hereupon, while our men were engaged on the work, a large number of the enemy came running down from the high ground and, as our men did not stop their work, a good many of them were wounded by the volleys of enemy missiles.

Then indeed, to quote Ennius, 'Our men did yield a little space.' Therefore when our men observed that they were giving way more than usual, two centurions of the Fifth legion crossed the river and rallied the line. Thanks to their gallant and ferocious fighting they were beginning to rout the enemy when one of the two fell under a hail of missiles from the higher ground. His companion had been fighting, but observing that he was being totally surrounded he began to withdraw, and in doing so he stumbled. As this gallant centurion fell, several of the enemy rushed to seize his insignia; but our cavalry crossed over and, operating from a lower position, began to drive the enemy back to their rampart. As a result of their excessive eagerness to carry the slaughter right in among the enemy guard-posts, they were cut off by cavalry squadrons and light infantry, and had they not displayed exceptional courage, they would have been captured alive; for they were so closely hemmed in by the fortifications of the outposts that there was scarcely room for a cavalryman to defend himself. In both types of fighting a good many were wounded, including Clodius Arquitius; but so energetic was their hand-to-hand fighting that none of our men was lost, except for the two centurions; and they acquitted themselves notably.

24. On the following day the forces of both sides moved towards Soricaria. Our men began to build lines of fortification. Pompeius observed that he was being cut off from the fort of Aspavia, which was about five miles from Ucubi; and this circumstance compelled him to come down and offer battle. However, he did not, but from a hillock*. . . . he attempted to take a lofty eminence, with the result that Caesar was compelled to approach at a disadvantage. Thereupon both sides made for this hill; the enemy were forestalled by our men, and driven down on the level ground. This turned the battle in our favour. The enemy were giving way on all sides and a fair number of them were being killed. It was the hill, not their valour, which helped to preserve them; for if evening had not come on, our men, though inferior in numbers, would have cut them off from all aid. In fact, 323 of the light infantry fell and 138 legionaries, and many others besides were stripped of their weapons and equipment. In this way vengeance was exacted from the enemy for the death of the two centurions on the previous day.

25. On the following day, Pompeius's force came in the same way to the same spot and employed the same tactics as before; for, apart from the cavalry, none of them ventured to present themselves on level ground. While our men were busy constructing fortifications, the enemy cavalry began making charges, while the legionaries yelled out demanding to be given their turn, as they were accustomed to follow up the cavalry. You might have

[* Text defective.]

supposed they were ready and eager to fight. Then our men advanced a considerable distance from a low-lying defile and halted on the level in a fairly favourable position. The enemy, however, quite clearly did not dare to come down on to the plain to engage on level ground – that is, except one man, Antistius Turpio; confident in his strength, he began boasting that there was not his match among his opponents. Then, like the legendary encounter between Achilles and Memnon[10], Quintus Pompeius Niger, a Roman knight from Italica, came forward from our ranks to engage with him. Antistius's ferocity had drawn everyone's attention away from the construction work; both battle lines were arrayed; for in this contest between two outstanding warriors, the outcome was uncertain, and it almost appeared that the fight between these two would bring the war to a conclusion.

Everyone was alert and eager, gripped by the enthusiasm of the partisans and supporters on his own side. The champions, with ready courage, came on to the plain to fight, their shields with engraved work, emblems of their renown, flashing*. . . . Their fight was on the point of being broken off straight away, had it not been for the yielding of the cavalry, as mentioned above*. . . . He posted the light infantry on guard not far from the defence-works*. . . . near [?] the camp. Our cavalry were withdrawing to camp when the enemy pursued rather too enthusiastically; and our men raised a shout and made a massed charge. The enemy were terrified and, losing a good many men in their flight, they returned to camp.

26. As rewards for valour, Caesar presented to the squadron of Cassius 13,000 sesterces, to the commanding officer five gold torques and to the light infantry 12,000 sesterces. On the same day, Aulus Baebius, Gaius Flavius and Aulus Trebellius, Roman knights from Asta, with their horses almost totally covered in silver, deserted to Caesar. They reported that all the Roman knights in Pompeius's camp had conspired to desert. A slave had informed on them and they had all been put under guard, but they themselves had seized an opportunity to escape. On the same day, a dispatch from Pompeius to Urso was intercepted. It read: 'Greetings. Such is our good fortune that we have hitherto repelled our

[* Text defective.]

opponents, as we wished, and if they had afforded an opportunity of battle on even ground, I should have brought the war to an end sooner than you expected. But they do not dare to bring their army of raw recruits down on to the plain and, pinned down so far by our forces, they are prolonging hostilities. They have invested individual towns and from these they draw supplies. Accordingly, I shall spare the communities which support me and I shall bring the war to as speedy a conclusion as possible. I intend to send you*... cohorts. When we move we shall deprive them of supplies and they will be forced to come down and fight.'

27. Subsequently, when our men were engaged in work on the fortifications, several cavalrymen on a wood-gathering party were killed in an olive grove. Some slaves deserted, who reported that since the battle near Soricaria on 5 March there had been great apprehension; and that Attius Varus was in charge of the forts in the area. On that day Pompeius moved camp and halted in an olive grove opposite Spalis. Before Caesar set out for the same area, the moon was visible, at about three p.m.

After moving camp, Pompeius instructed the garrison which he had left to set fire to Ucubi, and when the town was burned out to return to the main camp. Subsequently, Caesar proceeded to attack the town of Ventipo; when it surrendered he marched to Carruca and encamped opposite Pompeius. Pompeius set fire to the town for having closed its gates against his garrison; and a soldier who had murdered his brother in camp was captured by our men and beaten to death with cudgels. Caesar marched on from here to the plain of Munda and camped opposite Pompeius.

2. The victory of Munda

28. On the following day Caesar was intending to continue the march with his forces, when word was brought by scouts that Pompeius in the small hours of the morning had deployed his battle-line. At this news, Caesar hung out the flag as the signal for battle. Pompeius's reason for leading out his forces was as follows. He had previously written to the people of Urso, who

[* Text defective.]

were his supporters, saying that Caesar was reluctant to come down into the valley because the bulk of his army consisted of raw recruits. (This dispatch did a great deal to strengthen the morale of the townsfolk.) It was from this conviction that Pompeius believed he could achieve anything; and indeed he had in his favour the nature of the terrain, besides the fortifications of the town itself, where he had pitched camp. For, as we showed above*, it is a high-lying region, consisting in hills with an occasional plain intervening, as in this instance.

29. There was a plain between the two camps some five miles in extent; Pompeius's auxiliaries were protected by two things – the town and the elevated nature of the ground. Extending from here, the nearest part of the plain levelled out and ran down to a stream which flowed in front and greatly impeded access for Caesar's men, as the ground to the right of its course was marshy and full of bog-pits. Seeing the battle line deployed, Caesar was quite sure that his opponents intended to advance into the centre of the plain to engage. This area was in full sight of all. Moreover, the place was tempting to the cavalry, by its very flatness, and the calm sunny weather, so that it almost seemed as if the immortal gods themselves had given this marvellous, longed-for opportunity for battle.

Our men were delighted, though some also were apprehensive, reflecting that the fate and fortunes of them all were being brought into a situation in which it was uncertain what, an hour later, chance would prove to have bestowed on them. Our men, then, advanced to battle, as we also expected the enemy to do; they, however, did not venture to advance far from the fortifications of the town – on the contrary they stationed themselves on the defensive near the walls. So, our men advanced. From time to time the favourable nature of the ground strongly urged our opponents to press on, under such conditions, to victory; but they did not in fact abandon their usual practice, so as to move away from the high ground or the town. When our men came up to the stream in close formation, the enemy persisted on the defensive on the slope.

30. Their battle line was drawn up under thirteen legionary

[* Ch. 8.]

eagles. The wings were covered by cavalry with 6,000 light infantry and roughly the same number of auxiliaries. Our forces comprised eighty cohorts and 8,000 cavalry. So, when our men advanced on to the unfavourable ground at the far end of the plain, the position of the enemy on the higher ground made it extremely dangerous for our men to proceed up towards them. Observing this, Caesar began to restrict the area of manoeuvre, in order to avert the danger of a blunder through rashness or error. When this came to the men's ears they were very annoyed and bitter because, in their view, they were being hindered from bringing the fight to an issue. The delay gave their opponents all the more encouragement; they believed that it was fear that was delaying Caesar's forces in joining battle. They deployed themselves and afforded our men the opportunity of attacking them on the steep ground; but it was very hazardous to approach them. On our side the Tenth legion was in its normal position, i.e. the right wing, while the Third and Fifth were on the left, together with the rest, the auxiliaries and cavalry. A shout was raised, and they engaged.

31. Now, our men were superior in courage, but the enemy from their position of advantage were defending themselves energetically. So vigorous was the shouting on both sides, the discharge of javelins and the subsequent engagement, that our men almost lost confidence. In fact, in the shouting and the engaging at close quarters – the two aspects of a battle which are most effective in terrorizing an enemy – the sides were on even terms. And so, though both sides showed equal vigour in both these aspects, when the javelins were thrown, vast numbers of the enemy were hit and fell in heaps. As we said, the Tenth held the right wing; though few in number, their spirit was such that their efforts struck terror into their opponents; for they began forcibly to drive back the enemy from his position, so that the latter, to avoid being outflanked by our men, began to bring a legion across to the right. As soon as this legion moved, Caesar's cavalry began pushing hard on the left wing so that, no matter how courageously the enemy might fight, he was afforded no opportunity of bringing reinforcements up into the line. So, when shouting, mingled with groans and the clash of swords, was borne to their

ears, the minds of the inexperienced were numbed with fear. Thereupon, to quote Ennius, 'foot pressed hard by foot, arms clashed with arms', and despite our opponents' vigorous resistance, our men began to drive them back. The town was their salvation.

And so, on the day of the Liberalia[11] (17 March), they were routed and put to flight, and would have been annihilated had they not taken refuge in the place from which they had sallied out. In this battle there fell about 30,000 men, or if anything more, as well as Labienus, Attius Varus (both of whom received burial on the spot) and about 3,000 Roman knights, some from Rome and some from the province. Our losses amounted to about 1,000, partly cavalry, partly infantry. The enemy's thirteen eagles were captured, and in addition Caesar took the following standards and rods of office*....

3. 'Mopping-up'

32. . . . Those who, in their retreat, had taken refuge in the town of Munda. Our men were obliged to blockade them. Shields and spears from the enemy's weapons were set up as a stockade and bodies in place of a turf rampart. On top were set severed heads on sword-points, all facing towards the town, within sight of the enemy, so as both to intimidate them and to display our prowess, and also in order to surround them with a siege-work. Once they had thus encircled the town with a wall of corpses, the Gauls began attacking with throwing-darts and javelins. From this battle the young Valerius escaped to Corduba with a few cavalrymen and reported what had happened to Sextus Pompeius, who was at Corduba. On receiving the news, Sextus distributed such money as he had on the spot among the cavalry he had there and told the townsfolk that he was going to Caesar to negotiate for peace. He left the town late in the evening. Gnaeus Pompeius, with a small number of cavalry and some infantry, made off in the opposite direction to the naval garrison at Carteia, a town about 170 miles from Corduba. When he got within eight miles, Publius Caucilius, who had previously been Pompeius's camp-commander, sent a message, at Pompeius's dictation, that he was not too well,

[* Text defective.]

and they were to send a litter so that he could be carried to the town. Litter-bearers were dispatched and Pompeius was carried to Carteia. His supporters gathered at the house to which he had been conveyed, under the impression that he had entered the town in secret, to make inquiries of him about the war. When a large number had assembled, Pompeius left the litter and put himself in their hands.

33. After the battle, Caesar invested Munda with lines of fortifications, and proceeded to Corduba. Those who had fled there from the field of slaughter took possession of the bridge. On Caesar's arrival, they began to jeer at our men, saying we were the handful who had survived the battle and asking us where we were running off to. Then they began fighting from the bridge. Caesar crossed the river and pitched camp.

The ringleader of the resistance and leader of a gang of slaves and freedmen was Scapula, who had come to Corduba after the battle. He called the slaves and freedmen together, had a pyre built for himself, and ordered the best possible dinner, with the finest coverlets spread. He personally presented his slaves with money and silver plate. He presently dined, and anointed himself repeatedly with resin and nard. Then he gave orders to a slave and to a freedman, his concubine; the one was to cut his throat, the other to set light to the pyre.

34. As soon as Caesar pitched camp over against the town, the inhabitants began quarrelling, to such an extent that the noise of the brawling between supporters of Caesar and of Pompeius could be heard in our camp. There were two legions here, made up partly from deserters and partly from slaves belonging to the townsfolk, to whom Sextus Pompeius had given their freedom. These fell at variance on the arrival of Caesar. The Thirteenth began to defend the town; the Ninth, after they started fighting, took possession of some of the bastions, and the wall. Finally, they sent a deputation to Caesar, asking him to send legions in to help them. Learning this, the fugitives began to set fire to the town. They were overpowered by our men, and about 22,000 were killed, besides those who died outside the wall. So Caesar took possession of the town. While he was detained here, the people whom, as mentioned above, he had invested after the battle

made a sally and were driven back into the town with severe losses.

35. Caesar was pressing on towards Hispalis when he was met by a deputation begging his forgiveness. So, when he came to the town, he installed his lieutenant Caninius with a garrison, while he himself camped beside the town. There was a fairly large body of support there for Pompeius, and these people were very angry that the garrison had been admitted without the knowledge of a certain Philo. This Philo had been the most energetic supporter of the Pompeian cause – he was, besides, very well known throughout Lusitania. He now set out without the knowledge of the garrison and near Lennium he joined Caecilius Niger, a native, who had a large force of Lusitanians. He went back to Hispalis and was re-admitted into the town by night; he and his force killed the garrison and the sentries, barred the gates, and began fighting again.

36. Meanwhile, a deputation from the people of Carteia reported that they had Pompeius in their power. Since they had previously closed their gates against Caesar, they hoped by this good turn to offset their former bad behaviour. At Hispalis, the Lusitanians went on fighting continuously. Caesar learned this; but he was afraid that, if he attempted to take the town, they might in desperation set fire to it and destroy its fortifications. He therefore deliberately allowed the Lusitanians to break out by night, although they did not realize that this was done intentionally. So they broke out and set fire to the ships which were by the river Baetis. While our men were delayed by the fire, the Lusitanians tried to make their escape, and were cut down by the cavalry. Caesar thus recovered the town, then marched to Asta. A deputation came from this town to surrender. At Munda, after a prolonged blockade, many of the people who had taken refuge after the battle surrendered. These were enrolled into a legion and formed a conspiracy that, at a given signal, those in the town should sally out, while they themselves conducted a massacre in the camp. The plot was discovered and on the following night, in the small hours, when the pass-word was given they were all cut down outside the rampart.

37. While Caesar was on the march and attacking various other

towns, the people of Carteia began to quarrel over Pompeius. Some of them had sent the deputation to Caesar, while there were others who supported Pompeius's cause. Trouble flared up and they took sides. There was a great deal of bloodshed. Pompeius was wounded; and commandeering twenty warships he fled. Didius, who was in command of the fleet at Gades, hurried after him as soon as he received the news. From Carteia the infantry and cavalry advanced rapidly in pursuit. After three days' sailing the Pompeians were forced to put in to land, as they had left Carteia without making preparations and had no water. While they were getting some, Didius came up quickly with his fleet, set fire to their vessels and captured several.

38. Pompeius fled with a few men and seized a natural strong-point. The infantry and cavalry who had been dispatched in pursuit sent scouts ahead to reconnoitre, while they kept on the move night and day. Pompeius had received serious wounds in the shoulder and in the left leg. He had also sprained an ankle, which was a serious handicap. He was therefore carried to the bastion in a litter and continued to be so conveyed. A Lusitanian, who had been sent out from his force, according to normal military practice, as a scout, was observed by Caesar's force and was quickly surrounded by the cavalry and cohorts.

Now, the place was difficult of access; for Pompeius had deliberately chosen a natural strong-point so that, no matter how many men were brought up, a few could defend it from their position of advantage. On arrival, our men approached, only to be driven back by missiles. As they gave ground the enemy came in pursuit enthusiastically and soon checked their advance. This happened several times, until it was realized that it involved considerable hazard for our men. The enemy began to build a defence-wall round themselves; our men with equal speed began constructing lines of fortification along the high ground, so that they could come to grips with their opponents on an equal footing. Observing this, the latter sought refuge in flight.

39. Pompeius, as mentioned above, was wounded and had a sprained ankle, which hampered him in flight; moreover, the difficulty of the terrain made it impossible for him to use a horse or a vehicle to make his escape to safety. Our men dealt out

slaughter indiscriminately. Pompeius, debarred from his fortifications and having lost his supporters, attempted to conceal himself in a gully, where the rock was eroded away to form a cave, and he would not easily have been found had not prisoners revealed his whereabouts. So he was killed there. While Caesar was at Gades Pompeius's head was brought to Hispalis on 12 April and publicly exhibited.

40. At the death of young Gnaeus Pompeius, Didius, whom we mentioned above, was delighted. He withdrew to the nearest fort, beached several ships for repairs and*. . . . The Lusitanians who survived the battle rallied to their standard and once a pretty large force had gathered they marched against Didius. Conscientious as Didius was in guarding the ships, he was quite often tempted out of the fortress by their frequent raids; as a result, they fought almost daily, and the enemy laid a trap for him, dividing their forces into three. There were men ready to set fire to the ships, and to beat off attempts at rescue once they had been set on fire. These were out of sight; others, in full view, marched to battle. And so, when Didius advanced from the fort with his forces to beat them off, the Lusitanians hoisted the signal and the ships were set on fire. At the same time, while the forces which had emerged from the fort to do battle were pursuing the fleeing ruffians, they were cut off by an ambush, obeying the same signal, which raised an outcry in the rear. Didius died fighting bravely, with many others. In the fighting, several seized the dinghies which were on the beach, while a good many swam out, and so they made their way to the vessels which were lying off shore. They lifted anchor and began to row out to sea, and this action saved their lives. The Lusitanians took possession of the booty. Caesar hurried back from Gades to Hispalis.

41. Fabius Maximus, whom Caesar had left behind to attack the garrison at Munda, invested it in continuous operations by night and day. The besieged began fighting among themselves, and after considerable bloodshed they made a sally. Our men did not fail to take advantage of the opportunity to seize the town and captured the survivors, numbering 14,000, alive. They proceeded to Urso, a town which was surrounded by massive fortifi-

[* Text defective.]

cations, so that the place appeared naturally suited for assailing an enemy. Moreover, apart from the water supply within the town itself, there was none for seven miles around, a circumstance which was a great help to the townsfolk. In addition, the materials for earth-works* . . . and timber for constructing towers and screens could not be found less than six miles away. And Pompeius, to protect himself further against an attack on the town, had cut down all the timber around the town and conveyed it inside. Our men were therefore obliged to split up their forces, in order to convey timber from Munda, the nearest source of supply.

42. During these events at Urso and Munda, Caesar summoned a meeting the day after his return from Gades to Hispalis, and addressed it thus: 'At the start of my quaestorship[12] I determined that this above all provinces should be my especial concern and I lavished on it such good offices as were at that time in my power. Later in a more exalted position as praetor I secured from the Senate remission of the taxes imposed by Metellus[13] and freed the province from that payment. Once I had undertaken the patronage of the province I protected it, introducing many deputations into the Senate and undertaking many lawsuits, both public and private, and so incurring the enmity of many men. As consul too, although absent, I did what good I could for the province. I have found you, both in the course of this war and in earlier times, unmindful of all these benefits and ungrateful both to me and to the Roman people.

'Acquainted though you are with the principles of international equity and with the laws of the Romans, like barbarians you have time and again raised your hands against the sacred magistracies of the Roman people. You impiously determined to kill Cassius in broad daylight in the middle of the forum. You have always so detested peace that at no time have the legions of the Roman people ceased to be stationed in this province. You consider kindnesses as injuries, wrongs as benefits. As a result, you have never been able to maintain either harmony in peace-time or a resolute spirit in time of war. You admitted young Gnaeus Pompeius, while a fugitive and a private citizen; you let him seize the rods of office and military power for himself. After killing many

[* Lacuna in text.]

citizens he got together a force to attack the Roman people, and with your encouragement he ravaged the countryside of the province. In what conflict do you emerge as victors? Did you not realize that, even if I were destroyed, the Roman people has legions which could not only stop you, but could even bring the skies tumbling down about you? Thanks to their courage and renown...'

TRANSLATOR'S NOTE

Here the manuscript ends. Caesar stayed several months in Spain. Communities which had been hostile were ordered to pay extra taxes or deprived of some of their land; loyal communities were rewarded with the status of Roman colonies, or even grants of Roman citizenship, and exemption from taxes. Plans were prepared for the founding of several new colonies.

Sextus Pompeius went into hiding and survived, to be a thorn in the flesh of the triumvirs, another ten years.

Caesar returned to Rome in September, 45 B.C. He was assassinated six months later.

NOTES

1. *dispatch from Gaius Caesar.* This was brought from Ravenna by Curio ('Fabius' of the MSS is an error). It contained an offer from Caesar to resign his command if Pompey would do the same; if the offer were rejected, he said, he would be obliged to defend his own rights and those of the State.

2. *Pompey was near by.* By law, a proconsul with *imperium* had to remain outside the city; Plutarch tells us Pompey was in his house to the north-west of the city.

3. *comitium.* An open space beside the Forum, where the Roman people assembled to vote in certain elections.

4. *a relative ... by marriage.* Pompey had been married to Caesar's daughter, Julia, who died in 54 B.C. In the following year he rejected Caesar's offer of the hand of his great-niece, Octavia, and married Cornelia, a daughter of Scipio and widow of Crassus's son.

5. *ten legions ready.* Presumably two from Caesar, seven in Spain, and one with Domitius.

6. The chronology here is left vague – perhaps deliberately so. In fact, Caesar must have summoned the remaining legions from their winter quarters in Gallia Belgica and the territory of the Aedui some three weeks before the official break with the Senate; however, he is concerned to represent himself as reluctantly forced to arms, and so wishes to avoid the appearance of premeditation or preparation.

7. *the business for which he had come.* The nature of this business and its official status, if any, have exercised modern commentators. It is a plausible suggestion that Lucius was the bearer of some private offer from Pompey.

8. *six months of my command.* By the *Lex Sempronia* of Gaius Gracchus, the annual allocation by the Senate of consular provinces had to take place before the election of the consuls who were to hold them. However, by the *Lex Pompeia Licinia* of 55 B.C., Caesar's command was excluded from allocation for five years. The precise formulation of this law is uncertain, but what it probably amounted to was that his province could not be allocated before 1 March 50 B.C. – that is, it could be allocated to one of the consuls

for 49 B.C. The consul was not likely to leave Rome and go to take
over the province until after the consular elections for 48 B.C., at
which Caesar had been given permission to be a candidate *in
absentia*. So long, therefore, as the *Lex Sempronia* was in operation,
Caesar could hope to retain his province at least until he was
consul-elect.

Pompey in 52 B.C. had made into law a senatorial decree of the
previous year, to the effect that a five-year interval must elapse
between the holding of the office of consul or praetor and tenure
of a province. This had the effect of cancelling the Sempronian
law, since it made available for immediate assignment to provinces
ex-consuls and praetors of more than five years' standing who had
not yet held a province (the orator, Cicero, was among those
affected). In Caesar's eyes, these persons were private individuals –
see Part 1.6. Caesar's supporters, with some help from Pompey himself, managed to block discussion of the allocation of his province
on 1 March 50. Now, in January 49 B.C., Caesar has received a senatorial ultimatum ordering him to abandon his province; this, he
protests, robs him of the six further months on which he could
have relied, under the operation of the previous laws, and also of
the privilege of candidature *in absentia*.

9. *the treasury reserve.* Maintained by the proceeds of the five-per-
cent tax on the freeing of slaves; to be used only in emergency.
According to some other sources, the treasury was forced open by
Caesar himself.

10. *the Julian law.* Passed in Caesar's consulship (59 B.C.) this law had
assigned unoccupied State lands, including the fertile Campanian
territory, for distribution among needy citizens.

11. *prefectures.* Communities without independent municipal status,
administered by prefects in the name of Rome.

12. *prefects.* Cavalry officers. *military tribunes.* Legionary officers (six
per legion), a post usually held prior to entry into the Senate.

13. *college of pontiffs.* This consisted at this time of the Pontifex
Maximus or chief priest of Rome (Caesar himself) and fifteen
others. In the first century B.C., pontiffs were chosen by a combination of co-option and election; two candidates were nominated by
the college, and voted on by seventeen of the thirty-five Roman
tribes, selected by lot.

14. *proposals to Pompey.* Cicero (letters to Atticus, 9. 13A) preserves a
letter from Caesar: 'I have camped at Brundisium; Pompey is here.
He has sent N. Magius to me to discuss peace terms. I have replied
as I see fit. . . . I shall let you know at once, when I come within

sight of a settlement.' This appears at first sight to conflict with Caesar's version. We should not, however, hastily accuse Caesar of bad faith. It is possible that Magius was in fact sent *twice*: Caesar's letter does not divulge the nature of Pompey's proposals, which may have been unsatisfactory. In his narrative here, Caesar may simply have omitted the abortive set of negotiations.

15. *gratitude to Pompey*. After campaigning against Sertorius in Hither Spain Pompey in 72 B.C. gave Roman citizenship to a number of Spaniards.

16. *the statutory interval*. Fixed, by a law of Sulla, at ten years.

17. *Pompey ... was consul then*. In 52 B.C.

18. *tributary*. Each city in a Roman province was responsible for the administration of a large extent of surrounding territory. Those inhabitants of the territory who were not regarded as fit for full municipal citizenship were 'attributed' to the city, i.e. they were placed under its authority and had certain financial and other responsibilities to it.

19. *leading centurion*. The legion of Caesar's day was divided into ten cohorts, each containing six centuries arranged in three groups of two, corresponding to the three lines of the usual battle formation. The cohorts had a descending order of seniority, from First to Tenth, and promotion for a centurion was from cohort to cohort. The senior centurion of the whole legion was the *primipilus*, or centurion of the first front-line century of the first cohort. This rank was held by Caecilius. Fulginius's title was *primus hastatus*. At this period, the *Principes* and *Triarii* seem to have taken precedence over the *Hastati*; Fulginius, then, was presumably centurion of the senior company of *hastati* in the first cohort.

20. *as shown above*. An oversight. This is not mentioned previously.

21. *price of corn*. There is little evidence for the price of corn in the first century B.C. Large purchases to relieve a famine at Rome in 75 B.C. produced scarcity in Sicily in the following year and prices rose to 5 denarii (20 sesterces). From Cicero's Third Verrine Speech, it appears that an average price in Sicily around 70 B.C. was ¾ denarius (3 sesterces). Josephus mentions a famine price of 11 denarii on one occasion in Judaea. These prices are a long way behind the 50 denarii which is the interpretation of the MSS. accepted by most modern scholars and which is followed in the translation. Possibly the reading XL should be interpreted as 40 sesterces, i.e. 10 denarii.

22. *large fleets*. Cato had prepared one in Sicily (1.30). Probably also

reference is intended to the fleet at Massilia and that assembled by Varro in Spain (II.18).

23. *experienced commanders.* e.g. Afranius, Petreius, Varro, Domitius, Vibullius Rufus.

24. *rights of magistrates . . . tampered with*, cf. note 8 above. The reference is to Pompey's law of 52 B.C. on the allocation of provinces.

25. *siege-walls on two sides.* Caesar does not mention, what must surely have been done earlier, the building of a contravallation (cf. Lucan, III. 383–7). The two siege-walls would presumably be at right-angles to this wall.

26. *'tortoise'.* An outsize mantlet, i.e. a long, tunnel-like shed.

27. *previous setback.* Part I. 58.

28. *experience elsewhere.* There is no indication in the *Gallic War* that the Gallic tribes had any missile engines, and Caesar says (op. cit. IV. 25) that the Britons had none. Rice Holmes (*The Roman Republic* vol. III, p. 88, n. 1) thinks that the reference is to experience gained in the course of this siege.

29. *covered gallery.* A long, open-ended hut – not unlike the 'tortoise' of Ch. 2.

30. *bands* (fillets). White woollen strips worn on the head, usually as token that one is under the protection of the gods. Here, the inhabitants are claiming the sacrosanctity due to suppliants.

31. *skilled orators.* Massilia was the chief intellectual centre of Transalpine Gaul, and famous for its schools of rhetoric.

32. *the island.* Gades was situated on an off-shore island.

33. *benefits.* cf. Part I. 61.

34. *'Colonials'.* Levied in the Roman colonies.

35. *'Homebred'.* Composed of inhabitants of the province.

36. *Castra Cornelia.* The site of the camp of P. Cornelius Scipio in the campaign against Hannibal. According to Appian, the Africans, thinking that Curio would camp there in emulation of the great Scipio, poisoned the water in the neighbourhood; the consequent illness of his army made him move camp, marching through the marshes, to the neighbourhood of Utica.

37. *State property.* This proposal had been made by Curio in 50 B.C.; it amounted to declaring the kingdom a Roman province.

38. *imperator.* This was originally an honorific title bestowed on a victorious general by the acclamation of his troops, to signify his fitness to command. In the imperial period, it also formed part of the official nomenclature of the emperor (and is the source of the latter word).

39. *military oath.* Soldiers were required to take an oath of loyalty to their own particular commander, and to promise never to desert their standards.

40. The text here is very corrupt. For the readings adopted, see Appendix I.

41. *Sicily and Africa.* These were the main sources of corn supply for Rome; an enemy in control of these could starve the city.

42. *symbols of office.* In particular the *fasces*, part of the insignia of senior magistrates and military commanders in the field.

43. *loss of rights.* Prisoners of war were technically regarded as having forfeited their rights of citizenship.

44. *legally become consul.* See note 16. Caesar was consul in 59 B.C., and could not therefore legally be consul again until 48 B.C. His insistence on this point may be intended to point the contrast with Pompey, who was consul in 55 and again in 52.

45. *a law of Pompey's.* The *Lex Pompeia de ambitu*, against corruption, carried during Pompey's period as sole consul in 52 B.C. Like the law on cases of violence carried at the same time, it instituted a new abbreviated form of trial. The penalties also were increased. According to Asconius, three days were allowed for the hearing of witnesses. On the fourth, a panel of 360 judges was announced. From these, eighty-one were chosen by lot on the following day, and the plaintiff and defendant spoke before them. Before sentence was passed, both the plaintiff and the defendant could reject up to fifteen of the jury, thus leaving a panel of fifty-one to deliver verdict. Strictly, all 360 would have heard the evidence; but in practice this might not have been so. It would be difficult to secure the attendance of all on each day, and members of the panel might not be particularly attentive, if they were aware that they stood a good chance of not being called upon to deliver verdict.

46. *Latin holidays.* An annual festival in honour of Jupiter was celebrated on the Alban mount. Originally celebrated jointly by the members of the Latin League, it continued under the presidency of Rome after the dissolution of the League in 338 B.C. In the early republic, dictators were appointed not only in times of crisis (e.g. war or sedition) but also, when the consuls for some reason were unable to discharge their functions, for performing the essential duties of the conduct of the elections and of the Latin festival. Caesar's first dictatorship therefore resembles those of the old republic rather than that of Sulla.

47. *twelve legions.* Nine from Gaul (of which three fought at Massilia, six in Spain) and three new ones.

48. *Antonius's old troops.* The reference is to the brother of Mark Antony. An incident not mentioned by Caesar in Part II is that, while he himself was on his way to Spain, a naval squadron in the Adriatic under Dolabella was driven away by Pompeians from the Dalmatian coast. Antonius tried to help, but was forced to put in at Corcyra Nigra. He was betrayed to the Pompeians by an officer and forced to surrender together with fifteen cohorts.

49. *Seven legions . . . as indicated above.* If this referred to the 15,000 legionaries of Ch. 2, Caesar's forces would have been very severely depleted indeed. As the total strength of eighty cohorts (equivalent to eight legions) at Pharsalus, after a costly campaign, was 22,000 men (Ch. 89), these seven legions must have numbered more than 15,000. A possible explanation is that Caesar's original estimate allowed for the accommodation of slaves and heavy baggage, and that the exclusion of these made room for many more troops.

50. *Winter was now approaching.* The Roman calendar had got out of step with the seasons. Caesar sailed in January by the current calendar, i.e. actually in November.

51. *a brief space of time and a sheer coincidence.* Calenus might not have received the dispatch in time.

52. *private quarrels with Caesar.* Bibulus was aedile, praetor and consul in the same years as Caesar. As aediles, they shared the expenses for the games put on, but Bibulus complained that Caesar took all the credit. The particular causes of friction in their praetorship are unknown, but may have concerned their attitudes to the Catilinarian conspirators. As consul in 59 B.C. Bibulus attempted to block Caesar's agrarian legislation, but was forcibly prevented from doing so. When his complaints to the Senate produced no result he ceased to attend meetings. Shutting himself in his house, he gave out that he was observing the sky for omens. Technically, this should have caused the suspension of all public business; in fact, Caesar ignored him and governed Rome alone, while Bibulus vented his feelings by issuing vituperative proclamations about Caesar.

53. *Lucceius and Theophanes.* These were apparently acting as confidential counsellors to Pompey. Theophanes, of Mytilene, had been awarded Roman citizenship by Pompey in 62 B.C. Both Lucceius and Theophanes were writers of history.

54. *fugitives from the Pyrenean mountains.* The remnants of the army of Sertorius.

55. *urban praetor.* This magistrate had the jurisdiction of lawsuits between Roman citizens. Caelius, as *praetor peregrinus*, should

have concerned himself only with lawsuits between Romans and non-citizens.

56. *debarred from political life.* By stripping him of his praetorship and expelling him from the Senate.

57. *Milo.* See Introduction, p. 16. Milo had gone into exile in Massilia, though there is no evidence for his presence there during the siege. At the time of his trial he had had the support of Caelius, then tribune.

58. *herdsmen.* Large gangs of slaves, mostly of the rougher, more intractable sort, kept to look after herds on the large estates of southern and central Italy. They were housed in prison-like compounds and barracks.

59. *winter was well advanced.* The latter part of March by the unreformed calendar (i.e. January). 'Many months' is something of an exaggeration.

60. *assigned the town . . . had it fortified.* Presumably Caesar did this in virtue of his position as proconsul of Illyricum.

61. *imperator.* cf. II. 26. Caesar is being sarcastic at Scipio's expense; the title was not normally bestowed for *defeats*.

62. *Marcus Crassus.* Killed at Carrhae (53 B.C.). See Introduction, p. 16.

63. *Marcus Bibulus.* Proconsul in Syria in the latter half of 51 and the beginning of 50 B.C.

64. *the province.* The province of which Scipio was governor was Syria; Pergamum was in the province of Asia. Scipio had no business to exact levies of money in Asia, but his general behaviour in the province is somewhat high-handed; and the governor of Asia may have been offered some financial inducement to persuade him to acquiesce in these exactions.

65. *meat . . . they held in great esteem.* Cereal foods were the staple diet; meat became the main part of the diet, as here, only in default of grain.

66. See note 67.

67. *six engagements.* Of the engagements at the fortifications, two are described in Ch. 52, and the last part of one in Ch. 51. The description of the first part of this engagement and of the fighting at Dyrrachium does not appear in our text. It appears that a portion of the text, after the end of Ch. 50, is missing. This is further indicated by Caesar's reference in Ch. 58 to a previous statement that the approaches to the town were narrow; this is not in the existing text.

The missing section probably describes Pompey's attempt to force the blockade by sending some of his cavalry to Dyrrachium by sea.

Appian says that Caesar took a small force to Dyrrachium, hoping for the betrayal of the town, and Dio adds that he did so by night; however, he was trapped and attacked in the narrow passages and barely escaped.

Back at the fortifications, Pompey made an attack in force on one of Caesar's forts; the cohort stationed there resisted four hours, until the arrival of Sulla.

68. *Scaeva.* Several ancient sources carry, with variations in detail, the story of the courage of Scaeva, although his name suffers alteration: Scaeva (Florus, Lucan); Cassius Scaeva (Suetonius); Minucius (Appian – although a Scaeva appears in the same battle, losing an eye); Caesius Scaeva (Valerius Maximus).

69. *as shown above.* See Ch. 35 for Aetolia. Amphilochia and Acarnania are not mentioned in our extant text; Cassius's success may have been related in the lost portion.

70. See note 67.

71. *the Senate.* This is generally explained as referring to the tribal Senate of the Allobroges. However Rice Holmes (*The Roman Republic* vol. III, p. 148, n. 2) pertinently asks whether this would have been an 'extraordinary' appointment for the sons of a chieftain. He suggests that Caesar may have adlected some aliens into the Senate in his first dictatorship as well as later.

72. *'hedgehog'.* This was the name given to a barrier consisting of a wooden beam studded with sharp spikes.

73. *as we saw.* See note 48. The incident is not in fact related in our text of the *Civil War.*

74. *laurel wreath.* Pompey apparently had scruples about displaying an honour gained by a victory over Roman citizens.

75. *neighbouring provinces.* i.e. Sicily and Sardinia; or possibly those 'neighbouring' Dyrrachium – i.e. Thessaly, Aetolia, Macedonia.

76. *Gergovia.* cf. the *Gallic War*, VII. 2.

77. *ruler of Thessaly.* Caesar uses the Roman term *praetor*; the Greek word was *tagos*, until about 369 B.C., and thereafter *archon*.

78. *sharing the honour of command.* Scipio and Pompey both had the title of *proconsul* and therefore were officially of equal rank.

79. *claiming the houses and property.* This is confirmed by Cicero (*ad* Att. XI. 6).

80. *to fine them.* This is a variation on the normal procedure, under which the third tablet bore the letters N.L. (*non liquet*). This verdict (correspondingly roughly to 'not proven') entailed adjournment and successive further hearings until a positive verdict was reached.

81. *the levies of the last few years.* Caesar had also levied troops in Umbria, Picenum and other parts of Italy.

82. *the First ... the Third.* When under Caesar's command, they were known as the Sixth and the Fifteenth.

83. *the legion from Cilicia.* Formed from veterans of the two legions commanded by Cicero as proconsul in 51–50 B.C.

84. *as we said* – not in our text.

85. *special-duty corps.* In Latin, *beneficiarii.* These were attached to a superior officer for the execution of a particular task and were exempt from normal duties.

86. *22,000.* Plutarch and Appian agree on this figure.

87. *their instructions.* According to Plutarch (*Pompey* 69), they were told to strike at the faces of the enemy cavalry.

88. *his flag.* The red flag usually hoisted over the general's tent.

89. *King Ptolemy.* Ptolemy XIV, aged about fourteen. His father, Ptolemy Auletes, had been deposed by his subjects in 57 B.C.; he went to Italy, where he was the guest of Pompey. The money for an attempt to restore him was supplied by Rabirius Postumus, and Pompey had the task of restoration assigned to the proconsul of Syria, Aulus Gabinius. A body of troops was left in the kingdom to prop up the monarchy.

90. *etesian winds.* The regular yearly trade-winds.

91. *He burned all these vessels.* It is commonly believed that this fire, spreading out of control, destroyed the great library of Alexandria; certainly, our sources agree that hundreds of thousands of books were destroyed upon this occasion. It is, however, very doubtful whether the great library was anywhere near the docks, and more likely that the books in question were in store in warehouses by the docks.

92. *the Pharos.* One of the Seven Wonders of the ancient world.

93. *the younger daughter of Ptolemy.* Arsinoe.

THE ALEXANDRIAN WAR

1. *the Nabataeans.* These had long been hostile to the Egyptians; Pompey in 63 B.C. had contemplated an expedition against them. Through his lieutenant, Aemilius Scaurus, he had obtained a formal submission from their king; this apparently rankled with the present king, Malchus.

2. *straight streets.* Alexandria, designed by the architect Dinocrates of Rhodes, was laid out on a 'grid' plan, with streets intersecting at right-angles.

3. *island.* Pharos could not be described as 'to the right'; 'the island' may have been an alternative name for the Delta.

4. *Pompey's surrendered troops.* cf. C.W. III. 99.

5. *all the ships they had ready.* Presumably such as had escaped the conflagration described in C.W. III. 111.

6. This chapter seems to imply that this was the first naval action on the part of the Alexandrians, whereas Dio Cassius (42. 38) speaks of constant raids into the Great Harbour. The author's narrative appears to simplify the course of events.

7. *the mouths of the Nile.* Seven in number.

8. *colonnades.* A regular feature of Greek public architecture. They consisted of long, roofed galleries, open along one side and supported by columns, which provided some shelter from the sun and were used as social rendezvous or for more serious purposes such as the delivery of public lectures.

9. *ships from Rhodes . . . Asia.* According to C.W. III. 106, Caesar, when he first arrived at Alexandria, had ten Rhodian ships and a few Asiatic. In Ch. 1 of the *Alexandrian War*, we are told that Caesar summoned ships from Rhodes, Syria and Cilicia. Caesar does not mention the wreck of one vessel on the coast. The author may have made a mistake in Ch. 1. Alternatively, no further squadron arrived from Rhodes, but Syria and Cilicia did accede to the request mentioned in Ch. 1; Caesar's fleet, excluding the Rhodians, now amounts to twenty-five ships.

10. *deployed shrewdly and skilfully.* If a ship offered a broadside it exposed itself to the danger of being rammed. Another tactic was to race towards a vessel, then quickly ship oars while running close alongside; the victim had the blades of its oars snapped off.

11. *the island.* Pharos.

12. *the causeway.* The Heptastadion, so called from its length of seven stades (roughly three-quarters of a mile).

13. *arch.* There was one at either end of the Heptastadion, to allow ships to pass through between the Great Harbour and the Harbour of Eunostos.

14. *foreigners and runaway slaves.* Contrast C.W. III. 109, where the nature of the enemy is held by Caesar to make it desirable that he should have the king in his camp. Either the author has made an unfortunate guess or, as Rice Holmes suggests (*The Roman Republic* vol. III, p. 197, n. 1), Caesar had changed his opinion on finding that possession of the person of Ptolemy gave him no advantage.

15. *starting box.* At the start of races, horses were confined in stalls (*carceres*).

16. *his younger brother*. Ptolemy XV Neoteros.
17. *the rest*. i.e. the Twenty-seventh and Twenty-eighth and the legion sent by Domitius Calvinus. Perhaps also 'the Gabinians'.
18. The non-Roman legions are regarded as needing extra support. *The remaining cohorts* may be those fetched by Patisius from Cilicia.
19. *a punishment more wretched than death itself*. Castration. Ch. 70.
20. *Illyricum*. There had been a number of insurrections in the province in recent years. Matters had remained quiet during the summer of 48 B.C., but after Pharsalus troubles had begun again.
21. *his own auspices*. The commander in whom *imperium* had been invested by the Roman people had the duty of taking the auspices (omens) before entering upon action; his also was the credit for success. A delegated subordinate officer, or lieutenant (*legatus*), did not have this status.
22. *sails . . . lowered*. Rowing admitted of more precise manoeuvring in battle.
23. *the Fifth*. Caesar had originally given him four legions – the Native, the Second and (from Italy) the Twenty-first and Twentieth.
24. *proconsul*. In fact, Trebonius was propraetor, having just held the office of urban praetor; his consulship did not fall until 45 B.C.
25. *dangerous disturbances*. cf. C.W. III. 20–22. In October 48, Mark Antony landed at Brundisium, was nominated Master of the Horse (i.e. Deputy Dictator) by Servilius and took over government. The tribunes were the only regular magistrates then at Rome. One of them, Dolabella, resumed the demagogic tactics of Caelius, promising abolition of debts and suspension of rents. He was opposed by a rival tribune, Trebellius. Popular feeling ran high and rioting became common.
26. *breaches of . . . discipline*. There was a mutiny of the legions in Campania. Antony went to deal with it, leaving his uncle, Lucius Caesar, in charge at Rome. Failing to quell the mutiny, he returned to Rome to find disorder there. He refrained from intervention, leaving Trebellius and Dolabella to fight it out, until finally the Senate called on him to restore order. This he did by bringing in the one legion which had not mutinied. He used the troops to prevent the passing of Dolabella's bills and had some of the ringleaders in the riots arrested and put to death. Order was still not fully restored when Caesar returned.

27. *Bellona.* The title of an Italian goddess of war; identified by the Romans with a moon-goddess worshipped in Cappadocia.

28. *on trial in court.* It was not uncommon for parties to a lawsuit to appear in court in mourning – clothes and person unwashed, hair unkempt – in an attempt to excite pity.

29. *public decree when he was consul.* i.e. the decree of 59 B.C. confirming Pompey's Eastern settlement, which included grants of land to Deiotarus.

30. *Lentulus and Marcellus.* The consuls of 49 B.C., followed in 48 by Caesar and Servilius.

31. *the victory of Mithridates.* In 72 B.C. he defeated Lucullus's lieutenant, Triarius, who was killed in the battle.

32. *the immortal gods.* A sentiment unexampled in Caesar.

33. *Mithridates.* See Ch. 26. Bosphorus was, however, in the hands of a rebel satrap, Asander, and Mithridates was killed in attempting to take over his kingdom.

THE AFRICAN WAR

1. Dio Cassius, 43. 1–2, and Appian, II. 95 ff., give rather different versions of this engagement. According to Dio, Petreius and Labienus killed many of the Caesarians. The survivors made a stand on high ground and would have been cut to pieces, if Petreius and Labienus themselves had not been wounded. According to Appian, the Caesarians were completely routed. The pursuit was abandoned when Labienus's horse was wounded and threw him, Petreius wishing to allow Scipio the final honour of victory.

2. *tributaries. Stipendiarii,* i.e. paying a tax in kind on the produce of their farms.

3. *enrolled in the Senate.* Presumably during his stay in Rome in 47 B.C. (Dio 42. 51).

4. *Messalla.* In August 47 B.C., he and Sallust were sent to order certain legions to concentrate in Sicily for the African campaign; they were mutinously received.

5. Gaius Marius had married Caesar's aunt, Julia. The fathers or grandfathers of the present Gaetulians had presumably served under Marius in the war against Jugurtha (109–106 B.C.) and received rewards, together with the status of 'clients'. This expressed a relation of more or less informal reciprocal duty and obligation between client and 'patron'; Marius, as the latter, would, for instance, make representations on their behalf at Rome when occasion arose.

6. *nearly all the Roman citizens.* The terms in which the Sixth and Fourth Legions are referred to suggest that they contained some non-citizen troops as well.

7. *thirty-six years.* Not all of this, of course, could have been spent under Caesar, but the total length of service itself is not un-exampled.

8. *the Pleiades had set.* This marked the beginning of winter (early November) and was usually accompanied by some stormy weather. Since the setting was now some weeks past, more settled weather might have been expected.

9. A full account is given of the dispositions on either side, although no battle took place. Possibly, as suggested by M. Bouvet (Budé edition, Introduction, p. xxv), this reflects the technical interest and eye-witness knowledge of a serving soldier. It also serves to illustrate Caesar's merit as a general. His forces being considerably less than those of Scipio, specially in cavalry, particular care was needed in their deployment.

10. *ceremonial purification.* If the Latin (*lustrato exercitu*) is to be taken in this technical sense and not more generally, as 'a review of the army', there is presumably some connexion with the custom apparently observed at Rome of holding a series of ceremonies of purification of the instruments of warfare (the horses, the arms and the trumpets) in the course of the month of March. (This is discussed by Warde Fowler in the essay 'Lustratio' in *Anthropology and the Classics*, ed. R. J. Marett.) March marked the traditional beginning of the campaigning season. Caesar has already started campaigning, but the ritual is nevertheless observed.

11. As Thapsus stood on a cape it was possible to cut it off by land with a crescent-shaped line of works. The lake referred to is the Marsh of Moknine. Scipio came up from the south, camped at the bottom end of the corridor between the marsh and the coast, then made a detour round the marsh and approached Thapsus from the west. Juba and Afranius were left in the double camp sealing off the lower end of the corridor. See sketch-plan 3, p. 360.

12. *the Julian law.* Nothing is known of the provisions of this law, which was perhaps carried in Caesar's consulship, 59 B.C.

13. *the Three Hundred.* The meaning of this term is uncertain; they were probably some sort of representative council of the community of Roman businessmen at Utica.

14. *persuading a slave to kill him.* The account given here conflicts with versions in other sources, according to which Petreius killed

Juba first, or they killed each other, or Juba committed suicide and Petreius followed suit.

15. *Meanwhile*. The author of the *Bellum Africum* is characterized by a certain poverty of vocabulary and clumsiness in transition from one topic to another; in particular, he grossly overworks the word *interim* ('meanwhile'). The translation attempts to preserve this feature of his style.

16. *declared the kingdom a province*. Western Numidia was granted to Bocchus and Sittius. The latter founded a colony at Cirta, and his followers were settled there.

THE SPANISH WAR

1. *his triumphs*. Caesar celebrated four triumphs – over Gaul, Egypt, Pontus and Africa – i.e. for his campaigns against foreign enemies; victory over his fellow-citizens could not fittingly be the subject of a triumph.

2. *a great deal of business*. It was probably now that a census was taken for the revision of the lists of those eligible for the corn-dole. Arrangements were put in train for the allocation of land to veterans. A new forum and court-house were inaugurated. The Julian reformed calendar was introduced, and a sumptuary law and various other pieces of social legislation were carried. Great offence was given by the installation of Cleopatra in a house on the Janiculum, and the placing of her statue in the new temple of Venus Genetrix.

3. *sometimes theirs*. The northern end of the permanent bridge must have been controlled by Sextus Pompeius, who was holding Corduba. Caesar camped on the north side of the river, constructed a pile bridge and began to extend a fortified line from the southern end of the pile bridge towards the permanent bridge, in an attempt to prevent Gnaeus Pompeius from crossing by the latter.

4. *Homebred*. See C.W. II. 20 and note.

5. *slaves and auxiliaries*. I have adopted Mommsen's reading *vernacula et secunda* (see Appendix I). The legion 'raised among the Roman colonists' will then be the Fifth, raised by Cassius (Al. Ch. 50). The Second, part of the Fifth, and the native legion had earlier joined in the mutiny against Cassius and had been willing to fight in Pompey's name (Al. Ch. 57–8).

6. *Camp of Postumius*. Probably named after Lucius Postumius Albinus, governor of Further Spain, 180–179 B.C.

7. *Cato and Antonius*. See Appendix I for the reading here and in

Ch. 18. The text at the beginning of Ch. 18 is very corrupt. The situation seems to demand at least three envoys; two (of whom Tiberius was one) who fled to Caesar, and Cato, who was apparently in disagreement with Tiberius. A plausible reconstruction is offered by A. G. Way (Loeb edition, p. 402). Tiberius and Antonius would have been willing to offer unconditional surrender, but Cato opposed. In fear of being denounced by Cato as a traitor, Antonius decided at the last moment not to go back into the town. When Cato tried to use force, Tiberius came to the rescue and he and Antonius fled to Caesar. From the end of Ch. 19 it appears that they later returned to the town and carried their point.

8. *wearing a belt*. This would allow weapons to be hidden on their persons.

9. *seven denarii a month*. This is based on Klotz's reading (see Appendix I). The point seems to be that the deserters were given a good deal less than the standard legionary rate of pay. In the time of Polybius (mid second century B.C.) this had been one third of a *denarius* per day, i.e. ten *denarii* a month. The *denarius* was originally equivalent to ten *asses* but was later made equivalent to sixteen *asses*. Pliny assigns this change to the time of the first Punic War, though it may have taken place anything up to a century later. For military pay, however, says Pliny, the old scale, one *denarius*=ten *asses*, was retained. He is mistaken on the latter point; in A.D. 14 the pay stood at ten *asses* per day, but these were calculated at the rate of sixteen to the *denarius* (i.e. a rate of 18·75 *denarii* per month). According to Suetonius, Caesar at some point during his Gallic command 'doubled' the legionary pay. Since no other increase is attested before A.D. 14, his measure was presumably the one which raised the pay to ten *asses* a day (when it was extended to the remaining legions is unknown). On the old reckoning, this would be *three* times the Polybian pay; but the 3⅓ *asses* per day with which the troops had been credited were worth 5⅓ on the revised standard. If what Caesar actually did was nominally to treble the pay by raising it to ten *asses* but at the same time to bring the *as* for military pay on to the revised standard, the change could be represented as (roughly) doubling the pay.

Mommsen suggested '*asses* VII' instead of the 'XVII' of the text; Klotz's reading, however, is closer to the original and gives a satisfactory meaning.

10. *Achilles and Memnon*. Memnon, king of Ethiopia, son of Eos (Dawn) and Tithonus, went to help Priam in the Trojan War. He killed Antilochus, son of Nestor, and was then killed by Achilles,

but by his mother's entreaties Zeus was persuaded to raise him among the immortals. The story was probably first recounted in one of the lost poems of the Epic Cycle, the *Aethiopis*, and is mentioned as well known in extant Greek literature. .

11. *Liberalia*. The festival of Liber, or Bacchus.

12. *quaestorship*. Caesar served as quaestor in Further Spain in 68 B.C.

13. *Metellus*. Quintus Caecilius Metellus Pius was consul in 80 B.C. and sent out afterwards to govern Further Spain; his failure to suppress the rebellious Sertorius, governor of Hither Spain, resulted in the mission of Pompey as his colleague in 77 B.C. The rebellion was finally crushed in 72, and the taxes mentioned were probably imposed by Metellus as a punishment on the provincials who had helped Sertorius. Caesar was praetor in 62 B.C., and then in 61–60 B.C. governor of Further Spain. There, besides the remission of taxes here mentioned, he made regulations for the relief of debtors. Many provincials had no doubt been driven into the hands of Italian moneylenders in order to pay the taxes.

APPENDIX I. THE TEXT

I HAVE followed the readings of the Oxford Classical Text of Renatus du Pontet, except in the instances listed below.

O.C.T. READING	READING ADOPTED

THE CIVIL WAR · PART I

	O.C.T. READING	READING ADOPTED
6.6	[quod superioribus annis acciderat]	*delete*
6.7	ex urbe proficiscuntur lictoresque ... privati	antequam ex urbe proficiscuntur, lictores . . . paludatos
14.4	tutum esse [omnibus] videtur	tutum esse videtur

THE CIVIL WAR · PART II

	O.C.T. READING	READING ADOPTED
5.3	publicis custodiisque	publicis locis custodiisque
29.3–4	nam etiam Caesaris beneficium consuetudo †qua offerrentur. . . . municipia etiam diversis partibus coniuncta . . . neque enim ex Marsis Paelignisque veniebant ut qui superiore nocte in contuberniis commilitesque . . . †non nulli graviora sermones militum; dubia durius accipiebantur, non nulli etiam etc.	nam etiam Caesaris beneficium mutaverat consuetudo qua offerretur; municipia etiam diversis partibus coniuncta, aeque enim ex Marsis Paelignisque veniebant. et qui superiore nocte e contuberniis commigraverunt, de eis commenti sunt non nulli graviora sermones militum. dubia durius accipiebantur, non nulla etiam ab eis qui diligentiores videri volebant fingebantur.

THE CIVIL WAR · PART III

	O.C.T. READING	READING ADOPTED
6.3	arbitrabantur	arbitrabatur
8.4	Curici	Corcyrae
9.8	[hic fuit oppugnationis exitus]	*delete*
10.6	Curictam	Corcyram

305

	O.C.T. READING	READING ADOPTED
13.5	civitatis	civitates
16.4	se[d]	se
18.3	†reversus est†	e re visum est
19.6	submissa	superbissima
22.2	eo cum a Q.Pedio praetore cum legione ...	*sc.* excluderetur
38.4	†[hostium] in his fuit	*delete* unus fugit
44.4	†videbant† [timebant]	providebant *delete*
48.1	†a valeribus†	in vallibus
49.5	†subterere†	succedere
53.5	vespeciariis	veste, cibariis
63.3	munitiones	munitione
63.6	[exercitus adventus exstitit]	*delete*
79.3	[Senticam]	*delete*
101.1	Vibone	ad Vibonem
112.2	regionibus	regibus
112.6	†deauxit†	dimisit

THE ALEXANDRIAN WAR

1.5	urbis divisa acies,	urbs divisa, acies
12.1	†quibus et superioribus locis sublevabantur, ut ex aedificiis defendi possent†	ut vix ex aedificiis defendi posse confiderent, quibus et superioribus locis sublevabantur
15.3	†Caesaris† animum advertit	Caesaris cunctationem animum advertit
22.2	†manum comprehendi multum operibus†	manum conserere prohibitum operibus
26.2	adducit	advenit
27.5	[constantiaque virtutum et Alexandrinorum imprudentia]	*delete*
39.1	†sine causa†	si negatis

	O.C.T. READING	READING ADOPTED
40.2	†acies secundo†	ac transcendere
47.3	in eum	in ea
49.1	in ea	antea
55.1	†legiones V in castra remittit cohortibus XXX retentis†	legiones in castra remittit quinque cohortibus tricesimae retentis
57.2	†noctu†	Naevam
66.5	terreret †Ariobarzani attribuit	terreret Ariobarzanen, partem Armeniae Minoris concessit, eumque Ariobarzani attribuit
70.3	[non]	*delete*
73.3	†agerentur†	agerent
77.1	†quodque	eoque

THE AFRICAN WAR

2.3	Lilybaeo . . . commoratus	Lilybaeo milia passum X; ipse paucos dies ibi commoratus
15.2	†non conatur†	non moratur
18.1	†M C†	†M D C†
18.4	circumdatis	circumitis
19.3	†quis in illorum† †Brundisio†	qui in illorum numero Buthroto
21.1	alternas	alteras
26.3	gerere . . . instituit	gerere, hieme gerere instituit
30.2	[Iuba]	*delete*
31.1	processerant †quique pabulandi aut lignandi†	processerant pabulandi aut lignandi causa
32.4	[Gaetulos]	*delete*
38.1	post Caesar	postquam Caesar
38.2	postquam	et postquam
50.2	[Caesari subito se ostenderet]	*delete*
57.2	cum †nihilo minus eius ser-	cum eius sermonem nuntius

	O.C.T. READING	READING ADOPTED
	monem nuntius ad se referret† sed restaret	ad se referret sed nihilo minus
59.2	[in cornibus autem duplex esse existimabatur]	*delete*
60.2	†fere ipsum dextrum cornu secundam autem aciem fere in earum legionum parte†	in suo autem dextro cornu ex secunda acie veteranarum legionum partem
61.3	deserta †act†	deserti
66.1	†VIII†	III
77.1	[male]	*delete*
77.4	V [III]	V
80.2	III . . . praesidio relicto	III cohortium praesidio relicto
81.1	quinque legiones	quintae legionis
83.2	†itata†	iactatu
97.1	irrogatis	locatis

THE SPANISH WAR

1.1	qui ex his proeliis cum adulescente Cn. Pompeio profugissent, cum . . . et ulterioris Hispaniae potitus esset	qui ex his proeliis ⟨superfuissent⟩ cum ⟨ad⟩ adulescente⟨m⟩ Cn. Pompeium profugissent, cum ⟨Baleares appulisset⟩ et ulterioris Hispaniae potitus esset.
1.4	ita pacis commoda hoste †hortato† maiores augebantur copiae	ita paucis commoda ab hoste orta; eo maiores augebantur copiae
2.1	multis †iterante diebus coniectis†	multis ante iter rebus confectis
2.2	facerent . . . multa	facerent, ipse suum eius adventus metum significasset; multa
6.1	quos †quoniam a avia†	quo eos quomodo ab Ulia
6.2	facultatem . . . et angustias	facultatem nactus est, linquens montes et angustias

O.C.T. READING	READING ADOPTED
ib.	†multosque lanistas†	mulos onustas
7.2	†in munitionibus ceterisque† quae ad oppidum	interim munitionibus confectis quae ad oppugnandum
7.4	vernaculae	vernacula et secunda
7.5	auxiliares	auxiliariisve
9.1	[loci difficultatem]	*delete*
11.2	[sicut omne genus quibus ignis per iactus solitus est mitti]	*delete*
12.2	et Trebonio	et a Trebonio
12.6	†.l.	hi
14.1	†eius praeteriti temporis†	eius diei praeterito tempore
14.4	recepti	excepti
14.4	†ex simili†	eximia
15.3	[pedes equestre]	*delete*
16.1	[ad]	*delete*
17.1	Catone Lusitano	Catone et Antonio
17.2	praesidi ... et	praesidi simus et
17.2	dedimur	demur
ib.	[victoriam]	*delete*
17.3	petimusque ut' ...	petimusque ut vitam nobis concedas,' quibus Caesar respondit
18.1	venissent, Ti. Tullius. . . . et cum introeuntem †C. Antonius†	venissent, Ti. Tullius introiit; et cum introeuntem Catonem Antonius
18.8	†fune crure de ligno†	fine ⟨diei⟩ turrem ligneam
22.3	†adversione†	aversione
22.7	XVII	.X.VII
23.4	†huius concidentis temporis aquari†	in huius concidentis centurionis ac viri
24.5	saluti fuit. quo subsidio, ut, nisi	saluti fuit subsidio. quod nisi
25.7	ob opere. . . . castra	ab opere prope castra
26.2	tecti †equites†	tectis equis

	O.C.T. READING	READING ADOPTED
26.4	†freti†	fixi
28.4	†interim nulla planitia edividit†	intervallo planitiei dividi
29.4	†equitatum ornaret et diei solisque serenitatem†	equitatum evocaret et diei solisque serenitate
29.6	†in quo sibi prope murum adversariis†	immo se ibi prope murum adversarii
31.4	[ut]	*delete*
32.2	ex hostium armis pro caespite cadavera collocabantur, scuta et pila pro vallo; insuper †occisi et gladio ut mucro et† capita hominum ordinata ad oppidum conversa universa, timorem ...	ex hostium armis scuta et pila pro vallo, pro caespite cadavera collocabantur; insuper abscisa in gladiorum mucrone capita hominum ordinata ad oppidum conversa omnia, ut et ad hostium timorem
34.1	†feret†	rixae
34.2	†descenderet†	discordare
34.3	†non†	nonani
34.4	denuo	denique
35.2	†magnum†	magna manus
37.2	[ad quem]	*delete*
37.2	†partim pedibus†	Carteia pedites
38.3	more militari cum Caesaris praesidio fuisset conspectus	more militari ex eius praesidio speculator missus, cum etc.
38.4	[propter suo praesidio fuisset conspectus celeriter]	*delete*
ib.	†deductit†	adducta
39.2	†exclusat†	exclusus
40.2	†quodvis essent bracchium ex utrisque partibus†	*delete*
40.4	ut a nullo ... conspectu	ut a nullo conspici possent; reliqui in conspectu
41.1	circum †sese interclusi inter	circumsedit. interclusi inter

	O.C.T. READING	READING ADOPTED
	se decernere . . . facta caede bene magna . . . faciunt†	se decernere armis coeperunt. facta caede bene magna eruptionem faciunt
41.3	†aditus†	datus
41.4	†appeteret†	appareret
41.5	†agit†	ac vineas facere
ib.	†hac Pompeius ad oppidum oppugnationem	ac Pompeius, ut se ad oppidi oppugnationem
42.7	[decem]	*delete*

APPENDIX II. THE ULTIMATE DECREE

THE *senatusconsultum ultimum*, the formal wording of which is given by Caesar, C.W. I. 5, was taken by the Romans as equivalent to a declaration that a state of emergency existed and that, therefore, since it was likely that the normal processes of law were inoperable or inadequate, the magistrates would be justified in dealing summarily with the situation as they saw fit.

The status of the decree and the question of the legal liability of persons who had acted under it were for a long time in dispute. On the occasion of its first issue, it could be claimed that the consul acting under it was in fact setting aside existing law. Gaius Gracchus in his first tribunate had carried a bill making it illegal for any magistrate, without a vote of the people, to pronounce that a citizen had forfeited his civil rights (which included the right of appeal to the people against the sentence of a magistrate). The bill was intended to prevent a renewal of the dangerous precedent by which the special commission set up by the Senate had not only summarily tried and condemned to death, but had executed sentence on the adherents of his murdered brother. Gaius intended that such powers should be dependent upon the decree of the people as a whole. Two years later there was rioting when Gracchus and his supporters attempted to prevent the repeal of his bill for the colonization of Carthage, and someone was killed. The Senate thereupon called upon the consul to see that the State took no harm. The consul, Opimius, went into action, and put to death many of the Gracchans.

After order had been restored, Opimius himself was impeached before the assembly, but acquitted. The legal status of the decree remained obscure. The senatorial court was not in fact pronouncing upon a point of law, but condoning the consul's action. The decree, strictly speaking, amounted to no more than an exhortation to the magistrates to do what was in any case their duty, i.e. to protect public safety and order; it neither conferred nor, strictly, could confer any additional legal powers, nor did it specifically accord exemption from the laws. It amounted to no more than an expression of the approval and support of the Senate for any action the magistrate might take. Opimius's acquittal meant that a dangerous precedent had been created.

The decree was next employed over twenty years later, in the second tribunate of Saturninus. A candidate for the consulship, Gaius Memmius, had been assassinated to clear the way for the (unconstitutional) candidature of the praetor Glaucia. The violence previously employed by Glaucia and Saturninus and their associates had already alienated the Senate; the decree was passed with a view to preventing things going any further. Marius was charged to restore public order, and imprisoned Glaucia and Saturninus; their actual deaths were not his fault, as a mob broke into their place of confinement and pelted them to death. This incident was, as we shall see, to have a curious connexion with the career of Caesar thirty-seven years later.

The decree was passed again in 77 B.C. in face of the menace of Lepidus at the head of an army. The young Pompey was called in to help the consuls, nominally as a subordinate officer with the army. Suetonius tells us that Lepidus offered Caesar various inducements to participate in his revolt, but the latter refused. The emergency decree need hardly have been passed; the consuls and Pompey had little trouble in quelling the armies of the rebel. It is possible that the rebellion and civil war of the previous decade had shaken the nerve of the Senate. This time, the question of the legality of action taken consequent upon the decree did not arise; Lepidus had been in arms against the State and those killed were killed under arms.

In 63 B.C. a prosecution was instituted against an elderly senator, Gaius Rabirius, on the charge that he had taken part in the killing of Saturninus in 100 B.C. The ostensible accuser was Labienus; the real instigator was Caesar. The unfortunate Rabirius was put through two trials. He was first condemned by a special panel of judges, but the Senate quashed the sentence. He was then brought before the assembly of the people by centuries (the traditional tribunal for capital charges), where the consul, Cicero, spoke in Rabirius's defence and represented the case as an attack on the validity of the ultimate decree of the Senate. Before the vote on the verdict could be taken, the praetor Metellus Celer (on whose instructions it is not known) ordered the red flag on the Janiculum to be lowered. The lowering of this flag was the traditional signal for the dispersal of assemblies on the Field of Mars outside the city boundary. In remote antiquity it had served as a warning of the approach of Rome's hostile neighbours, the Etruscans. In 63 B.C., it had lost all such significance; and the fact that the prosecutor allowed this to put an end to the case is a strong indication that the real motive of the trial was not the punishment of Rabirius but a political manoeuvre.

The whole business had an air of unreality. It was thirty-seven years since the events in question; Rabirius was prosecuted by an archaic procedure, involving a sentence of such bizarre barbarity that the feelings of the Romans were revolted; and the whole thing was ended by a piece of meaningless, archaic ritual. Clearly, the prosecution was meant as a political demonstration, although what Caesar intended to convey is rather less clear. His political manoeuvrings at this period have a curious clumsiness about them. After the failure of the proposed Rullan land bill, which would, if put into effect, probably have given Caesar a special commission, with the use of military forces, he attempted in 64 B.C. to have proceedings instituted against two of Sulla's executioners. This, like the Rabirius trial, was a raking-up of old history; its only immediate result was a counter-charge against another former Sullan, Catiline. In any case, Sulla's agents had been amnestied.

Only a tentative explanation can be offered. The period since the Gracchi had seen several instances of the use or condoning by the Senate of summary force to deal with political opposition. Caesar's aim may have been to demonstrate the danger of leaving unresolved the question of the permissibility of such procedures, and perhaps to go on to impose legal safeguards on the use of force by the State. If so, he failed. The decree was passed again in 63 B.C.

The occasion was the discovery of the existence of the Catilinarian conspiracy and preparations for armed conflict. It was brought to the attention of the consul, Cicero, on 20 October through anonymous letters. Two days later the Senate passed the ultimate decree. In mid November, the Senate proclaimed Catiline and his lieutenants public enemies. Firm evidence of the plot was obtained on 3 December and a number of Catiline's associates were arrested (he himself had left the city). On the following day, the conspirators in custody were declared to be public enemies. On 5 December a senatorial debate was held on their punishment; Caesar was for sparing their lives, but the majority, including Cicero, were for execution. Cicero saw that it was done immediately.

Cicero was impeached five years later, on the charge of having executed Roman citizens without trial, by Clodius. The latter may have intended in part to question the validity of the ultimate decree, but he had certainly a personal grudge against Cicero. In any case, the question of legality was again left unresolved, for Cicero went into voluntary exile. It is unfortunate that this was so, for the circumstances of the case deserved examination. The executed conspirators were at the time in custody. It was at least arguable whether a state of emergency could really be said still to exist. Cicero might have defended himself on the lines of his arguments in the senatorial debate preceding the execution – that their deaths were necessary to deter the others: certainly, much of the armed strength raised by Catiline evaporated at news of the executions. Such an argument, however, would not really counter the objection that the prisoners could have been committed for trial. Cicero's speech on 4 December (the Fourth Catiline Oration) perhaps indicates the lines on which the Senate might have attempted, if compelled, to justify the ultimate decree. In the speech, especially Ch. 5, Cicero declares that public enemies have forfeited the rights of citizenship.

This argument, however, does not really advance matters any further. The mere proclamation by the Senate had no power to strip a citizen of his rights as citizen, the most important of which was the right to a trial. Only the person actively resisting the State under arms would lose this right, and that by his own action.

The decree was passed yet again in 62 B.C. The occasion was a mere skirmish in the forum when the praetor, Metellus, attempted to ignore the veto of Cato as tribune. Caesar, Metellus's colleague, and Metellus himself were declared by the Senate to be suspended from office. The Senate's mood seems to have been hysterical; popular resentment brought the likelihood of rioting, and order was restored only by the moderating influence of Caesar.

At the end of 53 B.C. quarrels between the followers of Milo and of Clodius after the murder of the latter were attended with such a degree of public disorder that it was found impossible to hold the consular elections, at which Milo was to be candidate. The Senate passed the ultimate decree and authorized the magistrates and Pompey to restore order, giving Pompey permission to levy troops in Italy. The Senate subsequently appointed him sole consul. The presence of his armed forces was enough to cow the opposition as he passed a series of judicial bills and bills relating to public order and then brought Milo to trial.

These were the only instances of the passing of the decree until it was passed against Caesar himself at the start of the Civil War. The name by which it is now commonly referred to, *senatusconsultum ultimum*, is first used by Caesar himself (C.W. I. 5.) The terms in which he there refers to the decree are worth examination. The legal question is ignored. He says merely that the decree 'was never employed before except when the city was on the verge of destruction and when everyone expected inevitable ruin at the hands of unscrupulous law-makers'. This is certainly an exaggeration; but, even allowing for the propagandist intent of the whole passage, it would be reading too much into it to say that Caesar intended, in the context, to cast a smear on the activities of Cato in 62 B.C. or to condemn the policies and principles of Gaius Gracchus. His prime concern is to point a contrast with the situation in 50 B.C. He was not threatening the city with imminent destruction nor was he attempting to subvert or distort the laws. This is, in effect, a restatement of the two main points of his defence in Part I. Firstly, he always sought to avert armed hostilities; secondly, far from breaking the laws, he himself was being debarred from what he considered his legal dues.

APPENDIX III. PHARSALUS

THE battle of Pharsalus is the most famous engagement of the Civil War between Caesar and Pompey; and yet the ancient accounts of it have left many essential details shrouded in obscurity. Caesar himself never mentions Pharsalus; in fact, in his whole narrative of events immediately preceding and following the battle, and the battle itself, he mentions no place at all except Larissa. Such topographical information as is given in his account and in other sources is of little help in identifying the site of the battle; and the strategic considerations underlying the actions of either side have to be inferred.

While some ancient sources refer to 'the battle of Pharsalus', Frontinus, Eutropius, Orosius and the author of the *Alexandrian War* give the additional detail that it was fought somewhere near 'Old Pharsalus', a stronghold on a hill in the territory of Pharsalus proper. Pharsalus is generally agreed to be the modern Fersala about three miles south of the river Enipeus. The site of Old Pharsalus is disputed.

There has been much controversy among modern scholars as to the site of the battle. It seems most probable that it was fought on the north bank of the river, at the western end of the plain, which is almost entirely closed on the remaining sides by hills. Pompey was camped on a hill at the western end of the plain, Caesar in the plain itself, farther east. Old Pharsalus was across the river, not far from the site of Caesar's camp. (This is the view taken by T. Rice Holmes in *The Roman Republic* and by F. E. Adcock in the *Cambridge Ancient History*, vol. IX.)

Caesar had reached the area first, and the position in which he was camped, while putting him at a tactical disadvantage for battle, gave him, initially at least, strategic superiority. His camp commanded the fertile plain round the river; he had good lines of communication and, for the present, an adequate corn supply. His successes at Gomphi and Metropolis had secured him supplies from those towns and, we are told, had disposed the rest of Thessaly with the exception of Larissa to be favourable to his cause. The corn in the plain itself was not yet ripe. Pompey, on the other hand, despite the advantage of a position on high ground was dependent on keeping open his lines of communication with Larissa.

Caesar seems to have decided against an attempt to cut Pompey's lines of communication, which would involve the risk of being pursued and perhaps being forced to give battle at a disadvantage. He therefore offered Pompey the alternatives of forfeiting his tactical superiority and coming down to battle on the plain, or settling down to a war of attrition. Pompey's repeated refusal to accept the daily challenge to battle heightened the morale of Caesar's army.

When we come to the actual day of the battle itself, however, Caesar's account records the apparent coincidence that Pompey decided to offer battle on the very day when Caesar himself was moving away, but does not adequately explain the motives for the decision on either side. Much of the account is clearly propagandist in intent. He stresses the arrogant self-confidence of the Pompeian officers, and indeed of Pompey himself. The questions preoccupying them were not those of the current military situation but the apportionment of offices and privilege at Rome after their victory. No doubt the intention is to make the defeat of the Pompeians appear a just retribution, pride suffering a fall; but the long delay, followed by the ultimate decision to offer battle, remains unexplained. Caesar does not suggest that there might have been special strategic reasons for the timing of Pompey's decision; but from a phrase in his report of his own reasons for striking camp and moving off, it is possible to infer that there were such reasons.

Caesar's alleged aims, in deciding to move off, were: (i) to make it easier to get corn; (ii) to seek some opportunity on the march for battle; (iii) to wear out Pompey's army, since they were unaccustomed to exertion, by daily marches.

The third reason is utterly unconvincing; after all, Pompey's army, like Caesar's, had marched from Dyrrachium to Asparagium and thence to Macedonia and Thessaly. The portion of their forces under Scipio and Domitius, respectively, had likewise both covered approximately the same ground. The second reason has more plausibility; if the Pompeians could be induced to abandon their strong position and follow, there might be an opportunity of battle on some occasion when the Caesarians had the advantage of position. To expose oneself to the possibility of attack while actually on the march, however, was to take something of a risk.

One is inclined to suspect that the first reason was the most influential. Caesar, we were previously told (III. 84), had secured the corn supply. However, when he first camped by the Enipeus, the crops in the area were not yet ripe (III. 81). It looks suspiciously as though Caesar had gambled on being able to rely on stores of grain in the area until the crops were ripe; but supplies had not in fact lasted out.

Pompey may also have been banking on this. No doubt he was able through scouts to get information on the state of Caesar's commissariat, and was able to calculate how long he was likely to hang on. But Caesar's version represents Pompey as having already decided to offer battle that day, before the Caesarians began to strike camp. He leaves this unexplained; that Pompey should have decided on that day, just as Caesar decided to move off, appears the merest coincidence.

Appian's account of the preliminaries to the battle contains little or nothing of all this, and indeed has some actual mistakes. It is interesting, however, that in Appian's version Pompey has excellent lines of communication and abundant supplies, whereas Caesar is hard-pressed to find food. Pompey, in Appian, is throughout waging a war of attrition against Caesar, not vice versa.

I would suggest that Appian's version, though incorrect as applied to the whole of the time spent near Pharsalus, is true of the final stages, and that this final stage has been suppressed by Caesar. Pompey knew that Caesar must move soon because his supplies were failing. Then, one morning, it was observed that the Caesarians were beginning to strike camp. Pompey had his men in readiness, his tactical orders issued, and at once advanced on to the plain and offered battle. The forfeiting of a position of advantage on high ground would be partially offset by the advantage to be gained by taking the enemy by surprise and forcing them to prepare for battle unexpectedly. (The order to his men to await the enemy charge and not to charge themselves was perhaps intended to gain a further advantage, but failed of its object thanks to the training and discipline of Caesar's legions.)

On this view, there was no coincidence. Pompey had succeeded in forcing Caesar to abandon his position; when he saw the opportunity had come, then he offered battle.

APPENDIX IV

CHRONOLOGICAL OUTLINE OF
THE CAREERS OF POMPEY
AND CAESAR

POMPEY

B.C. 106 Born.

    83 Under Sulla, military command in Italy.

    82 Under Sulla, military command in Sicily.

    80 Under Sulla, military command in Africa. Triumph.

    77 Military command against Lepidus.

77–71 Military command in Spain. Triumph.

    70 Consul.

    67 Special command for suppression of pirates.

    66 Special command against Mithridates. Organization of the Eastern provinces.

    62 Return to Rome.

    61 Triumph.

    60 First triumvirate formed.

    59 Ratification of Eastern settlement. Marries Caesar's daughter.

57–52 Controller of the corn supply.

    55 Consul.

54–49 Governor of the Spanish provinces.

    52 Consul.

    49 Military command against Caesar.

    48 Killed in Egypt.

CAESAR

B.C. 100 (traditional date) Born.

81–78 On Governors' staffs in Asia and Cilicia.

    81 Envoy to King Nicomedes of Bithynia.

    73 Elected to college of priests.

    68 Quaestor in Spain.

    65 Aedile.

    63 Elected head of college of priests (*pontifex maximus*).

    62 Praetor.

    61 Governor of Further Spain.

THE CAREERS OF POMPEY AND CAESAR

60 First triumvirate formed.

59 Consul.

58–49 Governor of Cisalpine Gaul, Transalpine Gaul and Illyricum. Conquest of Gallia Comata.

49 Dictator.

48 Dictator and Consul.

47 Dictator.

46 Dictator and Consul. Quadruple triumph.

45 Dictator and Consul. Triumph.

44 Dictator and Consul; declared dictator in perpetuity. 15 March – assassinated.

GLOSSARY OF PERSONS AND PLACES

C.W.=Civil War. *Af.*=African War. *Al.*=Alexandrian War. *Sp.*=Spanish War.

Roman figures refer to Parts of C.W., Arabic figures to numbered sections.

ACARNANIA (C.W. III. 56, 58): Region of Greece between Gulf of Ambracia and Gulf of Corinth.

ACHAEA (C.W. III. 3, 4, 56, 57, 106; Al. 44): Strictly, the northern part of the Peloponnese; used also of the Roman province, embracing the Peloponnese, Aetolia, Phocis and Locris, Boeotia, Attica, Euboea and the Megarid.

ACHILLAS (C.W. III. 104, 108–12; Al. 4, 26): Egyptian general, an adviser of Ptolemy XIV; arranged murder of Pompey; led rebel forces of Arsinoe; killed on the latter's orders.

ACILIUS, Manius (C.W. III. 15, 16, 39, 40): A Caesarian officer.

ACROCERAUNIA (C.W. III. 6): A mountainous region on the coast of Epirus.

ACUTIUS RUFUS (C.W. III. 83): A partisan of Pompey.

ACYLLA (Af. 33, 43, 67): An African coastal town; site disputed.

ADBUCILLUS (C.W. III. 59): A chieftain of the Gallic tribe, the Allobroges; father of Roucillus and Egus.

AEGIMURUS (Af. 44): An island in the Gulf of Tunis (mod. Djamour).

AEGINIUM (C.W. III. 79): Town in Epirus in upper valley of river Enipeus, near Thessalian frontier.

Lucius AELIUS Tubero (C.W. I. 30, 31): Historian, friend of Cicero. Prevented from taking up command in Africa, 49 B.C. With Pompey at Pharsalus; reconciled to Caesar afterwards.

Marcus AEMILIUS Lepidus (Introd.): Elected consul for 78 B.C. In an attempt to undo Sulla's legislation, he raised an army in Cisalpine Gaul and marched on Rome. Proconsul Catulus defeated him in battle, while Pompey dealt with the forces under his lieutenant. Lepidus fled to Sardinia and died there; the remnants of his army joined Sertorius in Spain.

Marcus AEMILIUS Lepidus (C.W. II. 21; Al. 59, 63, 64): Son of the consul of 78 B.C. As praetor in 49 B.C. had Caesar proclaimed dictator; governor in Hither Spain 48–47 B.C. and triumphed; consul with Caesar 46 B.C.; governor of Gallia Narbonensis and Hither Spain 44–43 B.C.; Caesar's successor as Pontifex Maximus. Joined Octavian and Antony on the Dictator's death to form the Second Triumvirate; consul 42 B.C.; governed Africa 40–36 B.C.; forced by Octavian to retire into private life.

AETOLIA (C.W. III. 34, 35, 56, 61): A region of Greece to north of Gulf of Corinth.

Lucius AFRANIUS (C.W. I. 37–43, 48–53, 60–76, 84, 87; II. 17, 18; III. 83, 88; Af. 69, 95): Served as lieutenant with Pompey against Sertorius and Mithridates; his lieutenant in Spain from 55 B.C. Waged campaign against Caesar round Ilerda; defended camp at Pharsalus. Joined Pompeians in Africa; killed in a mutiny after Thapsus.

AFRICA (C.W. I. 30, 31; II. 23, 28, 32, 37; Al. 9, 14, 28, 47, 51, 56; Af. passim): The Roman province established by Scipio in 146 B.C.; roughly corresponding to modern Tunisia. Name sometimes applied in general to coastal district of North Africa.

AGGAR (Af. 67, 76, 79): African town, several miles south of Thapsus; site disputed.

AHENOBARBUS: See Domitius.

ALBA (C.W. I. 15, 24): Italian town in territory of Marsi, to north-west of Fucine Lake.

ALIBICI (C.W. I. 34, 56–8; II. 2, 6): Hill tribe north-east of Massilia.

ALESIA (C.W. III. 47): Town in Côte d'Or (Alise-Sainte-Reine) where Gallic chief Vercingetorix surrendered in 52 B.C. after a long siege.

ALEXANDRIA (C.W. III. 4, 103–12; Al. passim): Capital of Ptolemaic kingdom of Egypt, situated west of Nile delta, between the sea and Lake Mareotis.

ALIENUS (Af. 2, 26, 34, 44): Lieutenant of Q. Cicero in Asia 60 B.C., praetor 49 B.C.: governor of Sicily 48 B.C.

ALLOBROGES (C.W. III. 59, 63, 79): A Gallic tribe living between the Rhône and the Isère.

AMANTIA (C.W. III. 4): A town in north-west Epirus.

Mount AMANUS (C.W. III. 31): A mountain in the Taurus chain in the province of Asia.

AMBRACIA (C.W. III. 36): A town in south Epirus.

AMPHILOCHIANS (C.W. III. 56): Inhabitants of Amphilochia, region of Greece north of Aetolia.

AMPHIPOLIS (C.W. III. 102): A town in Macedonia at eastern end of Via Egnatia. Colonized by Athens in 437 B.C., it occupied a strategically important position as a centre of communications.

Titus AMPIUS Balbus (C.W. III. 105): Praetor in about 59 B.C.;

adherent of Pompey. Historical writer, cited by Suetonius in criticism of Caesar; banished by the latter after Pharsalus, but apparently pardoned in 46 B.C. on the intercession of Cicero.

ANAS (C.W. I. 38): River in Spain (mod. Gaudiana).

ANCONA (C.W. I. 11): Town in north-east Italy, on Adriatic coast.

ANDROSTHENES (C.W. III. 80): Thessalian commander-in-chief; refused to admit Caesar to Gomphi.

Titus ANNIUS Milo (Introd.; C.W. III. 21, 22): Tribune 57 B.C., praetor 55. Exiled after murder of Clodius 52 B.C.; returned in 49 B.C., joined Caelius in an attempted revolt and was killed.

ANQUILLARIA (C.W. II. 23): Site of disembarkation of Curio in Africa; variously identified.

ANTIOCH (C.W. III. 102, 105): Capital of Syria.

ANTIOCHUS (C.W. III. 4): Ruler of Commagene, a small state north of Syria and east of Cilicia.

ANNIUS SCAPULA (Al. 55): A Spaniard who took part in the plot against Q. Cassius Longinus.

ANTISTIUS TURPIO (Al. 25): A Pompeian soldier.

ANTONIUS (Sp. 18): An envoy from Ategua.

Gaius ANTONIUS (C.W. III. 4, 10, 67): Younger brother of Mark Antony. An officer of Caesar in the Civil War; tribune c. 46 B.C., praetor 44 B.C. Forestalled by Brutus in reaching his province Macedonia in 43 B.C.; captured by Brutus and killed on his orders in 42 B.C.

MARK ANTONY (Marcus Antonius) (C.W. I. 2, 11, 18; III. 24-30, 34, 40, 46, 65, 89): Elder brother of Gaius; born c. 82 B.C. Caesar's lieutenant in Gaul 52-51 B.C.; tribune at Rome 49 B.C.; controlled Italy as Caesar's deputy for a time after Pharsalus; consul with Caesar in 44 B.C. After Caesar's death, secured confirmation of his acts; formed Second Triumvirate with Octavian and Lepidus. Lepidus was forced out; estrangement between Octavian and Antony developed into Civil War, in which Antony had the support of Cleopatra. Defeated at Actium, 31 B.C.; committed suicide the following year.

APOLLONIA (C.W. III. 5, 11-13, 25, 26, 30, 75, 78, 79): Town in north Epirus.

APONIANA (Af. 2): One of the Aegates islands, off coast of Sicily near Lilybaeum.

Lucius APPULEIUS Saturninus (Introd.; C.W. I. 7): Tribune 103 B.C., 100 B.C. and tribune-elect for 99 B.C. Associated with Marius and Glaucia. Forced through a series of demagogic and revolutionary measures by violent means. Finally Marius, as consul, was requested by the Senate to restore order; he besieged Saturninus and his supporters on the Capitol and imprisoned them, but was unable to save Saturninus from the mob, who pelted him to death (10 December 100).

APSUS (C.W. III. 13, 19, 30): A river in South Illyricum flowing into the Adriatic north of Apollonia.

APULIA (C.W. I. 14, 17, 23): Region in south Italy.

Quintus AQUILA (Af. 62, 63, 67): A Caesarian officer.

Marcus AQUINUS (Af. 57, 89): A senator, supporter of Pompey.

AQUITANIA (C.W. I. 39): The south-west division of Gaul, over-run by the younger Crassus in 56 B.C.

ARELATE (C.W. I. 36, II. 5): Situated on the Rhône, about twenty miles from the mouth (mod. Arles).

ARGUETIUS (Sp. 10): A Caesarian officer.

ARIARATHES (Al. 66): Brother of Ariobarzanes, king of Cappadocia.

ARIMINUM (C.W. I. 8, 10, 11, 12): Town in north-east of Umbria on the Adriatic coast (mod. Rimini).

ARIOBARZANES (C.W. III. 4; Al. 34, 66): King of Cappadocia, 52-42 B.C.; supported Pompey, but submitted to Caesar after Pharsalus.

ARMENIA MINOR (Al. 34-6, 67): Region between Armenia, Cappadocia and Pontus; granted by Senate as a kingdom to Deiotarus. Became a Roman province under Trajan.

ARQUITIUS: See Clodius.

ARRETIUM (C.W. I. 11): Town in Etruria, modern Arezzo.

ARSINOE (Al. 4, 33): Younger daughter of Ptolemy XIII Auletes and sister of Cleopatra.

ASCULUM (C.W. I. 15): Chief town in Picenum.

ASCURUM (Af. 23): A town in Mauretania.

ASIA (C.W. I. 4; III. 3-5, 42, 53, 105-7; Al. 13, 34, 40, 65, 78): The Roman province, comprising the western part of Asia Minor, Mysia, Lydia, Caria and Phrygia.

ASPARAGIUM (C.W. III. 30, 41, 76): Town in Illyricum in the territory of Dyrrachium.

ASPAVIA (Sp. 34): A Spanish stronghold near Ucubi.

ASPRENAS: See Nonius.

ASTA (Sp. 26, 36): Spanish town, perhaps the modern Mesa de Asta, about twenty miles from Cadiz.

ATEGUA (Sp. 6-8, 22): A Spanish town.

Gaius ATEIUS (Af. 89): A supporter of Pompey.

ATHAMANIA (C.W. III. 78): South-eastern district of Epirus.

Titus ATIUS Labienus (C.W. I. 15; III. 13, 19, 71, 87; Af. passim; Sp. 18, 31): Caesar's lieutenant in Gaul 58-49 B.C. Joined Pompey in 49 and fought on the Pompeian side throughout the Civil War. Killed at Munda.

Quintus ATIUS Varus (C.W. III. 37): Cavalry commander under Gnaeus Domitius Calvinus.

Publius ATRIUS (Af. 68, 89): A Roman knight, supporter of Pompey, from the community at Utica.

Publius ATTIUS Varus (C.W. I. 12, 13, 31; II. 23–36, 43, 44; Af. 44, 62–4, 90; Sp. 27, 31): Praetor 53 B.C., governed Africa 52. Took over Africa again in 49 and fought against Curio and Caesar; later went to Spain and was killed at Munda.

ATTIUS, a PAELIGNIAN (C.W. I. 18): A Pompeian officer from the district inhabited by the Paeligni (near Corfinium).

Lucius AURELIUS Cotta (C.W. I. 6): Consul 65 B.C., Censor 64 B.C.

Marcus AURELIUS Cotta (C.W. I. 30): Governed Sardinia for Pompeians in 49 B.C.

AUSETANI (C.W. I. 60): A tribe in Hither Spain, living near the Pyrenees in part of modern Catalonia.

AUXIMUM (C.W. I. 12, 13, 14): Town in Picenum.

AVARICUM (C.W. III. 47): Modern Bourges.

Gaius AVIENUS (Af. 54): A military tribune in Caesar's army, cashiered for inefficiency and disaffection.

Aulus BAEBIUS (Sp. 26): Roman knight from Asta.

BAETIS (Al. 59, 60; Sp. 5, 36): A Spanish river, the modern Guadalquivir.

BAETURIA (Sp. 22): District in Spain between the rivers Anas and Baetis.

BAGRADAS (C.W. II. 24, 26, 38, 39): Principal river of the Roman province of Africa.

BALBAS: See Cornelius.

BELLONA (Al. 66): Goddess of War, with a famous shrine at Comana in Cappadocia.

BERONES (Al. 53): A Celtic people of Hither Spain.

BESSI (C.W. III. 4): A Thracian tribe living on the upper course of the river Hebrus.

BIBULUS: See Calpurnius.

BITHYNIA (C.W. III. 3; Al. 65–6, 78): Territory lying between the Black Sea, Propontis, Phrygia, Galatia and Paphlagonia. First organized as a Roman province in 74 B.C.; extended in 64 B.C. by the addition by Pompey of parts of Pontus.

BOEOTIA (C.W. III. 4): District in eastern Greece to north-east of the territory of Athens (Attica).

BOCCHUS (*Af.* 25): King of East Mauretania; a supporter of Caesar.

BOGUS (*Al.* 59, 62; *Af.* 23): King of West Mauretania; a supporter of Caesar.

BOSPHORUS (*Al.* 78): Part of the hereditary kingdom of the kings of Pontus, in the Crimean area; awarded by Caesar to Mithridates of Pergamum.

BRUNDISIUM (*C.W.* I. 24–8, 30; III. 2, 6, 8, 14, 23–5, 87, 100; *Al.* 44, 47): Port in south Italy at end of Via Appia; on the Adriatic coast (mod. Brindisi).

BRUTTIUM (*C.W.* I. 30): District of south Italy.

BRUTUS: See Junius.

BUTHROTUM (*C.W.* III. 16; *Af.* 19): Town in Epirus opposite Corcyra.

BYLLIS (*C.W.* III. 40): Town in Epirus.

Lucius CAECILIUS Metellus (*C.W.* I. 33): Tribune 49 B.C. Tried to oppose Caesar when the latter opened the treasury at Rome (an incident not reported in *C.W.*); banished from Italy by Caesar.

Quintus CAECILIUS Metellus Pius (*Sp.* 42): Consul 80 B.C.; governor of Further Spain and fighting against Sertorius 79–71 B.C.

Quintus CAECILIUS Metellus Pius SCIPIO Nasica (*C.W.* I. 1, 2, 4, 6; III. 4, 31, 33, 36–8, 57, 78–83, 88, 90; *Af. passim*): Son of Publius Cornelius Scipio Nasica; adopted by Quintus Caecilius Metellus Pius. Became father-in-law of Pompey 53 B.C.; consul with him 52; governor of Syria 49 B.C. Commanded the centre at Pharsalus. Led Pompeian resistance in Africa; defeated at Thapsus. Committed suicide to avoid capture.

CAECILIUS NIGER (*Sp.* 35): A Spaniard from Lusitania. Pompeian supporter.

Lucius CAECILIUS Rufus (*C.W.* I. 23): Half-brother of Sulla. Captured and released by Caesar at Corfinium.

Titus CAECILIUS (*C.W.* I. 46): A leading centurion in Afranius's army, killed at Ilerda.

CAECINA (*Af.* 89): Probably Aulus Caecina, friend of Cicero and a man of learning. Supported Pompey; wrote a pamphlet attacking Caesar and was exiled. In exile he wrote an encomium of Caesar, but this did not earn him pardon.

Marcus CAELIUS Rufus (*C.W.* I. 2; III. 20–22): Young Roman nobleman. Accused of assassination in 56 B.C., defended by Cicero (*Pro Caelio*) and acquitted. Supported Caesar for opportunistic reasons; turned against him when his ambitions were not realized. Killed in 49 B.C. while attempting to raise a revolt in Italy.

CAELIUS VINICIANUS (Al. 77): A Caesarian officer.

CAESAR: See Julius.

CALAGURRIS (C.W. I. 60): A town in Hither Spain.

CALENUS: See Fufius.

Marcus CALIDIUS (C.W. I. 2): As praetor in 57 B.C. supported recall of Cicero. A supporter of Caesar, he died in 47 B.C. while governor of Cisalpine Gaul.

Marcus CALPURNIUS Bibulus (C.W. III. 5, 7, 8, 14–18, 31; his son – C.W. III. 110): Aedile, praetor and consul in the same years as Caesar, and his inveterate opponent. Governed Syria 51–50 B.C.; commanded the Pompeian fleet in the Adriatic 49–48; died early 48.

Gnaeus CALPURNIUS Piso (Af. 3, 18): A Pompeian cavalry commander; survived to become consul in 23 B.C.

Lucius CALPURNIUS Piso Caesoninus (C.W. I. 3): Became Caesar's father-in-law in 59 B.C. Consul 58 B.C., governor of Macedonia 57–55, censor 50. After Caesar's death, he attempted to mediate between Antony and Cicero. Died c. 43 B.C.

CALPURNIUS SALVIANUS (Al. 53, 55): One of the conspirators against Q. Cassius Longinus.

CALVINUS: See Domitius.

Gaius CALVISIUS Sabinus (C.W. III. 34, 35, 56): A Caesarian officer; later governor of Africa, 45–44 B.C., consul 39 B.C., commander of fleet against Sextus Pompeius, 38 B.C. Triumphed in 28 B.C. after his governorship in Spain.

CALYDON (C.W. III. 35): A town in south Aetolia, near Gulf of Corinth.

CAMERINUM (C.W. I. 15): A town in Umbria.

CANDAVIA (C.W. III. 11, 79): A district to the east of Dyrrachium, crossed by the Via Egnatia.

Gaius CANINIUS Rebilus (C.W. I. 26; II. 24, 34; Af. 86, 93; Sp. 35): Caesarian officer; in Gaul 52 B.C., Italy 49, Africa, with Curio, 48; besieged Thapsus in 46; in Spain 45 B.C. Notorious for consulship lasting a single day (end of 45 B.C.).

CANOPUS (Al. 25): Town on an islet at mouth of the western branch of the Nile.

CANTABRIANS (C.W. I. 38): Tribe living on northern coast of Spain.

Lucius CANULEIUS (C.W. III. 42): A Caesarian officer.

CANUSIUM (C.W. I. 24): A town in Apulia.

CAPPADOCIA (C.W. III. 4; Al. 34, 35, 40, 66): A district of Asia Minor, between Pontus and Cilicia.

CAPUA (C.W. I. 10, 14; III. 21, 71): The main town of Campania in Italy, at some distance from the modern town of the same name.

CARALIS (*C.W.* I. 30; *Af.* 98): Modern Cagliari; the capital of Sardinia.

CARFULENUS (*Al.* 31): A Caesarian officer.

CARMO (*C.W.* II. 19; *Al.* 57, 64): Town in Further Spain about thirteen miles from Seville.

CARRUCA (*Sp.* 27): A Spanish town.

CARTEIA (*Sp.* 32, 36, 37): A Spanish town (mod. El Rocadillo), not far from Gibraltar.

CASILINUM (*C.W.* III. 21): A town in Campania.

Gaius CASSIUS Longinus (*C.W.* III. 5, 101): Quaestor with Crassus in Syria; tribune 49 B.C.; left Rome with Pompey. After the latter's death, joined Caesar; praetor 44 B.C. A ringleader in the conspiracy to assassinate Caesar. Died at Philippi, 42 B.C.

Lucius CASSIUS Longinus (*C.W.* III. 34–6, 56): Young brother of Gaius (above); was sent with a legion to hold Thessaly for Caesar in 48 B.C.

Quintus CASSIUS Longinus (*C.W.* I. 2; II. 19, 21; *Al.* 48–64; *Sp.* 42): Brother of the two foregoing. Tribune 49 B.C. Commander in Hither Spain with four legions 49–47 B.C. Roused hatred of provincials; after an attempted assassination, he was recalled by Caesar to help the campaign in Africa; died in a shipwreck.

Quintus CASSIUS (*Al.* 52, 57): An officer of the above.

CASTOR: See Tarcondarius.

CASTULO, Pass of (*C.W.* I. 38): A pass in the Sierra Morena.

CATO (*Sp.* 17, 18): An envoy from Ategua.

CATO: See Porcius.

Publius CAUCILIUS (*Sp.* 32): A Pompeian officer.

Lucius CELLA (*Af.* 89): A Pompeian supporter.

CELTIBERIA (*C.W.* I. 38, 61): A mountainous region of Hither Spain with a very savage population.

CERCINA (*Af.* 8, 34): An island off the African coast.

CHERSONESUS (*Al.* 10): A promontory in Egypt, west of Alexandria.

CICERO: See Tullius.

CILICIA (*C.W.* III. 34, 88, 102, 110; *Al.* 1, 13, 25, 26, 34, 65, 66): A Roman province on the south-east coast of Asia Minor.

CINGA (*C.W.* I. 48): Modern Cinca; a stream in Hither Spain; rises in the Pyrenees and flows into the Sicoris.

CINGULUM (*C.W.* I. 15): A town in Picenum.

CINNA: See Cornelius.

CIRTA (*Af.* 25): A capital of the kingdom of Numidia (mod. Constantine).

Lucius CISPIUS (Af. 62, 67): A Caesarian officer.

Gaius CLAUDIUS Marcellus (C.W. I. 6, 14; III. 5; Al. 68): Consul 49 B.C.; cousin of the consul of the same name of 50 B.C. and brother of Marcus Marcellus. Probably died before Pharsalus.

Marcus CLAUDIUS Marcellus (C.W. I. 2): Consul 51 B.C. Inactive in the Civil War; after Pharsalus, lived in exile in Mytilene till 46 B.C. Cicero's Pro Marcello was delivered in gratitude to Caesar. However, Marcellus was assassinated at Piraeus on his way back to Italy.

Marcus CLAUDIUS Marcellus Aeserninus (Al. 57–64): Quaestor of Cassius Longinus in Spain 48 B.C. Chosen leader by mutinous legions; voluntarily joined Lepidus when the latter arrived to arbitrate.

Tiberius CLAUDIUS Nero (Al. 25): Father of the emperor Tiberius; commanded a Caesarian fleet in Egypt in the Civil War.

CLEOPATRA (C.W. III. 103, 107; Al. 33): Elder daughter of Ptolemy XIII Auletes of Egypt and sister of Ptolemy XIV.

Aulus CLODIUS (C.W. III. 57, 90): Friend of Caesar and Scipio; sent by former to latter on an abortive peace mission in 48 B.C.

Publius CLODIUS Pulcher (Introd.; C.W. III. 21): A member of the patrician Claudii; became a demagogic figure and affected the plebeian spelling of the name. Murdered 52 B.C.

CLODIUS Arquitius (Sp. 23): A Caesarian cavalry officer.

CLUPEA (C.W. II. 23; Af. 2, 3): A town on the north coast of Africa.

Gaius CLUSINAS (Af. 54): Caesarian centurion, cashiered for indiscipline.

COMANA (a) (Al. 66): A town in Cappadocia, with a famous shrine of Bellona. (b) (Al. 34, 35): A town in Pontus.

Quintus COMINIUS (Af. 44, 46): A knight, supporter of Caesar.

COMMAGENE: See Antiochus.

COMPSA (C.W. III. 22): Town in Italy, in the upper valley of the river Aufidus.

Gaius CONSIDIUS Longus (C.W. II. 23; Af. 3–5, 33, 43, 76, 86, 93; his son, Af. 89): Governor of Africa in 50 B.C. Came back in 49 as commander for the Pompeians; stayed till after Thapsus. Assassinated on his way to Numidia.

Gaius COPONIUS (C.W. III. 5, 26): Probably served with Crassus in 53 B.C. Commanded the Rhodian fleet in 48 B.C. for Pompey.

CORCYRA (C.W. III. 3, 7, 11, 15, 16, 58, 100): An island in the Ionian Sea near the coast of Epirus (mod. Corfu).

CORCYRA (Nigra) (C.W. III. 8, 10): An island off the Adriatic coast of Greece.

GLOSSARY OF PERSONS AND PLACES

CORDUBA (C.W. II. 19–21; Al. 49, 52, 54, 57–61, 64; Sp. 2–4, 6, 10–12, 32, 33): A town in Spain on the river Baetis; capital of Further Spain (mod. Cordova).

CORFINIUM (C.W. I. 15, 16, 19, 20, 23, 24, 25, 34; II. 28, 32; III. 10): Town in Paelignian territory; commanded approaches to south Italy. In Social War (90 B.C.) it was for a time the federal capital of the Italians.

Lucius CORNELIUS Balbus (C.W. III. 19): Spanish in origin, nephew of Caesar's captain of engineers of the same name. With Caesar in Greece 48 B.C. Quaestor of Asinius Pollio in Spain 44 B.C. and suspected of embezzlement. Was later raised to consular rank by Augustus, governed Africa and held a triumph in 19 B.C. He was the first person of non-Roman origin to do so, and the last person outside the imperial family. His uncle was Rome's first consul of foreign origin (40 B.C.).

Lucius CORNELIUS Cinna (Introd.): Consul in 87, 86, 85, and 84 B.C. He used military force to secure Marius's recall to Rome. In his consulships he forced through a series of democratic measures; he was killed in a mutiny while preparing to encounter Sulla on the latter's return from Greece.

Lucius CORNELIUS Lentulus Crus (C.W. I. 1, 2, 4, 5, 14; III. 4, 96, 102, 104): Consul 49 B.C.; a violent opponent of Caesar. He landed in Egypt just after Pompey's murder, was arrested and killed in prison.

Publius CORNELIUS Lentulus Marcellinus (C.W. III. 62, 64, 65; Al. 68): Quaestor with Caesar in 48 B.C.; perhaps died that year.

Publius CORNELIUS Lentulus Spinther (C.W. I. 15, 16, 21–3; III. 83, 102): As consul in 57 B.C. he worked for Cicero's return. He supported the Pompeians in the Civil War.

Publius CORNELIUS Sulla (C.W. III. 89, 99): Nephew of the dictator. Accused of complicity with Catiline and defended by Cicero (62 B.C.). Served with Caesar at Dyrrachium and Pharsalus. Died 45 B.C.

Lucius CORNELIUS Sulla Faustus (C.W. I. 6; Af. 87, 95): Son of the dictator and son-in-law of Pompey. Killed by Caesarians after Thapsus.

Lucius CORNELIUS Sulla Felix (Introd.; C.W. I. 4, 5, 7; Af. 56): The dictator. Held power in Rome 82–80 B.C. Died 78 B.C.

Publius CORNELIUS (Af. 76): A recalled veteran; a Pompeian supporter.

Quintus CORNIFICIUS (Al. 42–44, 47): A Caesarian supporter. Possibly praetor in 45 B.C.; governor of Africa 44–42 B.C.

COSA (a) (C.W. I. 34): Town in Etruria. (b) (C.W. III. 22): Town near Thurii.

Marcus COTTA: See Aurelius.

COTYS (C.W. III. 4, 36): King of Thrace; sent his son to help Pompey in 48 B.C.

CRASSUS: See Licinius and Otacilius.

Gaius CRASTINUS (C.W. III. 91, 99): Ex-leading centurion in Caesar's army; died bravely at Pharsalus.

CREMONA (C.W. I. 24): Town in Cisalpine Gaul.

CRISPUS: See Marcius and Sallustius.

CURIO: See Scribonius.

CURIUS: See Vibius.

CYCLADES (C.W. III. 102, 106): An archipelago of islands in the south Aegean.

CYRENE (C.W. III. 5): Capital of Cyrenaica on North African coast. From 68 B.C., Cyrenaica constituted a joint province with Crete.

DALMATIANS (C.W. III. 9): A barbarian people on the Adriatic coast of Illyricum.

DAMASIPPUS: See Licinius.

DARDANIANS (C.W. III. 4): A tribe to the east of Illyricum, in modern Yugoslavia.

Lucius DECIDIUS Saxa (C.W. I. 66): A Spaniard enfranchised by Caesar and serving as an officer in his army. Was tribune in 44 B.C., lieutenant of Antony in Syria 42–40 B.C., then governor; killed in Syria.

Gaius DECIMIUS (Af. 34): A Roman senator on the Pompeian side.

DEIOTARUS (C.W. III. 4; Al. 34, 39, 40, 67–70, 77, 78): Tetrarch of part of Galatia. Helped Rome against Mithridates; rewarded by Pompey with grants of land in eastern Pontus and title of 'King' (59 B.C.). Brought troops to help Pompey 48 B.C.; reconciled with Caesar after Pharsalus. 45 B.C., accused of plotting against Caesar; defended by Cicero. Died c. 40 B.C.

Gaius DIDIUS (Sp. 37, 40): A Caesarian officer.

DIOSCORIDES (C.W. III. 109): An influential Greek at the Ptolemaic court; sent by the king to negotiate with Achillas, who had him killed.

Lucius DOMITIUS Ahenobarbus (Introd.; C.W. I. 6, 15–23, 25, 34, 36, 56–8; II. 3, 18, 22, 28, 32; III. 83, 99): Consul 54 B.C. Opponent of Caesar; failed to hold (a) Corfinium, (b) Massilia; commanded left wing at Pharsalus; killed after battle. His son (C.W. I. 23) took part in the assassination conspiracy 44 B.C.; consul 32 B.C.; died before Actium.

Gnaeus DOMITIUS (C.W. II. 42): A Roman knight.

Gnaeus DOMITIUS Calvinus (C.W. III. 34, 36–8, 78, 79, 80; Al. 9, 34–40, 65, 69, 74; Af. 86, 93): A Caesarian officer; commanded in Macedonia in 48 B.C.; commanded the centre at Pharsalus; campaigned in Asia against Pharnaces; consul 53 and 42; celebrated triumph after governorship in Spain 39–36 B.C.

DOMNILAUS (C.W. III. 4): Tetrarch of Galatia; a supporter of Pompey.

DYRRACHIUM (C.W. I. 25, 27; III. passim; Al. 48): Harbour on coast of Illyricum (mod. Durazzo).

EGUS (C.W. III. 59, 79): Gallic chieftain, son of Adbucillus.

ELIS (C.W. III. 105): Town – capital of district of same name in north-west Peloponnese.

Quintus ENNIUS (Sp. 23, 31): 239–169 B.C. First of the great Roman poets. Wrote more than twenty tragedies, but his fame rested above all on his national epic, the Annales, a poem in eighteen books in which the Greek hexameter verse was first acclimatized to Latin. The Annales, probably the source of the lines quoted in the text, recorded the history of Rome from Aeneas's arrival in Italy down to Ennius's own day. For Caesar's contemporaries, the poem was the greatest classic of Latin literature.

EPHESUS (C.W. III. 33, 105): Town in Asia Minor, capital of the Roman province of Asia, with a celebrated temple of Artemis (Diana).

EPIDAURUS (Al. 44): Town on Dalmatian coast.

EPIRUS (C.W. III. 4, 12, 13, 42, 47, 61, 78, 80): District of north-west Greece opposite Corfu.

Marcus EPPIUS (Af. 89): A senator, on the Pompeian side.

EUPHRANOR (Al. 15, 25): A Rhodian admiral in Caesar's service.

Gaius FABIUS (C.W. I. 37, 40, 48): Governor of Asia, 58–57 B.C. Caesar's lieutenant in Gaul from 54 B.C. Fought in Spain 49 B.C. and perhaps died that year.

Quintus FABIUS Maximus (Sp. 2, 12, 41): A Caesarian officer of praetorian rank; suffect consul 45 B.C.

FABIUS, a Paelignian (C.W. II. 35): A centurion in Curio's army.

FANUM (C.W. I. 11): Town on the Adriatic coast of Italy.

FAUSTUS: See Cornelius.

Marcus FAVONIUS (C.W. III. 36, 57): Praetor 49 B.C.; supported

Pompey in Civil War. Proscribed after the death of Caesar, he was captured and put to death at Philippi.

FIRMUM (C.W. I. 16): Town in Picenum on the Adriatic coast of Italy.

FLACCUS: See Munatius and Valerius.

Gaius FLAVIUS (Sp. 26): A Roman knight from Asta.

Gaius FLEGINAS (C.W. III. 71): A Caesarian knight from Placentia.

Aulus FONTEIUS (Af. 54): A military tribune in Caesar's army, cashiered for indiscipline.

FRENTANI (C.W. I. 23): A tribe in central Italy, on the Adriatic coast.

Quintus FUFIUS Calenus (C.W. I. 87; III. 8, 14, 26, 56, 106; Al. 44): A Caesarian supporter; governed Greece after Pharsalus; consul 47 B.C.; supported Antony after the death of Caesar; governed Narbonensis 41 B.C., died 40 B.C.

Quintus FULGINIUS (C.W. I. 46): A Caesarian centurion.

FULVIUS Postumus (C.W. III. 62): An officer in Caesar's army.

Gaius FUNDANIUS (Sp. 11): Roman knight on the Pompeian side who deserted to Caesar.

Aulus GABINIUS (C.W. III. 4, 103, 110; Al. 3, 42, 43): Proposed *lex Gabinia* 67 B.C. (Pompey's command against the pirates). Pompey's lieutenant in east 66–63 B.C., consul 58, restored Ptolemy XIII to Egyptian throne for a payment of 10,000 talents, 55 B.C. Exiled from Rome 54 B.C. after condemnation for extortion; amnestied 49 B.C. Caesar's officer in Illyricum 48–47 B.C.; died at Salonae.

GADES (C.W. II. 18, 20, 21; Sp. 37, 39, 40, 42): The modern Cadiz.

GAETULIANS (Af. 25, 32, 35, 43, 55, 56, 61, 62, 67, 93): An African tribe living mainly in the hinterland south of Mauretania and Numidia.

GALLOGRAECI (C.W. III. 4; Al. 67, 78): Galatians, from Asia Minor.

Gaius GALLONIUS (C.W. II. 18, 20): Roman knight in Spain on business 49 B.C., assigned to command of Gades.

GALLUS: See Tuticanus.

GANYMEDE (Al. 4, 5, 12, 23, 33): An Egyptian eunuch, tutor to Arsinoe, who commanded her military forces. According to a scholium on Lucan, he was captured and later led in Caesar's triumph.

GAUL (C.W. I. and III. *frequent refs.*; II. 1; Al. 17): Roughly equivalent to modern France.

(a) *Narbonensian Gaul* (capital Narbonne): also called Trans-alpine Gaul; province since 120 B.C.; corresponded to modern Provence.

(b) *Cisalpine Gaul*: the basin of the river Po, at the north of the Italian peninsula. Southern part (*Cispadana*) received Roman citizenship probably 89 B.C.; northern part (*Trans-padana*) in 49 B.C.

(c) *Gallia Comata* ('Long-haired Gaul'): Caesar's conquest; cor-responds with most of modern France, except Provence and Belgium. Divided by Augustus into three regions – Aquitania, Lugdunensis (capital Lyons) and Belgica.

Aulus GRANIUS (*C.W.* III. 71): Roman knight from Puteoli, killed at Dyrrachium.

GENUSUS (*C.W.* III. 75, 76): River in Illyricum.

GERGOVIA (*C.W.* III. 73): A Gallic stronghold in the country of the Arverni, a few miles south of Clermont Ferrand; Caesar at-tacked it unsuccessfully in 52 B.C. (see *Gallic War*, Bk VII).

GERMINII (*C.W.* III. 6): A tribe in Epirus.

GOMPHI (*C.W.* III. 80, 81): Town on the western edge of Thessaly.

GRACCHI (Introd.; *C.W.* I. 7): The brothers Tiberius Sempronius Gracchus and Gaius Sempronius Gracchus, tribunes respectively in 133 B.C. and 123–122 B.C., whose attempts to introduce radical policies of reform resulted in their deaths by violence.

HADRUMETUM (*C.W.* II. 23; *Af.* 3, 21, 24, 33, 43, 62, 63, 67, 89, 97): A town on the east coast of Tunisia.

HALIACMON (*C.W.* III. 36, 37): A river of Macedon.

HEGESARETOS (*C.W.* III. 35): A Thessalian from Larissa; leader of support for Pompey, but reconciled to Caesar after Pharsalus.

HELVII (*C.W.* I. 35): A Gallic tribe from the Cevennes.

HERACLIA (*C.W.* III. 79): A town in Macedonia.

Mount HERMINIUS (*Al.* 48): A mountain range in Spain (mod. Sierra Estrella).

HIEMPSAL (*Af.* 56): Father of King Juba.

HIPPO REGIUS (*Af.* 96): Town on Numidian coast (mod. Bône).

HIRRUS: See Lucilius.

HISPALIS (*C.W.* II. 18, 20; *Al.* 56, 57; *Sp.* 35, 36, 39, 40, 42): Mod-ern Seville, on the Guadalquivir.

IACETANI (*C.W.* I. 60): A tribe on the coast of Spain between the Ebro and the Pyrenees.

IADERTINI (*Al.* 42): Inhabitants of a town in Illyricum.

IGILIUM (C.W. I. 34): Small island off the coast of Etruria.

IGUVIUM (C.W. I. 12): A town in Umbria.

ILERDA (C.W. I. 38, 41–9, 56, 59, 63, 69, 73, 78; II. 17): A town in north-east Spain on right bank of river Sicoris, a tributary of the Ebro (mod. Lerida).

ILIPA (Al. 57): A Spanish town on the right bank of the Guadalquivir.

ILLURGAVONENSES (C.W. I. 60): A Spanish tribe on the coast south of the Ebro.

ILLYRICUM (C.W. III. 9, 78; Al. 42–4): Territory on north-east coast of Adriatic (part of modern Yugoslavia). Southern part formed into a province with Macedon in 146 B.C. Northern part not fully subjugated until 9 B.C.; command of province of Cisalpine Gaul included responsibility for this area.

INDO (Sp. 10): A Spanish chieftain, ally of Caesar.

ISSA (C.W. III. 9; Al. 47): Island off the coast of Illyricum.

The ISTHMUS (C.W. III. 56): The Isthmus of Corinth.

ITALICA (C.W. II. 20; Al. 52, 57; Sp. 25): A Spanish town on the Guadalquivir, north of Seville; the oldest Roman foundation in Spain, established 206 B.C. by Publius Cornelius Scipio (later Africanus). Ruins near modern Santaponce. Later famous as the birthplace of the emperors Trajan and Hadrian.

ITYREANS (Af. 20): A people of Coele-Syria (north of Palestine).

JUBA (C.W. I. 6; II. 25, 26, 36–44; Al. 51; Af. passim): King of Numidia and Gaetulia since before 50 B.C. Supported the Pompeian side in the Civil War. Committed suicide after defeat of Thapsus; kingdom became a province.

Gaius JULIUS Caesar (passim): The dictator.

Lucius JULIUS Caesar (C.W. I. 8, 10; II. 23; Af. 88, 89): Second cousin of the dictator. Took Pompeian side in Civil War; died in Africa after Thapsus.

Sextus JULIUS Caesar (C.W. II. 20; Al. 66): Grandson of the consul of 91 B.C., who was the dictator's uncle. Caesarian supporter; assassinated 46 B.C. by Caecilius Bassus.

JUNIUS (Sp. 16): A Pompeian who protested at the massacre of the townsfolk in Ategua.

Decimus JUNIUS Brutus (C.W. I. 36, 56, 57; II. 3, 5, 6, 22): Officer with Caesar in Gaul, commanded fleet against Veneti 56 B.C. Commanded fleet at Massilia 49 B.C. Governed Transalpine Gaul 48–46 B.C. In the assassination conspiracy 44 B.C. Proconsul in Cisalpine Gaul 44–43 B.C. Killed en route to Macedonia 43 B.C.

Lucius JUVENTIUS Laterensis (Al. 53–5): One of the conspirators against Cassius Longinus.

LABIENUS: See Atius.

LACEDAEMON (C.W. III. 4): Sparta.

Decimus LAELIUS (C.W. III. 5, 7, 40, 100): Son of Pompey's lieutenant in Spain 77 B.C.; served with Pompey 62 B.C. On Pompeian side at beginning of Civil War; reconciled with Caesar after Pharsalus. Possibly governed Africa 43 B.C.; died by violence 42 B.C.

LARINATES (C.W. I. 23): An Italian tribe, main town Larinum.

LARISSA (C.W. III. 80, 96–8): Town in Thessaly on the river Peneus.

LATERENSIS: See Juventius.

LENNIUM (Sp. 35): A Spanish town in Lusitania.

LENTULUS: See Cornelius.

LEPIDUS: See Aemilius.

LEPTIS (C.W. II. 38; Af. 7, 9, 10, 29, 61–3, 67, 97): A town on the east coast of the province of Africa, between Hadrumetum and Thapsus.

LIBURNIA (C.W. III. 5, 9): A district in Illyricum, which gave its name to a type of fast, light warship.

Marcus LICINIUS Crassus (Introd.; C.W. III. 31: The triumvir; killed at Carrhae, 53 B.C., in battle against the Parthians.

LICINIUS Damasippus (C.W. II. 44; Af. 89, 96): Senator on the Pompeian side; with Juba in Africa 49 B.C., died there 46 B.C. after Thapsus.

Lucius LICINIUS Squillus (Al. 52, 55): One of the conspirators against Cassius Longinus.

Publius LIGARIUS (Af. 64): A Pompeian knight, amnestied by Caesar in Spain, later executed.

Quintus LIGARIUS (Af. 89): A Pompeian supporter; commanded in Africa pending arrival of Varus. Cicero tried to secure permission from Caesar for his return to Rome, and defended him on a charge of treason in 46 B.C. He was allowed to return.

LILYBAEUM (Af. 1, 2, 34, 37): A port in the west of Sicily.

LISSUS (C.W. III. 26, 28, 29, 40, 42, 78): Coastal town in Illyricum (mod. Alessio).

Lucius LIVINEIUS Regulus (Af. 89): A young Roman on Caesar's side; started political career 43 B.C.

Marcus LIVIUS Drusus (Introd.): Tribune in 91 B.C.; championed the cause of enfranchisement of Rome's Italian allies. Strong senatorial opposition resulted in his legislation being declared invalid, and soon after he was murdered.

LONGINUS: See Cassius.

LONGUS: See Considius.

LUCANIA (*C.W.* I. 30): District of south Italy, between Tyrrhenian Sea and Gulf of Tarentum.

Lucius LUCCEIUS (*C.W.* III. 18): Ran jointly with Caesar for consulship of 59 B.C. but failed to secure election. Historian and friend of Cicero, who tried to get him to write a special monograph on the subject of his consulship, exile and recall. Supported Pompey in Civil War; reconciled to Caesar after Pharsalus. Probably died 43 B.C.

LUCERIA (*C.W.* I. 24): Town in Apulia.

Gaius LUCILIUS Hirrus (*C.W.* I. 15; III. 82): A Pompeian supporter. Tribune 53 B.C.

Quintus LUCRETIUS (*C.W.* I. 18): Roman senator, died at Sulmo.

Quintus LUCRETIUS Vespillo (*C.W.* III. 7): Roman senator, Pompeian supporter. Reconciled with Caesar after Pharsalus. Proscribed 43 B.C., but went into hiding; later spared, and survived to become consul 19 B.C.

LUSITANIA (*C.W.* I. 38; *Al.* 48; *Sp.* 18, 35, 36, 38, 40): Part of the province of Further Spain; corresponding roughly to modern Portugal, south of Oporto, and part of western Spain.

LYCOMEDES (*Al.* 66): A noble Bithynian.

MACEDONIA (*C.W.* III. 4, 11, 33, 34, 36, 57, 79, 102; *Al.* 42): Territory to the north of Thessaly. A Roman province since 146 B.C.; western part 'free Macedon'.

Numerius MAGIUS (*C.W.* I. 24, 26): Pompey's chief engineer.

MALACA (*Al.* 64): Town in Spain (mod. Malaga).

MALCHUS (*Al.* 1): King of the Nabataeans.

MANILIUS Tusculus (*Al.* 53): One of the conspirators against Cassius Longinus.

Lucius MANLIUS Torquatus (*C.W.* I. 24; III. 11; *Af.* 96): Son of the consul of 65 B.C., friend of Cicero; probably the bridegroom in Catullus's Epithalamium (LXIII); literary dilettante. Pompeian supporter; died with Scipio after Thapsus.

MARCELLUS: See Claudius.

Quintus MARCIUS (*Sp.* 11): A Pompeian officer who deserted to Caesar.

MARCIUS Crispus (*Af.* 77): Senator on the Caesarian side; governed Bithynia and Pontus 45 B.C., Syria 44–43.

MARCIUS Rufus (C.W. II. 23, 24, 43): Quaestor with Curio in Africa; took survivors back to Sicily.

Lucius MARCIUS Philippus, *pater* (C.W. I. 6): Consul 56 B.C. Nephew of Caesar by marriage, step-father of Octavius, father-in-law of Cato; neutral in Civil War.

Lucius MARCIUS Philippus, *filius* (C.W. I. 6): Son of the above; a very wealthy senator; suffect consul 38 B.C., governor in Spain 34–33 B.C.

Gaius MARIUS (Introd.; Af. 32, 35, 36): The famous general, conqueror in the wars against Jugurtha (106 B.C.) and the Cimbri and Teutones (101 B.C.), and consul seven times.

MARRUCINI (C.W. I. 23; II. 34): A central Italian tribe.

MARSI (C.W. I. 15, 20; II. 27, 29): A people living by the Fucine Lake, east of Rome.

MASSILIA, MASSILIOTES (C.W. I. 34–6, 56–8; II. 1, 3–7, 14, 15, 17, 18, 21, 22): Modern Marseille and its inhabitants; a Greek foundation (c. 600 B.C.).

MAURETANIA (C.W. I. 6, 39, 60; Al. 51, 52, 59; Af. 22, 23, 95): Country in North Africa west of Numidia (corresponds to western Algeria and Morocco), divided in two kingdoms. Annexed to Roman empire in A.D. 40 and divided into provinces of Mauretania Tingitana and Mauretania Caesariensis.

MAXIMUS: See Fabius.

MAZACA (Al. 66): Chief town of Cappadocia.

MEDOBREGA (Al. 48): A Spanish town in Lusitania.

MENEDEMUS (C.W. III. 34): A Greek chieftain from Free Macedonia.

MESSANA (C.W. II. 3; III. 101): A port in Sicily (mod. Messina).

Lucius MERCELLO (Al. 52, 55): One of the conspirators against Cassius Longinus.

MESSALLA: See Valerius.

Gaius MESSIUS (Af. 33, 43): Friend of Cicero and Pompey. Tribune 57 B.C., tried to secure Cicero's return from exile; proposed that Pompey as curator of corn supply should have unlimited powers. Appointed lieutenant of Caesar in Gaul 54 B.C.; recalled to answer charges of corruption. On Caesarian side in Civil War.

METELLUS: See Caecilius.

METROPOLIS (C.W. III. 80): Now Palaeo-Kastro; town about fifteen miles south-east of Gomphi.

MILO: See Annius.

Gaius MINUCIUS Reginus (Af. 68): Roman knight, friend of Scipio.

MINUCIUS Rufus (C.W. III. 7): Joint commander of Pompeian fleet at Oricum in 49 B.C.

MINUCIUS Silo (Al. 52, 53, 55): One of the conspirators against Cassius Longinus.

Quintus MINUCIUS Thermus (C.W. I. 12): A Pompeian officer, expelled from Iguvium 49 B.C. Governed Asia 52–50 B.C.

MITHRIDATES (Al. 72, 73, 78): 'The Great', king of Pontus. His aggressive expansionist policy led to three wars with Rome (88–64 B.C.). He was finally defeated by Pompey, and committed suicide in 63 B.C. in consequence of a revolt led by his son Pharnaces.

MITHRIDATES OF PERGAMUM (Al. 26–8, 78): Reputedly the natural son of Mithridates the Great, but more probably the son of one Menodotus and a Galatian princess. He was brought up at Mithridates' court. His help to Caesar was rewarded by the grant of the kingdom of Bosphorus. In attempting to take it over, he was killed by the usurping Asander, who had already killed the previous possessor, Pharnaces.

MOORS (Af. 3, 6, 7, 83): Inhabitants of Mauretania.

MUNATIUS Flaccus (Al. 52): Citizen of Italica; one of the conspirators against Cassius Longinus.

Lucius MUNATIUS Flaccus (Sp. 19): A Pompeian officer in charge of Ategua in 45 B.C.

Lucius MUNATIUS Plancus (C.W. I. 40; Af. 4; Sp. 19): Caesar's lieutenant in Gaul. After Caesar's death, governed Transalpine Gaul; founded colonies at Augst and Lyons. Consul 42 B.C.; initially supported Antony in Civil War, later transferred to Octavian. Held the office of censor 22 B.C.

MUNDA (Sp. 27, 32, 33, 36, 41, 42): Spanish town; scene of the decisive battle in 45 B.C.

MURCUS: See Statius.

MYTILENE (C.W. III. 102): Chief town of the island of Lesbos.

NABATAEANS (Al. 1): A people of Arabia Petraea, west of Sinai; conquered by Pompey and Aemilius Scaurus in two campaigns.

NAEVA (Al. 57): A town in Spain.

NARBO (C.W. I. 37; II. 21): Modern Narbonne, chief town of the province of Gallia Narbonensis.

Lucius NASIDIUS (C.W. II. 3, 4; Af. 64, 98): A Pompeian supporter.

NAUPACTUS (C.W. III. 35): Modern Lepanto; town at the entrance to the Gulf of Corinth.

NERO: See Claudius.

NICOPOLIS (Al. 36, 37): A town in Armenia Minor.

NIGER: See Caecilius and Pompeius.

NONIUS Asprenas (Af. 80; Sp. 10): A Caesarian officer.

NORICUM (C.W. I. 18): A kingdom between the Danube and the Alps; became a province in 16 B.C.

NUMIDIA (C.W. II. 25, 38, 39, 41; Al. 51; Af. passim): A kingdom in North Africa, between Mauretania and the Roman province of Africa; inhabitants famous for their skill as cavalrymen.

NYMPHAEUM (C.W. III. 26): A coastal town in Illyricum.

OBUCULA (Al. 57): A town in Spain.

Marcus OCTAVIUS (C.W. III. 5, 9; Al. 42–7; Af. 44): A Pompeian officer.

OCTOGESA (C.W. I. 61, 68, 70): A Spanish town on the Ebro.

Marcus OPIMIUS (C.W. III. 38): A cavalry officer in Scipio's army.

OPPIUS (Af. 68): A Caesarian officer.

ORCHOMENUS (C.W. III. 56): A town in Boeotia.

ORICUM (C.W. III. 7, 11–16, 23, 34, 39, 40, 78, 90): A town in Epirus.

OSCA (C.W. I. 60): A Spanish town, about sixty miles north-west of Ilerda.

OTACILIUS Crassus (C.W. III. 28, 29): A Pompeian officer.

PACIAECUS: See Vibius.

PACIDEIUS (Af. 13, 78): Two brothers in Pompeian army, one of whom commanded the cavalry at Tegea.

PAELIGNIANS (C.W. I. 59; II. 29): An Italian people, living east of the Marsi.

PALAEPHARSALUS (Al. 48): 'Old Pharsalus' in Thessaly; a stronghold near the site of Caesar's victory over Pompey.

PALAESTE (C.W. III. 6): A town in Epirus.

PARADA (Af. 87): An African town, between Thapsus and Utica.

PARAETONIUM (Al. 8): A place on the Egyptian coast west of Alexandria.

PARTHIANS (C.W. I. 9; III. 31, 82): A powerful Eastern nation, whose empire extended from the Euphrates to the Indus.

PARTHINI (C.W. III. 11, 41, 42): A tribe living near Dyrrachium.

Quintus PATISIUS (Al. 34): A lieutenant of Domitius Calvinus, sent to Cilicia for troops.

Quintus PEDIUS (C.W. III. 22; Sp. 2, 12): A relative of Caesar's; his lieutenant in Gaul 58 B.C.; aedile 54 B.C.; served in Caesar's army in Civil War and triumphed in 45 B.C.; suffect consul 43 B.C.

PELUSIUM (C.W. III. 103, 108): A town at the mouth of a branch of the Nile.

PERGAMUM (C.W. III. 31, 105; Al. 78): A town in Mysia in Asia Minor, formerly capital of the Seleucid kingdom.

PETRA (C.W. III. 42): A rocky height south of Dyrrachium.

PETRAEUS (C.W. III. 35): Leader of Thessalian support for Caesar.

Marcus PETREIUS (C.W. I. 38–43, 53, 61–7, 72–6, 87; II. 17–18; Af. 18–20, 24, 91, 94, 97): Pompey's lieutenant in Spain 55–49 B.C.; probably in Greece 49–47 B.C.; in Africa 46 B.C. and committed suicide with Juba after Thapsus.

PHARNACES (Al. 34–41, 65, 69–78; Sp. 1): Son of Mithridates the Great. He rose against his father in 63 B.C. and was given the kingdom of Bosphorus by the Romans as a reward. He took advantage of the Civil War to overrun Cappadocia, Armenia Minor and Pontus, but was finally defeated by Caesar at Zela.

PHAROS (C.W. III. 111, 112): An island off Alexandria and joined to the latter by a causeway, the Heptastadion; on the island stood the famous Pharos lighthouse.

PHILIPPUS: See Marcius.

PHILO (Sp. 35): A Pompeian supporter from Lusitania.

PHOENICIA (C.W. III. 101): Coastal district of the Roman province of Syria.

PICENUM (C.W. I. 12, 15, 29): Region of Italy between the Apennines and the Adriatic, extending roughly from Ancona in the north to Hatria in the south.

PISAURUM (C.W. I. 11, 12): A town on the Adriatic coast of Italy, about twenty miles south-east of Rimini (Ariminum).

PISO: See Calpurnius.

PLACENTIA (C.W. III. 71): A Roman colony on the river Po (mod. Piacenza).

Gaius PLAETORIUS (Al. 34): Quaestor of Domitius Calvinus in Pontus, 48 B.C.

PLAETORIUS Rustianus (Af. 96): A Pompeian supporter.

PLANCUS: See Munatius.

Marcus PLOTIUS (C.W. III. 19): Caesarian officer wounded near river Apsus, 48 B.C.

POMPEIA (Af. 95): Wife of L. Sulla Faustus.

POMPEIUS Rufus (Af. 85): A Caesarian officer.

Gnaeus POMPEIUS, filius (C.W. III. 4, 5, 40; Af. 22, 23; Sp. passim): Elder son of Pompey; led Pompeian resistance in Spain after Pharsalus; captured and executed after Munda.

Sextus POMPEIUS (Sp. 3, 4, 32, 34): Younger son of Pompey. Survived the Civil War; amnestied 44 B.C. by Lepidus; appointed commander of the fleet 43 B.C. Amnesty revoked the same year. He threatened Italy with a naval blockade, and was formally declared governor of Sicily, Sardinia and Achaea, 39 B.C. Hostilities continued until 36 B.C., when he was defeated by Octavian's admiral, Agrippa. He escaped to Asia Minor, but was captured by an officer of Antony's and executed, 35 B.C.

Quintus POMPEIUS Niger (Sp. 25): Roman knight from Italica, on Caesarian side.

POMPEY (Gnaeus POMPEIUS Magnus, pater) (passim): The triumvir.

Marcus POMPONIUS (C.W. III. 101): Pompey's lieutenant in the Pirate War; on Caesar's side in Civil War.

PONTUS (C.W. III. 3, 4; Al. 13, 14, 34, 35, 39–41, 65, 67, 69, 70, 72, 77): Formerly the kingdom of Mithridates: at the time of the Civil War attached to Bithynia.

Marcus PORCIUS Cato (later Uticensis) (Introd.; C.W. I. 4, 30, 32; Af. 22, 36, 87, 88, 93; his son, Af. 89): Born 93 B.C. Supported Cicero's measures against Catilinarians, 63 B.C.; his opposition to the requests of Caesar, Crassus and Pompey instrumental in bringing about formation of the first triumvirate. Constant opponent thereafter. Advocated consulship of Pompey, 52 B.C. Tried to avert bloodshed in Civil War, while supporting Pompey. In command of Utica during the final campaign in Africa; committed suicide after Thapsus. Venerated as a 'martyr' by the Stoic opposition in the early Empire.

POSTUMIUS, Camp of (Sp. 8): Site of a camp of Lucius Postumius Albinus, proconsul in Spain in 179 B.C., during campaign against the Celtiberians.

POSTUMUS: See Fulvius, Rabirius.

POTHINUS (C.W. III. 108, 112): Tutor of King Ptolemy XIV.

PTOLEMY (a) XIII AULETES (C.W. III. 4. 103, 107–10, 112; Al. 4, 33): King of Egypt, 73–51 B.C. Expelled 58 B.C. and restored with Roman help in 55 B.C.

(b) XIV DIONYSUS (C.W. III. 103, 104, 106–9, 112; Al. 23–33): Son of the above.

PTOLOMAIS (C.W. III. 105): A town in Phoenicia (mod. Acre) named after Ptolemy I.

Titus PULEIO (C.W. III. 67): Roman centurion; with Caesar in Gaul and with Pompey in Civil War.

Lucius PUPIUS (C.W. I. 13): A leading centurion on the Pompeian side; arrested at Auximum and set free.

PUTEOLI (C.W. III. 71): An Italian port on the bay of Baiae, near Naples (mod. Pozzuoli).

QUINCTIUS Scapula (Sp. 33): Leader of mutinous Caesarian troops; committed suicide after Munda.

Sextus QUINTILIUS Varus (C.W. I. 23; II. 28): Quaestor 49 B.C.; on Pompeian side. Committed suicide after Pharsalus.

Gaius RABIRIUS (Introd.): A Roman prosecuted in 63 B.C. for his part in the death of Saturninus, 100 B.C.

RABIRIUS Postumus (Af. 8, 26): Roman banker who administered financial affairs of Ptolemy XIII; prosecuted in 54 B.C. on charge of receiving; defended by Cicero and acquitted. Taken up by Caesar; praetor by 48 B.C. and served with Caesar in the Civil War.

Lucius RACILIUS (Al. 52, 53, 55): One of the conspirators against Cassius Longinus.

RAVENNA (C.W. I. 5): Town in Cisalpine Gaul, on the Adriatic coast.

REBILUS: See Caninius.

REGINUS: See Minucius.

RHASCYPOLIS (C.W. III. 4): Thracian chieftain who brought 200 troops to help Pompey.

Lucius ROSCIUS Fabatus (C.W. I. 3, 8, 10): Caesar's lieutenant in Gaul; praetor 49 B.C.; Caesarian in Civil War. Died 43 B.C.

ROUCILLUS (C.W. III. 59, 79): A Gallic chieftain, son of Adbucillus.

Lucius RUBRIUS (C.W. I. 23): A Pompeian senator captured at Corfinium.

RUFUS: See Acutius, Caelius, Marcius, Minucius, Sulpicius, Vibullius.

RUSPINA (Af. 6, 9–11, 20, 28, 33–7, 53, 67): African coastal town.

RUTENI (C.W. I. 51): A Gallic tribe; their chief town was Segodunum (mod. Rodez).

Publius RUTILIUS Lupus (C.W. I. 24; III. 56): Praetor 49 B.C.; held the Peloponnese for Pompey in 48 B.C.

SABINUS: See Calvisius.

SABURRA (C.W. II. 38–42; Af. 48, 93, 95): A general of Juba.

Marcus SACRATIVIR (C.W. III. 71): Roman knight from Capua on the Caesarian side; killed at Dyrrachium.

SADALA (C.W. III. 4): Son of King Cotys of Thrace.

SAGUNTUM (*Sp.* 10): Sea-coast town in Hither Spain.

Titus SALIENUS (a) (*Af.* 28): Caesarian centurion captured and put to death by Pompeians.

(b) (*Af.* 54): a centurion cashiered by Caesar.

Gaius SALLUSTIUS Crispus (*Af.* 8, 34, 97): Tribune 52 B.C.; expelled from Senate 50 B.C. for alleged immorality. Reinstated by Caesar two years later. A Caesarian officer in the Civil War and governor of the new province of Africa 45 B.C. Spent rest of his life in retirement from politics. Published monographs on the Jugurthan War and the Catilinarian conspiracy, as well as five books of *Histories*.

SALLYES (*C.W.* I. 35): A Gallic tribe living on the Durance.

SALONAE (*C.W.* III. 9; *Al.* 43): A town near modern Spalato (Split) on the Adriatic coast.

SALVIANUS: See Calpurnius.

SARSURA (*Af.* 75, 76): Inland African town.

SASON (*C.W.* III. 8): A small island north of the promontory of Acroceraunia.

Gaius SASERNA (*Af.* 9, 29, 57): A Caesarian officer, left to garrison Leptis.

Publius SASERNA (*Af.* 10): Brother of the preceding.

SATURNINUS: See Appuleius.

SCAEVA (*C.W.* III. 53): A Caesarian centurion.

SCAPULA: See Annius and Quinctius.

SCIPIO: See Caecilius.

Lucius SCRIBONIUS Libo (*C.W.* I. 26; III. 5, 15–18, 23, 24, 90, 100): A Pompeian supporter, stepfather of Sextus Pompeius. 49 B.C., expelled Dolabella from Illyricum and captured C. Antonius. Commanded a fleet, 48 B.C. Consul 34 B.C. His sister was Octavian's first wife.

Gaius SCRIBONIUS Curio (Introd.; *C.W.* I. 12, 18, 30, 31; II. 3, 23–43; III 10; *Af.* 19, 40): Young Roman nobleman whose support was earned by Caesar by the latter's payment of his debts. Tribune 50 B.C.; killed with his army in Africa 49 B.C.

SEGOVIA (*Al.* 57): A town in Spain.

Lucius SEPTIMIUS (*C.W.* III. 104): A centurion in the Pirate War under Pompey; remained in Egypt with Gabinius's troops after 55 B.C. Pompey's assassin.

SERAPION (*C.W.* III. 109): An influential Greek at the court of Ptolemy. Sent to negotiate with Achillas, who had him killed.

Quintus SERTORIUS (Introd.; *C.W.* I. 61): Appointed governor of Hither Spain 83 B.C.; maintained himself there as a rebel until 73; assassinated.

Publius SERVILIUS Isauricus (*C.W.* III. 1, 21): Son of consul of 79 B.C.; Caesar's colleague in the consulship, 48 B.C.; governed Asia 46–44; consul II. 41 B.C.

Publius SESTIUS (*Al.* 34): Ex-praetor, governed Cilicia 49–48 B.C.; lieutenant of Domitius 48–47 B.C.

Quintus SESTIUS (*Al.* 55): One of the conspirators against Cassius Longinus.

SICORIS (*C.W.* I. 40, 48, 61–3, 83): A tributary of the river Ebro (mod. Segre).

SILO: See Minucius.

SINGILIS (*Al.* 57): A tributary of the river Baetis.

Publius SITTIUS (*Af.* 25, 36, 48, 93, 95, 96): A Roman bankrupt, turned mercenary captain. Fought against Juba; rewarded by Caesar with territory in Africa.

SORICARIA (*Sp.* 24, 27): A Spanish town.

SPAIN (*passim*) (a) *Hither Spain*: Roman province, comprising the valley of the Ebro and the eastern coastal district to a point south of Carthago Nova.

(b) *Further Spain*: Roman province, the Baetis valley south of the Sierra Morena.

SPALIS (*Sp.* 27): A Spanish town; site not identified.

SPARTACUS (Introd.): A gladiator, leader of a large-scale revolt of slaves which broke out in Italy in 73 B.C. The slave army is said to have grown to 90,000 and after defeating two Roman forces it was finally suppressed in 71 B.C., largely by Crassus, with some help from Pompey in 'mopping-up'.

Lucius STABERIUS (*C.W.* III. 12): A Pompeian officer.

STATIUS Murcus (*C.W.* III. 15, 16): A Caesarian officer. Governed Syria 44–43 B.C.; apparently later held a naval command with Sextus Pompeius.

SQUILLUS: See Licinius.

SULCI (*Af.* 98): In Sardinia (mod. Sol).

SULLA: See Cornelius.

SULMO (*C.W.* I. 18): A town of the Paelignians, famous later as the birthplace of Ovid.

Publius SULPICIUS Rufus (*C.W.* I. 74; III. 101; *Af.* 10): Lieutenant of Caesar in Gaul, and in Spain 49 B.C. Praetor 48 B.C. Governed Illyricum in 46 and Bithynia and Pontus the following year. Censor in 42 B.C.

Servius SULPICIUS (*C.W.* II. 44): Roman senator on the Pompeian side.

SYRIA (*C.W.* I. 4, 6; III. 3–5, 31, 32, 88, 101, 103, 105, 110; *Al.* 1,

25, 26, 33, 34, 38, 65, 66): Roman province established by Pompey in 63 B.C. Situated between Cilicia and Palestine; bounded on west by Mediterranean and on east by Mesopotamia (part of the Parthian empire) and Arabia.

TARCONDARIUS Castor (C.W. III. 4): Grandson of Deiotarus; his father was the ruler of part of Cilicia. Served in Pompey's army.

TARRACINA (C.W. I. 24): Town on coast of Latium in Italy.

TARRACO (C.W. I. 73, 78; II. 21): A port in Hither Spain (mod. Tarragona).

TARSUS (Al. 66): Chief town of Cilicia.

TAURIS (Al. 45): Island in the Adriatic.

TAUROIS (C.W. II. 4): A stronghold near Massilia.

TEGEA (Af. 78): Inland town in Africa.

Aulus TERENTIUS Varro (C.W. III. 19): A Pompeian officer.

Marcus TERENTIUS Varro (C.W. I. 38; II. 17, 19–21; Al. 58): A famous polymath. Governed Further Spain 49 B.C.; surrendered to Caesar. Not present at Pharsalus; fled to Spain after the battle. Returned to Rome 46 B.C. and was put in charge of the new library in Caesar's forum. Died 25 B.C.

THABENA (Af. 77): Coastal town in Numidia.

THAPSUS (Af. 28, 44, 46, 53, 62, 67, 79, 80, 85, 86, 89, 97): African coastal town; scene of the decisive battle in the campaign of 46 B.C.

THEBES (C.W. III. 56): Capital of Boeotia.

THEOPHANES (C.W. III. 18): A Greek from Mytilene, given citizenship by Pompey in 62 B.C. Historical writer and confidential adviser of Pompey. According to Plutarch (Life of Cicero, 38) he was Pompey's chief of engineers in the Illyrian campaign.

THERMUS: See Minucius.

THESSALY (C.W. III. 4, 5, 34–6, 79–82, 100, 101, 106, 111): A region of north-east Greece, south of Macedonia but attached to the province of that name.

Titus THORIUS (Al. 57, 58): Caesarian officer from Italica, chosen as leader by the mutinous troops of Cassius.

THRACE (C.W. III. 4, 95): A region between the Danube and the Aegean, east of Macedon; became a Roman province in A.D. 46.

THURII (C.W. III. 22): A town in south Italy on the Gulf of Tarentum, also called Thurium.

THYSDRA (Af. 36, 76, 86, 93, 97): Inland town in Africa.

TIBERIUS: See Claudius and Tullius.

Lucius TIBURTIUS (C.W. III. 19): A Caesarian officer.

Lucius TICIDA (Af. 44, 46): A Roman knight, supporter of Caesar; doubtfully identified with the poet of that name.

Quintius TILLIUS (C.W. III. 42): Caesarian officer.

Marcus TIRO (Af. 54: A Caesarian centurion cashiered for indiscipline.

Lucius TITIUS (Al. 57): Military tribune of the native legion levied in Spain.

TITII (Af. 28): Two Spanish brothers, tribunes of the Fifth legion; possibly sons of the preceding.

TORQUATUS: See Manlius.

TRALLES (C.W. III. 105): A town in Caria in Asia Minor.

Aulus TREBELLIUS (Sp. 26): A Roman knight from Asta.

Gaius TREBONIUS (C.W. I. 36; II. 1, 5, 13, 15; III. 20, 21; Al. 64; Sp. 7, 12): Tribune 55 B.C., proposer of the law assigning Syria to Crassus and Spain to Pompey; Caesar's lieutenant in Gaul thereafter; governed Further Spain 47–46 B.C.; suffect consul 45 B.C.; one of the conspirators for the assassination of Caesar. Governed Asia 43 B.C., put to death by Dolabella at Smyrna in 42 B.C.

TRIARIUS: See Valerius.

TUBERO: See Aelius.

Marcus TULLIUS Cicero (Introd.): Famous Roman orator and statesman. Leading legal pleader of his day. The first of his family to enter the Senate, he became consul in 63 B.C. and suppressed the conspiracy of Catiline. Exiled 58 B.C. but recalled the following year. Supported the triumvirs thereafter. Opted for Pompey at outbreak of Civil War, but took no active part. Pardoned by Caesar. After the latter's death, he violently opposed Mark Antony, who insisted on his proscription. Killed December 43 B.C.

TULLIUS Rufus (Af. 85): Ex-quaestor, on Caesarian side. Killed in 46 B.C. by Caesar's veterans as a suspected traitor.

Tiberius TULLIUS (Sp. 17, 18): An envoy from Ategua.

TULLUS: See Volcatius.

TURPIO: See Antistius.

TUSCULUS: See Manilius.

TUTICANUS Gallus (C.W. III. 71): A Caesarian senator, killed at Dyrrachium.

UCUBI (Sp. 7, 8, 20, 24, 27): A Spanish town.

ULIA (Al. 61, 63; Sp. 3, 4, 6): Spanish town, seventeen miles south of Corduba.

URSO (Sp. 22, 26, 28, 41, 42): Spanish town (mod. Osuna).

USSETA (Af. 89): African town.

UTICA (C.W. I. 31; II. 23–6, 36–8, 44): Principal town of the Roman province of Africa.

UZITTA (Af. 41, 51–9): African town.

VAGA (Af. 74): African inland town near Zeta.

VALERIUS (Sp. 32): A Pompeian supporter.

Marcus VALERIUS Messalla (Af. 28, 86, 88): Father of Messalla Corvinus; augur for fifty-five years and an authority on divination. Consul 53 B.C.; lieutenant of Caesar in the African campaign.

Lucius VALERIUS Flaccus (C.W. III. 53): Praetor 63 B.C., governor of Asia. Accused of extortion 59 B.C. and defended by Cicero.

Publius VALERIUS Flaccus (C.W. III. 53): Son of the preceding. Pompeian supporter, killed in battle at Dyrrachium, 48 B.C.

Gaius VALERIUS Triarius (a) (C.W. III. 5, 92): Naval commander under Pompey, 49–48 B.C.

(b) (Al. 72, 73): Lieutenant of Lucullus, defeated by Mithridates at Zela, 67 B.C.

Quintus VALERIUS Orca (C.W. I. 30, 31): Praetor 57 B.C.; governor of Africa 56 B.C.; Caesar's lieutenant in Sardinia 49 B.C.

Aulus VALGIUS (Sp. 13): Caesarian, son of a senator; deserted to join his brother among the Pompeians.

VAR (C.W. I. 86, 87): A river entering the Mediterranean a few miles west of Nice; it marked the south-east boundary of the Roman province of Transalpine Gaul.

VARRO: See Terentius.

VARUS: See Atius, Attius, Quintilius.

Titus VASIUS (Al. 52): One of the conspirators against Cassius Longinus.

Publius VATINIUS (Introd.; C.W. III. 19, 90, 100; Al. 43–7; Af. 10): A man with a chequered career. Prosecuted after being quaestor in 63 on a charge of extortion; notorious for his depredations as a lieutenant in Further Spain 62 B.C.; as tribune in 59 B.C., supported Caesar in hope of profitable political appointments; elected praetor for 55 B.C. by bribery; prosecuted 54 B.C. by Calvus and defended by Cicero; 51 B.C., Caesar's lieutenant in Gaul. Defended Brundisium in the Civil War; finally became consul, for a few months, in 47 B.C. Commanded the army in Illyricum from 45 B.C. and triumphed at the end of 43, although his army had already deserted.

Gaius VERGILIUS (Af. 28, 44, 79, 86, 93): Possibly the praetor 62 B.C.; Pompeian commander in charge of Thapsus.

VENTIPO (Sp. 27): A Spanish town.

VESPILLO: See Lucretius.

GLOSSARY OF PERSONS AND PLACES

Publius VESTRIUS (Af. 64): A Roman knight on the Pompeian side.

VETTONES (C.W. I. 38): A Spanish tribe living between the Duoro and the Guadiana.

VIBIUS Curius (C.W. I. 24): A cavalry commander of Caesar's.

Lucius VIBIUS Paciaecus (Sp. 3): Caesarian prefect of troops for the relief of Ulia, in 45 B.C.

VIBO (C.W. III. 101): Town on coast of Bruttium in Italy.

Lucius VIBULLIUS Rufus (C.W. I. 15, 34, 38): Prefect in Picenum under Pompey; in Spain 49 B.C.

VINICIANUS: See Caelius.

VOLCAE ARECOMICI (C.W. I. 35): A Gallic tribe; principal town Nemausus (Nîmes).

Lucius VOLCATIUS Tullus (C.W. III. 52): A Caesarian officer; became consul 33 B.C.

Gaius VOLUSENUS (C.W. III. 60): A Caesarian cavalry officer.

ZAMA (Af. 91, 92, 97): One of the capitals of Numidia.

ZELA (Al. 72): A town in south Pontus. After a rapid and victorious campaign, ending in the defeat of Pharnaces here, Caesar sent the dispatch famous for its terseness: 'Veni, vidi, vici'.

ZETA (Af. 68, 74): African inland town.

INDEX TO MAPS

INDEX TO MAPS

INDEX TO MAPS

ITALY

Miles

50   0   50   100

——— Principal roads

Ravenna
R. Rubicon
Ariminum
Pisaurum
Fanum
Ancona
Luca
Arretium
PICENUM
Auximum
Iguvium
Firmum
Camerinum
Asculum
Cosa
MARRUCINI
Igilium I.
Alba
Corfinium
PAELIGNI
FRENTANI
MARSI
Sulmo
ROME
Larinum
Luceria
Tarracina
Casilinum
Canusium
Capua
APULIA
Naples
Brundisium
LUCANIA
Tarentum
Thurium
Messana
BRUTTII
Lilybaeum
SICILY
Rhegium

354

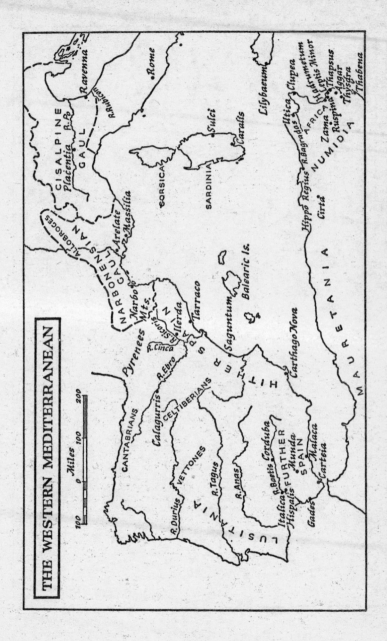

THE WESTERN MEDITERRANEAN

Miles

100   0   100   200

CISALPINE GAUL
Placentia
Ravenna
Rome
R. Rubicon
R. Po

ALLOBROGES
NARBONENSIAN GAUL
Arelate
Massilia
Narbo
Pyrenees

CORSICA
SARDINIA
Sulci
Caralis
Lilybaeum

HITHER SPAIN
Emporiae
Mts.
Ilerda
R. Sicoris
R. Cinca
Tarraco
Saguntum
R. Ebro
Carthago Nova
Balearic Is.

CANTABRIANS
Calagurris
CELTIBERIANS
VETTONES
R. Durius
R. Tagus
R. Anas
LUSITANIA
FURTHER SPAIN
Italica
Hispalis
R. Baetis
Corduba
Munda
Malaca
Carteia
Gades

MAURETANIA
NUMIDIA
AFRICA
Hippo Regius
R. Bagradas
Utica
Clupea
Hadrumetum
Leptis Minor
Thapsus
Aggar
Thysdra
Thabena
Zama
Ruspina
Cirta

355

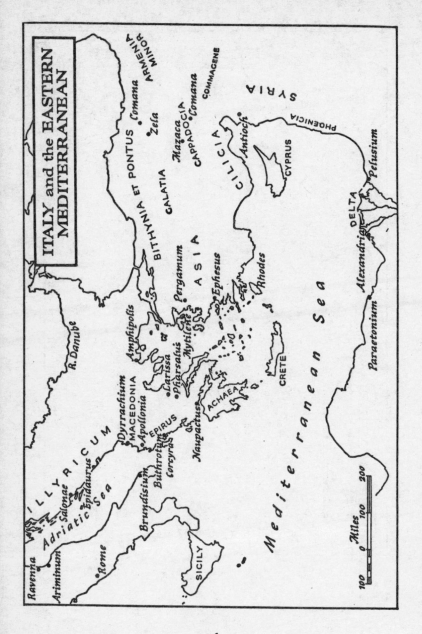

ITALY and the EASTERN MEDITERRANEAN

NORTHERN GREECE

Miles
25   0   25   50

Nymphaeum
• Lissus
PARTHINI
Dyrrachium
Asparagium
R. Genusus
CANDAVIA
Heraclia
Amphipolis
Egnatian Way
Thessalonica
Apollonia
• Byllis
• Amantia
Oricum
• Palaeste
ACROCERAUNIA
RAPSUS
ILLYRICUM
EPIRUS
MACEDONIA
R. Haliacmon
THESSALY
R. Peneus
R. Enipeus
Buthrotum
ATHAMANIA
Aeginium
Gomphi
Larissa
Corcyra
Metropolis
Pharsalus
• Ambracia
Amphilochia
ACARNANIA
AETOLIA
Orchomenus
Calydon
Naupactus
BOEOTIA
Gulf of Corinth

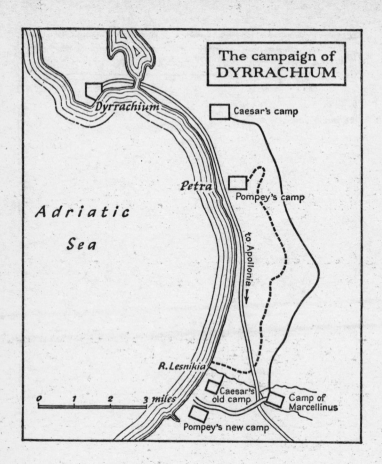

The campaign of DYRRACHIUM

Caesar's camp

Dyrrachium

Petra

Pompey's camp

Adriatic

Sea

to Apollonia →

Adriatic

Sea

R. Lesnikia

0   1   2   3 miles

Caesar's old camp

Camp of Marcellinus

Pompey's new camp

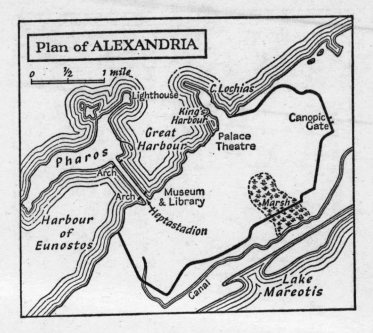

Plan of ALEXANDRIA

0   ½   1 mile

Lighthouse

C. Lochias

King's Harbour

Canopic Gate

Great Harbour

Palace
Theatre

Pharos

Arch

Arch

Museum
& Library

Heptastadion

Marsh

Harbour
of
Eunostos

Canal

Lake
Mareotis

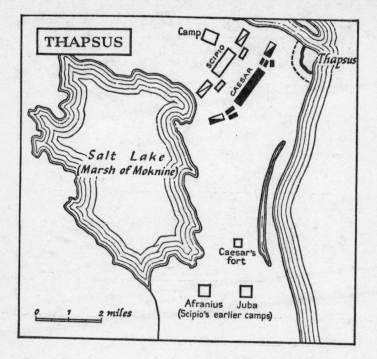

THAPSUS

Camp

SCIPIO

CAESAR

Thapsus

Salt Lake
(Marsh of Moknine)

Caesar's
fort

Afranius   Juba
(Scipio's earlier camps)

0   1   2 miles

READ MORE IN PENGUIN

In every corner of the world, on every subject under the sun, Penguin represents quality and variety – the very best in publishing today.

For complete information about books available from Penguin – including Puffins, Penguin Classics and Arkana – and how to order them, write to us at the appropriate address below. Please note that for copyright reasons the selection of books varies from country to country.

In the United Kingdom: Please write to *Dept. EP, Penguin Books Ltd, Bath Road, Harmondsworth, West Drayton, Middlesex UB7 0DA*

In the United States: Please write to *Consumer Services, Penguin Putnam Inc., 405 Murray Hill Parkway, East Rutherford, New Jersey 07073-2136.* VISA and MasterCard holders call 1-800-631-8571 to order Penguin titles

In Canada: Please write to *Penguin Books Canada Ltd, 10 Alcorn Avenue, Suite 300, Toronto, Ontario M4V 3B2*

In Australia: Please write to *Penguin Books Australia Ltd, 487 Maroondah Highway, Ringwood, Victoria 3134*

In New Zealand: Please write to *Penguin Books (NZ) Ltd, Private Bag 102902, North Shore Mail Centre, Auckland 10*

In India: Please write to *Penguin Books India Pvt Ltd, 11 Community Centre, Panchsheel Park, New Delhi 110017*

In the Netherlands: Please write to *Penguin Books Netherlands bv, Postbus 3507, NL-1001 AH Amsterdam*

In Germany: Please write to *Penguin Books Deutschland GmbH, Metzlerstrasse 26, 60594 Frankfurt am Main*

In Spain: Please write to *Penguin Books S. A., Bravo Murillo 19, 1°B, 28015 Madrid*

In Italy: Please write to *Penguin Italia s.r.l., Via Vittorio Emanuele 45/a, 20094 Corsico, Milano*

In France: Please write to *Penguin France, 12, Rue Prosper Ferradou, 31700 Blagnac*

In Japan: Please write to *Penguin Books Japan Ltd, Iidabashi KM-Bldg, 2-23-9 Koraku, Bunkyo-Ku, Tokyo 112-0004*

In South Africa: Please write to *Penguin Books South Africa (Pty) Ltd, P.O. Box 751093, Gardenview, 2047 Johannesburg*